Alexey Brodovitch

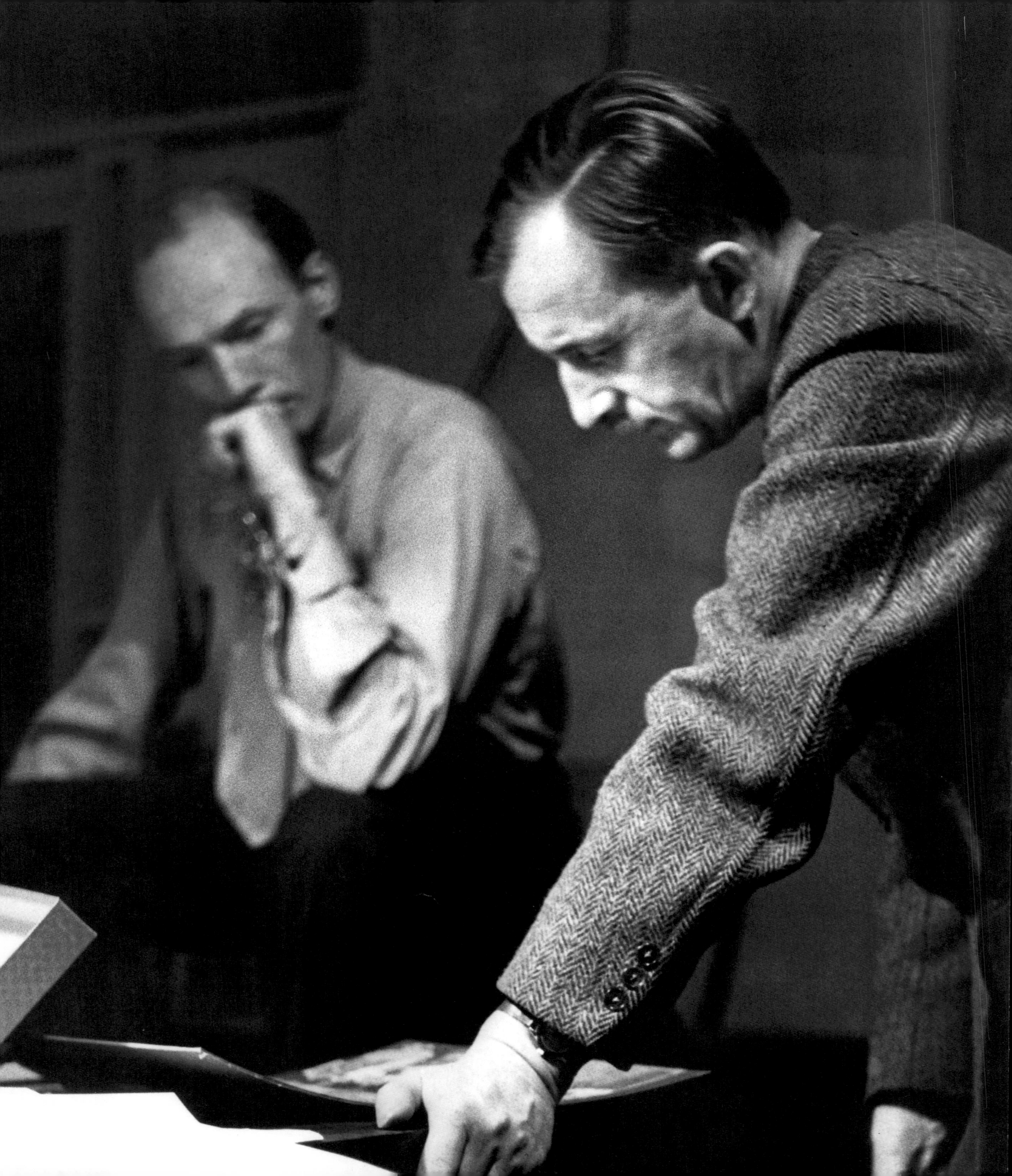

Alexey Brodovitch

Kerry William Purcell

Φ

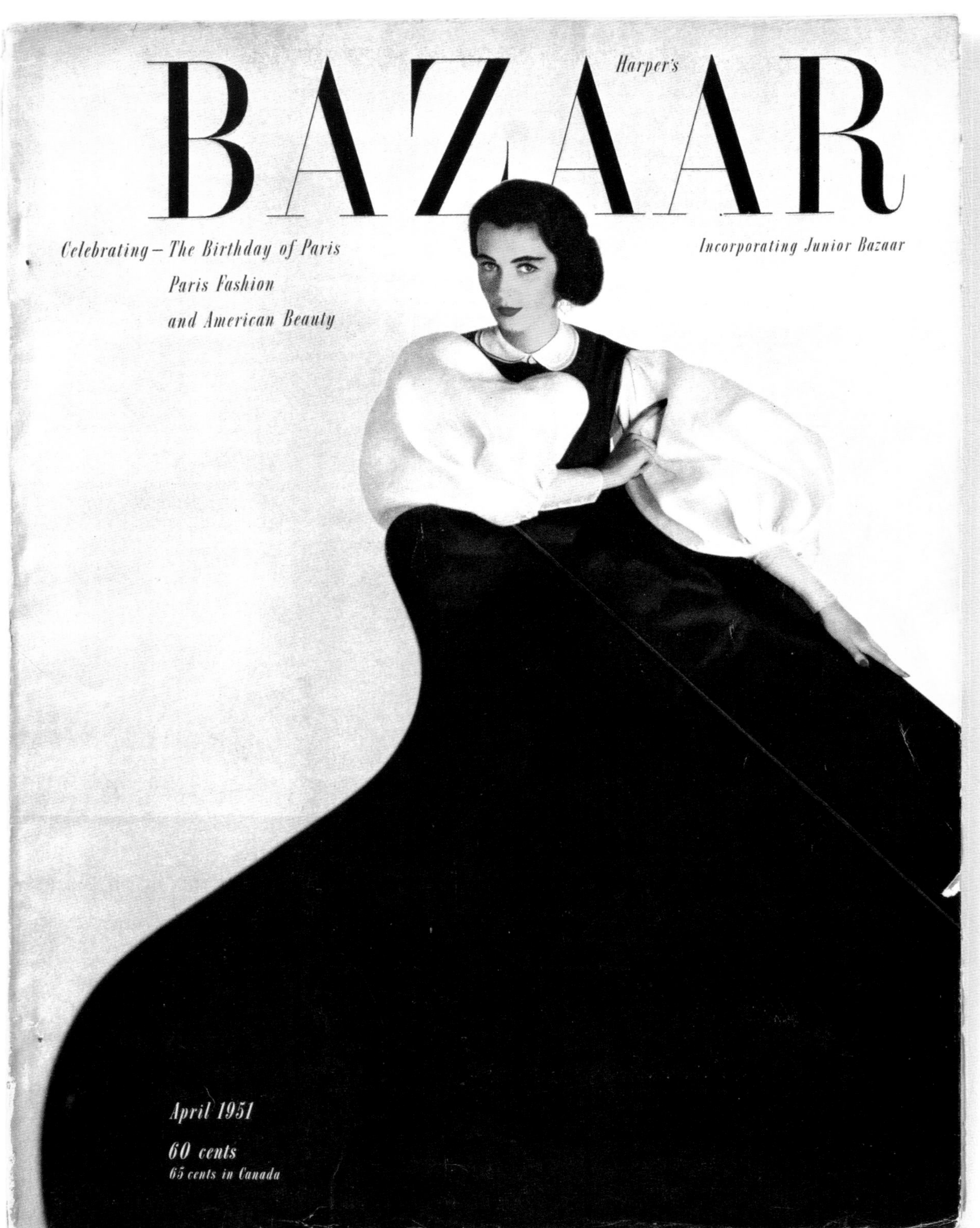

Above: *Harper's Bazaar,* April 1951. Photograph by Richard Avedon.

Frontispiece: Alexey Brodovitch teaching a workshop at Pennsylvania Museum School of Industrial Art, c.1938. Photograph by Arnold Roston.

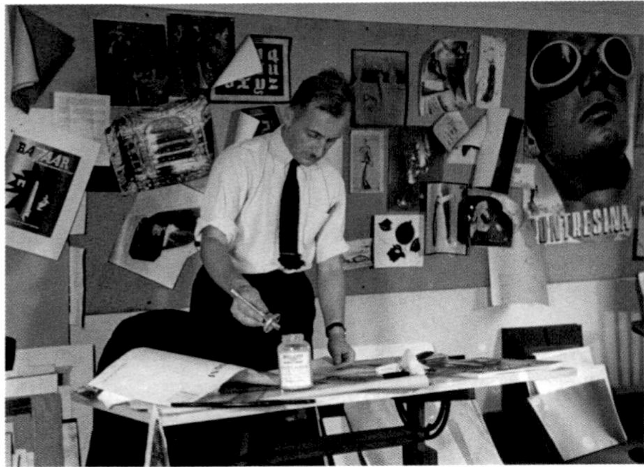

Brodovitch working on a layout at *Harper's Bazaar*, New York, 1937. Photograph by George Karger.

Introduction

In New York, from 1941 to 1966, Alexey Brodovitch taught a class for students of photography and the graphic arts titled the "Design Laboratory." Many evenings, following the end of the class, Brodovitch would invite a select group of students to his apartment for coffee. One of the students who frequently made this weekly pilgrimage was the photographer Harvey Lloyd. "One evening," Lloyd recounts, "we left the class with six or eight people, and went up to his place. When we arrived at the door everyone walked in and he looked and saw that [Bob] Adelman was coming in at my invitation, he hadn't invited him. He said: 'Goodnight Mr. Adelman.' Bob had to leave. I called him the next morning and said: 'Alexey, what in God's name are you doing? How can you be so rude?' I said: 'That was a really terrible thing to do.'... Nonetheless, later that year *Popular Photography* invited Brodovitch to select a 'Photograph of the Year.'... The photograph that appeared was Bob Adelman's photograph of the blacks in Birmingham being hit with a fire hose. I realized, nothing would interfere with his vision. His personal attitudes had nothing to do with his attitudes toward art."[1]

Such stories of Alexey Brodovitch's unswerving dedication to the values of originality and immediacy in the graphic arts are both legendary and numerous. In both meanings of the word, he was a seer. His ability to recognize when an individual had discovered something exciting, and foresee the possibilities this work held for the printed page, was uncanny. Even if, as above, the human values of concern and empathy frequently suffered in his constant search for the new and imaginative, the list of those touched by Brodovitch's creative life is a role call of pivotal innovators in the graphic arts: A. M. Cassandre, Salvador Dali, Brassai, Henri Cartier-Bresson, Robert Frank, Bill Brandt, Man Ray, Hans Namuth, and Richard Avedon, to name but a few. It was through his groundbreaking layouts as the revolutionary art director of *Harper's Bazaar* (1934–58) that Brodovitch's designs fused with the work of these artists, photographers, and designers. As a result of these creative encounters alone, Brodovitch's influence on twentieth century art and photography is both considerable and enduring.

Alexey Brodovitch's lasting legacy extends beyond the pages of *Harper's Bazaar*. In 1920, he arrived in Paris as an exile from the Bolshevik Revolution and was to play a part in that decade-long experiment that forever transformed our ways of seeing.[2] His years in Paris were central to his development as a graphic designer. In this environment, where aesthetic boundaries dissolved in a radical synthesis of the arts, Brodovitch's creative energy was absorbed and cultivated by unlimited opportunities. Whether painting sets for Diaghilev's Ballets Russes, or designing posters, fabrics, china, jewelry, and books, Brodovitch displayed a Renaissance-like mastery of the graphic arts. After only five short years in Paris he had established himself as a designer of repute. Yet, unlike many of his Parisian contemporaries, his eclectic approach to questions of form resulted in Brodovitch never developing a consistent theory toward the arts. Rather, he always approached each new project with the attitude "If you know yourself you are doomed."

It was his work during this period that eventually brought him to the attention of John Story Jenks. Then vice president of the Philadelphia Museum of Art, he persuaded Brodovitch to journey to America in 1930 to establish a department of advertising at the museum's School of Industrial Art. Over the coming decades Brodovitch's early assimilation into the world of American commercial art provided an entrée for many other translators of modernist ideas into American culture. Through *Harper's Bazaar*, *Portfolio*, and books such as *Observations* and *Ballet*, Brodovitch acted as a conduit of European art and design, introducing the influential ideas of Fernand Léger, de Stijl, and Surrealism to a traditionally conservative American audience. In this regard he was a pioneer.

Today, in an age where the line between art and commerce is casually traversed, Alexey Brodovitch's design influence is so pervasive as to be invisible. However, never afraid to contradict himself (and irritate those around him), he would have rejected this easy association between the creative and commercial. Once satirically noting that "Madison Avenue practices birth control on creative photography," he continually pushed those photographers and designers who entered his world to excite and provoke, never to simply satisfy. It is here that we find the true legacy of Alexey Brodovitch. That is, those students and colleagues who transformed the fields of photography and design throughout the twentieth century by responding to Brodovitch's goading to "constantly experiment. Constantly go forward," to never be satisfied or content with what one has produced.

One year after his death, the photographer Irving Penn recalled how Brodovitch sustained this energy to provoke right up until the end:

A number of years ago Brodovitch was in the hospital and they said he was dying. I went to the hospital thinking it would be my last visit. There he was lying on the bed and I said hello. He said, "Thank you, Penn, for sending me a copy of your book, but frankly, I must tell you it is terrible." I thought, is that the last word I would ever have from him? He really let me have it right there and I just took it.... You see, he was not charming. He was a special person and they don't come often. There isn't a designer or photographer in our time who hasn't felt the influence of Brodovitch. The waves that went out from Harper's Bazaar *since his first issue are still rippling.*[3]

Émigré: The Formative Years

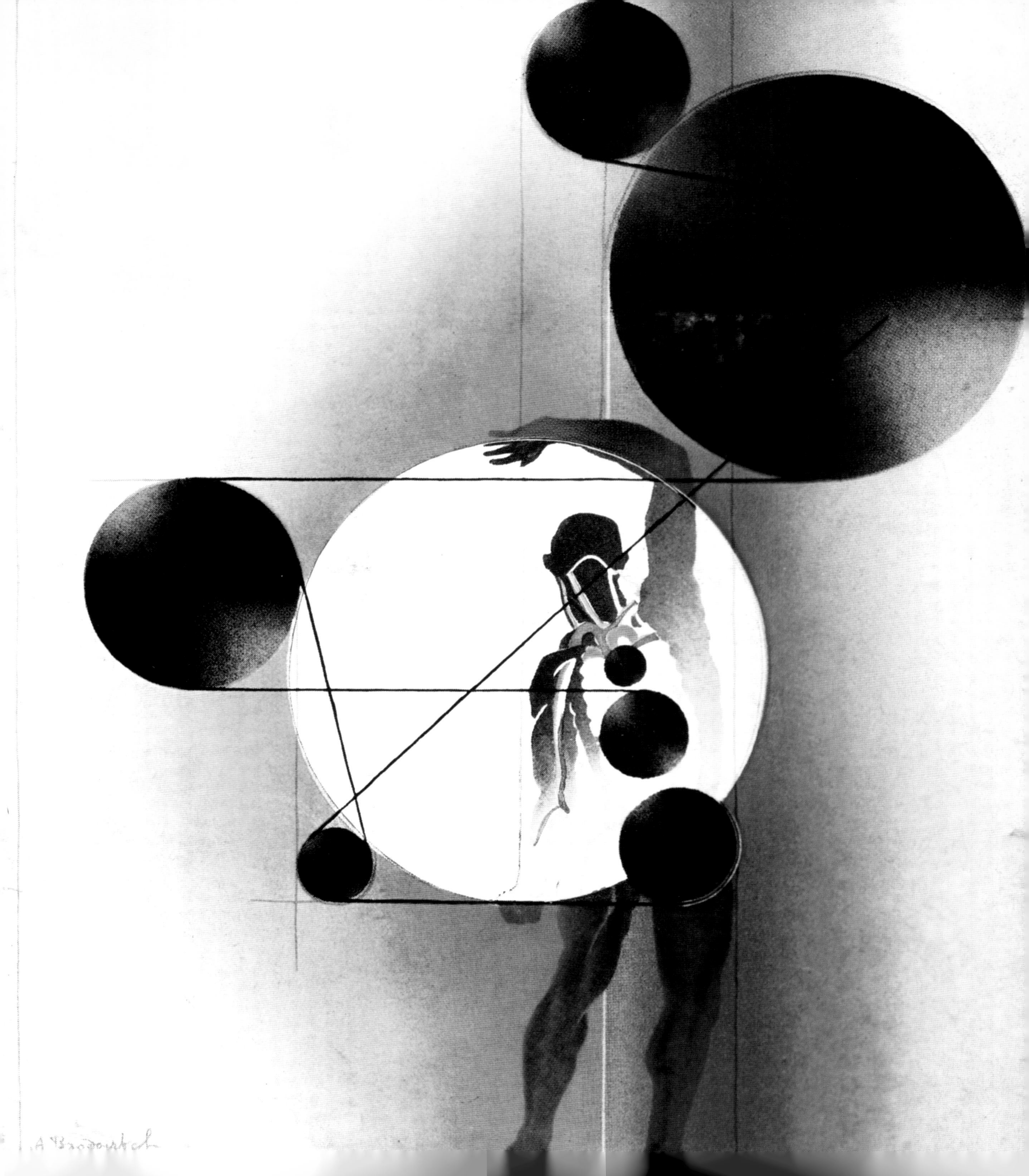

Once, at the restaurant opposite the Orthodox Russian Cathedral on the rue Daru, Stravinsky ordered his famous raw repast in the company of composer Nicolas Nabokov. Nabokov could not finish his cotelettes Pojarsky; *Stravinsky scooped the remainder of Nabokov's cutlet onto to his own plate, doused it with sour cream, and devoured the morsel saying, "I want to astonish the raw potato in my stomach."* – William Wiser, *The Crazy Years: Paris in the Twenties*

Russia

BORN in Ogolitchi in 1898, Alexey Brodovitch was to be forever marked by the conflicts of fin de siècle Russia. At a time when new, modern, and revolutionary ideas were developing throughout a country permeated by old, traditional, and conservative values, Brodovitch's early years in Russia (1898–1920) were riddled with inconsistencies and oppositions. His father, Cheslav Brodovitch, a Polish doctor, and his mother, an amateur painter and early influence on Brodovitch's future direction, attempted to provide the young Brodovitch with an even keel in those unbalanced times. By his own account, Brodovitch's father was a stern taskmaster. With a description sounding like an extract from a Pushkin short story, Brodovitch recounts the events surrounding his birth:

Shortly before I was born, [my father] persuaded my mother to join him on a hunting trip to North Russia ... where they lived in a comfortable but very primitive hunting lodge rented from the elders of the village; the temperature was below zero and there was lots of snow. Mother had narrow hips and my father ordered her to walk in the snow for exercise.

Two weeks later I was born, a healthy baby; my mother was alright. A week later, my father put me in deep snow for a few seconds and then dried me over an open fire, out of doors. The lodge was steaming hot ... I choked down my first vodka.[4]

As a doctor, Brodovitch's father was posted to various hospitals. In February 1904, Russia entered a disastrous conflict with Japan and, in early 1905, Cheslav Brodovitch was assigned to a Moscow hospital to tend the increasing number of sick and dying soldiers from the front. In Moscow the young Brodovitch had his first of many encounters with war. It was a rendezvous that not only sparked a youthful desire to enter the army but, indirectly, precipitated Brodovitch's interest in photography. Brodovitch's father had given the young Alexey a box camera, and the first photographs he took were in Moscow of Japanese prisoners of war.

Toward the end of 1905, following the short-lived fatuity that was the Russo-Japanese War, Brodovitch's grandfather died and bequeathed to his son, Cheslav Brodovitch, a large hotel, two restaurants, and an exclusive grocery store in St. Petersburg. To manage his inheritance, Cheslav Brodovitch transferred to St. Nicholas' Hospital in St. Petersburg, and moved his family to the city. St. Petersburg undoubtedly had a major influence on the young Brodovitch's mind. Continuing to take photographs with his box camera – he has referred to another series of images he took of patients within his father's hospital, this time a mental institution – Brodovitch found himself in a city that was, visually, a fertile seedbed for a young, creative imagination.[5]

Through an abrasive combination of the forced modernization of Russian society, but within a country that was still predominately populated by rural peasants, St. Petersburg found itself in a constant state of flux during the 1890s and 1900s.[6] During this period, those distinctively modern symbols of the forthcoming century, factories, grew in size and number. As a result, cities such as St. Petersburg were swelled by hundreds of thousands from rural towns and villages looking for work. The sudden influx of peasants into these showcases of modern industry transformed social behavior and dress, and most significantly, the subsequent development of modern commerce. Walking down Nevsky Prospekt, the central thoroughfare in St. Petersburg analogous to Regent Street in London or the Champs Elysées in Paris, Alexey Brodovitch would have found himself in the midst of modern Russia. In Andrei Bely's modernist masterpiece *Petersburg*, published in 1916 but set in 1905, the main character provides

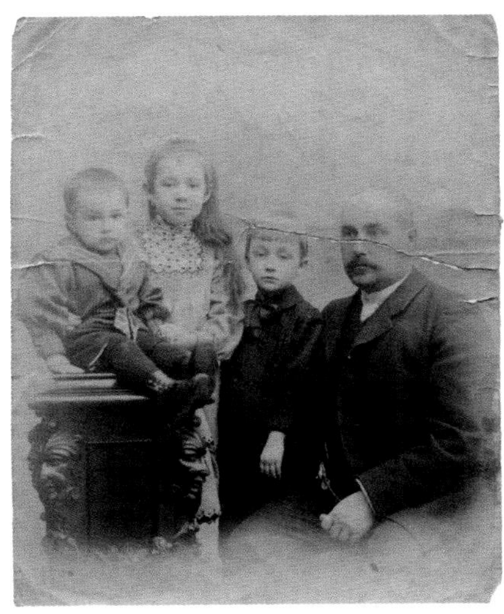

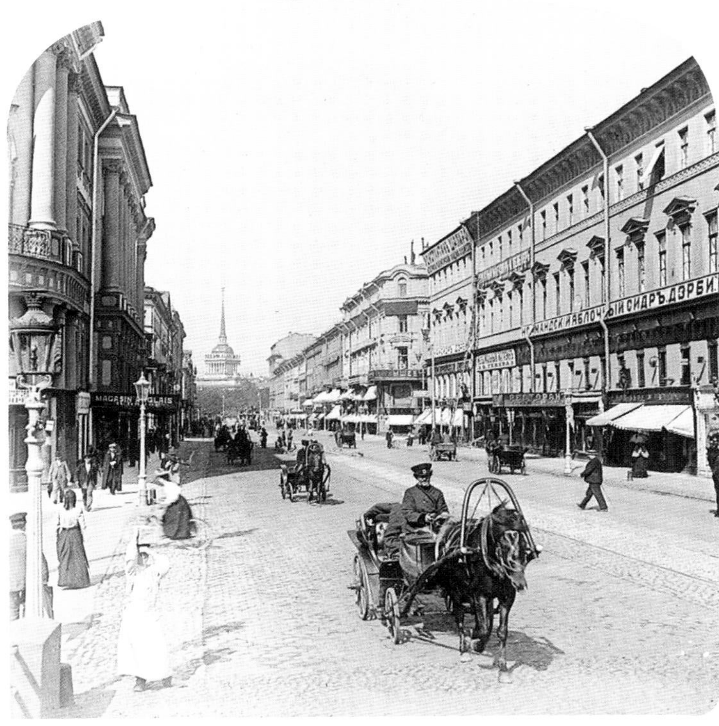

Page 9: Untitled Brodovitch design, Paris, c. 1928.

Above: Brodovitch family portrait, c. 1905.
From left, brother Nicholas, sister Natacha, Alexey, father Cheslav.

Right: St. Petersburg, view along the central thoroughfare, Nevsky Prospekt, c. 1905.
At the turn of the twentieth century, St. Petersburg changed profoundly as new forms of advertising, shops, streetcars, automobiles, and lights multiplied in the urban environment. These spectacles undoubtedly influenced a young, receptive Brodovitch.

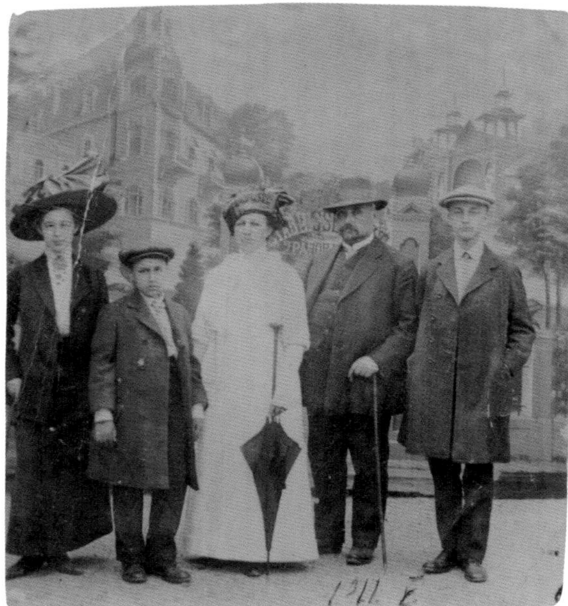

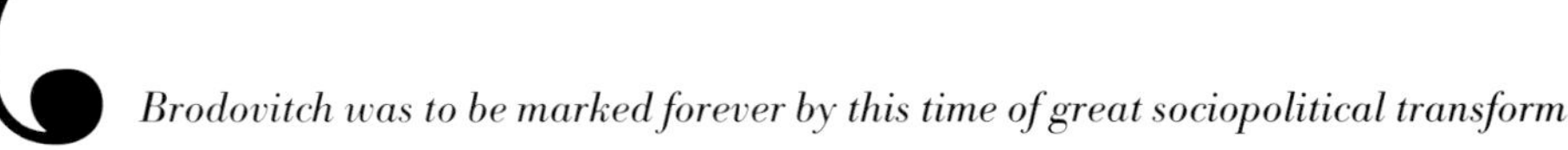

an expressive account of the spectacle Brodovitch would have apprehended on an evening walk along the Nevsky Prospekt:

In the evening the Nevsky is suffused with a fiery murk. And the walls of many houses burn with a diamond light: words formed from diamonds brightly scintillate: "Coffee House," "Farce," "Tate Diamonds," "Omega Watches." Greenish by day, but now effulgent, a display window opens wide on the Nevsky its fiery maw: everywhere there are tens, hundreds of infernal fiery maws: these maws agonizingly disgorge on to the flagstones their brilliant white light; they spew a turbid wetness like fiery rust. And the prospect is gnawed to shreds by rust. The white brilliance falls on bowlers, top hats, feathers; the white brilliance rushes onwards, toward the centre of the prospect, shoving aside the evening darkness from the pavement.[7]

In his 1903 essay "Metropolis and Mental Life," Georg Simmel concluded that the outcome of the visual "shocks" experienced by the individual in their migration to the city, resulted in the "essentially intellectualistic character of ... mental life."[8] The protection of this "inner life" from the roar of the urban everyday, engendered a demeanor of conscious detachment, a desire to see without being seen. The characteristics Brodovitch cultivated to cope with this sudden cacophony of sight and sound – a blasé manner expressing a spirit of indifference to everything around him – would forever define his formal and austere disposition.

It was a stance that was ideally suited to observing the products of modernity – the bright shop signs and advertisements, the plate-glass display windows, the motorcars and trams – and other spectators of the city. Akin to Baudelaire's acts of "*flânerie*" in Paris over thirty years earlier, the residents of the Nevsky Prospekt were offered a uniquely modern vocabulary.[9] It was a language in which shops, street lights, cars, and the like became letters of a visual alphabet, spelling new words and sentences. This phantasmagoria of urban life marked the beginning of Brodovitch's visual education. Although he never attended a traditional school of artistic instruction, his immersion in this age of "condensed" modernization clearly shaped his unique vision. He would forever draw on the intense quality of this period in both his teachings and designs.

From around 1906 it seems the Brodovitch family divided their time between winters in the city of St. Petersburg and summers on their farm in Ogolitchi. In an effort to steer him away from any direct encounter with the mounting political tensions of pre-revolutionary Russia, Brodovitch's parents sent him to the prestigious Prince Tenisheff School and then hired a private tutor. Regardless of their efforts, Brodovitch was to be a marked forever by this time of great sociopolitical transformation when change of one sort or another was the oxygen of public life.[10] As one historian of the period highlighted, everybody from

Opposite top: Brodovitch in Paris, 1928.

Opposite bottom: Poster for the Ballets Russes, 1923. Designer unknown.

Right: Léon Bakst, set design for the Ballets Russes, "Shehérezade," by Serge Diaghilev, 1909.
It was Diaghilev's ability to synthesize and orchestrate the arts of music, dance, and design that sparked Brodovitch's creative desire to collaborate across artistic boundaries. Brodovitch's love of the ballet would culminate in a book he later photographed and designed, *Ballet*, published in 1945.

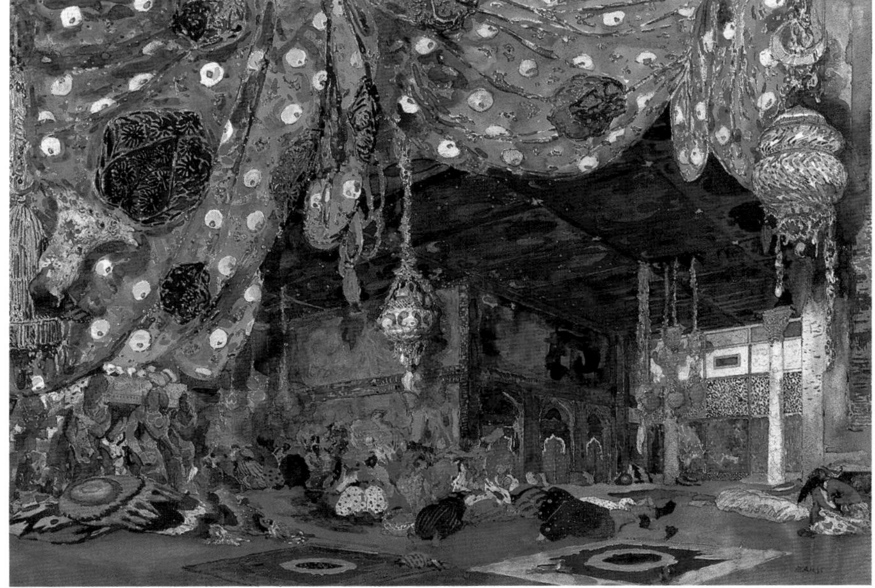

1920–1930," many of these Russian artists would "meet each other at the Académie Vassilieff founded in 1909 by Marie Vassilieff, or at the Académie Russe, located at number 54 Cosmopolitan." It was here that "Marie Vassilieff organised a canteen where Russian émigrés came in close contact with French artists."[21] At this café fellow artists such as Fernand Léger often gave talks and held conferences on a broad range of subjects. Brodovitch was probably introduced to the world of the Parisian avant-garde through this artistic group. This is not to say he would have been unaware of developments in the arts prior to arriving in Paris. Like most children of the European aristocracy, a brief schooling in the classical narratives of Western art was seen as fundamental to a rounded education. However, the radical artistic milieu of postwar France would have been something new to this twenty-two-year-old ex-solider. The contacts made among his fellow Russian artists eventually enabled Brodovitch to gain more creative forms of work. Within a few months of arriving he had obtained a short-term position as a painter of backdrops for Diaghilev's Ballets Russes. This rendezvous with Diaghilev would not only influence his move toward commercial art but, more importantly, spark a career that thrived on collaboration.

Serge Diaghilev's Ballet Russes gave its first performance at the Theâtre du Châtelet on 19 May 1909. It was a major event in terms of theater, stage design, and fashion. Throughout the 1910s and 1920s Diaghilev's far-reaching influence on popular design is legendary. His influence can be seen in Art Deco, haute couture, and music. Diaghilev's legacy to the 1920s was, however, more than the individual aspects of his productions. His lasting influence for Brodovitch, and many others, was his willingness to integrate completely all the arts in his productions. Blind to boundaries of craft or profession, his work was a total realization of the Wagnerian idea of "*Gesamtkunstwerk*," a synthesis of music, dance, and stage sets for an overall dramatic effect. The scholar Charles S. Mayer describes this synthesis of the arts in a Diaghilev production:

In the Ballets Russes productions, music, design, and dance were unified by means of an added emphasis on the spectacle, that is, costumes and decors. [One of Diaghilev's designers, Léon] Bakst equated designing a ballet to creating a painting and saw the ballet as a continually changing succession of frames of a large picture. These individual frames were coordinated through a sequence of interrelated rhythms expressed by music, choreography, color harmonies, and the plastic elements of the decors and costumes which had to express the specific emotional tone evoked by the music. These diverse elements were all subordinated to each other in order to create the "finished poem."[22]

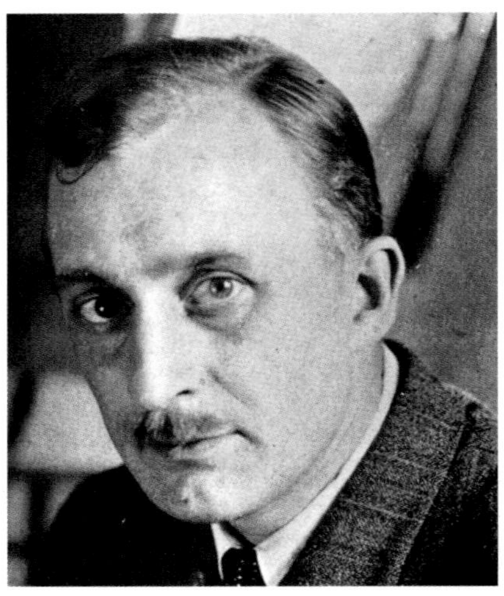

Diaghilev's integrated approach to design was obviously absorbed and understood by Brodovitch. It was a way of working that would eventually find its way onto the pages of *Harper's Bazaar* and its apogee in the conception and production of *Observations* and *Portfolio* (see chapters 4 and 5).

For many Russian artists the Ballets Russes operated as a vital link between Russia and the West. With the twofold advantage of being based in Paris and thus removed from the political turmoil of post-revolutionary Russia, Diaghilev's company offered many émigrés an opening into the artistic developments of European modernism. Thus, working at the Ballets Russes, like at the Académie Vassilieff, gave Brodovitch an opportunity to meet artists who would not only fuel his desire to learn but also generate a lifelong fascination with the new. Even though he was still unsure of what artistic direction he should take, meetings with Picasso, Anna Pavlova, Nijinsky, Massine, Derain, Christian Bérard, and Alexander Benois obviously contributed to his accelerated visual education. Brodovitch would forever draw on this intense period of learning, allowing it to satiate his creative appetite like a "movable feast."[23]

Unfortunately, we have no record of which Ballets Russes productions Brodovitch worked on. What is more important however, is that we know he was part of a ferocious climate of invention and collaboration, one not just limited to Diaghilev. In spare moments away from the Ballets Russes, at nights or weekends, Brodovitch began sketching designs for textiles, china, and jewelry. When the work with Diaghilev finished, he had already compiled an extensive portfolio to take to prospective clients. Visiting designers such as Patou, Poiret, Bianchini, Rodier, and Schiaparelli, Brodovitch was successful in selling his designs. Calling upon these renowned designers, Brodovitch apparently presented an image of the cultivated gentleman. Alexandre Alexeïeff, the Russian engraver and one of Brodovitch's many future collaborators, met Brodovitch in 1921 and painted this portrait of the young designer:

Alexey had a little moustache, he wore a broad checked greenish-grey jacket, the kind the rich used to wear for hunting; Alexey's jacket must have come from some charity collection of used clothes. He wore English-cut breeches and army leggings, relics of the war which were still commonly worn. Brodovitch also wore a Tyrolian-style hat, not a worker's hat (like us, like me). He took care of his looks.... I immediately noticed his good manners.[24]

It has been mentioned by some of Brodovitch's relatives that during the time he spent in Paris he was not an originator of the new, but, rather, tuned his astute antennae to the shifts in visual culture around him.[25] Commercial art, or what was to become known as the graphic/applied arts, was still in the process of

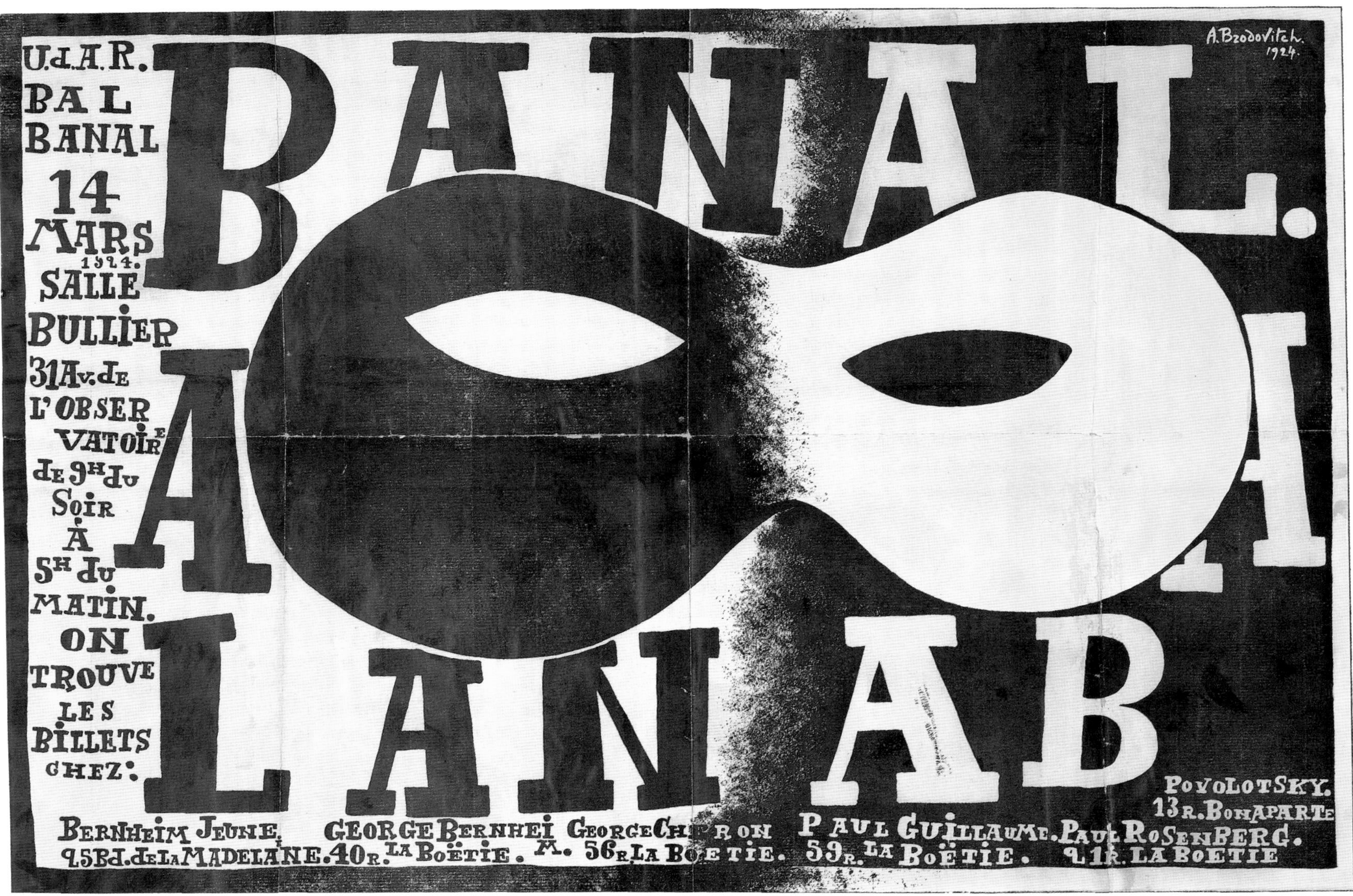

Opposite: Alexey Brodovitch, photographer unknown, c. 1928.

Above: Poster for the Bal Banal, 1924.
Produced on the occasion of a party for fellow Russian émigrés in Paris, the Bal Banal poster was Brodovitch's first illustration to receive widespread recognition and acclaim. For Brodovitch, it marked the beginning of his design career.

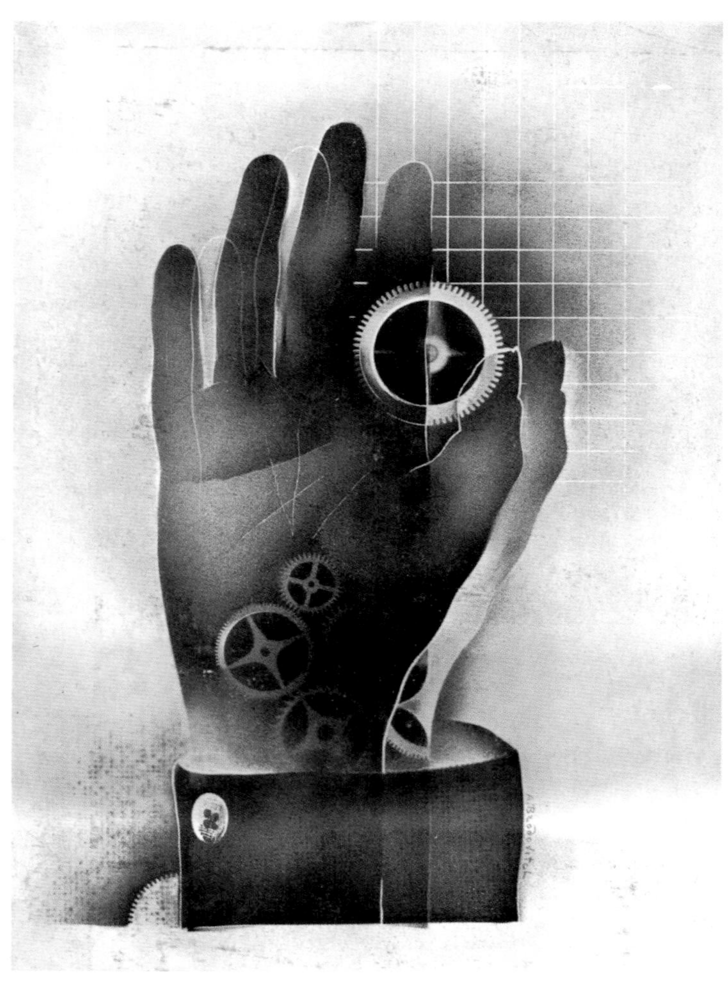

crystallizing into a singular discipline in the early 1920s. Thus, while his designs for textiles, porcelain, glass, and jewelry enabled Brodovitch and Nina to survive, the eclectic nature of his work is symptomatic of the ill-defined identity of the profession at the time. It was precisely because of its diffuse constitution, however, that commercial art was especially porous to the waves of radical movements and ideas flooding into the city through books, magazines, and journals. Paris operated as a willing recipient of all these competing theories of the visual. Brodovitch, alongside many other artists, was uniquely placed to absorb the key ideas of Cubism, Constructivism, Purism, and Surrealism. Embracing technical developments from the spheres of industrial design, photography, and contemporary painting, Brodovitch's broad curiosity began to assimilate the most interesting aspects of all these fields into his work, eventually making them his own. What he required was a medium that would enable him to synthesize these ideas into a manageable whole. Searching for a visual form that would allow his graphic sensibility to be permanently inventive, but also provide some continuity through which his ideas could take shape and develop, the turning point for Brodovitch was his entry into the Bal Banal poster competition.

On Friday, 24 March 1924, the Union of Russian Artists gave a party, the Bal Banal, organized to help undernourished compatriots in Paris. A poster competition, held in the Salle Bullier, was created to find the most innovatory design to publicize the event. With his eclectic approach favoring an openness to all forms of artistic production, Brodovitch entered the competition and won first prize. Together with a drawing by Picasso, which came second in the competition, Brodovitch's poster was exhibited on walls all over Montparnasse. The Bal Banal design is essentially a contemporaneous example of Art Deco. The amalgamation of type and illustration into a coherent overall pattern is characteristic of such posterists as Cassandre and Jean Carlu. The poster itself is the oldest piece of surviving work by Brodovitch. Yet, its importance arises not from its rarity but its significance marking the beginning of a shift in Brodovitch's career. From 1924 until leaving France for America in 1930, Brodovitch would focus more and more on the fields of graphic design, advertising, and illustration. As Andy

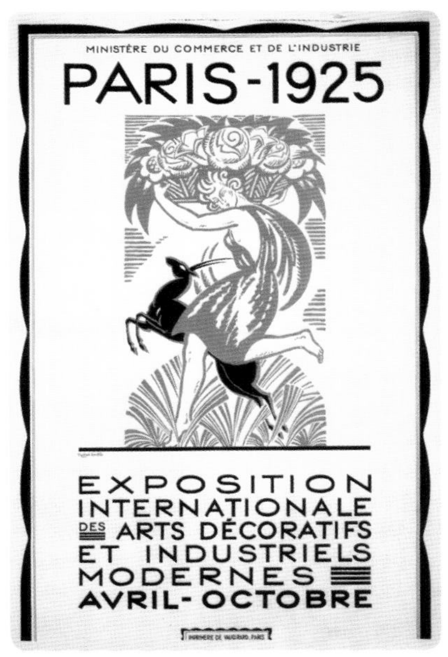

Opposite: Untitled Brodovitch design, c. 1930.
Brodovitch's artistic development paralleled the rise of modernity; hands were a frequent motif in his work.

Right: Poster for the Exposition Internationale Des Arts Décoratifs et Industriels Modernes, 1925. Design by Robert Bonfils.
Brodovitch was commissioned to create several designs for the historic Art Deco exhibition. Although he won five awards, no records exist of his work.

Grundberg recognized in his monograph *Brodovitch*, the Bal Banal poster's "graphic, light-to-dark inversion of its mask shape, type, and background not only suggests the positive-negative process of photography, but also symbolically represents the process of masking: one trades one's identity for another, contrary one."[26] The Bal Banal was, as Brodovitch commented, "the beginning of my career."[27] The poster was a piece of work that marked a transition from Brodovitch, the talented Russian artist, to Brodovitch, the graphic designer and art director.

In the early years of commerce's alliance with art, the poster provided a unique form through which to assess the possible value, for both business and artist, of this untried and untested partnership. Even though the 1890s marked the supposed "golden age" of the poster, following the Great War the growth in consumerism sparked a return to mass advertising throughout the West. The twenties witnessed the steady growth of a society in which leisure became a significant part of everyday life. French society was no exception; in 1919, the French government introduced the eight-hour workday. The average Parisian's experience of this growth in free time was heightened by the sheer multitude of entertainments on offer. Nearly anything could be bought on a street corner. Cinemas, department stores, cabarets, theaters, restaurants, and bars offered young people something their parents could only have dreamed of a decade previously. To attract the attention of a public bombarded by these spectacles of modern life, more emphasis was placed on the role of the "arts located in the street."[28] For many commercial artists, including Brodovitch, this growth of street art was considered a positive development. Bringing good design to a broader audience was a way of demystifying the otherwise inaccessible ideas of the avant-garde. However, the Parisian public was not altogether ready to accept the modernist dictates of Constructivism or de Stijl in their purist form. In 1925, the historic success of the exposition "Arts Décoratifs et Industriels Modernes" seems to confirm this reticence.

Planned for 1915 but postponed because of the war, the Art Deco exposition opened its doors to the public in April 1925. Because of the ten-year delay, the exhibition was immediately accused by some as being entirely at odds with the developments witnessed in the graphic arts over the preceding decade. As the design historian Steven Heller has noted, it was seen by some as more "a triumph of Moderne over Modern, of design linked to art, not to the machine."[29] Following his success with the Bal Banal, Brodovitch came to the attention of various designers, advertising agencies, and studios. Through collaborations with, for example, the famous couture house Becker Fils, Brodovitch was commissioned to create several designs for the Art Deco exhibition. Unfortunately, once again, no records exist of this

Untitled Brodovitch design, c. 1930.
Brodovitch's artistic development paralleled the rise of modernity; hands were a frequent motif in his work.

work. What we do know is that he won five awards: three gold medals for kiosk design and jewelry, two silver medals for fabrics, and the top award for the Becker Fils pavilion "Amour de l'Art."[30]

Aside from the criticism leveled by some artists that the exhibition was antiquated – the Hungarian photographer Brassai said it was "erecting a tombstone for art"[31] – the exhibition did display Art Deco's willingness to meet the developments of modernist design halfway. Including the glass pavilion of Konstantin Melnikov, and Le Corbusier's "Pavilion d'un Espirit Nouveau," the exhibition endeavored to represent some of the ideas of the "machine age," if only in a perfunctory manner.[32] For Brodovitch, the exhibits by Melnikov and Le Corbusier seemed to have played a major role in reinforcing his emerging belief in the need for harmony and purpose in design. Alongside the key ideas of Fernand Léger, Constructivism, and the Bauhaus, Amédée Ozenfant's and Le Corbusier's Purist arguments, through their review *L' Espirit Nouveau*, were highly influential on Brodovitch. (Some biographical material suggests that Brodovitch actually studied at Amédée Ozenfant's Académie de l'Art Moderne, and Brodovitch once referred to working with Le Corbusier on the design of the Voisin automobile. However, no evidence exists to support either of these claims.) The shift from the unpolished style of the Bal Banal poster to the more pure and machine-like designs in the second half of the twenties makes it possible to assert that in 1925 Brodovitch began to synthesize the various modernist strands into a unified approach to design and illustration. This consolidation of influences enabled him to focus the totality of his creative commitment in one direction: advertising.[33] "One thing is sure," as Le Corbusier said, "1925 marks the decisive turning point in the quarrel between the old and the new." For some, this turning point signaled the end.[34] For Brodovitch, success at the 1925 exhibition provided him with new opportunities to put these radical ideas into action.

With the growth of commercial design, many aspects of the avant-garde were being appropriated and synthesized by designers like Brodovitch, specifically through the medium of the poster. One of the consequences of this was that many of the elitist connotations associated with these movements were being democratized (and depoliticized) through their utilization in the promotion of mass-produced commodities. At the forefront of these appropriations were department stores and advertising agencies. Following the 1925 exhibition, Brodovitch was solicited by the famous Parisian stores Printemps and Bon Marché to produce posters and lavish catalogues for forthcoming collections. Succeeding this was a request by the ad agency Maximilien Vox (owned by the renowned typographer and designer of the same name) for a poster advertising Martini Vermouth. Highlighting the impact of the simple geometric forms of early 1920s Constructivist graphics on his work, Brodovitch created a 1926 Martini poster similar in style to the Constructivist productions of El Lissitzky. Against a white background, Brodovitch utilizes a sparse but elegant combination of text, circle, and square to create an uncomplicated and pure design. Like most of Brodovitch's other work, however, these individual creations offered him little control over their final application or display. Witnessing Diaghilev's orchestration of the Ballets Russes five years before, Brodovitch would have clearly recognized the advantage of being able to direct all aspects of a creative production. A commission in 1926 by the seafood restaurant Prunier to design the restaurant, menus, and layout provided Brodovitch with the first occasion to realize this particular modus operandi.

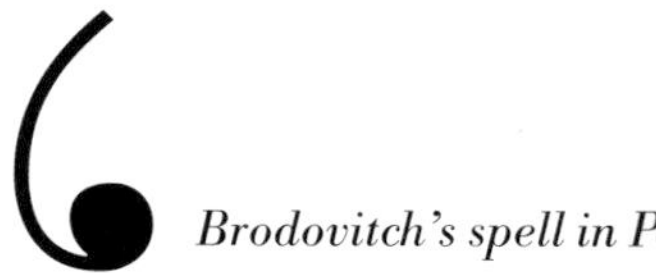

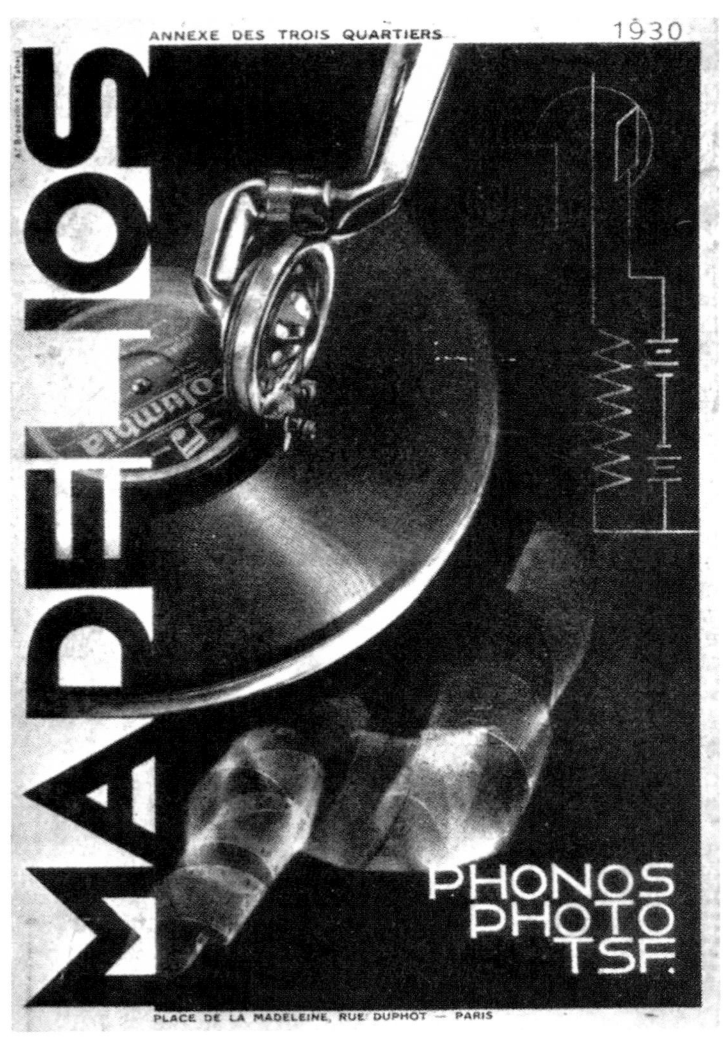

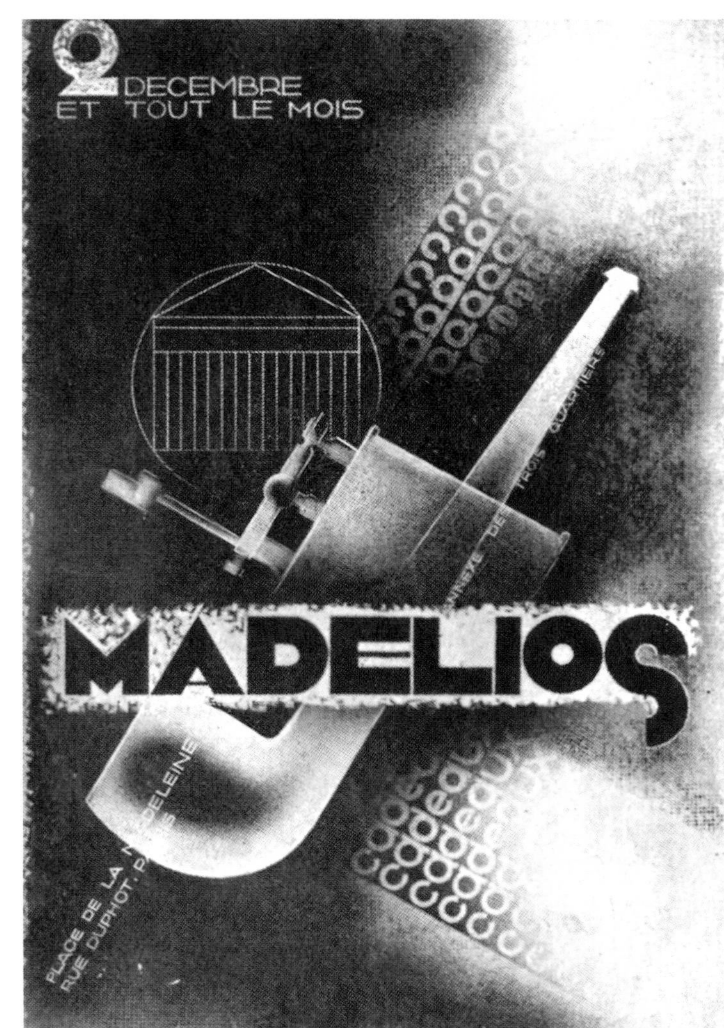

Aside from being the design department for Aux Trois Quartiers, the Athélia studio also offered interior design services to the store's customers.[42] Considering the circumspect nature of the Parisian public's desire for stark modernist design, Brodovitch's Athélia advertisements cleverly blend classical busts within an inventive layout. These traditional-modern motifs can also be witnessed in the recurring use of a portico throughout the advertisements for Madelios. Located at 10, place de la Madeleine on the rue Duphot, Madelios was close to the famous building of Madeleine. Ever conscious of Robert Block's imperative that all commercial designs should "impress themselves on the brain by continual repetition," Brodovitch cleverly incorporated details of Madeleine's portico in most of the Madelios designs. Ultimately, through constant iteration, these emblems eventually came to function "both as a kind of logotype for the store and as a signpost of its location."[43]

Designs for Athélia, interior design studio of Aux Trois Quartiers department store, Paris, c. 1928–1930. Athélia was under the artistic directorship of architect Robert Block, whose theories about design and advertising greatly influenced Brodovitch. Recognizing that many of Athelia's customers were fairly traditional in their design tastes, Brodovitch cleverly utilized classical motifs to moderate the impact of his radical designs.

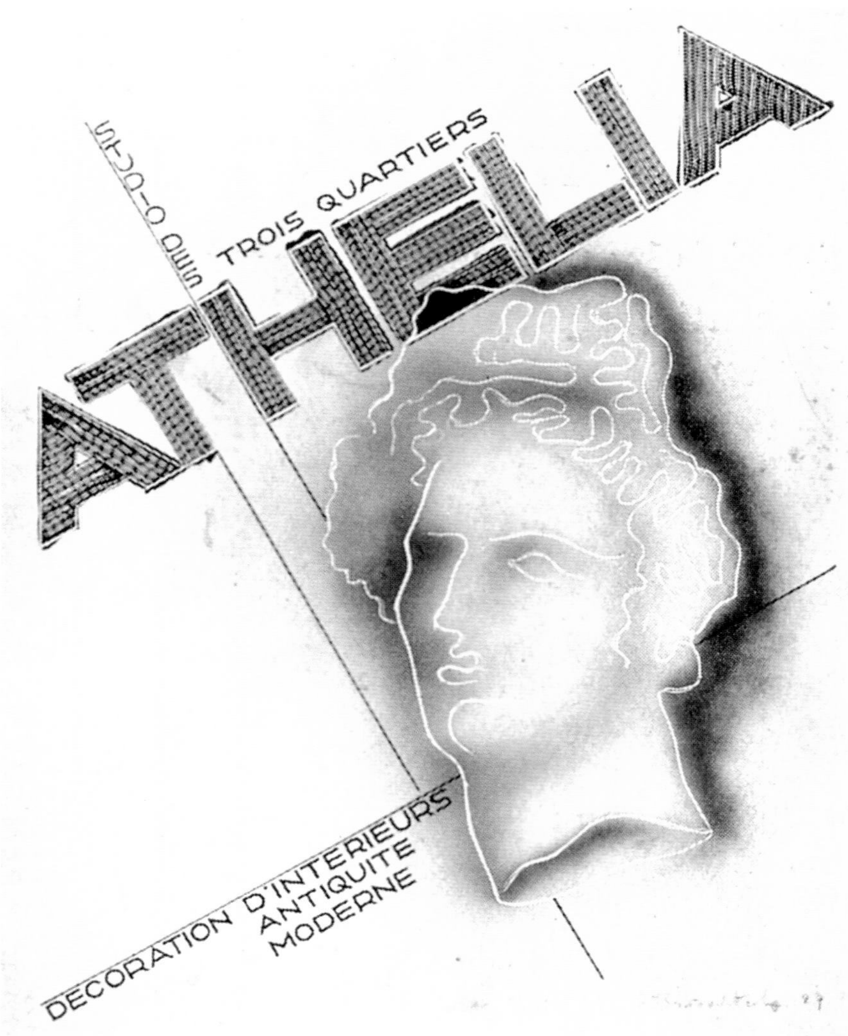

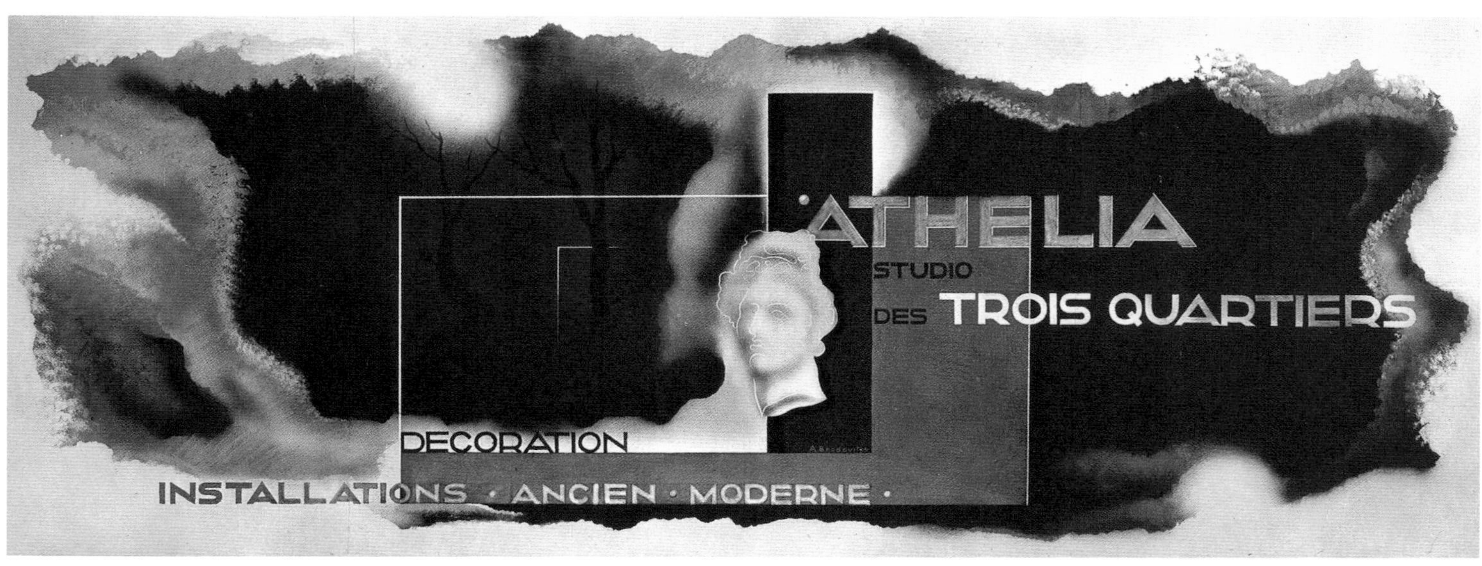

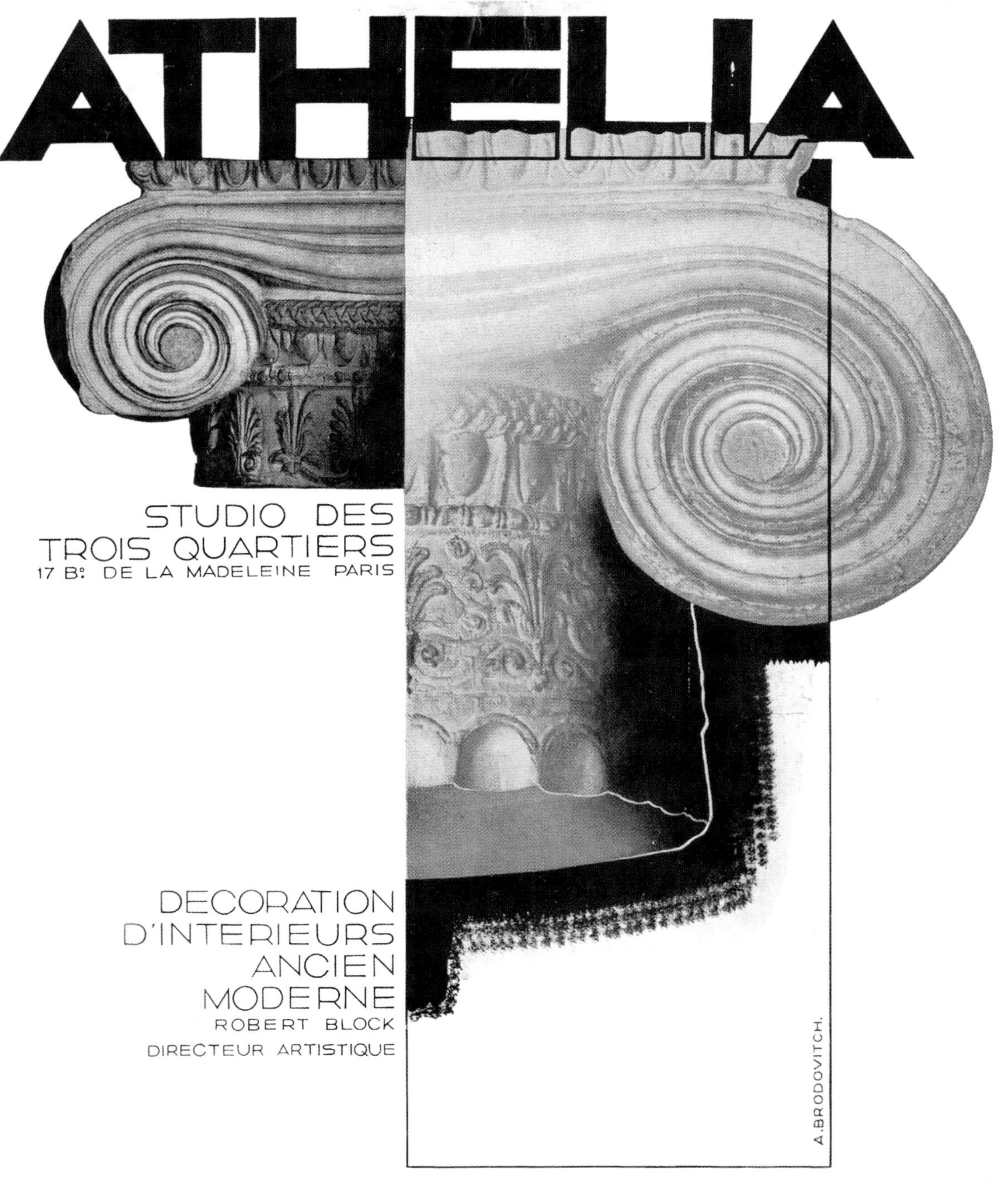
ATHELIA
STUDIO DES
TROIS QUARTIERS
17 B.D DE LA MADELEINE PARIS
DECORATION
D'INTERIEURS
ANCIEN
MODERNE
ROBERT BLOCK
DIRECTEUR ARTISTIQUE
A.BRODOVITCH.

Even though Brodovitch was employed full-time by the Athélia studio from 1928 to 1930, he continued to offer and develop his services as a freelance graphic designer during this same period. Working through his own studio, L'Atelier A.B., Brodovitch produced posters for various clients, including Union Radio Paris and Boucheron/Cartier/La Cloche. His most well known commission was his poster for the Cunard shipping company. Despite this growth in work, the problem for Brodovitch seems to have been that most clients now wanted their services associated with the dominant Art Deco style. Faced with these demands – and as with the other work he created through L'Atelier A.B. for Donnet cars, Nicolet gloves, and Nitrolac enamel – the Cunard poster seems to simply ape the style of the day. With Brodovitch probably regarding this sort of design passé, he doubtless would have devised and completed the illustration very quickly. Alongside L'Atelier A.B., Brodovitch also worked with Le Cercle, an association of commercial designers. Based at 4, square de Port-Royal, its members included Brodovitch's old friend Alexandre Alexeïeff, as well as the photographer Roger Parry.[44] As Cattaruzza has noted, Brodovitch's influential position at Aux Trois Quartiers now enabled him to provide his collaborators at Le Cercle with some design commissions. Little is known about his own work at Le Cercle. But Brodovitch did produce two designs for the association itself, the most important being the logo for the collective, which has echoes of a solar eclipse. It has also been said that, working through these studios, Brodovitch created editorial layouts for periodicals such as *Arts et Métiers Graphiques* and *Cahiers d'Art*.

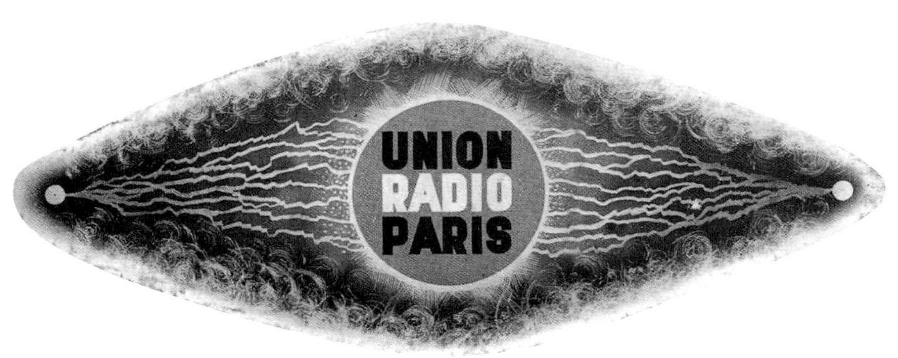

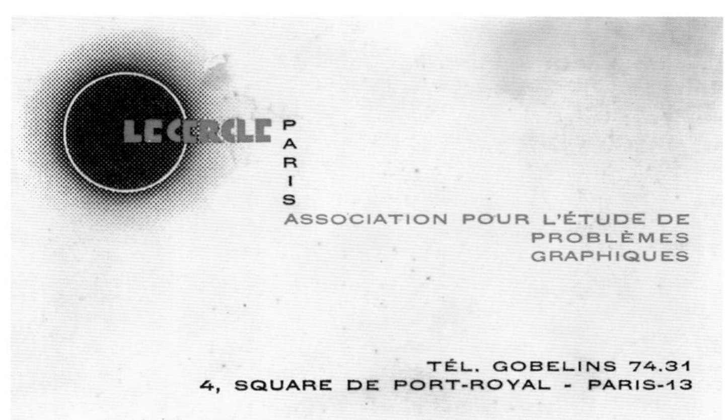

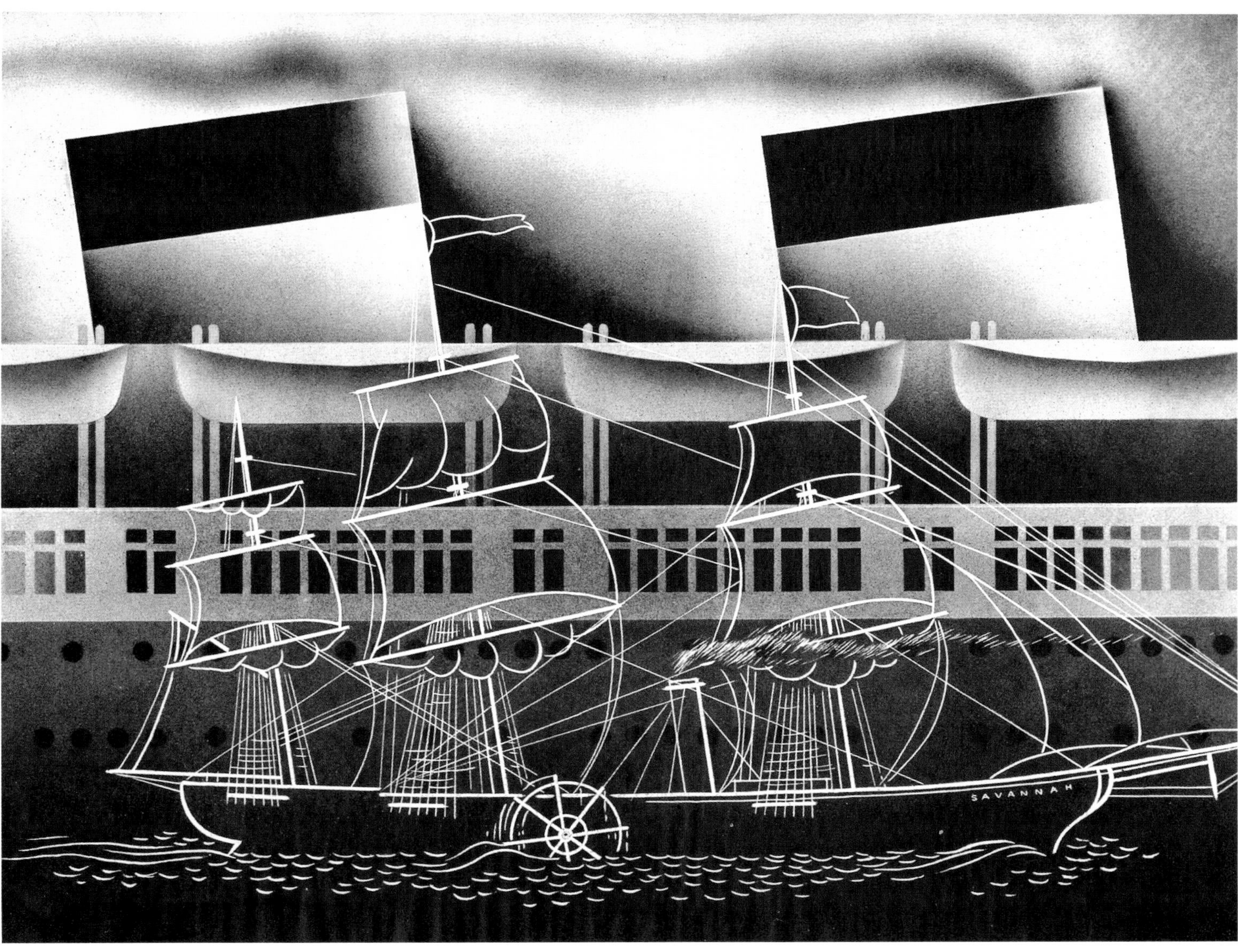

Opposite left: Logo for Union Radio Paris, c. 1929.

Opposite right: Le Cercle business card, Paris, c. 1929.
While still contracted to Aux Trois Quartier department store, Brodovitch worked with Le Cercle, an association of graphic designers, and designed the group's logo.

Above: Untitled Brodovitch design, c. 1928.

CE LIVRE, LE DIXIÈME DE LA COLLECTION « LES AUTEURS CLASSIQUES RUSSES » A ÉTÉ TIRÉ A 1.600 EXEMPLAIRES, DONT : 50 EXEMPLAIRES SUR HOLLANDE VAN GELDER, NUMÉROTÉS DE 1 A 50, 1.550 EXEMPLAIRES SUR VÉLIN DU MARAIS, NUMÉROTÉS DE 51 A 1.600, ET 50 EXEMPLAIRES HORS COMMERCE.

EXEMPLAIRE N° 948

F. DOSTOÏEVSKY

CONTES FANTASTIQUES

TRADUCTION DE
B. DE SCHLŒZER ET J. SCHIFFRIN
ORNEMENTS DE A. BRODOVITCH

ÉDITIONS DE LA PLÉIADE
J. SCHIFFRIN, 2, RUE HUYGHENS - PARIS

RÊVE D'UN HOMME RIDICULE

façon absolument affirmative : « Oui. » C'est-à-dire : je me tuerai. Je savais à coup sûr que cette nuit-là je me tuerais. Mais combien de temps encore resterais-je ainsi devant cette table, — cela je n'en savais rien...

Et je me serais tué, c'est certain, n'eût été cette petite fille.

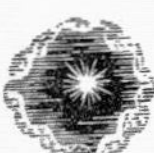

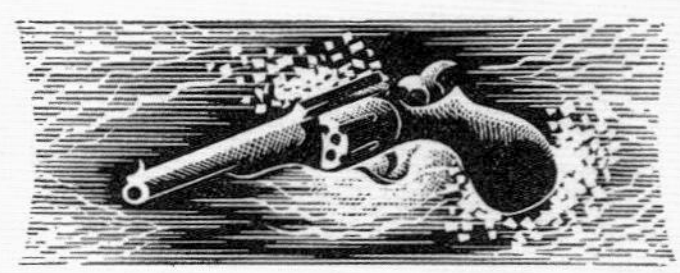

CHAPITRE II

VOYEZ-VOUS, bien que tout me fût égal, j'étais sensible, par exemple, à la douleur. Si quelqu'un m'eût frappé, j'eusse ressenti une douleur. De même dans le domaine moral : s'il me fût arrivé quelque chose de triste, j'en eusse éprouvé un sentiment pénible, — comme au temps où tout ne m'était pas encore égal dans la vie. Aussi avais-je ressenti tout à l'heure de la pitié; je serais certes toujours venu en aide à un enfant. Pourquoi donc n'avais-je pas secouru cette petite? A cause d'une idée

147

Opposite: Title page (top) and inside spread from *Contes Fantastiques*, by F. Dostoïevsky, [Fyodor Dostoyevsky]. Illustrations by Brodovitch. Paris: Editions de La Pléiade, 1929.
By way of his own studio, L'Atelier A.B., Brodovitch was commissioned to illustrate several limited-edition books throughout the late 1920s. These designs were distinctive because they alluded to aspects of the books' narratives while maintaining their singularity as significant works of art in themselves.

Right: Selected illustrations from *A Brief History of Moscovia*, by John Milton. Illustrations by Brodovitch. London: Blackmore Press, 1929.
Like his designs for Prunier restaurant in Paris, these illustrations allude to the Russian popular print to depict various places in Moscovia (Russia).

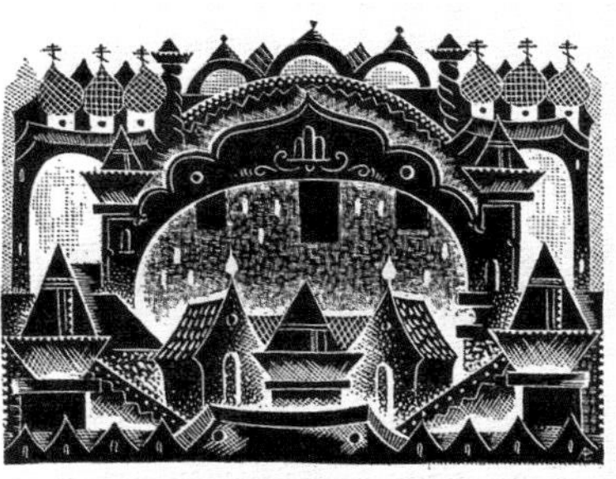

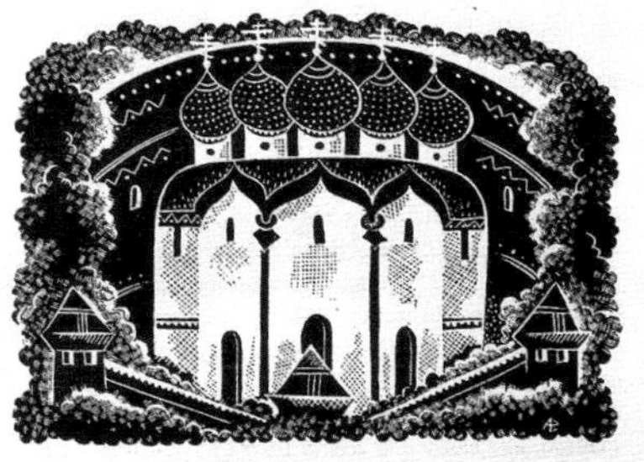

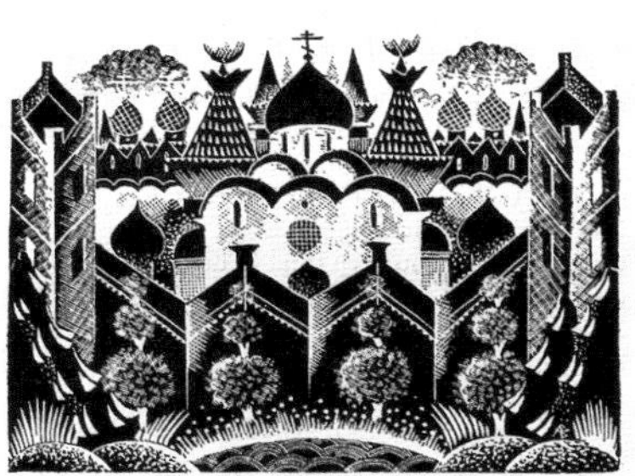

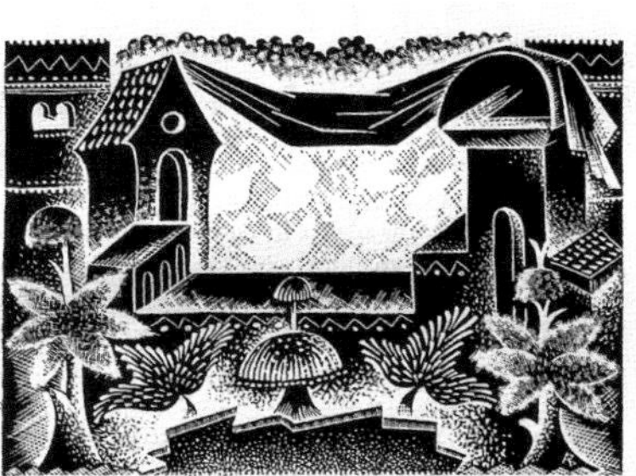

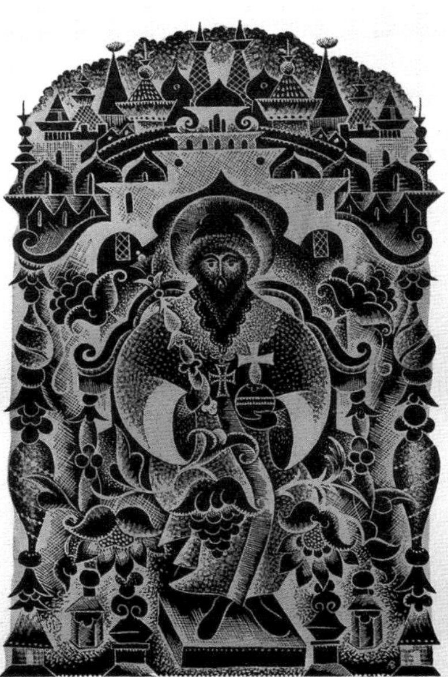

In 1928 and 1929, Brodovitch was also commissioned by the Parisian publishing house La Pléiade to illustrate three books: *Nouvelles* by Aleksander Pushkin, *Contes Fantastiques* by Fyodor Dostoyevsky, and *Monsieur de Bougrelon* by Jean Lorrain. Additional book commissions came from Blackmore Press in London to illustrate one of John Milton's lesser known works, *A Brief History of Moscovia*,[15] from André Delpeuch Press to design Franz Toussaint's *La Sultane de L'Amour*, and from Briffaut Press to illustrate another Toussaint title, *Le Ramayana*. All produced during the same period as Brodovitch's Madelios work, the mastery of these illustrations lies in their ability to achieve an aesthetic harmony with the books' contents. Offering a backward glance to earlier design forms, the seven designs for *A Brief History of Moscovia* are, for instance, like the Prunier designs, reminiscent of the Russian *lubok*. Utilizing the semantic perspective characteristic of the *lubok* – where objects are represented according to their narrative importance – the bookplate for Moscovia shows Brodovitch's oversized impression of a Russian Orthodox priest. Making use of the same method of "reverse perspective," the other six illustrations are a collection of figurative designs of churches and imperial palaces throughout Moscovia (Russia). In Fyodor Dostoyevsky's anthology *Contes Fantastiques*, Brodovitch use the same method. These decorative plates illustrate the book's content through their delicate ornamentation of chapter headings. One of Brodovitch's most interesting book illustrations was for Jean Lorrain's *Monsieur de Bougrelon*. In a drawing of two men, the harsh lines and elongation of their faces are emphasized in an austere angular style. Once again, like the Madelios designs, Brodovitch created a sense of depth and solidity throughout the drawing by the gradual disintegration of these dense lines into a blinding white space. This contrasting use of white space would eventually become a trademark of Brodovitch's work at *Harper's Bazaar* – where, it was reported, he was loath to allow any corruption of its unadulterated surface by type or image (see chapter 2).

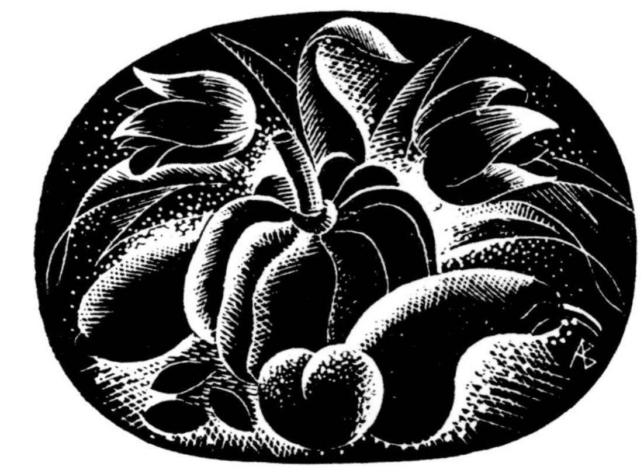

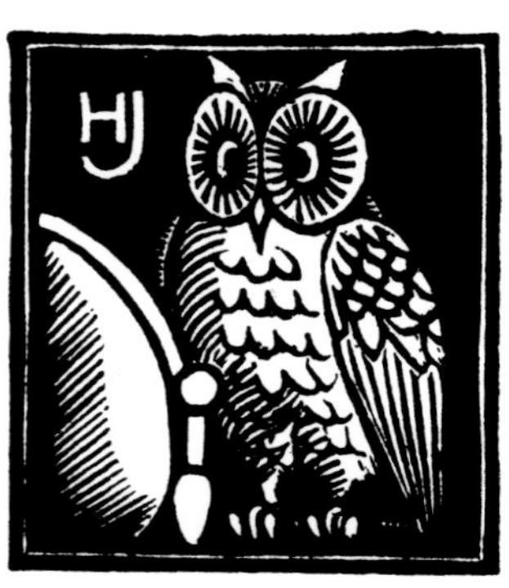

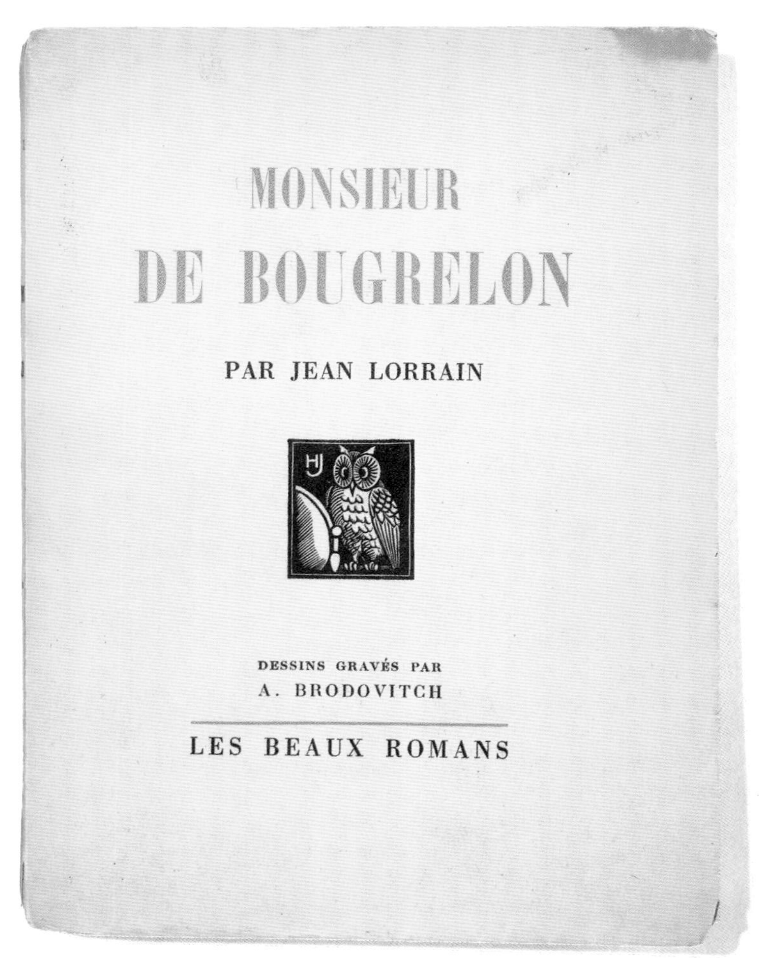

MONSIEUR
DE BOUGRELON

PAR JEAN LORRAIN

DESSINS GRAVÉS PAR
A. BRODOVITCH

LES BEAUX ROMANS

Above and left: Cover and selected illustrations from *Monsieur de Bougrelon*, by Jean Lorrain. Illustrations by Brodovitch. Paris: Les Beaux Romans, 1928.

Opposite: Illustration from *Monsieur de Bougrelon*.

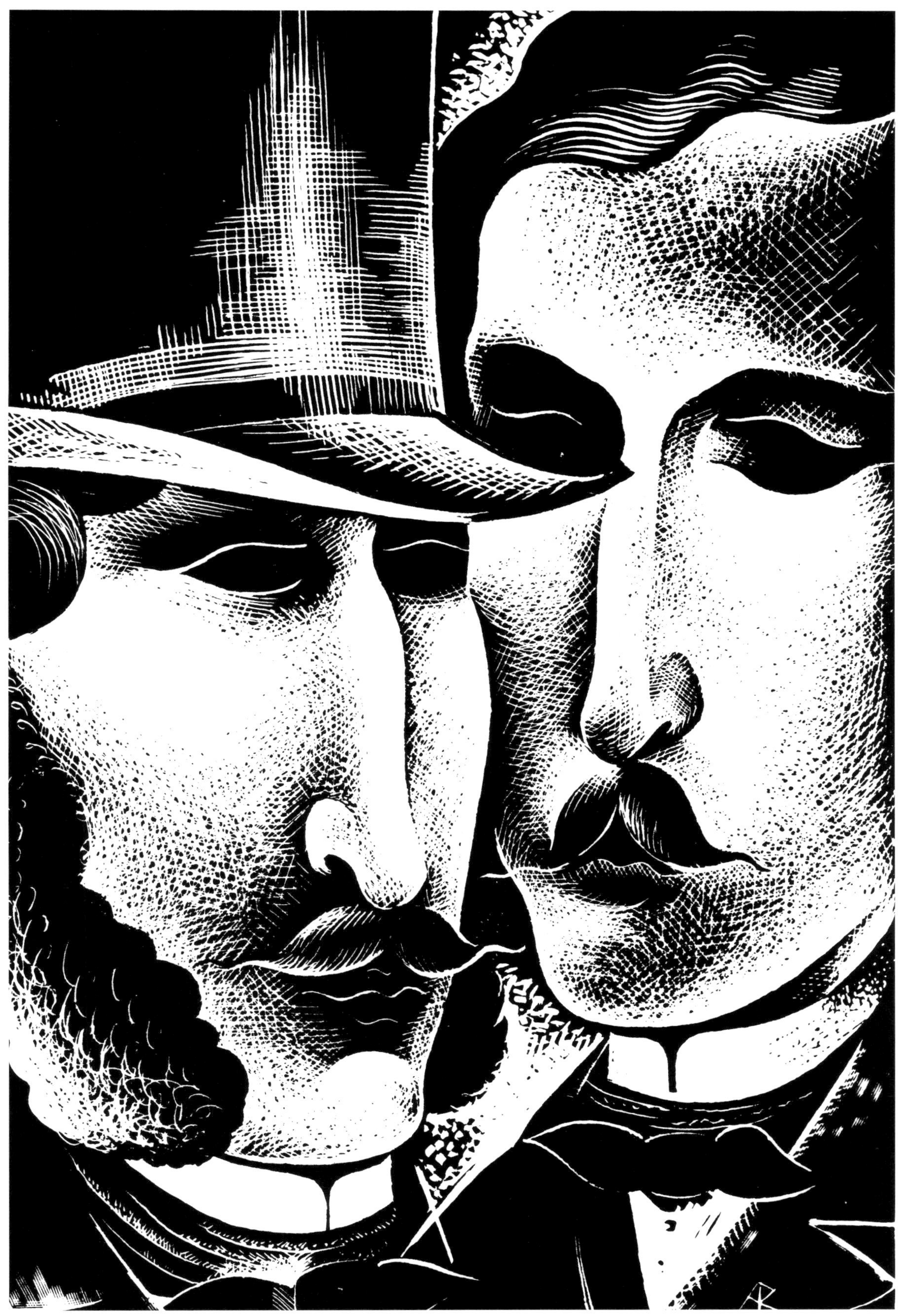

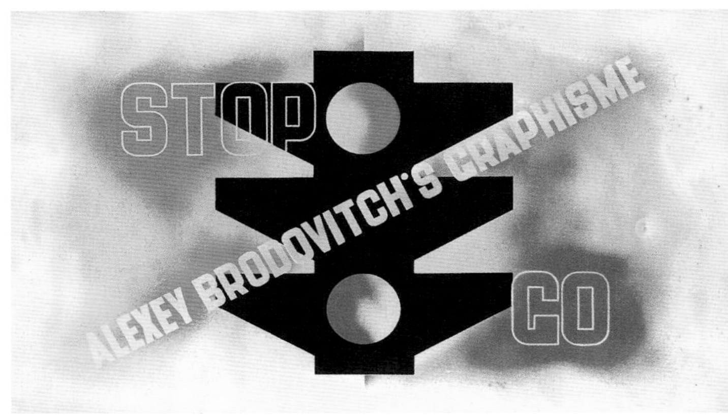

Above: Alexey Brodovitch's Graphisme, c. 1929. Brodovitch used the word *"graphisme"* to refer to those designs that successfully illustrated his ideas. *"Graphisme"* was also the title of a May 1929 article in *Arts et Métiers Graphiques* by Pierre Mac Orlan that was illustrated by Brodovitch.

Opposite top: Brodovitch family in Paris, 1930. Back: Alexey, father Cheslav, brother Georges. Front: Sister Marguerite, mother Ludmilla.

Opposite bottom: Brodovitch, his wife Nina, and his son Nikita, France, 1931.

Alexey Brodovitch was both a captive witness and an enthusiastic participant in the symphony of artistic experiments that was Paris in the twenties. Without any formal artistic training, Brodovitch's spell in Paris initiated a lifelong journey of self-education that would compel him to be permanently "inventive to the extreme." Producing posters, china, jewelry, textiles, advertisements, and paintings, Brodovitch had been perfectly attuned to the synthesis of the arts that infused every creative act. Eventually specializing in advertising and graphic design by the end of the decade, at the age of thirty-two Brodovitch had become one of the most respected designers of commercial art in Paris. Yet, by 1930, Paris had begun to lose the spirit of adventure and experimentation that had initially made it so attractive to young artists and immigrants from around the world. The international reverberations of the Wall Street crash and the beginnings of political upheaval throughout Europe resulted in a widespread reversion to the safety of traditional values, both artistically and socially. Diaghilev's death in 1929 just seemed to punctuate this sense of the end of an era. While still occupying the position of art director of Aux Trois Quartiers, Brodovitch had received many job offers from Parisian publishers. The sense of disillusionment throughout Paris must have been palpable, and Brodovitch presumably turned down many opportunities as he began to look elsewhere for the chance to advance new design ideas.

Despite its manifest parochialism, Brodovitch's work was beginning to reach an international audience of fellow designers and artists toward the end of the 1920s. This was especially so in America. Believing in the modernist triad of perpetual "progress, novelty, change," Brodovitch began to look across the Atlantic for new experiences and opportunities.[46] In the spring of 1928, he met the president of Pennsylvania University Museum and vice president of the Pennsylvania Museum of Art, John Story Jenks. John Story and his wife, Isobella, asked Brodovitch if he would be willing to take their daughter Ann Morton Jenks to lectures, exhibits, and museums throughout Paris, and he gladly acquiesced. While it is not known which artists she met or what exhibitions she attended with Brodovitch, it is clear that she was very impressed by his

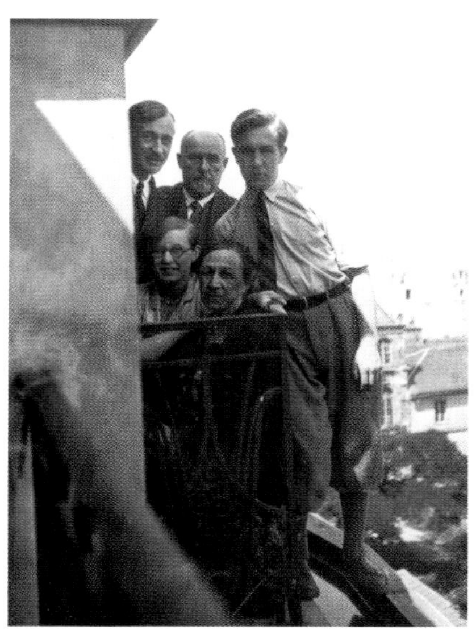

wide-ranging knowledge of art, design, and photography – so much so that she recommended to her father that Brodovitch come to Philadelphia to teach. Consequently, John Story Jenks asked Brodovitch if he would be interested in coming to Philadelphia to organize advertising classes in a school of industrial art. Brodovitch accepted the post immediately.[17] From Russia to Paris, historical events had propelled Brodovitch into a period of artistic invention that had cultivated his unique visual perspicacity. Modernism was on the move in the 1930s and history was about to launch him into a new arena. This time it was a place where his singular capacities would effect a major transformation in the essential quality of American design for decades to come.

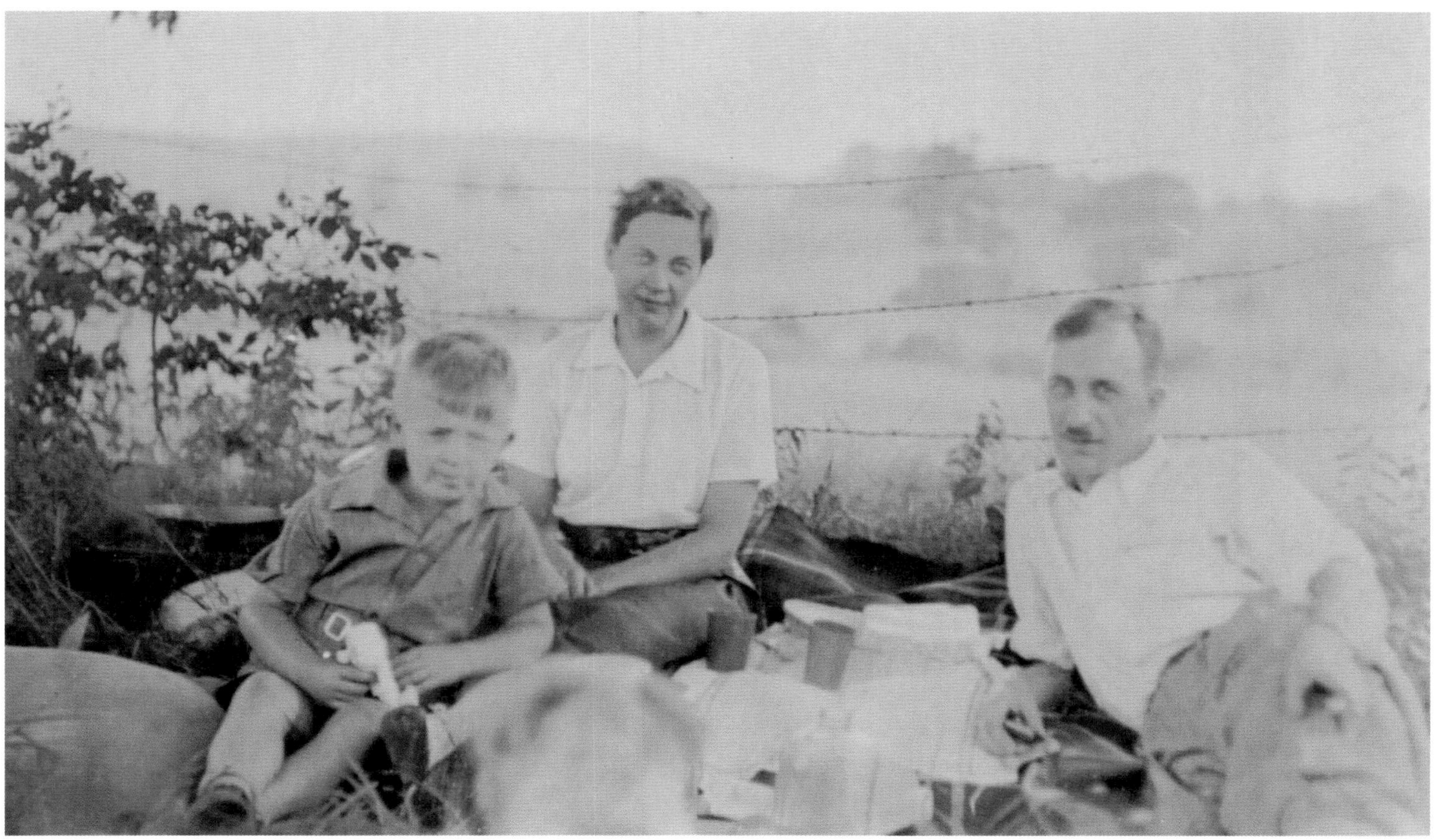

Harper's Bazaar: Paper Movies

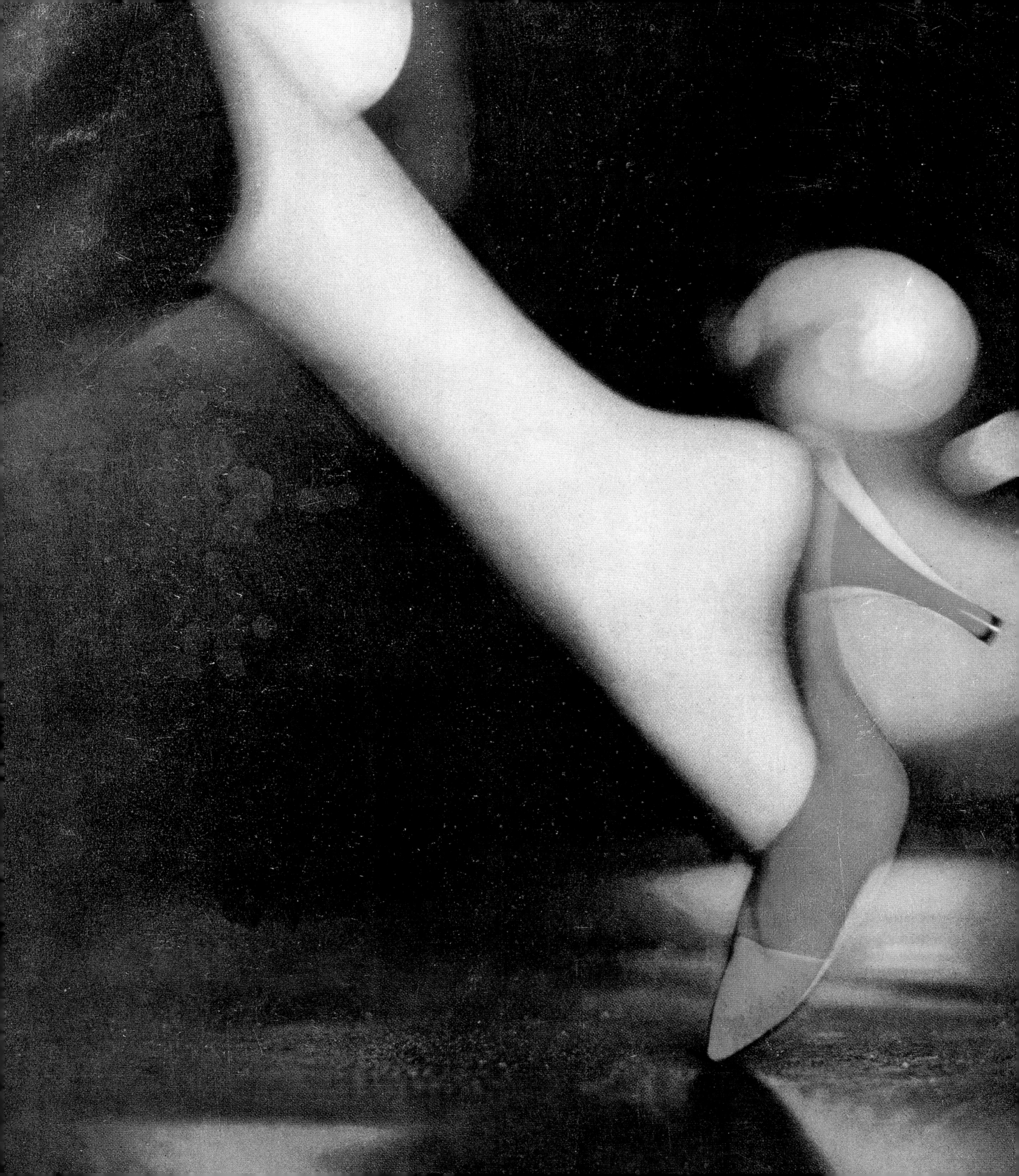

He was obsessed with change… I think it was a state of perpetual optimism. – Marvin Israel

Philadelphia

A myth perpetuated in historic accounts of European migration is the belief that America was the ideal home for radical modernists because it lacked the oppressive history and tradition associated with Europe. This may have been true for many in the artistic community, but for commercial artists the reality was different. Applied design in America of the late twenties and early thirties gravitated toward the twin values of conservatism and stability, not those of radical experimentation. More so than it did in Paris, the Wall Street crash of 1929 had a reactionary effect on the commercial arts. Confronted with the trauma of socioeconomic collapse, many companies shied away from pioneering designs and reverted to tried and trusted methods in advertising their products. It was as if returning to the publicly acceptable ornamentation of Art Nouveau "the discovery of commonalties could give meaning to the worth of the nation and reassure Americans of their ability to endure and triumph."[1]

Arriving at the Pennsylvania Museum School of Industrial Art in September 1930, Alexey Brodovitch was sheltered from this economic storm. As he was to discover, however, the conservatism of design prevalent in the commercial sphere was not just the result of the depression. It seemed that modern European typography, illustration, and design familiar to Brodovitch in Paris had yet to make an impact on the teaching of applied arts

Page 39: *Harper's Bazaar*, September 1956. Photograph by Richard Avedon.

at PMSIA. "When Brodovitch appeared at Pennsylvania," Virginia Smith noted in her 1994 essay "Launching Brodovitch," "students there were still rendering illustrations in the magazine style of N.C. Wyeth and Howard Pyle. Those beautiful, technically flawless pictures evolved from a nineteenth-century tradition of romantic realism.... News of the arrival of a Russian painter who had lived among modern artists in Paris intrigued the students. One of them reconnoitred Brodovitch's classes and was bowled over by the new things she saw in his classroom. When she told her classmates, twelve transferred...class into Brodovitch's."[2]

The initial attraction for students to Brodovitch's class seems to have been his diverse approach to what constituted design education. Breaking away from the repetitious practice of simply copying the "old master," Brodovitch's teaching method emphasized the dynamics of modern life as a valuable source for graphic ideas. In an early declaration of his thinking featured in the August 1930 edition of the British graphics periodical *Commercial Art*, Brodovitch pointed the way with the article "What Pleases the Modern Man":

Blinking lights of a city. The surface of the revolving phonograph record, the fantastic reflection of the red tail light and the tread of an automobile tyre on the wet pavement, the heroism and daring in the silhouette of an aeroplane. The rhythm of the biographical or statistical diagram....In the monotony and drudgery of a work-a-day world, there is to be found new beauty and a new aesthetic.[3]

Lacking any single theoretical approach to industrial art, Brodovitch taught by visual examples. His first act was always to show the students copies of French and German magazines that were influential on himself. Opening a copy of *Arts et Métiers Graphiques* or *Gebrauchsgraphik* Brodovitch would highlight an artist's design and then provoke his students into questioning the work. He would ask: "Could the line be better? Could it be like, for example, Cocteau?" Then he would show Cocteau in one of the magazines.[4] An inveterate collector of magazine cuttings, photographs, and typography, Brodovitch would frequently produce envelopes stuffed with examples of type and layout and use these cuttings to illustrate possible variations of a design. Brodovitch titled this method of using visual cues to pose a series of graphic questions "*graphisme*." It was a method of working that would find its apogee in the "montage of attractions" that was *Harper's Bazaar*.

As he did with his own work, Brodovitch encouraged his students to look beyond the traditional tools of the artist and exploit the variety of implements used throughout modern industrial production. He promoted the use of new methods, recommending such devices as "industrial lacquers, perfected hard, flexible steel needles, surgical knives...even dental implements may also adequately take the place of watercolours, undurable and clumsy brushes and charcoal pens and crayons."[5] In Paris this synthesis of techniques was, if not common, highly prevalent among many artists. In Philadelphia, Pennsylvania, it was for most students a new and exciting way of approaching the questions of form, color, texture, and depth in design.

Beyond the classroom, Brodovitch focused his students' minds on the radical developments of modern industry through class excursions. Being sympathetic to Léger's "Aesthetic of the Machine" where "every object, picture, piece of architecture... has a value in itself,"[6] Brodovitch took his students to "factories, laboratories, the zoo, shopping centers, housing projects, [and] dumps." Following these outings he would then "instruct them to make a 'graphic impression' of what they had seen. It could be a photographic interpretation, a drawing of the experience, or an abstraction."[7] Never one to curtail his expectations of an individual's response to a project, Brodovitch would then proceed to critique the student's work in just the same manner as he approached the illustrations of Jean Cocteau or George Grosz on the pages of *Gebrauchsgraphik*. In his essay "Revolution on Pine Street," the renowned designer Charles Coiner observed that each "student was told that he had the seed of his particular form of expression within himself and that from this a way of working would evolve." Brodovitch would then proceed "to uncover each student's capabilities. The student with a modest talent would receive no less attention than the genius. In the end he could be a capable craftsman if he made the most of his ability."[8] The work they produced was in many instances a mix of the traditional and modern similar to Brodovitch's Madelios work toward the

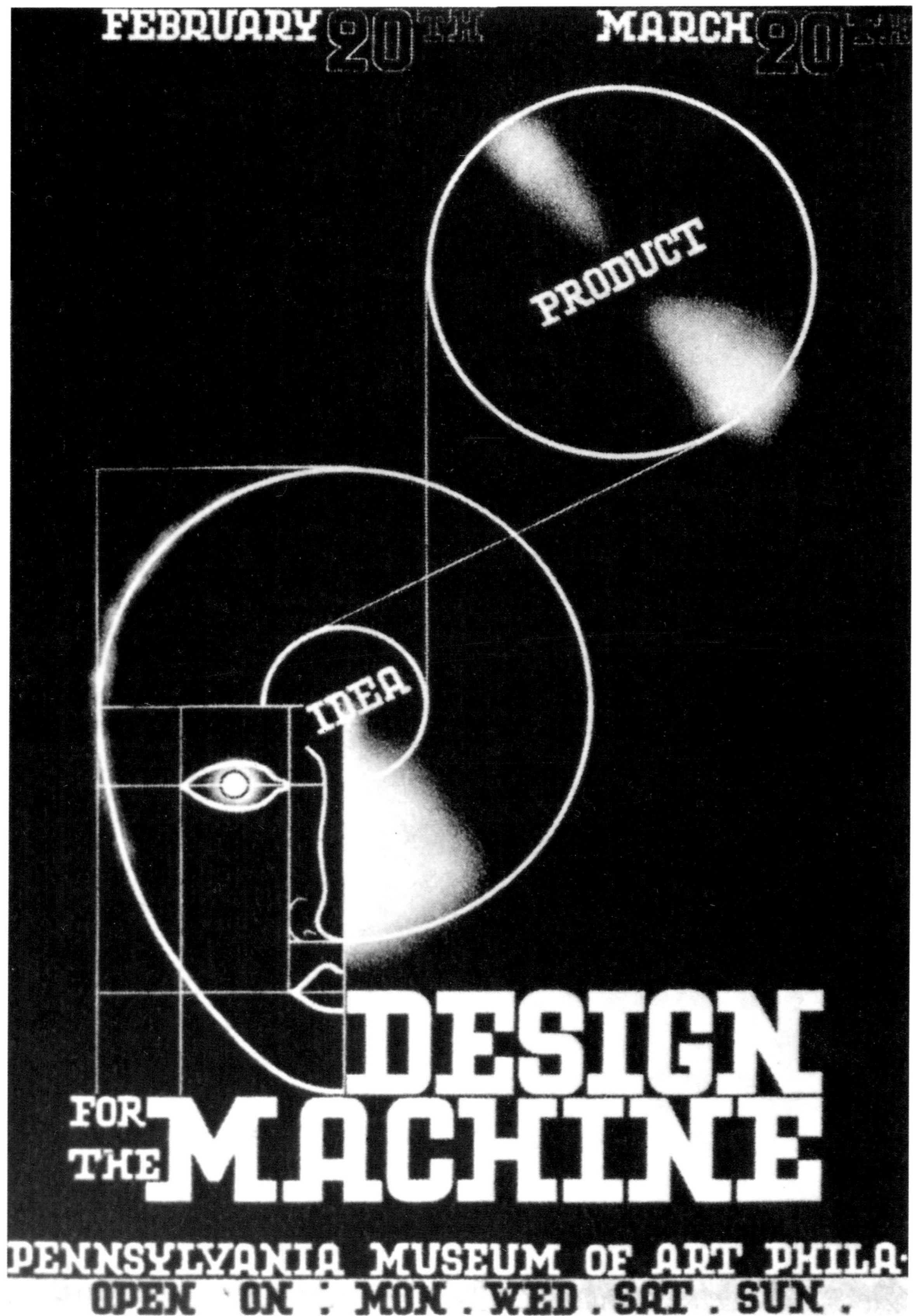
FEBRUARY 20TH MARCH 20TH
PRODUCT
IDEA
DESIGN
FOR THE MACHINE
PENNSYLVANIA MUSEUM OF ART PHILA·
OPEN ON : MON . WED . SAT . SUN .

Poster design for the exhibition "Design for the Machine Age" at the Pennsylvania Museum of Art, Philadelphia, 1937.

end of the 1920s. For example, according to Smith, achievements were frequently "inspired by the Surrealist art they had seen in the magazines – the unexpected pairing in a photograph of a massive Greek sculpture against piles of rubbish in a junkyard."[9] With his quiet and formal demeanor Brodovitch would provoke and question the student. His comments would be reduced to simple statements such as "Why not do dis?" or "Why not try dis way?" which would then be followed by a "loose sketch."[10] In general, Brodovitch's prompting was always an attempt to cultivate the inherent faculties of his students from below, not to impart knowledge from above.

Brodovitch's low Russian accent would compel students to focus on his comments. As Harvey Lloyd, a later student and friend of Brodovitch, once remarked, it seemed that he consciously exploited this need by students to make an extra effort to understand what he was saying. For Brodovitch, it was just another way of making them think for themselves:

I know that when [Brodovitch] walked into a room, especially when there were sixty people in the room chattering, shouting at each other and showing each other their work, he would walk in the room, this slight little man, there was a sudden hush.... Shhh. Not a sound. Until he spoke in his very low voice and said, "Thank you gentleman, we will begin now, let me see what you've done." And somebody in the back would say: "Mr Brodovitch, I can't hear you," [and not raising his voice, he would say] "Oh, I'm very sorry, I'll talk louder, can you hear me now." And that's the way it was, you want to hear him, get up front. The idea was he was not there so that you could get it the easy way. If you wanted it you went after it.[11]

Unaware of it at the time, his pressure on students to take more control of their artistic development represented the beginnings of the modernization and professionalization of the industrial artist. By underlining the importance of complete command over the creative process, Brodovitch played a major role in the shift from "commercial artist" or "layout man," who executed someone else's concepts, to graphic designer (and art director), who plays a central role in the conception of printed matter.[12] His time spent in Paris at Aux Trois Quartiers and Le Cercle had highlighted the value of overseeing a project from initial conception to finished article.

Through a series of exercises that compelled his students to articulate original ideas, Brodovitch's teaching was an illustration of these practical experiences. The result, as Coiner observed, was that "graduating students came out of the school with well-prepared and often inspired portfolios of their work, aimed at specific jobs or types of freelance work. The agency or publication art director was shown a comprehensive collection of work demonstrating a thorough knowledge of typography, photography, lettering, drawing, illustration, and in fact all the elements of good design."[13] For many of Brodovitch's Pennsylvania students these were skills well learned. Through his prompting, they had found their graphic voice. Many went on to become highly respected graphic designers and art directors at corporations throughout America.[14]

As his students discovered, Brodovitch's ideas on advertising were intimately entwined with the shifting experiences of modern life. This was made concrete in his poster Design for the Machine Age for an exhibition of the same title at the Pennsylvania Museum of Art in 1937. Using a fine drawing of an industrial belt connected at one end to a spindle and at the other to an individual's "mind," Brodovitch illustrates the importance of allowing a creative interdependence between the modern environment and a corresponding inner vision. Even though he always endeavored to represent his ideas with visual examples, Brodovitch did stop to produce a written record of his thoughts on design. Coming after several years teaching at PMSIA, his unpublished manuscript "Ideas on Advertising" is one of Brodovitch's rare moments of codification. It reads as follows:

We are living in the age of industry and mechanization.
We are spoiled by the quality and quantity – result of standardization and competition.
The comfort of our surroundings increases our demand (requirement).
The tempo of life is fast – new achievements open new horizons – our psychology and taste are in constant evolution.
The best medium to persuade to buy is to appeal to the common-sense of the consumer, knowing his weaknesses.
Studying the condition of the average buyer, knowing his habits,

the schedule of his day, his life and his customs, we find that the most direct medium to bring him the message is certainly by the space in the daily news and specifically in the Sunday papers, which are the bread and butter of human curiosity and pleasant leisure.

But it seems to me that up to now Newspaper Advertising is not staged to the highest degree. To follow logically the general idea, studying human psychology, the Advertisement must have a human appeal combined with novelty and originality in appearance.

Considering the amount of space in newspapers occupied by Advertising – to be logical and successful we must stress not only what we are announcing but how we present our announcement.

With all our weakness for sex and admiration for old-timers, no longer can we sell the cigarette, the liquor, or the perfume by announcing that "They are milder" and showing a nice-looking picture of a beautiful girl, or the traditional Colonel of Kentucky...

The Advertising idea of today must be prepared and presented in a dramatic, new, unusual, direct and logical manner.[15]

Conceived as a paper for a graduate show in 1935, these "thoughts" bear more than a passing resemblance to *Mise en Page*, a 1930 publication by Alfred Tolmer. Tolmer worked as a designer in Paris during the 1920s and it has been indicated elsewhere that he may have employed Brodovitch's services at one time.[16] From this information – even though Brodovitch had a rather "well-developed tendency for pastiche" – we could conclude that, rather than expropriating Tolmer's work, it is more likely that both he and Brodovitch were simply receptive to the same artistic and cultural influences shaping this newly emerging field.[17] However, if we were to argue that this is a clear-cut case of plagiarism, Brodovitch, like many other influential designers, would probably agree. The ability to adopt other people's work and make it his own was a highly developed skill he cultivated in that concentrated period of artistic embezzlement that was Paris of the 1920s. For Brodovitch, the idea of constructing a boundary to artistic appropriation would have been anathema to his creative spirit. The "only way to be creative is to try everything," he once said, "[w]e learn by making mistakes. We must be critical of ourselves and have the courage to start all over again after each failure. Only then do we really absorb, really start to know."[18] Likewise, as the designer Paul Rand noted in his *Thoughts on Design*, "great original artists...take a tradition into themselves. They have not shunned but digested it. Then the very conflict set up between it and what is new in themselves and in their environment creates the tension that demands a new mode of expression."[19]

Brodovitch's visual sensibility was permanently attuned to new modes of expression. The constant renewal of his interest in what was modern resulted in him abandoning painting by the mid-1930s. Following a 1928 exhibition of his work at the Povolotzky Gallery in Paris, he held two final exhibitions in 1933 at the Crillon Gallery and Cosmopolitan Club, in Philadelphia. One of Brodovitch's early students, Irving Penn, who became the celebrated fashion photographer, remembered his paintings "as gray, leaden scenes evocative of factories and steel mills."[20] For Brodovitch, photography was the medium of the future. As we know, Brodovitch had a keen interest in photography as a young man. But it was not until his designs for Madelios and Athélia that he had begun to witness the graphic potential of this medium. Now having a receptive audience eager for anything novel and fresh, he acknowledged the relevance of this visual language for commercial art; announcing that the new way of apprehending the modern landscape was not on the canvas, but through "the lens of a Kodak."[21]

Brodovitch always treated his students as equals in the learning process – even if this sometimes resulted in rather abrasive arguments. One of his favorite phrases when beginning a class was "I am student more than a teacher." Familiar with the European idea of actually putting apprentices to work on real jobs, he always encouraged his students to work with him on any professional assignment he obtained. Therefore, when he began to receive several design commissions, the open relationship he had forged with his students resulted in many wishing to assist him in fulfilling these accounts. At the time the

Opposite top: Self-assembled furniture, c. 1938.
During the 1930s Brodovitch produced a range of furniture with the help of his architect brother, Georges.

Opposite bottom: Brodovitch-designed chair, c. 1948.
Brodovitch won third prize for his chair in the International Competition for Low-cost Furniture Design at the Museum of Modern Art in New York in 1948.

Below: Cover for *3 Poems* by Tom Maloney. New York: W. Morrow & Co., c. 1935.

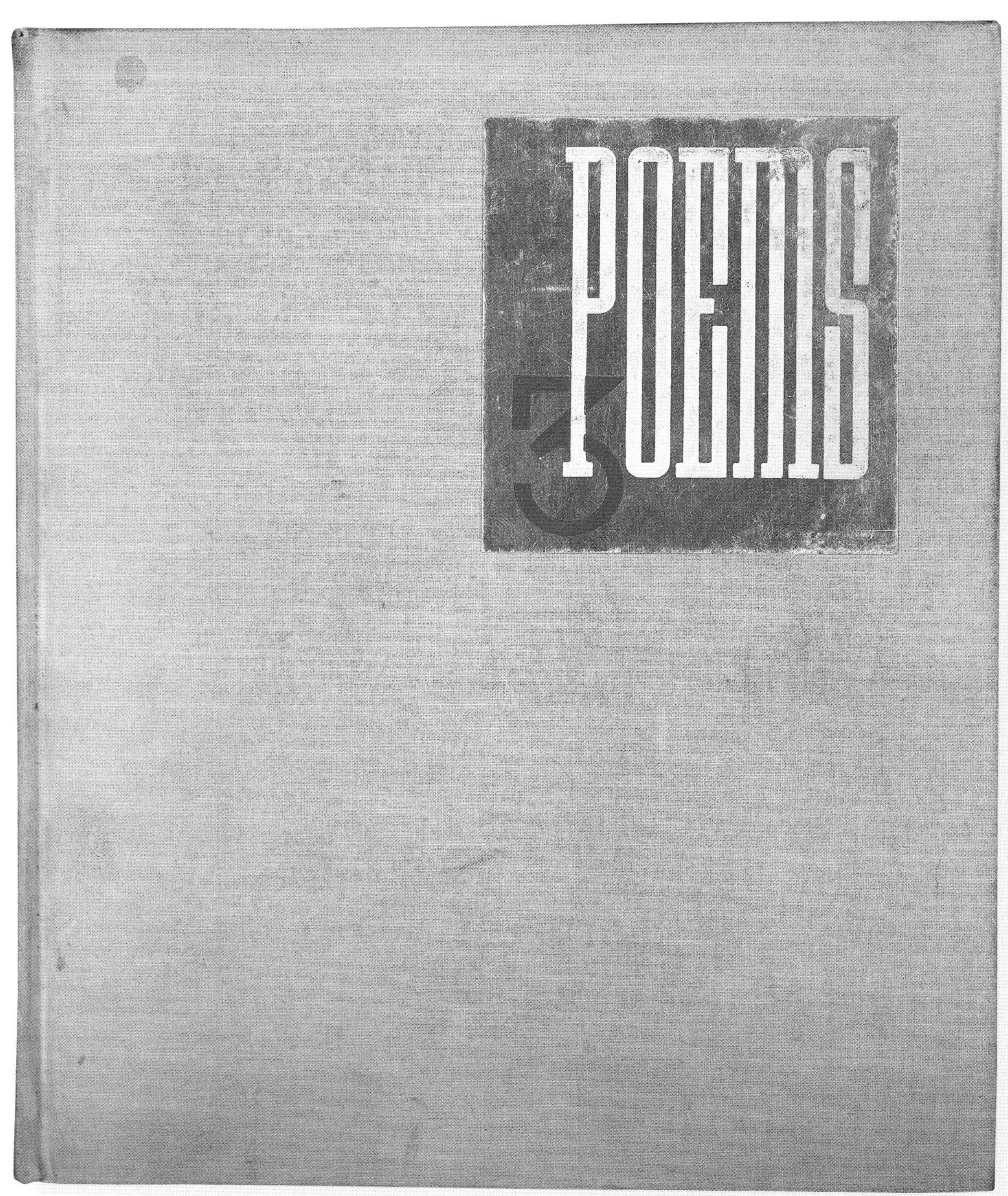

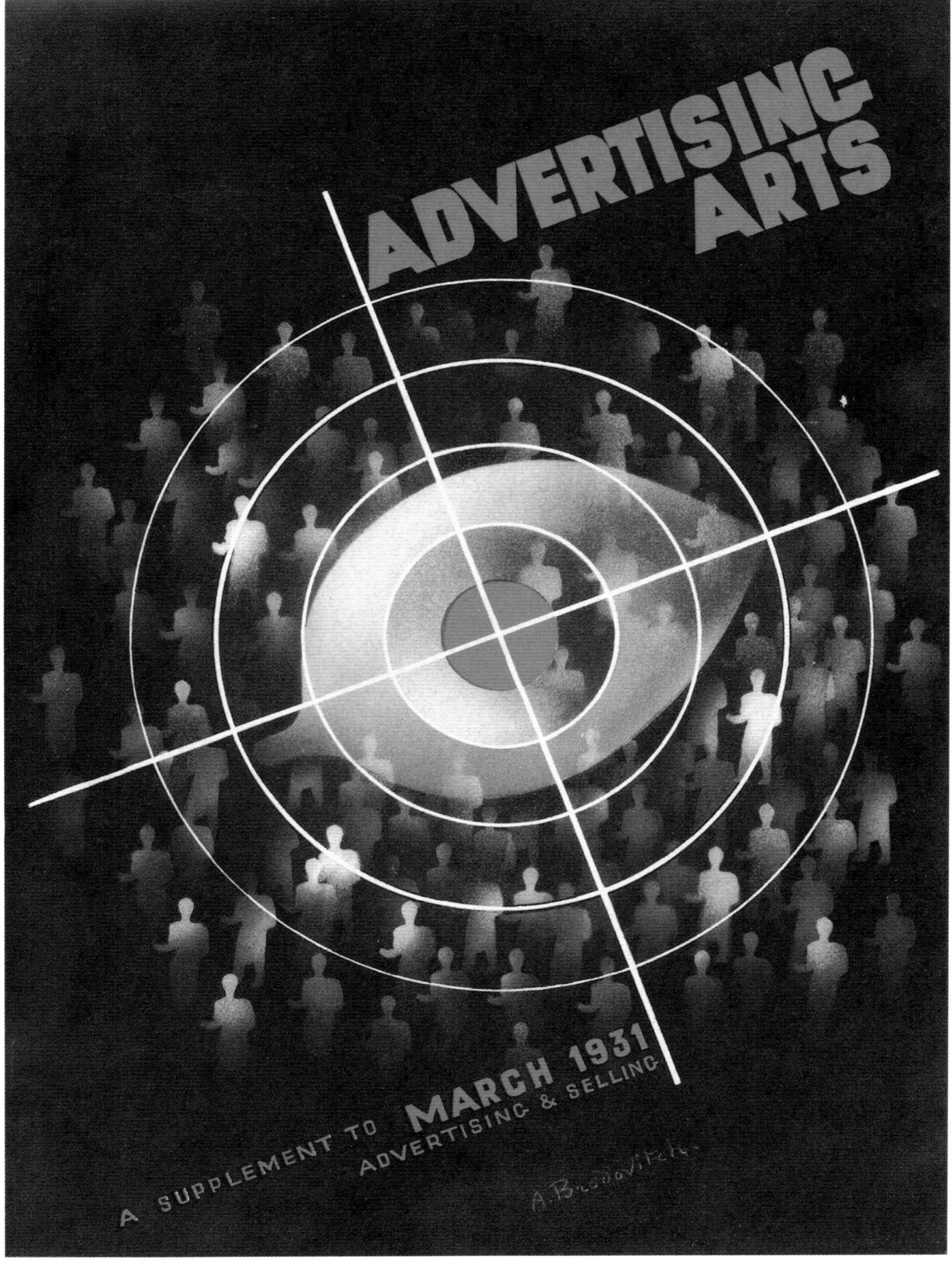

Left: Cover of *Advertising Arts*, March 1931.

Opposite: Advertisement for Bauer Type Foundry, New York, c.1933–35.
Brodovitch's favorite tool, the airbrush, is used simply but effectively in this advertisement.

How Brodovitch Made the Cover

He used an ordinary piece of Bristol Board.

He made no preliminary sketch. He merely visualized in his imagination what he was going to do.

With an air brush he covered the surface of the Bristol Board with black.

He used ordinary show-card colors.

He cut a stencil of the little man out of ordinary paper.

He air-brushed the figure in on the black background, using white paint and the stencil.

He worked out little details on tracing paper and made two stencils for the eye and again used the air brush.

The white circles were then made with a compass and ruling pen.

The lettering was worked out on tracing paper—a white pencil was used on the back of the tracing paper and the tracing of the lettering onto the drawing was done with an ordinary hard pencil.

The lettering was then put in with a brush.

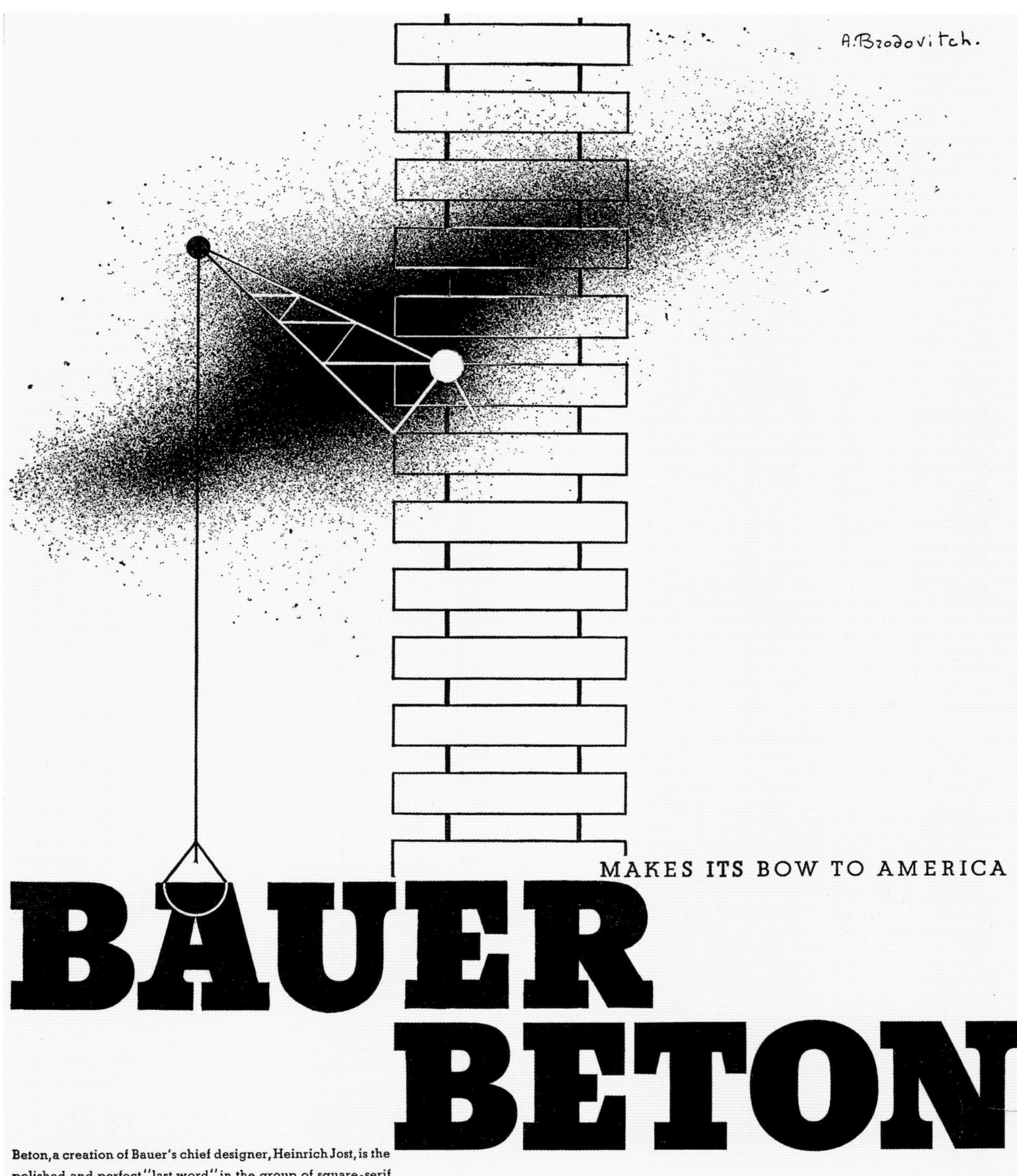
A. Brodovitch.
MAKES ITS BOW TO AMERICA
BAUER
BETON
Beton, a creation of Bauer's chief designer, Heinrich Jost, is the polished and perfect "last word" in the group of square-serif types. It retains its chiselled, diamond-fine clarity of outline even in 8 point size. The bold faces, massive and forthright, are the basso profundo of modern typography. If you are preparing printed material which seeks to express the concrete nature of our times, you cannot afford to do without Beton.
Bauer Beton is now available in light, medium, bold and extra-bold at our accredited agencies
THE BAUER TYPE FOUNDRY · INC
235 EAST 45TH STREET
NEW YORK CITY

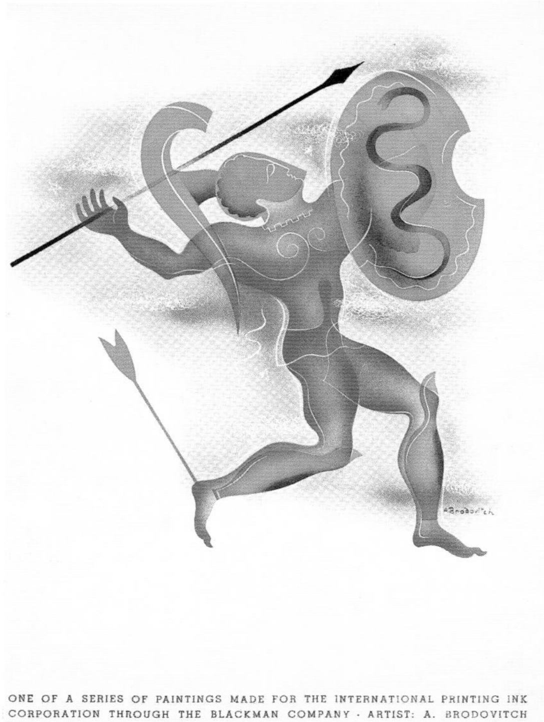

Left: Advertisement for International Printing Ink, c. 1935.

Opposite, clockwise from top left: Cover for *Dead Man's Music* by Christopher Bush. New York: Doubleday Doran, 1932; cover for *Fuller's Earth* by Carolyn Wells. New York: J.B. Lippincott, 1932; cover for *The Night of the 12th–13th* by André Steeman. Publisher unknown, c. 1933; cover for *The Jazz Record Book* by Charles Edward Smith. New York: Smith and Durrell, 1942. Brodovitch designed numerous book covers during his first decade in the United States, using type, illustration, and airbrush to create the illusion of depth and narrative.

In the ad "Bauer Beton," for the Bauer Type Foundry, Brodovitch once again utilizes his favorite tool from Paris, the airbrush. Fizzing across a skeletal illustration of a crane, the speckled paint from the airbrush provides a fluid contrast to the stark angularity of the drawing. Where the paint crosses the illustration we see a shift from positive to negative in the crane's structure that is reminiscent of his Bal Banal poster. Finally, with the crane actually lifting the letter "A" out of the word "Bauer," Brodovitch is once again making explicit his interest in the interaction of type, illustration, design, and the ideas of the machine age. With all these designs, we are witness to the fact that Brodovitch was one of the earliest translators of modernist ideas into the American popular culture.

Recognized for the exceptional work he had performed for Pléiade and Blackmore Press in Paris and London, Brodovitch was also invited to design several book covers during his first decade in America. These included Christopher Bush's publication *Dead Man's Music* (1932), Carolyn Wells's *Fuller's Earth* (1932), André Steeman's *The Night of the 12th-13th* (c. 1933), Tom Maloney's *3 Poems* (c. 1935), and *The Jazz Record Book* by C. E. Smith (1942). Of these designs, *Dead Man's Music* is the most graphically inventive. Similar to the design "Maximum Payload" Brodovitch utilizes an "x-ray" style, this time of a man's hand. It is a technique that creates the illusion of a three-dimensional narrative within the two-dimensional graphic space. The transparent hand provides a sense of depth above and below the illustration. This depth enables a series of associations to be made between the different designs. The piano keyboard trapping the skeletal hand, which in turn is positioned over a grave-like outline of a piano, perfectly illustrates the book's promotional slogan: "The clue was music. The crime was murder." We can see this tool utilized in many other Brodovitch designs, including the New Jersey Zinc advertisement. Achieving this construction of a narrative flow through a two-dimensional space was something Brodovitch would push to its logical extreme on the pages of *Harper's Bazaar*.

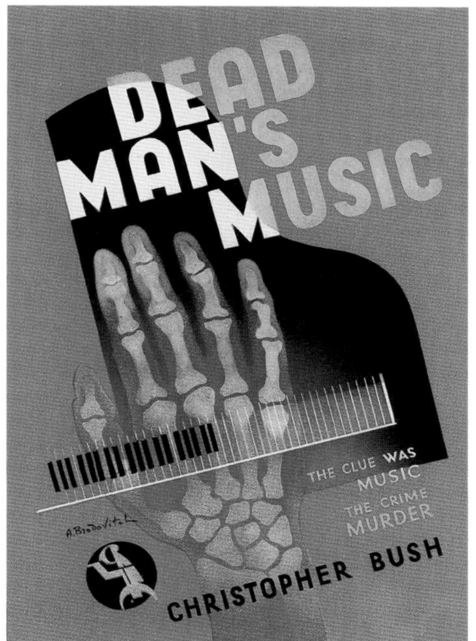
DEAD MAN'S MUSIC
THE CLUE WAS MUSIC
THE CRIME MURDER
CHRISTOPHER BUSH

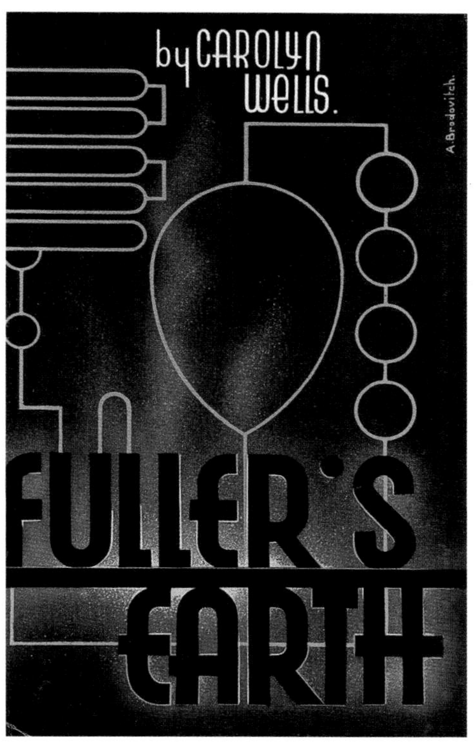
by CAROLYN WELLS.
A.Brodovitch.
FULLER'S EARTH

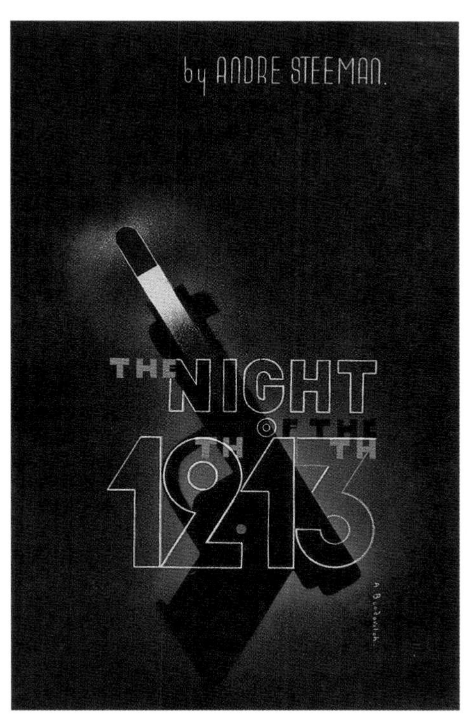
by ANDRE STEEMAN.
THE NIGHT OF THE 12TH 13TH

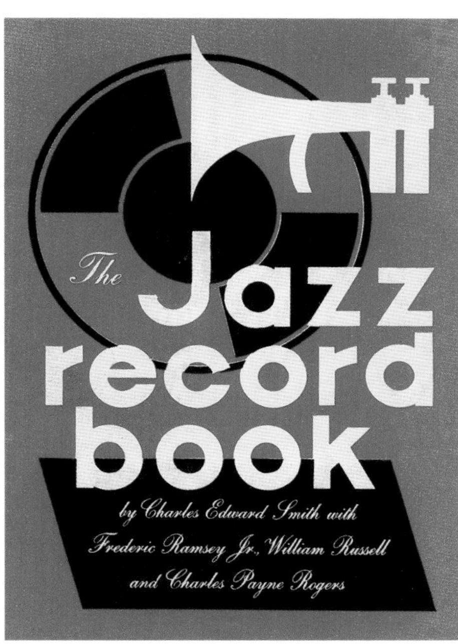
The Jazz record book
by Charles Edward Smith with
Frederic Ramsey Jr., William Russell
and Charles Payne Rogers

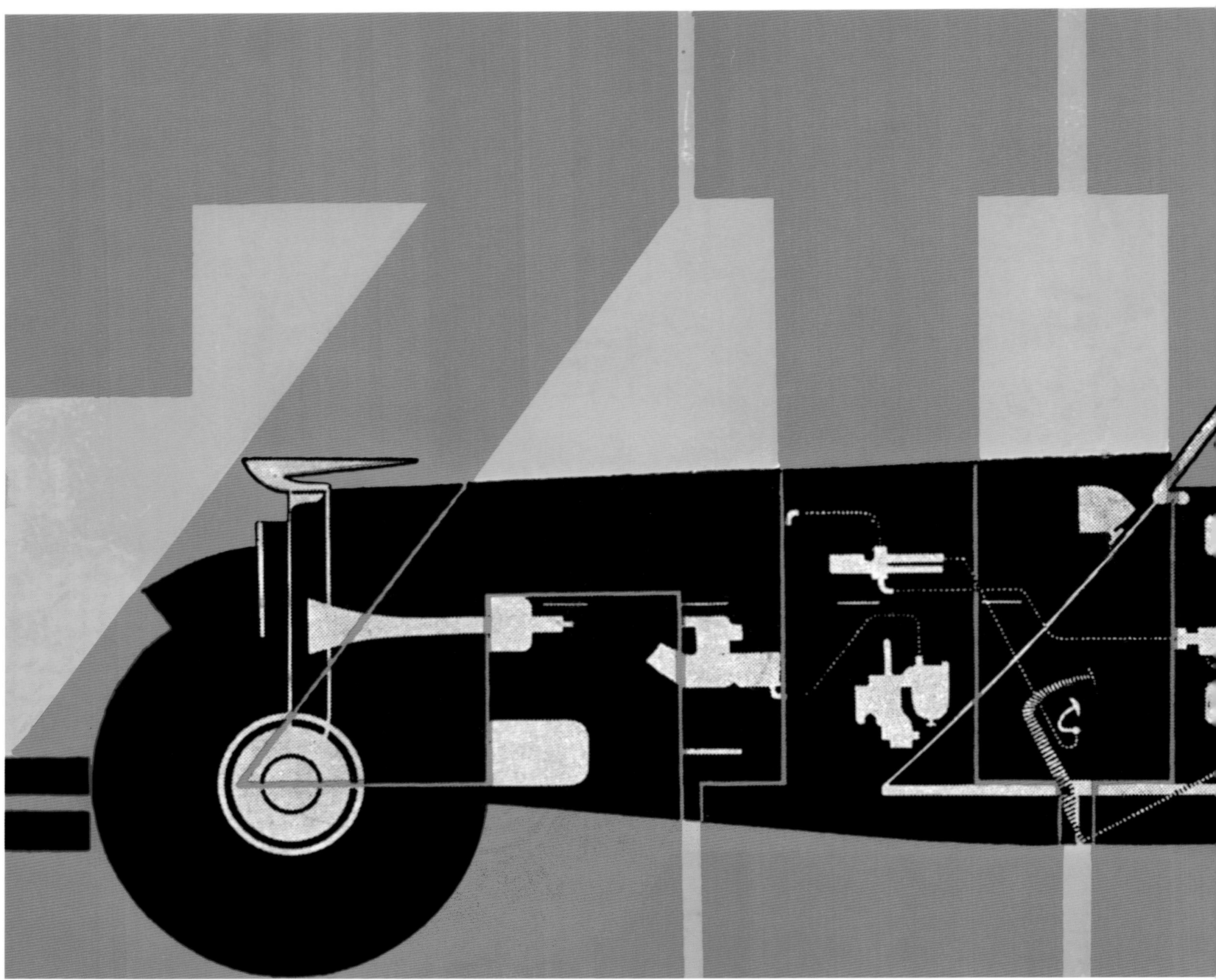

Opposite: *Harper's Bazaar* cover, January 1936. Illustration by Brodovitch.
In one of his few cover illustrations for *Bazaar*, Brodovitch uses a hand motif, a recurring theme in his work.

Below left: Catalogue for the "New Poster International Exposition," 1937.

Below right: "Play Safe." Poster for the Pennsylvania State Police, 1937.
The New Poster International Exposition was held in April 1937 at the Franklin Institute, Philadelphia. Brodovitch designed the catalogue, the poster, and the exhibition layout.

To an American audience, Brodovitch's transformation of *Bazaar* must have placed in stark relief the graphic formality of other magazines. Throughout the twenties and thirties, American magazines frequently displayed photographs and drawings within ornamented frames and boxes. When photographs were used, they were simply appended to articles as supporting evidence, perceived as lending weight to the written word. In these magazines the line where the text ended and illustration began was always clearly demarcated by wide white margins. On the whole, most publications were standardized and devoid of any aesthetic feeling or invention. This is not to say, however, that Brodovitch was the first art director to integrate image and text. *Vogue*, for instance, still contained the stylistic formalism of its origins as a society magazine before Dr. Mehemed Fehmy Agha became art director in 1929. Agha, born in the Ukraine two years before Brodovitch, was the chief assistant and layout man at German *Vogue* when he was hired by Condé Nast. Polly Devlin believed that Agha was the true pioneer in the liberation of the double-page spread. She has noted that with his designs he "removed the frames and sometimes the margins, and enlarged the photographs or filled whole pages with them, put together to tell one fashion story. He laced the pages with headlines, used bigger print, and gave them an enticing, accessible look. He matched content to layout, to give the unified look of a single unit of communication, with words and pictures matching."[36]

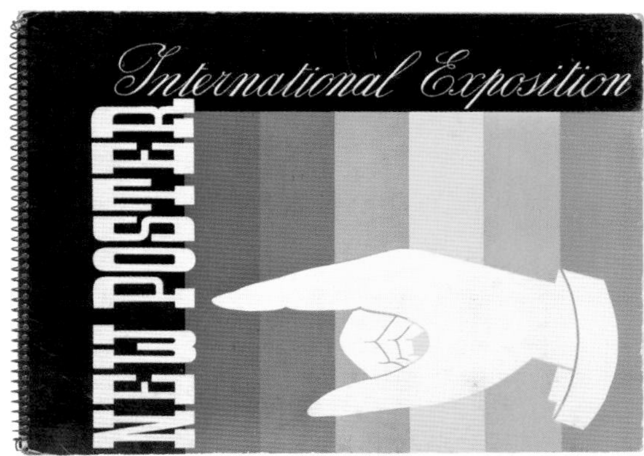

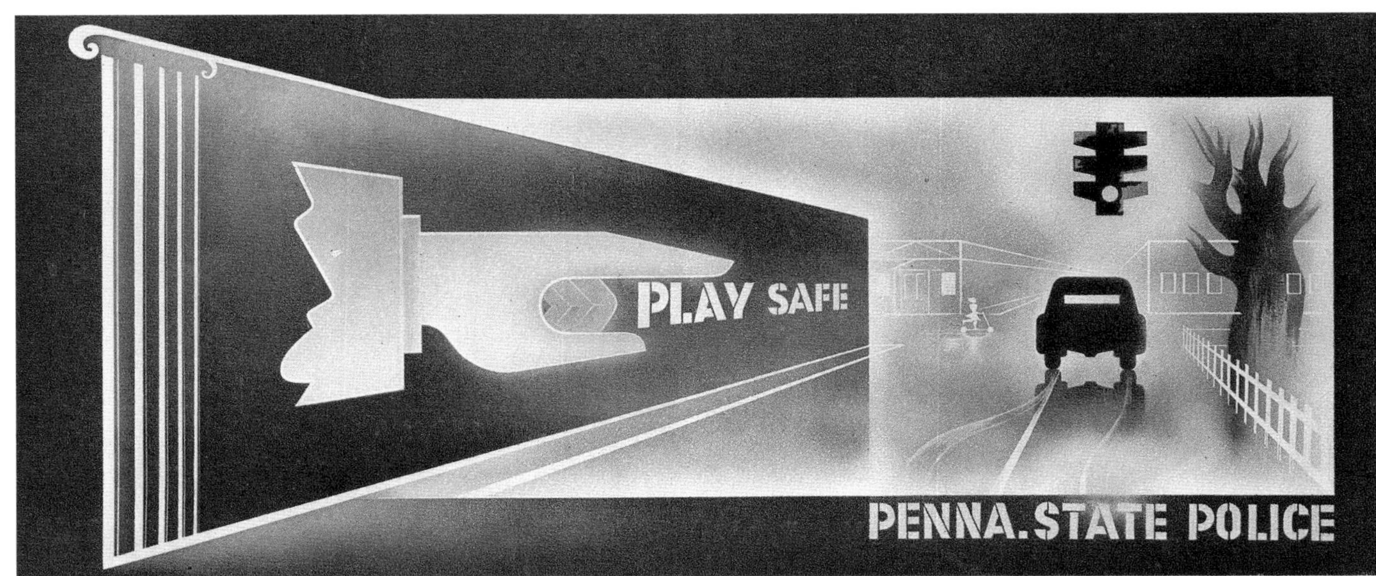

Through his transformation of *Vogue*, Agha has been credited by many as being the first to synthesize all aspects of magazine design. The truth is probably more a case of shared influences – with neither Agha nor Brodovitch being the first to utilize the techniques in question. During their time in Europe both would have been equally affected by the graphic innovations of magazines such as *Lef*, *Fotoauge*, *De 8 en Opbouw*, and *AIZ*.

Agha received his artistic education in Russia and France. He studied at the academy of fine arts in Kiev and with Le Corbusier in Paris. Influenced by the Constructivist ideas of Jan Tschichold, Bauhaus, de Stijl, and Futurism, both Agha and Brodovitch were in the vanguard of those émigrés who translated the radical ideas of 1920s Europe into commercially acceptable designs of 1930s America. Throughout this period many American editors wanted the look and feel of European (and Russian) avant-garde design, but minus the political dimension of such work. As the design historian Lorraine Wild recognized: "The political and ideological connotations of modern graphic design disappeared with its acceptance by business and industry here. The depoliticized 'futurism' of modern design suited the optimism of the American business man and the needs of society at large."[37] Agha himself put it more sardonically when he noted that the importance of European designers for American editors was their ability to produce "Attention Value, Snap, and Wallop; while in their spare time they were allowed to indulge in innocent discussions about the machine age, fitness to function, and objectivity."[38] Unlike many other modernist émigrés, however, Agha and Brodovitch did not simply personalize the objective ideas of modernist design. Their smooth acceptance into the sphere of American commerce was the result of their skillful ability to appropriate them for an individual end and purpose.

If we can trace any direct influence from Agha to Brodovitch, it probably came via the route of Carmel Snow. Snow had worked with Agha as fashion editor at *Vogue* during the late twenties. It was widely assumed at the time that Snow would eventually replace the long-standing editor of *Vogue*, Edna Woolman Chase. However, to Snow's growing frustration, Chase seemed reluctant to go. During this time William Randolph Hearst had made several requests for Snow to join *Bazaar*. After seeing no immediate route to an editorship at *Vogue*, Snow jumped ship in 1933 (with many at *Vogue* whispering "treason" as she went) to become editor of the rival magazine. While at *Vogue*, Snow had cultivated her knowledge of photography and design through her association with both Agha and the magazine's chief photographer Edward Steichen. With Agha, she encouraged his desire to use "bigger photographs…more white space and modern typography." While Agha's direction of photographers was at times rigid, it was at *Vogue* that Snow realized the creative benefits of allowing photographers carte blanche on any project. Steichen remembered Snow enforcing a "policy that a photographer should have whatever he required, and no questions asked."[39] This artistic freedom enabled Steichen to produce sparse angular images that signaled a move away from the lavishly ornate but antiquated photographs of *Vogue*'s previous photographer, Baron Adolph de Meyer. De Meyer's romantic style had imagined an aristocratic audience unchanged since *Vogue*'s beginnings as a society magazine. Unlike Steichen's images, his nostalgic vision was not responsive to the changing nature of fashion. Instead of simply signifying social class, clothes throughout the 1930s began to represent new ways of living or, as we now know it, "lifestyle." Steichen's images were attuned to this shift and eliminated the accoutrements of bourgeois life so central to de Meyer's photographic sets. No longer draped in furs and satins, Steichen's models spoke with the confidence and glamour of the new woman. When appointed editor-in-chief of *Harper's Bazaar*, Snow was quick to realize this change in demographics. Her first task was to dispense with the services of de Meyer – who had moved to *Bazaar* after leaving *Vogue* – and hire a photographer more in keeping with the new spirit.

Aware that *Harper's Bazaar* needed to offer the modern woman an image relevant to her own life, Snow's most significant appointment during her first few years was to hire the services of Hungarian photographer Martin Munkacsi. Munkacsi was originally a news photographer and as such "lacked the common prejudices about what a [fashion] photograph should look like."[40] Snow discovered Munkacsi's work while on one of her many

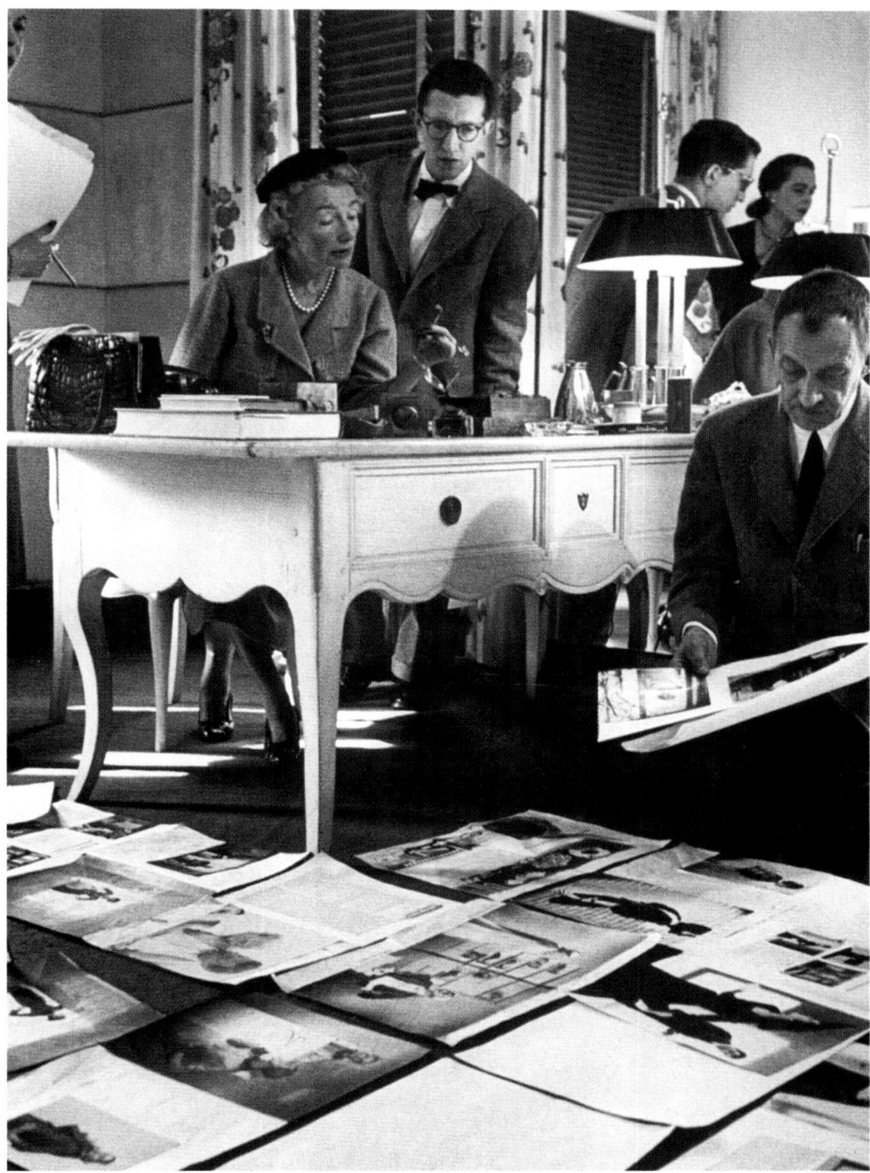

Brodovitch (far right) and Carmel Snow, editor of *Harper's Bazaar*, examining layouts in her office, New York, 1952. Photograph by Walter Sanders.

sorties to the Parisian fashion shows. What she saw both surprised and excited her. Compared to Steichen's studio-bound portraits, Munkacsi's images incorporated a spontaneity and fluidity that was both vibrant and modern. She recognized that in the 1930s Munkacsi's photography was a perfect visual accomplice to the rhythmic and melodic inventions of the swing era. It was as if he had allowed his ears to educate his eyes.

That Snow saw the potential for groundbreaking fashion photography in the work of this news photographer is to acknowledge the genius of her creative foresight. Going on a

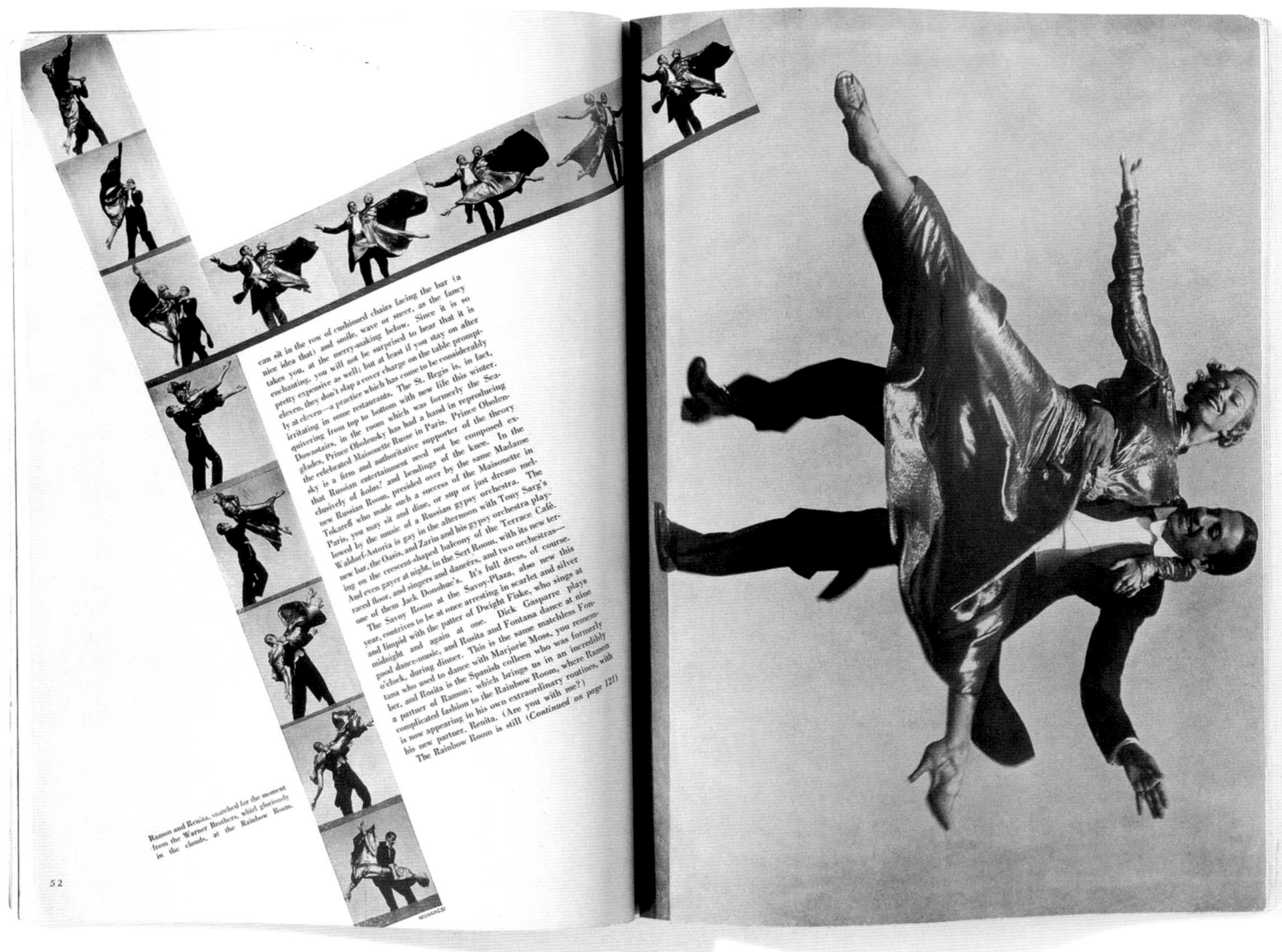

can sit in the row of cushioned chairs facing the bar (a nice idea that) and smile, wave or sneer, as the fancy takes you, at the merry-making below. Since it is so enchanting, you will not be surprised to hear that it is pretty expensive as well; but at least if you stay on after eleven, they don't slap a cover charge on the table promptly at eleven—a practice which has come to be considerably irritating in some restaurants. The St. Regis is, in fact, quivering from top to bottom with new life this winter. Downstairs, in the room which was formerly the Seaglades, Prince Obolensky has had a hand in reproducing the celebrated Maisonette Russe in Paris. Prince Obolensky is a firm and authoritative supporter of the theory that Russian entertainment need not be composed exclusively of *holas!* and bendings of the knee. In the new Russian Room, presided over by the same Madame Tokareff who made such a success of the Maisonette in Paris, you may sit and dine, or sup or just dream mellowed by the music of a Russian gypsy orchestra. The Waldorf-Astoria is gay in the afternoon with Tony Sarg's new bar, the Oasis, and Zarin and his gypsy orchestra playing on the crescent-shaped balcony of the Terrace Café. And even gayer at night, in the Sert Room, with its new terraced floor, and singers and dancers, and two orchestras—one of them Jack Donohue's. It's full dress, of course.

The Savoy Room at the Savoy-Plaza, also new this year, contrives to be at once arresting in scarlet and silver and limpid with the patter of Dwight Fiske, who sings at midnight and again at one. Dick Gasparre plays good dance-music, and Rosita and Fontana dance at nine o'clock, during dinner. This is the same matchless Fontana who used to dance with Marjorie Moss, you remember, and Rosita is the Spanish colleen who was formerly a partner of Ramon; which brings us in an incredibly complicated fashion to the Rainbow Room, where Ramon is now appearing in his own extraordinary routines, with his new partner, Renita. (Are you with me?)

The Rainbow Room is still (*Continued on page 121*)

Ramon and Renita, snatched for the moment from the Warner Brothers, whirl gloriously in the clouds, at the Rainbow Room.

52

MUNKACSI

Left: "Ramon and Renita," *Harper's Bazaar*, November 1935. Photographs by Martin Mur

Using individual frames in cinematic style, Brodovitch created

shoot with Munkacsi and a translator (Munkacsi could not speak English), Snow describes the creation of these now legendary images:

The day I took those two Hungarians to the Piping Rock Beach is a day I will never forget.... Munkacsi hadn't a word of English and his friend seemed to take forever to interpret us. Munkacsi began making wild gestures. What does Munkacsi want us to do?... It seemed that what Munkacsi wanted was for the model to run toward him. Such a "pose" had never been attempted before for fashion (even "sailing" features were posed in a studio on a fake boat).... The resulting picture of a typical American girl in action with her cape billowing out behind her made photographic history.[41]

Even though Alexey Brodovitch has traditionally been associated with the conception of these groundbreaking images, Snow's work with Munkacsi predates his arrival by one year. Thus, many of *Bazaar*'s photographic innovations were actually initiated by Carmel Snow. As Andy Grundberg has recognized, Snow was the guiding genius behind *Bazaar*'s editorial transformation and it is difficult to overestimate her influence on Brodovitch's twenty-four-year tenure at the magazine.[42]

have worked with Le Corbusier in Paris, and it has been said that he based his approach to layout on Le Corbusier's "Le Modular" system.[47] Whether this is true or not, it seems apt to view his designs as "architectural" constructions. Frank Zachary, editor of *Portfolio* magazine, adopted such an approach when assessing Brodovitch's contribution to the double-page spread. "His general philosophy obtains to this day," Zachary states. "The elegance and his lucidity of design, the arrangement of the work...it's architectural. He takes that white sheet [of paper], it's like the side of a building, [he'd] pierce it with a couple of windows, and a door, and it's a beautiful facade, page by page."[48] Other techniques Brodovitch used to lend an illusion of physicality to the layout included torn edges of photographs, photomontage, and the use of tone and shadow behind images to create a sense of depth.

Beyond the fundamental desire to be permanently inventive, Brodovitch's appropriation of these techniques had a more prosaic relevance to the average reader of *Harper's Bazaar*. The combination of Surrealist imagery and the imparting of architectural solidity to the page established a relationship between the realm of real objects and the existence of objects in the mind. As Alfred Tolmer recognized in *Mise en Page:* "The mingling of real life and imaginary life, of present and past, of probability and improbability, could only be expressed hitherto in surrealist poetry and by the technique of cinema. To-day it is one of the most powerful devices of the art of lay-out."[49] No longer wishing to be condescended to, the reader of magazines such as *Bazaar* and *Vogue* wished to be addressed as an equal. "A fashion-magazine reader," Roland Barthes once said, "is almost in a conversational situation; while two people talk, they understand each other very well, but at the same time they don't analyze their words grammatically. In the same way, the fashion-magazine reader isn't conscious of the mechanisms which produce these signs, but they reach her."[50] It was through Brodovitch's visual innovations that Carmel Snow attempted to establish a new dialogue between the reader and the magazine. Of course, at the heart of this dialogue lies a contradiction. That is, as Barthes again recognized, the language used "must be everything at once in order to represent the greatest possible number of women readers."[51] This need to speak to as many woman as possible found its perfect form in the expressionistic photography Brodovitch would pioneer throughout the forties and fifties. Via his graphic manipulation, these photographic compositions would the meet the reader halfway. While offering a glimpse of a lifestyle or experience, the nebulous nature of these photographs would also enable the readers to project their own desires into the empty white space.

As mentioned above, when Brodovitch was detached from the genesis of a photograph, he was always restricted in its imaginative application on the printed page. The problem was that many of the photographers he commissioned in his first few years as art director did not share his influences or vision. It wasn't until the mid-1940s, as William Owen identified in his book *Magazine Design*, that Brodovitch had the opportunity to encourage the photographer "to design the page in the lens, to use props and movement to create force and balance, and to use plain backgrounds which enabled the designer to bleed the picture across the entire page."[52] Brodovitch eventually achieved this synthesis between image and page because many of the photographers he began to commission during this period were also his students. In 1933, at PMSIA, Brodovitch had begun a class titled the Design Laboratory (see chapter 3). Following his move to *Bazaar*, the class continued for a short time in Pennsylvania until 1938. In 1941, it was relaunched at the New School for Social Research in New York. Throughout the forties and fifties this class functioned as a career launchpad for many young designers and photographers, such as Lillian Bassman, David Attie, and Leon Levinstein, with many going on to work for *Bazaar*. Brodovitch's tutelage encouraged these photographers to produce images in class that would fuse perfectly with his graphic approach to the printed page. This is not to say that creative moments of, in Brodovitch's words, "instantaneous combustion" never took place before this period.[53] The fusion of image and text within the same graphic space can be seen in the work of photographers who did not attend his classes, such as the photograph by Victor Leon for the double-page spread

"Diplomat's Wife" (February 1940). However, prior to the mid-forties, layouts such as these were relatively rare. As with this example – the white expanse of a snowy landscape provides an ideal canvas for the main body of text – their occurrence was a fortuitous case of the subject matter happening to lend itself to an integrated design. Unlike Leon's image, Brodovitch's work with photographers such as David Attie and Leslie Gill engendered images that were consciously produced with the page in mind. Their work responded to Brodovitch's request that when a photographer "looks at the ground glass, he should see not only the picture, but four or eight pages."[54] The outcome of such an approach can be seen in Leslie Gill's "The New Spirit" (April 1946), Ben Rose's "The 9-Minute Wonder Exercises" (April 1950), or Lillian Bassman's dreamlike "The New Brassiere Has–," (December 1949).

Diana Vreeland, then fashion editor at *Harper's Bazaar*, witnessed the close bond he forged with these photographers. She once commented that "he loved his photographers, and with them he blossomed. He treated them with such heart and intelligence and passionate interest, and with them he was totally instructive."[55] Ben Shultz, a Brodovitch student, remembered that

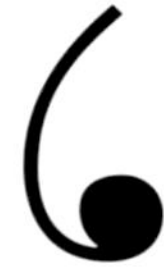

I saw a fresh, new conception of layout technique that struck me like a revelation: pages that bled beautifully cropped photographs, typography and design

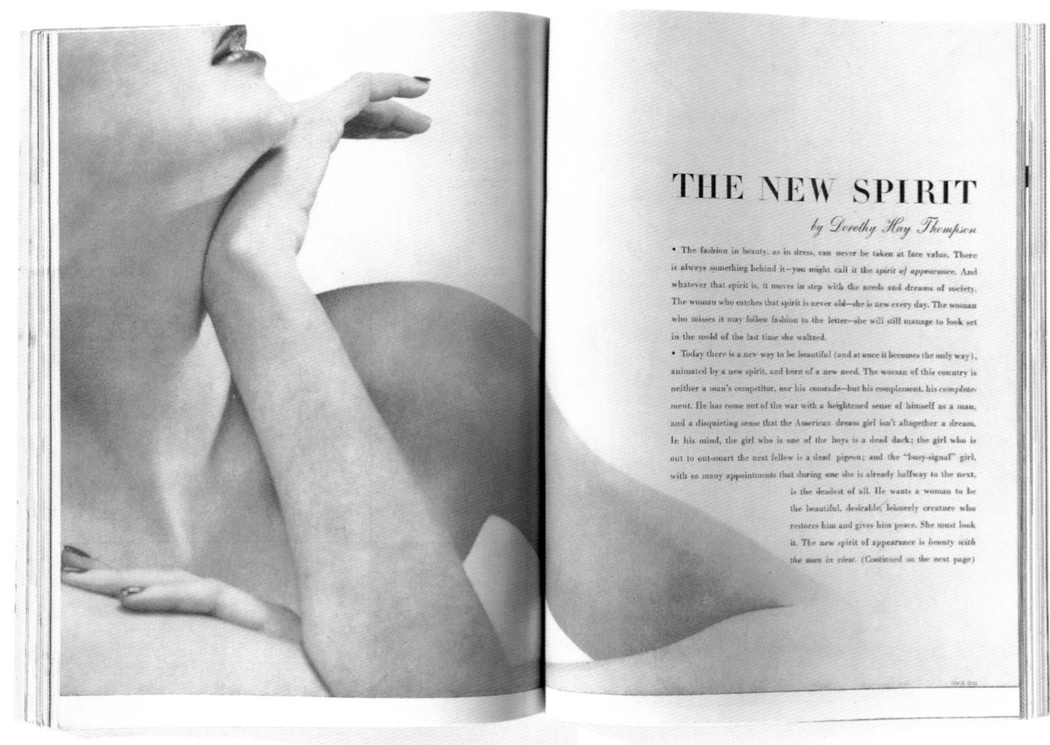

THE NEW SPIRIT

by Dorothy Hay Thompson

• The fashion in beauty, as in dress, can never be taken at face value. There is always something behind it—you might call it the *spirit of appearance*. And whatever that spirit is, it moves in step with the needs and dreams of society. The woman who catches that spirit is never old—she is new every day. The woman who misses it may follow fashion to the letter—she will still manage to look set in the mold of the last time she waltzed.

• Today there is a new way to be beautiful (and at once it becomes the only way), animated by a new spirit, and born of a new need. The woman of this country is neither a man's competitor, nor his comrade—but his complement, his *completement*. He has come out of the war with a heightened sense of himself as a man, and a disquieting sense that the American dream girl isn't altogether a dream. In his mind, the girl who is one of the boys is a dead duck; the girl who is out to out-smart the next fellow is a dead pigeon; and the "busy-signal" girl, with so many appointments that during one she is already halfway to the next, is the deadest of all. He wants a woman to be the beautiful, desirable, leisurely creature who restores him and gives him peace. She must look it. The new spirit of appearance is *beauty with the man in view*. (Continued on the next page)

Below: "The New Spirit," *Harper's Bazaar*, April 1946. Photograph by Leslie Gill.

Opposite top: "The New Brassiere Has–," December 1949. Photograph by Lillian Bassman.

Opposite bottom: "The 9-Minute Wonder Exercises," *Harper's Bazaar*, April 1950. Photograph by Ben Rose.
These spreads reflect Brodovitch's belief that fashion magazines such as *Bazaar* and *Vogue* should identify clothes with atmosphere and feeling rather than specific details.

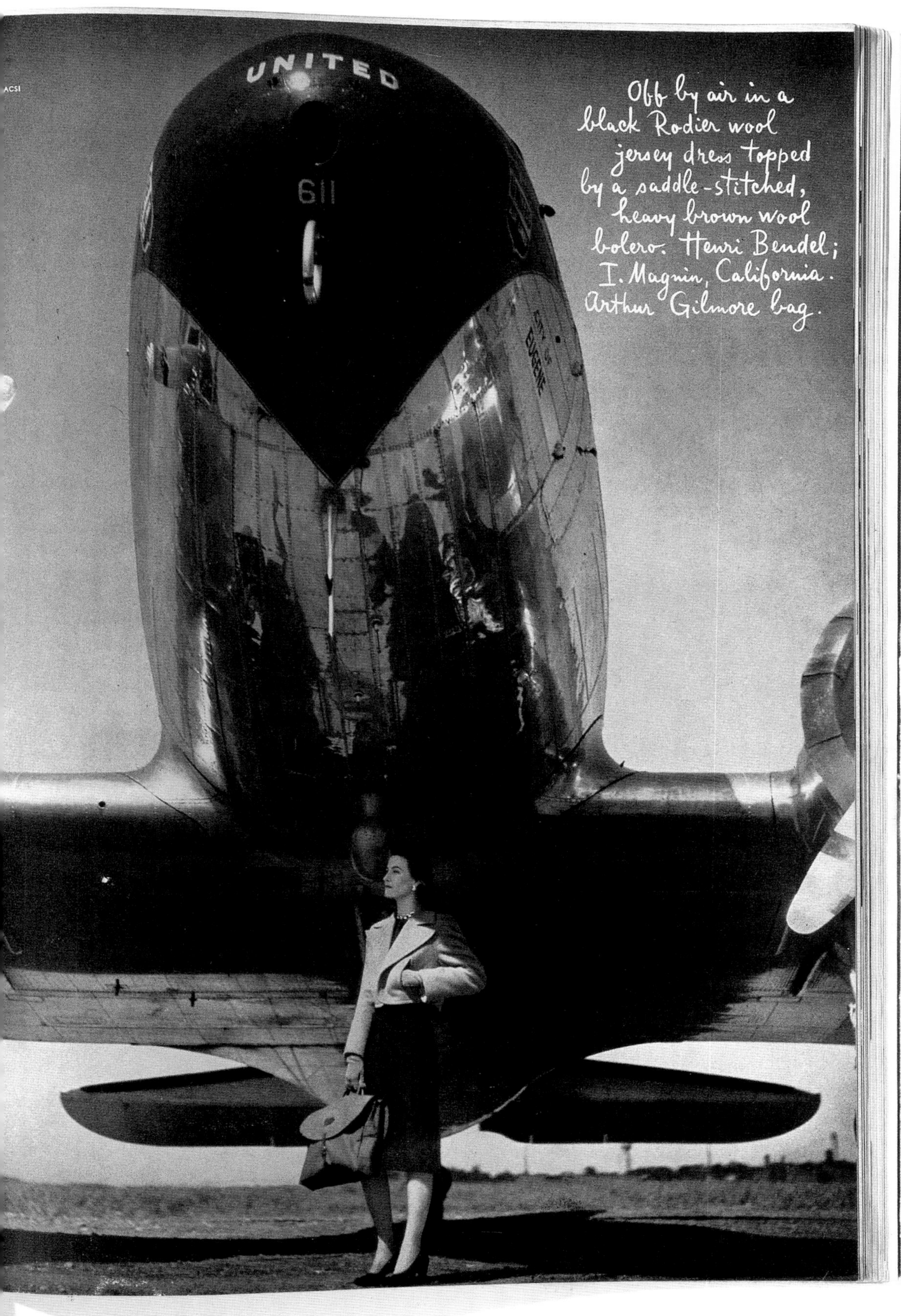

"K. T. Stevens in Molyneux's tweed suit...," *Harper's Bazaar*, October 1944. Photographs by Martin Munkacsi.
In many of his *Bazaar* layouts, Brodovitch would often use a disorientating change of perspective across a double-page spread to attract the reader's eye.

for many "serious photographers, *Bazaar* was a place to 'roost.' He took an interest in us. If you called him at the magazine, he answered the phone and said, 'Sure come up. I'd like to see what you've got.' "[56] One of the most unlikely photographers to visit Brodovitch's Madison Avenue office was Lisette Model. At the time Model was already well-known for her images of oversize bathers at New York's Coney Island and bizarre nightclub acts. While these photographs may have repulsed many other art directors, Brodovitch found something in them he liked. He established that her "particular genius was in photographing the bizarre quality of human beings and finding beauty in the grotesque. If she were asked to photograph a boy and girl kissing she would be a complete failure but when photographing fat ladies on the beach she was wonderful."[57] Even with such an unorthodox photographer for a fashion magazine, Brodovitch was still intensely loyal. Model became familiar with his unwavering allegiance when the famous photographer Weegee attempted to steal her job. Model recollected that: "Weegee said [to Brodovitch]: 'You have worked enough with Lisette Model. Now throw her out and take me.' So Brodovitch threw him out. And he went to *Vogue* magazine and *Vogue* took him."[58] This strong belief in the integrity of the individual photographer was also extended to include their opinions on how their images were presented on the page. As Charles Reynolds, one-time photography critic and friend of Brodovitch, once noted:

Brodovitch tried always to confer with each person about the cropping of his pictures, the quality of the prints, and the way the layouts would be made. If he and the photographer were not in agreement, several alternate layouts would often be made and discussed. In a few cases, Henri Cartier-Bresson, who usually does not allow his pictures to be cropped in any way, allowed Brodovitch to alter his photographs for a particular layout when he was shown it in comparison to another one in which the pictures were uncropped.[59]

Brodovitch assisted his photographers in any way possible. If their images were not suitable for *Bazaar*, he would make a phone call and send them to another magazine such as *Life*. He helped them attain much needed sponsorship. For example, unknown to many, Brodovitch was one of the five sponsors that recommended Robert Frank for a Guggenheim fellowship in 1954, which resulted in the now legendary book *The Americans* (1959). The outgrowth of such a close and trusting relationship with his photographers is most clearly represented in the work of one of Brodovitch's most celebrated pupils, Richard Avedon.

Fresh out of the merchant marines, where he had been working in the photographic department, Richard Avedon enrolled in Brodovitch's Design Laboratory class in 1944. Avedon had taken hundreds of photographs of the seamen with whom he had served and showed these photographs to Brodovitch. Like Snow in her

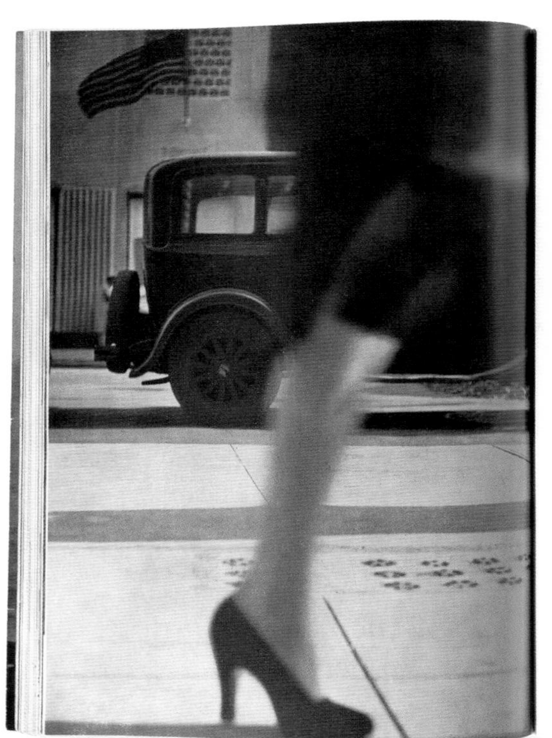

"New York," *Harper's Bazaar*, February 1946. Photograph by Lisette Model.

165

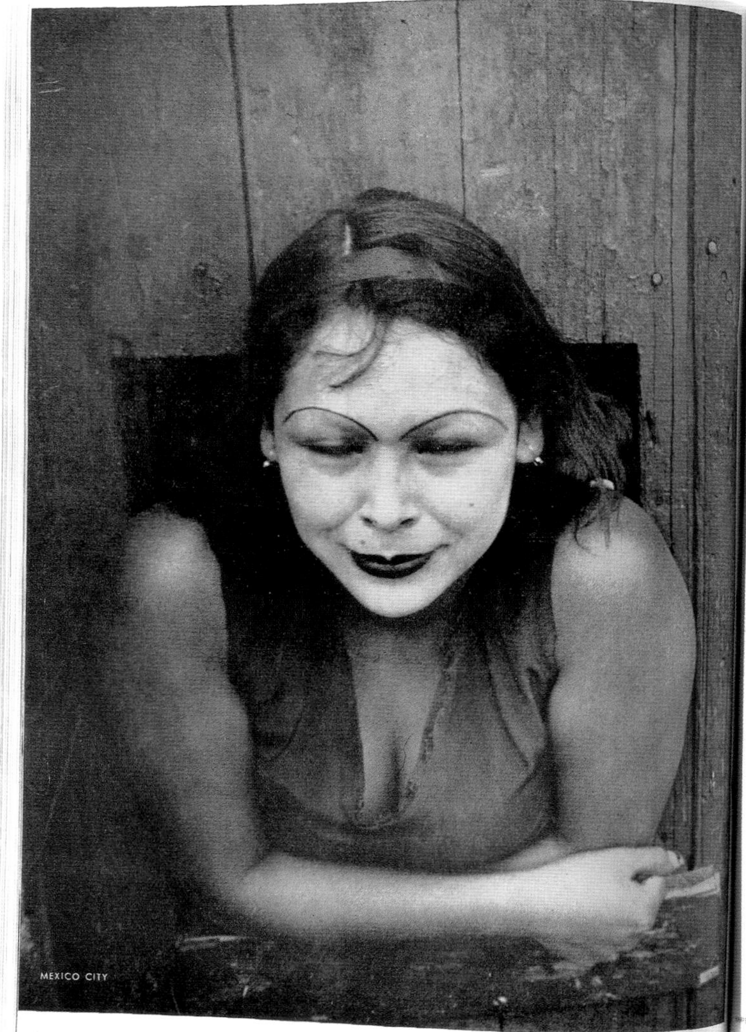

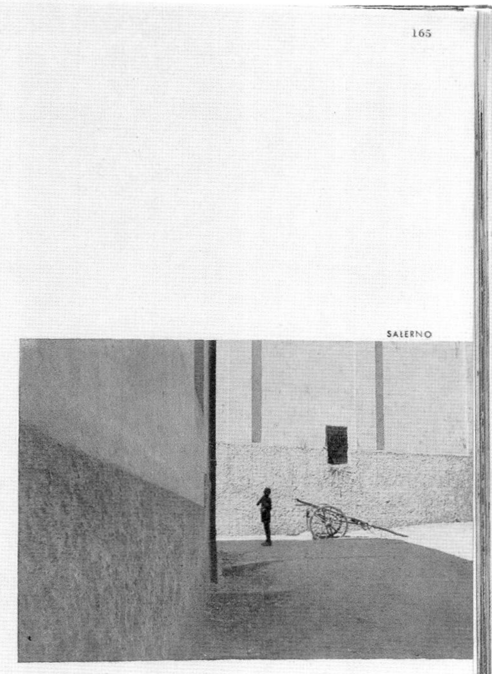

Henri Cartier-Bresson: 'Intruder on Tiptoe'

• These photographs and those on the next four pages are taken from *The Decisive Moment,* a collection of the work of Henri Cartier-Bresson, to be published this month in New York by Simon and Schuster and in Paris by Tériade. After spending much of his minority with a paintbrush in hand, Cartier-Bresson began, at twenty-two, his career as a photographer, which has taken him over a good part of the globe. During the war, as a camera-toting corporal in the French Army, he was captured and spent three years in a prison camp. On his third escape try, he made it. Equipped with false identity papers, he then organized underground photography units to document the German occupation and retreat.

In the text for *The Decisive Moment,* Cartier-Bresson describes the "elementary truths" of his profession. "In whatever picture-story we try to do," he says, "we are bound to arrive as intruders. It is essential, therefore, to approach the subject on tiptoe . . . alert with the brain, the eye, the heart." Soon after he started to use his favorite camera, the Leica, he took to prowling the streets, "strung up and ready to pounce." He adds, "I craved to seize the whole essence, in one single photograph, of some situation that was in the process of unrolling itself before my eyes." Innumerable times, some on record here, Cartier-Bresson has found the "whole essence" and, at the decisive moment, clicked the shutter.

HARPER'S BAZAAR OCTOBER 1952

"Henri Cartier-Bresson: 'Intruder on Tiptoe,'" *Harper's Bazaar,* October 1952. Photographs by Henri Cartier-Bresson.
Cartier-Bresson always declared that of all the art directors he worked with, he would allow only Alexey Brodovitch to crop his photographs.

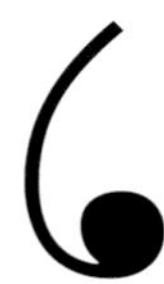

In the monotony and drudgery of work-a-day world, there is to be found new beauty and a new aesthetic. – Alexey Brodovitch

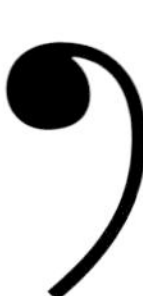

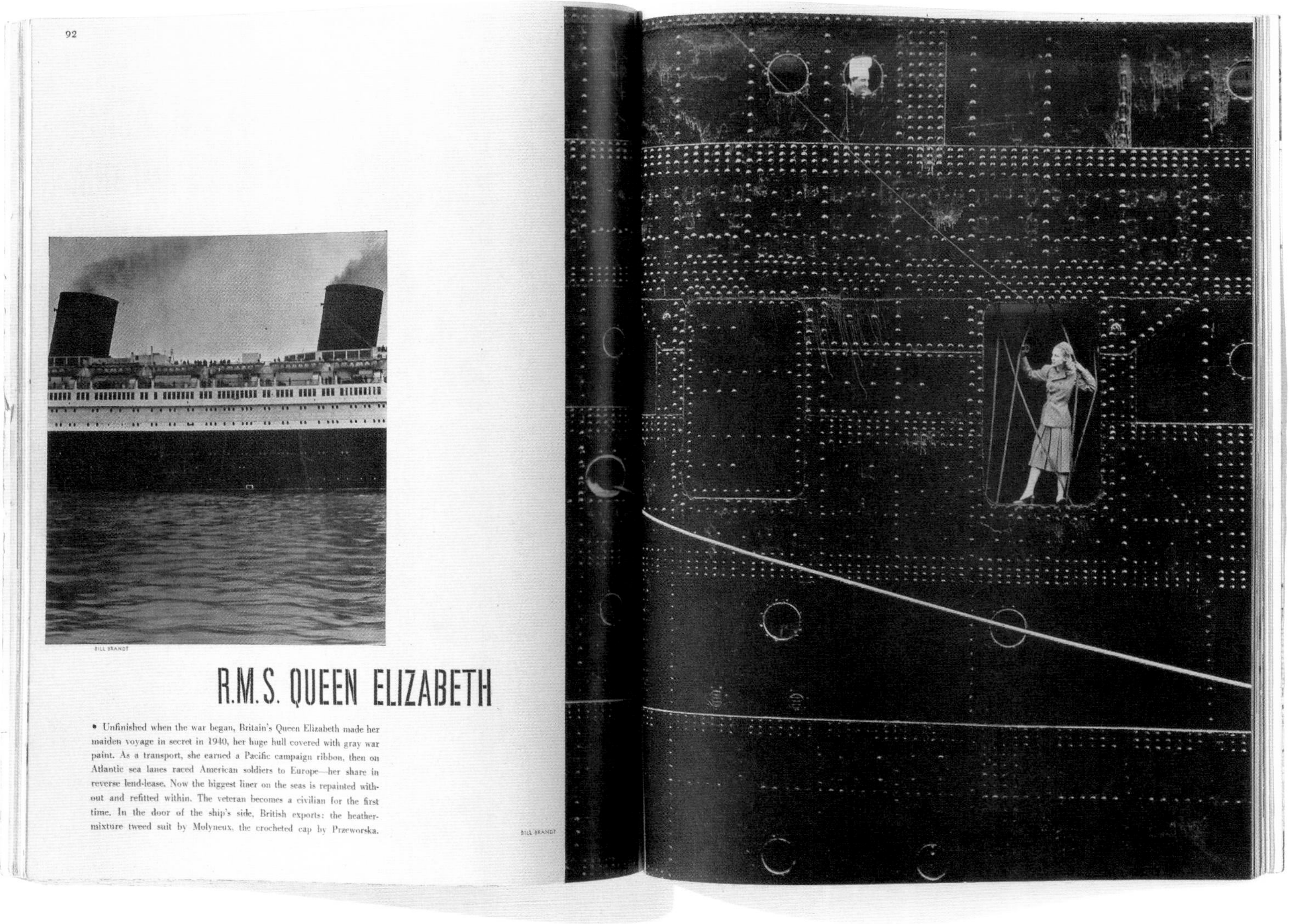

92

BILL BRANDT

R.M.S. QUEEN ELIZABETH

• Unfinished when the war began, Britain's Queen Elizabeth made her maiden voyage in secret in 1940, her huge hull covered with gray war paint. As a transport, she earned a Pacific campaign ribbon, then on Atlantic sea lanes raced American soldiers to Europe—her share in reverse lend-lease. Now the biggest liner on the seas is repainted without and refitted within. The veteran becomes a civilian for the first time. In the door of the ship's side, British exports: the heather-mixture tweed suit by Molyneux, the crocheted cap by Przeworska.

BILL BRANDT

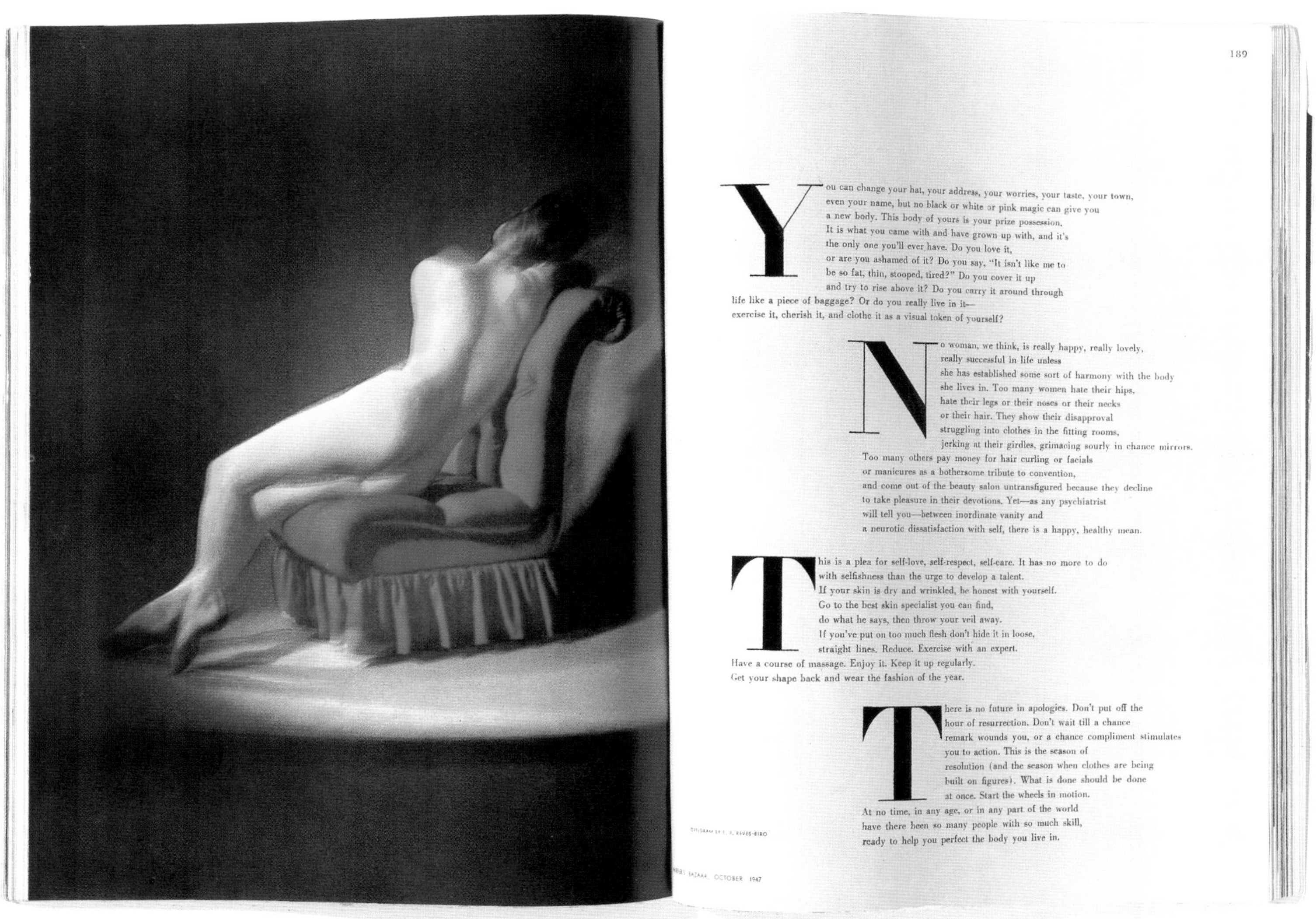
189

You can change your hat, your address, your worries, your taste, your town, even your name, but no black or white or pink magic can give you a new body. This body of yours is your prize possession. It is what you came with and have grown up with, and it's the only one you'll ever have. Do you love it, or are you ashamed of it? Do you say, "It isn't like me to be so fat, thin, stooped, tired?" Do you cover it up and try to rise above it? Do you carry it around through life like a piece of baggage? Or do you really live in it— exercise it, cherish it, and clothe it as a visual token of yourself?

No woman, we think, is really happy, really lovely, really successful in life unless she has established some sort of harmony with the body she lives in. Too many women hate their hips, hate their legs or their noses or their necks or their hair. They show their disapproval struggling into clothes in the fitting rooms, jerking at their girdles, grimacing sourly in chance mirrors. Too many others pay money for hair curling or facials or manicures as a bothersome tribute to convention, and come out of the beauty salon untransfigured because they decline to take pleasure in their devotions. Yet—as any psychiatrist will tell you—between inordinate vanity and a neurotic dissatisfaction with self, there is a happy, healthy mean.

This is a plea for self-love, self-respect, self-care. It has no more to do with selfishness than the urge to develop a talent. If your skin is dry and wrinkled, be honest with yourself. Go to the best skin specialist you can find, do what he says, then throw your veil away. If you've put on too much flesh don't hide it in loose, straight lines. Reduce. Exercise with an expert. Have a course of massage. Enjoy it. Keep it up regularly. Get your shape back and wear the fashion of the year.

There is no future in apologies. Don't put off the hour of resurrection. Don't wait till a chance remark wounds you, or a chance compliment stimulates you to action. This is the season of resolution (and the season when clothes are being built on figures). What is done should be done at once. Start the wheels in motion. At no time, in any age, or in any part of the world have there been so many people with so much skill, ready to help you perfect the body you live in.

Opposite: "R.M.S. Queen Elizabeth," *Harper's Bazaar*, January, 1947. Photographs by Bill Brandt.

Above: "You can change your hat...," *Harper's Bazaar*, October, 1947. Optigram by E. P. Reves-Biro.

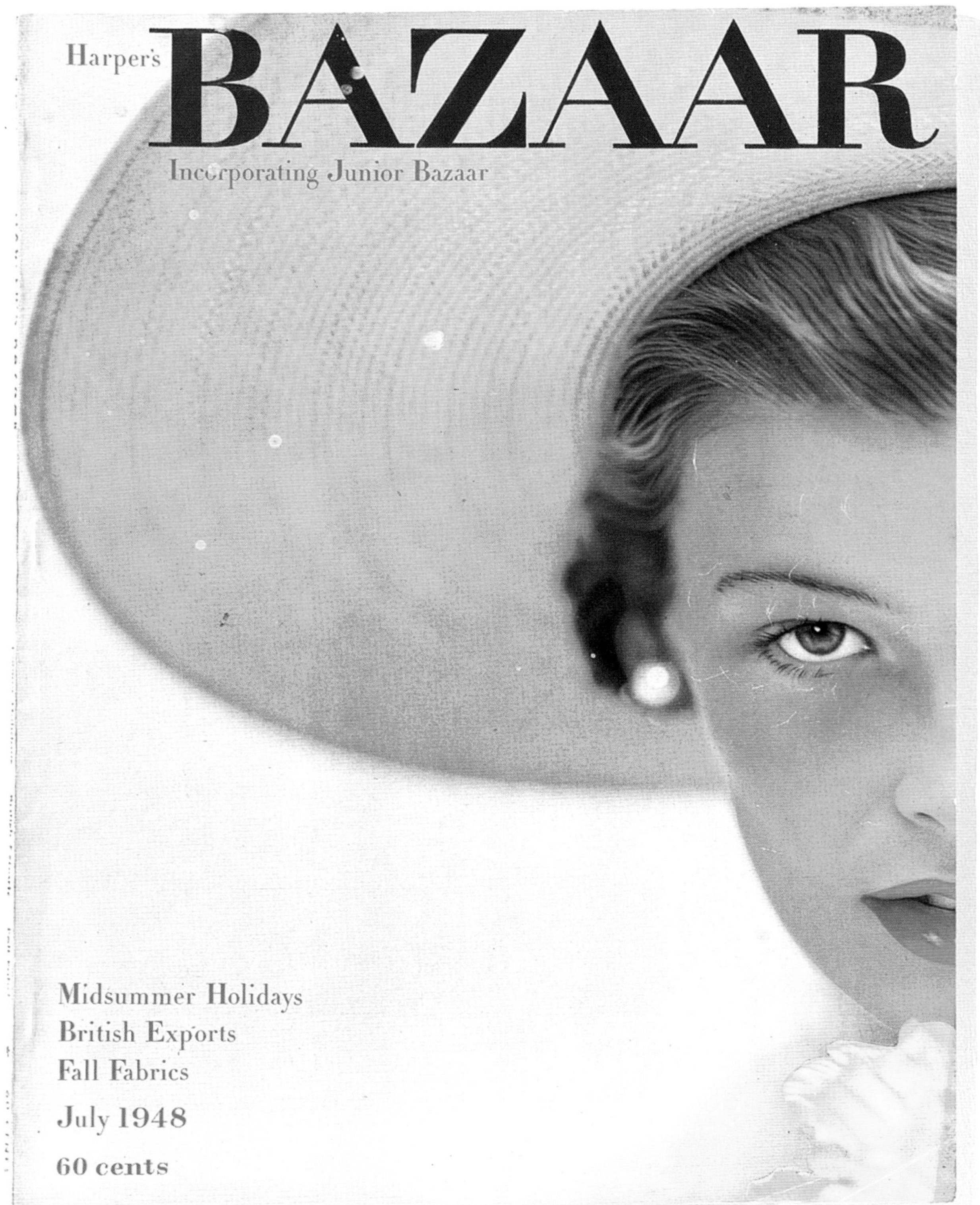
Harper's
BAZAAR
Incorporating Junior Bazaar
Midsummer Holidays
British Exports
Fall Fabrics
July 1948
60 cents

Harper's Bazaar cover, July 1948. Photograph by Richard Avedon.

response to Munkacsi's news photographs, Brodovitch saw in these images something that signaled Avedon's potential as a fashion photographer. Recounting this meeting to Jane Livingston in her seminal book *The New York School: Photographs 1936–1963*, Avedon said:

[I] brought my first attempts at fashion photography to Brodovitch, and, for good luck, I included an experiment I had done during my time with the Merchant Marine: a picture of twin brothers. Brodovitch dismissed all my carefully wrought attempts at fashion photography. They were completely derivative, he said, but if I could take some of the psychological power that was in the flatly lit yet complicated experiment and turn it into a fashion photograph, I might be ready to begin. He also helped me immediately to see that I could use technical means, even accidents or imperfections – objects in and out of focus, for instance – to achieve what I needed.[60]

Livingston goes on to say "Brodovitch somehow helped Avedon understand what kinds of demands one not only could place, but was obligated to place, on oneself as a creative person."[61] It was through these creative demands that Avedon pioneered a style of impressionistic fashion photography that concurred perfectly with what the modern woman was and what she dreamt of becoming; a form of photography ideally suited to the changing expectations of postwar life. The photography critic Janet Malcolm accurately summarized this aspect of Avedon's early work in her essay "Men without Props":

Avedon's achievement was to mark the passing of Art Deco and to grasp, before anyone else did, the outlines of its successor…in whose thrusting curvilinearities we can read a recoil from the deprivations and politics of the war years and a foreshadowing of the escapist tendencies that shaped the next two decades – the privatism and the acquisitiveness; the obsessions with food, sex, children, and objects; the search for the natural and the organic.[62]

Avedon's work first appeared in the newly launched magazine *Junior Bazaar*. Overseen by Brodovitch but art directed by the photographer Lillian Bassman, *Junior Bazaar* ran as a separate publication from *Harper's Bazaar* from November 1945 to May 1948. For Carmel Snow it became a "good proving ground for young fashion editors like Melanie Witt, young copy-writers like Maeve Brenann, young models like Fifi Wheeler; above all for Avedon."[63] The pages of the *Harper's* sister publication maintained the radical spirit of photographic innovation and experimentation. Using work by photographers such as Herman Landshoff and Avedon, it cultivated the texture and fluidity of Munkacsi's images to produce dynamic and exciting layouts. Following the traumas of World War II, Avedon's imagery in *Junior* and then *Harper's Bazaar* offered the American woman, in Brodovitch words, a much needed "vacation from life."[64]

Playing an integral part in the conception of Avedon's imagery enabled Brodovitch to move away from the contrived influences of Surrealism. No longer reduced to working with a photographer's "end product," he was able to reject the secondary manipulation of the photograph witnessed, for example, in his earlier fan spreads. The expansive white space of Avedon's work gave Brodovitch a license to zoom in beyond the borders of the photograph and explore the internal dynamics of the image. Using such tools as cropping, guttering, and bleeding the image to the edge of the page, he was able to frustrate any desire to read the photograph as a single entity. While this work resulted in Brodovitch receiving the Robert Leavitt Memorial award from the American Society of Magazine Photographers in 1954, such a radical approach to the printed page was not welcomed by all in the magazine world. Alexander Liberman, Agha's successor at American *Vogue*, saw Brodovitch's sparse designs as simply wasting valuable editorial space. "Elegance was Brodovitch's strong point," Liberman commented, "the page looked very attractive. But in a way, it seemed to me that Brodovitch was serving the same purpose that Agha had served, which was to make the page attractive to women – not interesting to women, attractive to women.… I thought there was more merit in being able to put twenty pictures on two pages than in making two elegant pages."[65]

Many commentators ascribe a cinematic quality to the fluidity of Brodovitch's designs from the forties and fifties. Viewing the layouts we can see that it is through the filmic techniques of duplication, fade-out, close-up, and long-shot that he achieves the visual freedom traditionally associated with film. For example,

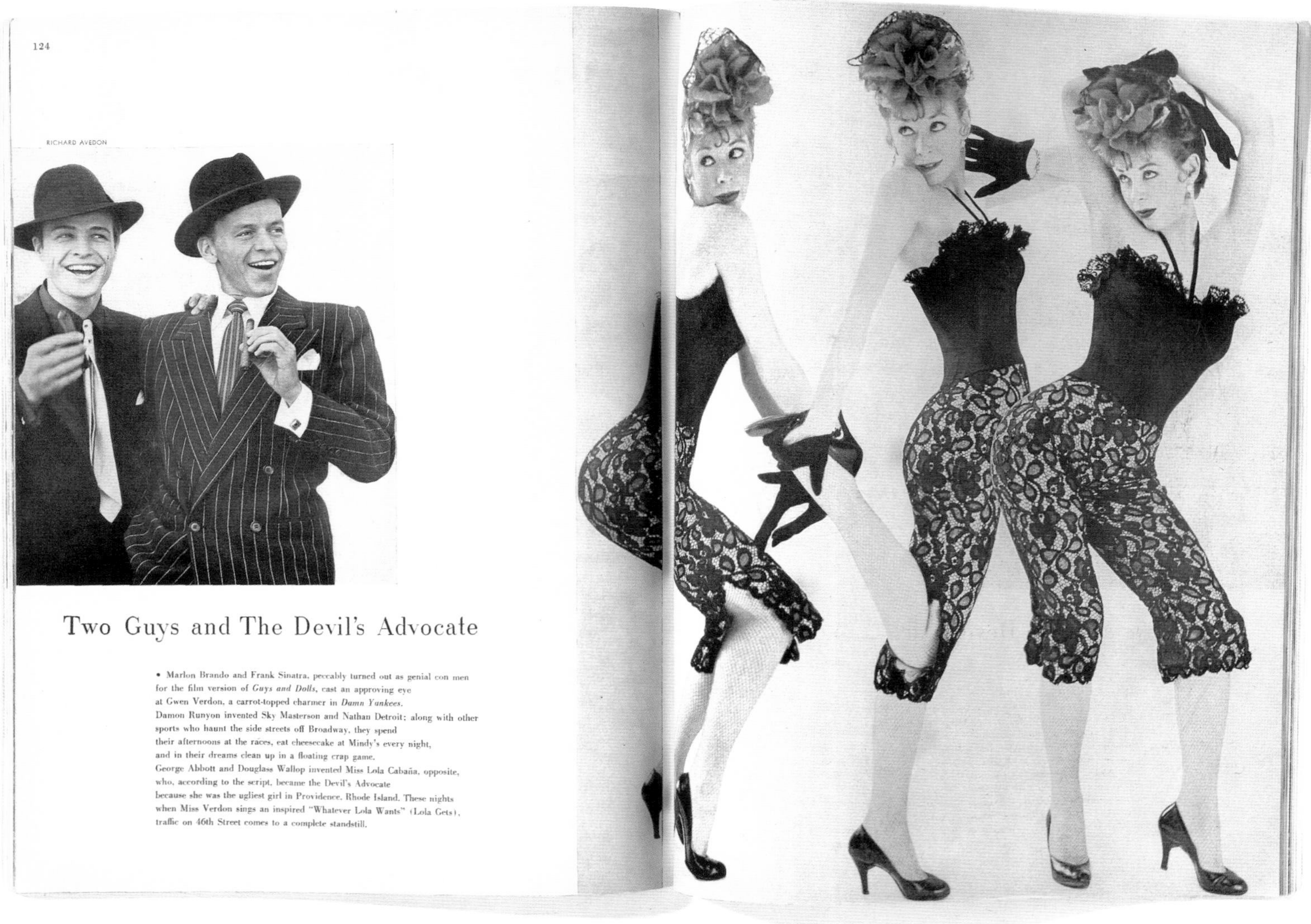

124

RICHARD AVEDON

Two Guys and The Devil's Advocate

• Marlon Brando and Frank Sinatra, peccably turned out as genial con men for the film version of *Guys and Dolls*, cast an approving eye at Gwen Verdon, a carrot-topped charmer in *Damn Yankees*.
Damon Runyon invented Sky Masterson and Nathan Detroit; along with other sports who haunt the side streets off Broadway, they spend their afternoons at the races, eat cheesecake at Mindy's every night, and in their dreams clean up in a floating crap game.
George Abbott and Douglass Wallop invented Miss Lola Cabaña, opposite, who, according to the script, became the Devil's Advocate because she was the ugliest girl in Providence, Rhode Island. These nights when Miss Verdon sings an inspired "Whatever Lola Wants" (Lola Gets), traffic on 46th Street comes to a complete standstill.

"Two Guys and the Devil's Advocate," *Harper's Bazaar*, August, 1955. Photographs by Richard Avedon.
These two Avedon photographs are unconnected – the Marlon Brando/Frank Sinatra image is from the film *Guys and Dolls*, while the photo of actress Gwen Verdon is from *Damn Yankees* – yet Brodovitch's sizing and placement creates a whimsical association.

in "Two Guys and The Devil's Advocate" (August 1955) Brodovitch creates a narrative connection over two pages by establishing a spatial flow between two separate Avedon images. Akin to the 180° law used in film editing (all the action advances smoothly from frame to frame along a single axis) Brodovitch creates a continuous link from the gaze of Sinatra and Brando to the images of Gwen Verdon. Similar to watching a film, Brodovitch physically directs our gaze from left to right by moving from a reduced medium-shot on the left-hand page to an enlarged long-shot on the right. Following the action, we become part of the visual story. This movement is given an added sense of momentum through the "jump-cut" repetition of the Verdon images. Their overlapping repetition enhances the graphic association and, by transgressing the spine of the magazine, they create a literal connection between the two pages. The singular experience of this graphic story is one of viewing a paper movie.

As "Two Guys and The Devil's Advocate" demonstrates, the cinematic device most closely allied with Brodovitch's designs is that of montage. In cinema, montage is regularly a synonym for editing. The film theorist David Bordwell characterized it as an approach to editing that "emphasizes dynamic, often discontinuous, relationships between shots and the juxtaposition of images to create ideas not present in either shot by itself."[66] The filmmaker most often associated with this technique is the Russian director Sergei Eisenstein, though it is impossible to say whether or not Brodovitch actually saw any of his films. In a 1923 article for *Lef* magazine, Eisenstein differentiated between traditional editing and his revolutionary theory of montage. It is a theory of film that could equally be applied to Brodovitch's manipulation and transformation of the photographic still. Eisenstein noted:

Instead of a static "reflection" of an event with all possibilities for activity within the limits of the event's logical action, we advance to a new plane – free montage of arbitrarily selected, independent (within the given composition and the subject links that hold the influencing actions together) attractions – all from the stand of establishing certain final thematic effects – this is montage of attractions.[67]

Through a series of graphic compositions Brodovitch's designs, like Eisenstein's films, emphasized the architectural aspects of the photograph and through this its dynamic features. Cropping images off-center, his layouts often registered as a frozen moment in a cinematic sequence. We can see this in the recurring image used to inform the reader of new shoe designs. In these photographs the model is arrested in midwalk. Used on covers or double-page spreads, the image is cropped in such a manner that it seems the model has just stepped onto the page. In the repetitive world of fashion magazines, such devices provided Brodovitch with a novel approach to the incessant seasonal fanfare of new dresses, bags,

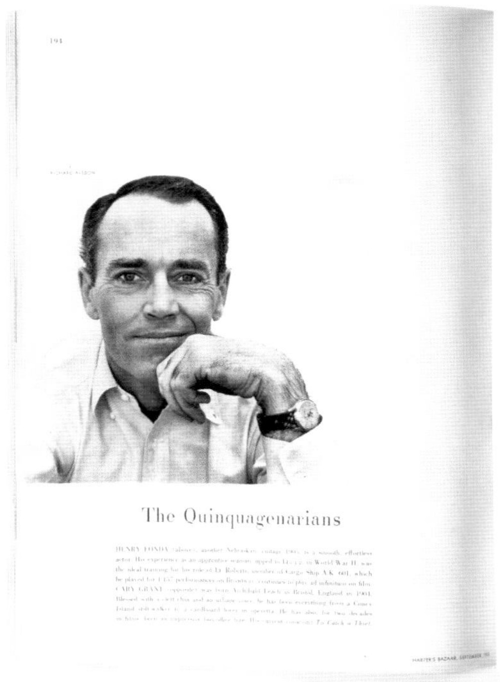

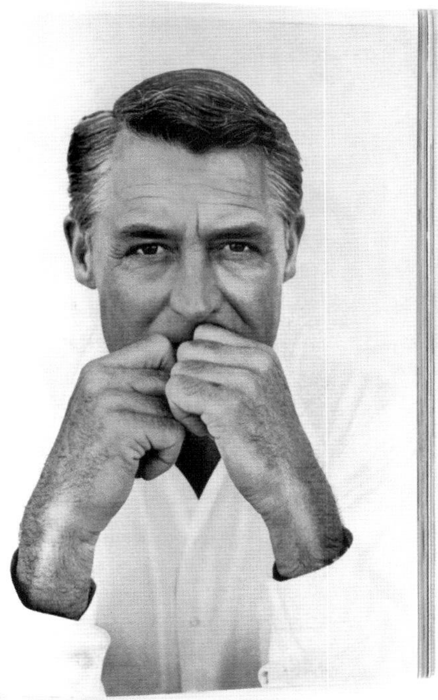

"The Quinquagenarians," *Harper's Bazaar*, September, 1955. Photographs by Richard Avedon.

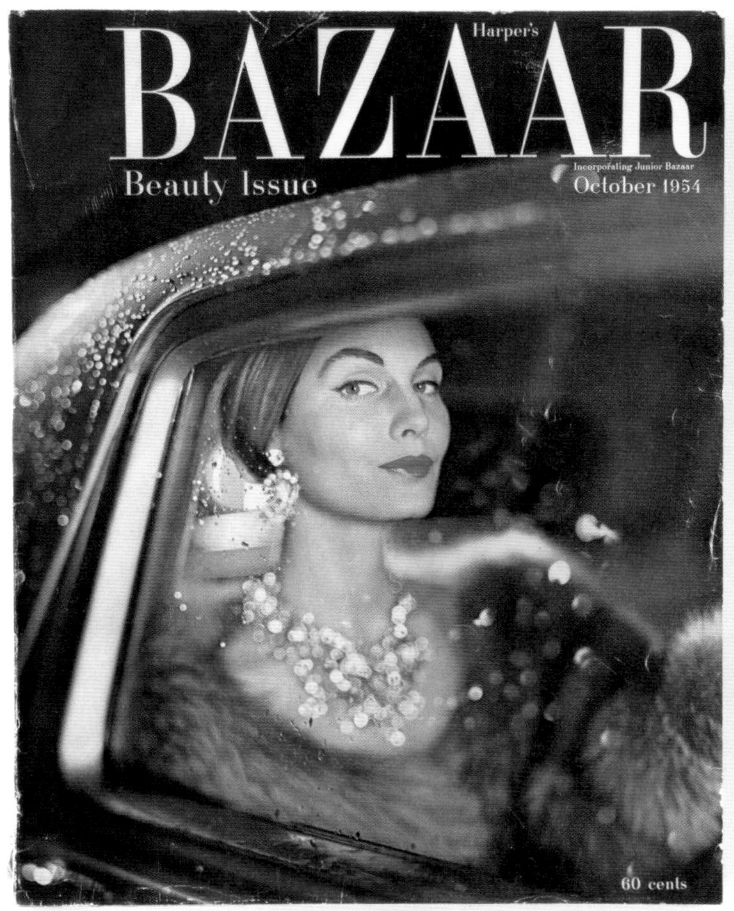

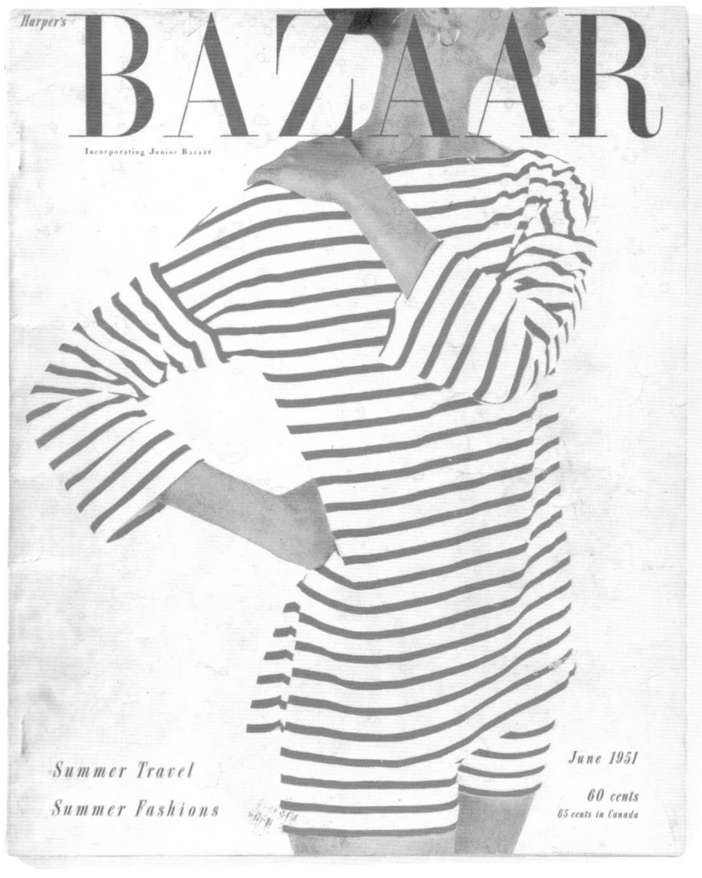

' *Brodovitch somehow helped Avedon understand what kinds of demands one not only could place, but was obligated to p*

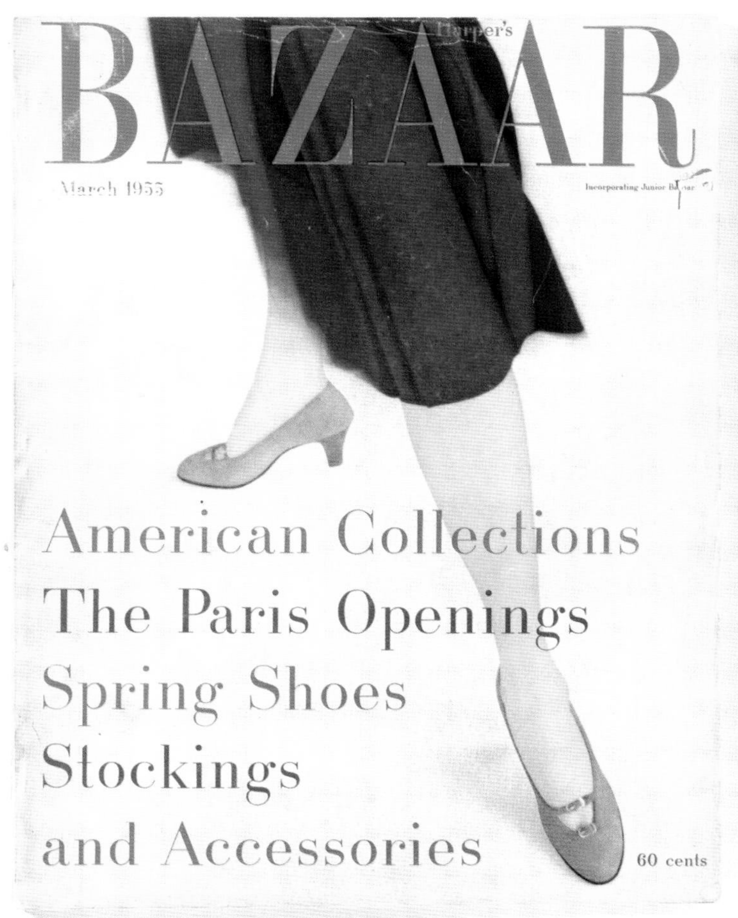

Harper's Bazaar covers photographed by Richard Avedon. Left to right: June 1951, October 1954, March 1955, February 1955.
Brodovitch's technique of cropping images unexpectedly or off-center brought a new dynamism to fashion layouts.

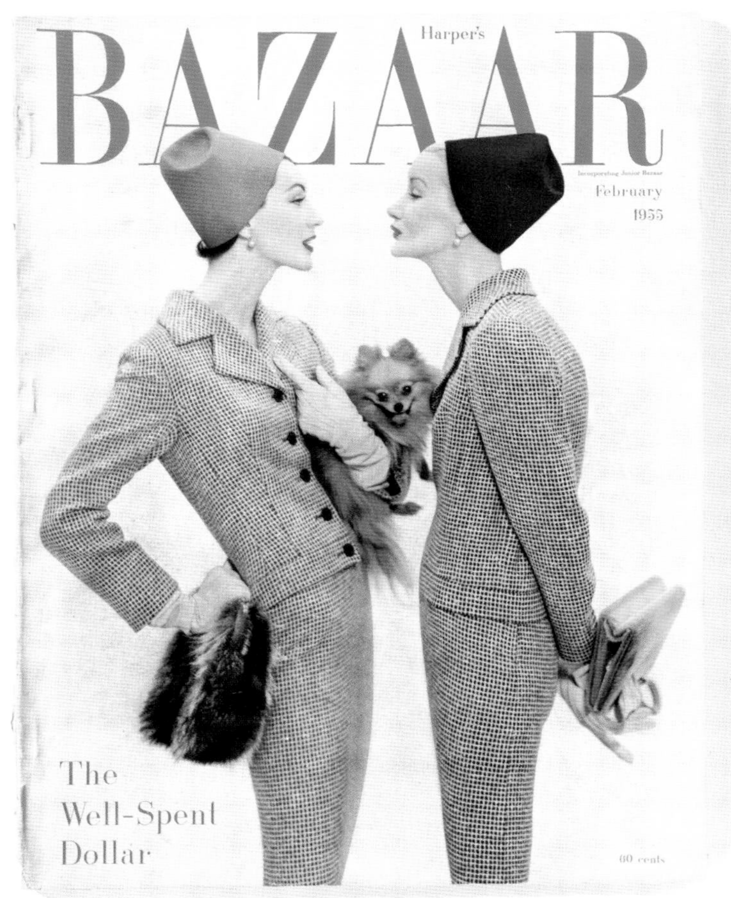

neself as a creative person. – Jane Livingston

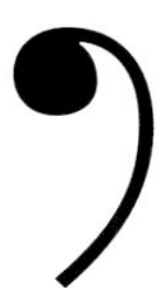

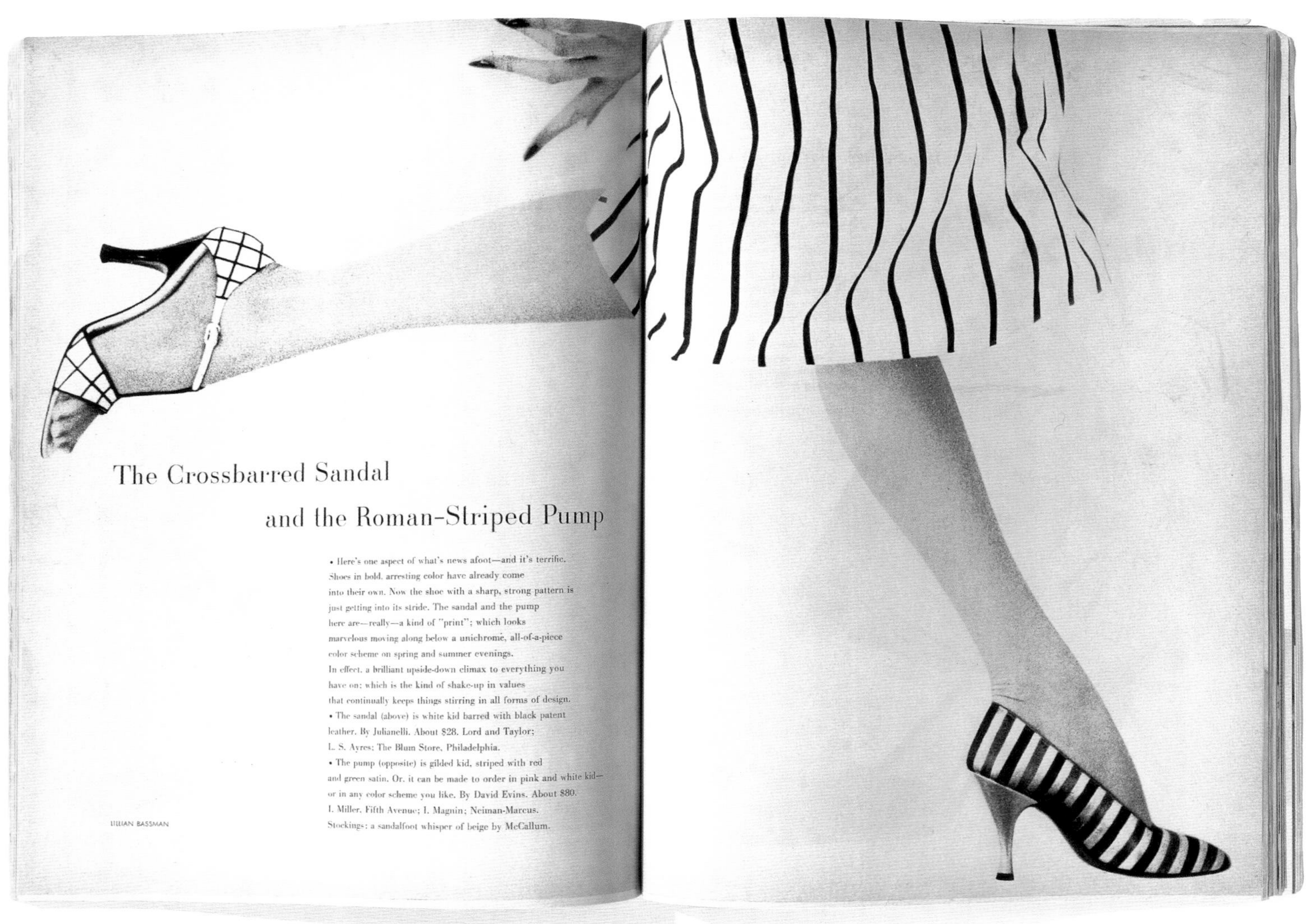

The Crossbarred Sandal
and the Roman-Striped Pump

• Here's one aspect of what's news afoot—and it's terrific. Shoes in bold, arresting color have already come into their own. Now the shoe with a sharp, strong pattern is just getting into its stride. The sandal and the pump here are—really—a kind of "print"; which looks marvelous moving along below a unichrome, all-of-a-piece color scheme on spring and summer evenings. In effect, a brilliant upside-down climax to everything you have on; which is the kind of shake-up in values that continually keeps things stirring in all forms of design.

• The sandal (above) is white kid barred with black patent leather. By Julianelli. About $28. Lord and Taylor; L. S. Ayres; The Blum Store, Philadelphia.

• The pump (opposite) is gilded kid, striped with red and green satin. Or, it can be made to order in pink and white kid—or in any color scheme you like. By David Evins. About $80. I. Miller, Fifth Avenue; I. Magnin; Neiman-Marcus. Stockings: a sandalfoot whisper of beige by McCallum.

LILLIAN BASSMAN

Left: "The Crossbarred Sandal...," *Harper's Bazaar*, March, 1954. Photograph by Lillian Ba

Lillian Bassman was a student in Brodovitch's Design Laboratory in New York. She eventually became Brodovitch's apprent

or hats. As with Eisenstein, it was a way of working that was "always, in some way, intuitively employed, but not on a plane of montage or construction, but as part of a 'harmonic composition.'"[68]

Beyond Eisenstein, comparisons have also been made between Brodovitch's designs and the Constructivist ideas of El Lissitzky. In publications such as Mayakovsky's book of poems *For the Voice* (1923) or his own *Moi Parizh* (1933), Lissitzky illustrated his theory of the "kinetics of succeeding pages" or the "cinematic book." Speaking about *For the Voice*, Lissitzky's comments about the relationship between his manipulation of type and Mayakovsky's poems echoes Brodovitch's treatment of image and text: "My pages stand in much the same relation to the poems as an accompanying piano to a violin. Just as the poet in his poem unites concept and sound, I have tried to create an equivalent unity using the poem and typography."[69] Based on simple geometric forms and their relationship with the clean white space of the page, Lissitzky's work seems to have been a key reference point in Brodovitch's *Bazaar* designs.

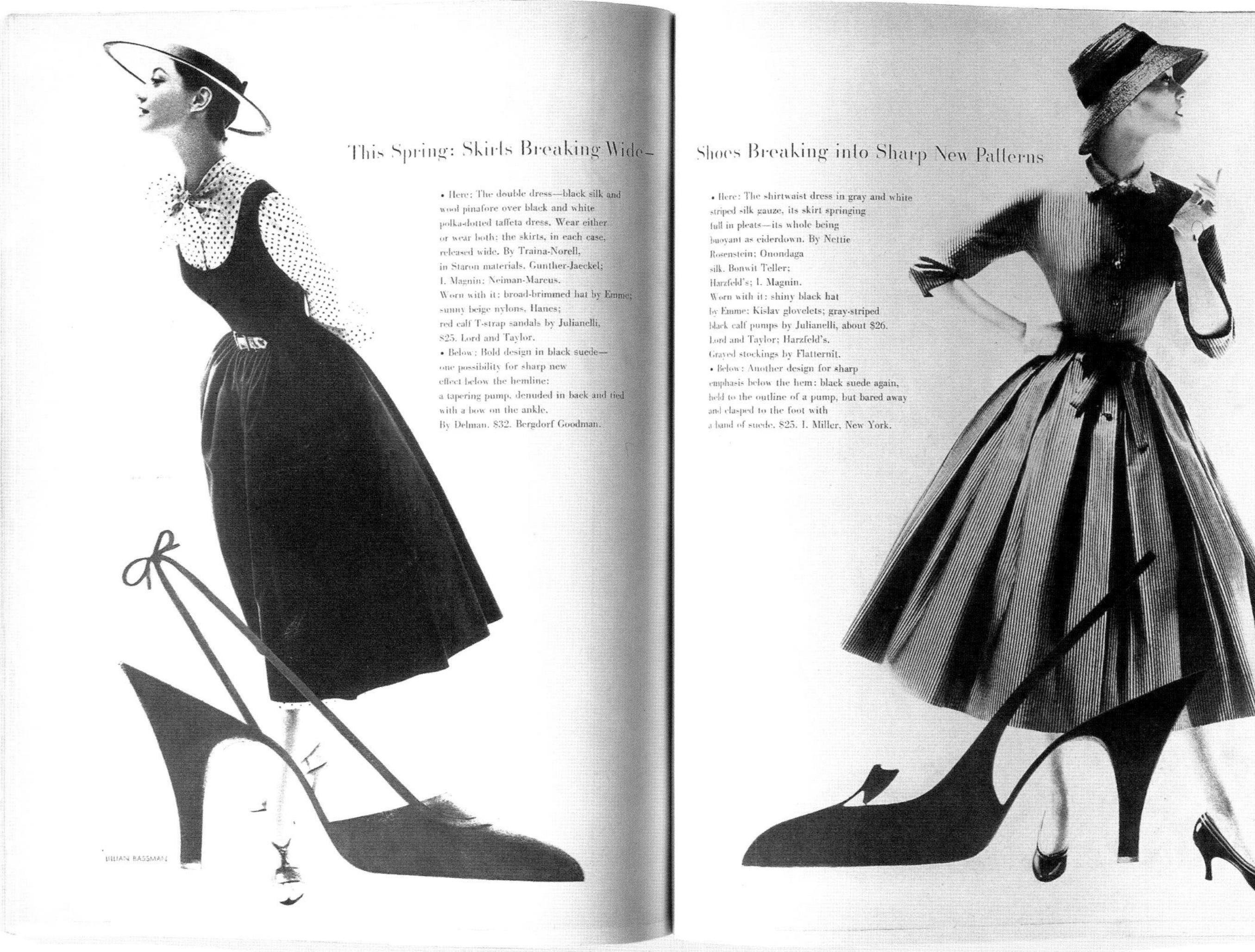

This Spring: Skirts Breaking Wide–

• Here: The double dress—black silk and wool pinafore over black and white polka-dotted taffeta dress. Wear either or wear both: the skirts, in each case, released wide. By Traina-Norell, in Staron materials. Gunther-Jaeckel; I. Magnin; Neiman-Marcus.
Worn with it: broad-brimmed hat by Emme; sunny beige nylons, Hanes; red calf T-strap sandals by Julianelli, $25. Lord and Taylor.
• Below: Bold design in black suede—one possibility for sharp new effect below the hemline: a tapering pump, denuded in back and tied with a bow on the ankle. By Delman. $32. Bergdorf Goodman.

Shoes Breaking into Sharp New Patterns

• Here: The shirtwaist dress in gray and white striped silk gauze, its skirt springing full in pleats—its whole being buoyant as eiderdown. By Nettie Rosenstein; Onondaga silk. Bonwit Teller; Harzfeld's; I. Magnin.
Worn with it: shiny black hat by Emme; Kislav glovelets; gray-striped black calf pumps by Julianelli, about $26. Lord and Taylor; Harzfeld's.
Grayed stockings by Flatternit.
• Below: Another design for sharp emphasis below the hem: black suede again, held to the outline of a pump, but bared away and clasped to the foot with a band of suede. $25. I. Miller, New York.

: "This Spring...," *Harper's Bazaar*, March 1954. Photograph by Lillian Bassman.

r's *Bazaar* and art directed *Bazaar's* sister publication *Junior Bazaar*.

Frances McFadden, at various times the literary and managing editor at *Harper's Bazaar*, witnessed firsthand Brodovitch's natural instinct when constructing a "harmonic composition":

It was a pleasure to watch him work. He was so swift and so sure. In emergencies, like the time the Clipper bearing the report of the Paris Collections was held up in Bermuda, his speed was dazzling. A quick splash or two on the cutting board, a minute's juggling of the photostats, a slather of art gum, and the sixteen pages were complete. His layouts, of course, were the despair of copywriters whose cherished tone poems on girdles or minks had to be sacrificed to his sacred white space. Just before we went to press, all the layouts were laid out in sequence on Carmel Snow's floor and there, under his eye, rearranged until the rhythm of the magazine suited him.[70]

Aspiring to divest the photograph of its value as a distinctive and individual object, Brodovitch used the term "flow" to identify this approach to magazine layout. Subordinating the single image to the overall look of the magazine, the reader of Brodovitch's

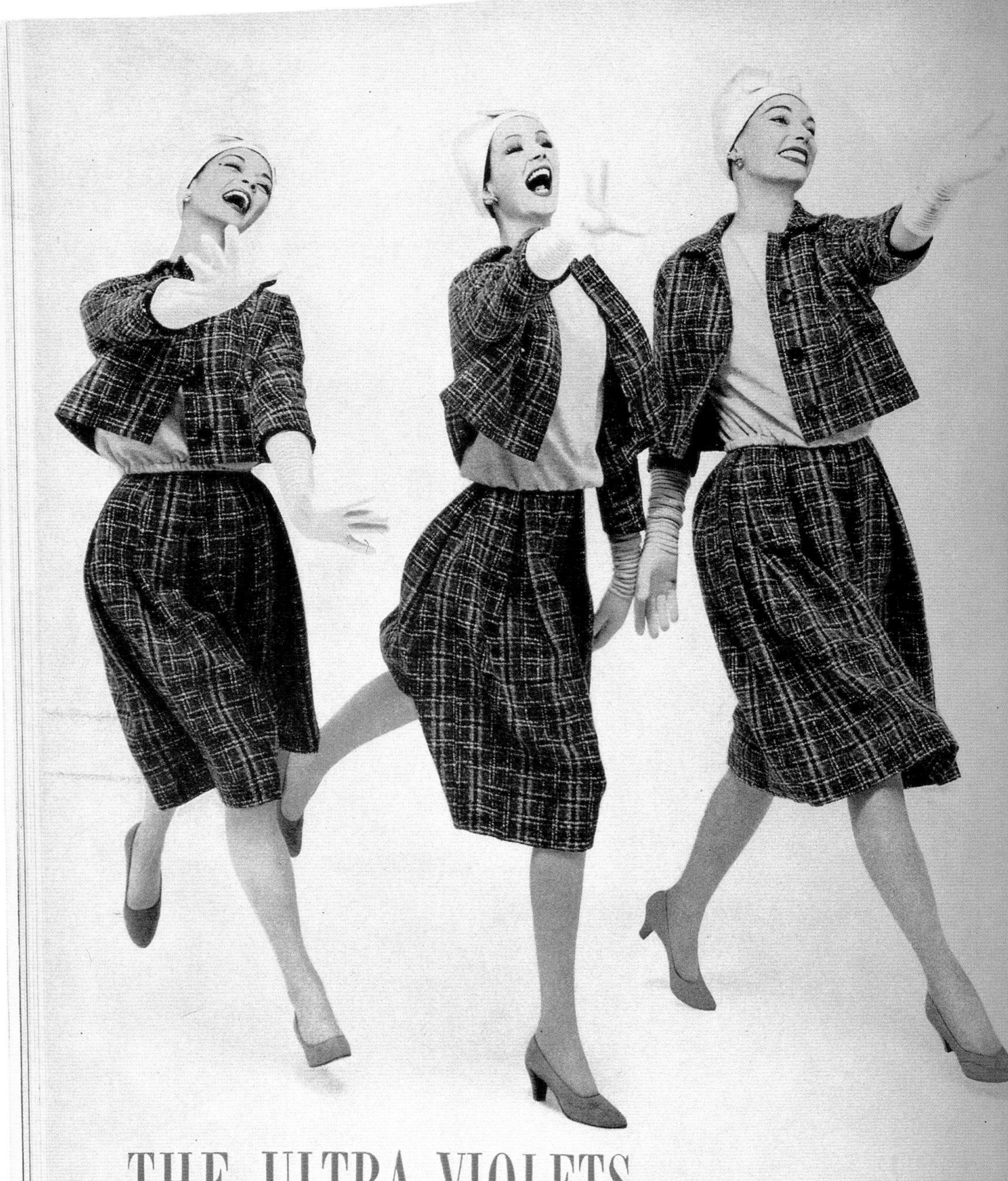

THE ULTRA VIOLETS

• Above: Nelly de Grab's wide swath of flecked Strong Hewat wool (a mix of violet with green, red, white) may be taken in part (the jacket, about $23, the skirt, about $25, and the beige wool overblouse for about $15), but we prefer the look of the whole, which is about $63. At Bloomingdale's; R. H. Stearns, Boston; Stix, Baer and Fuller, St. Louis.

• Opposite: Towncliffe has shaped magenta tweed into a particularly able exposition of the blouson-jacket suit, holds the waistline with elastic. At Bloomingdale's; Kaufmann's, Pittsburgh; Dayton's, Minneapolis; I. Magnin. About $80. Stockings, Van Raalte. Shoes, I. Miller. Madcaps hats, opposite and above, at Bloomingdale's.

RICHARD AVEDON

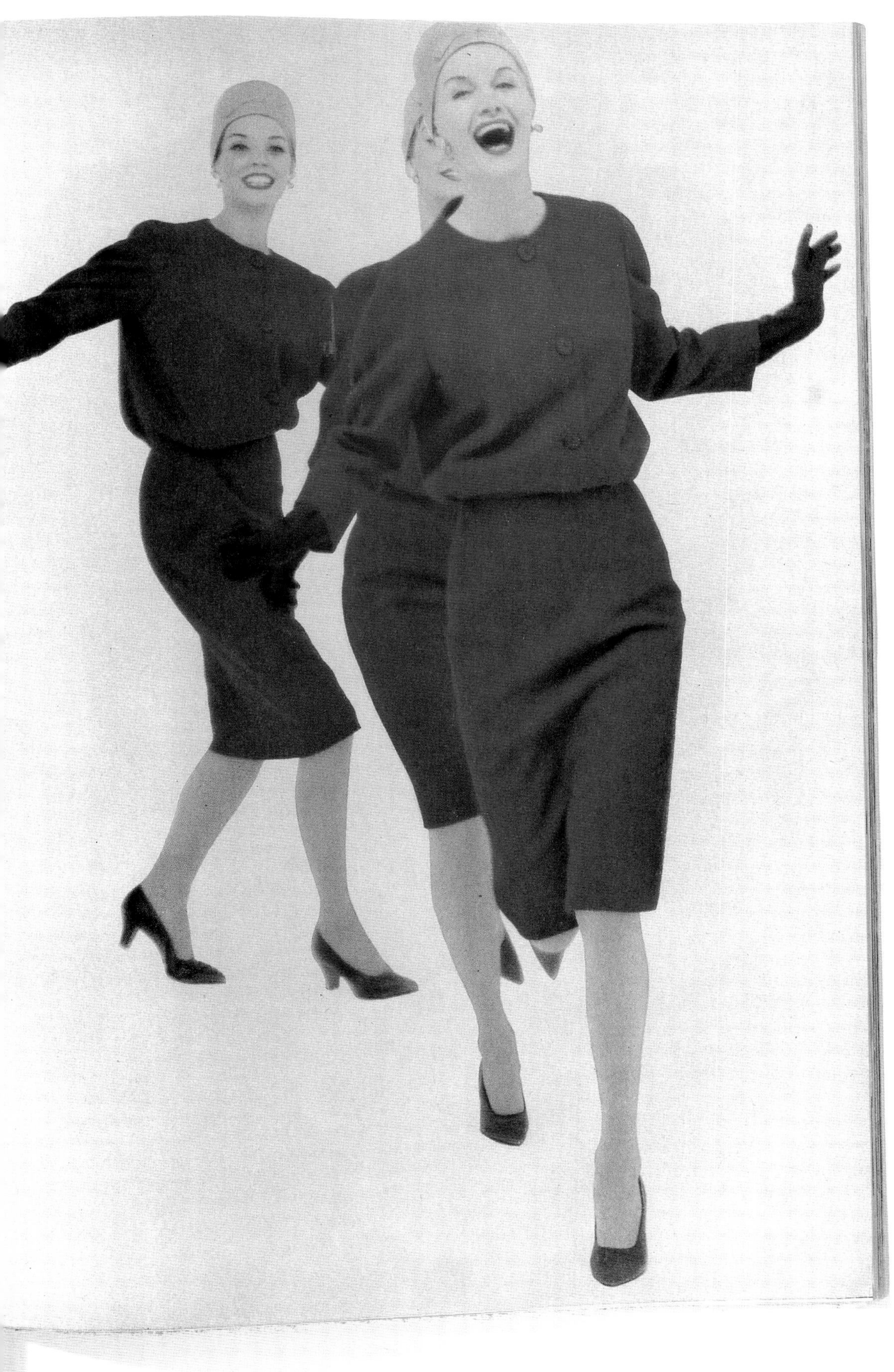

"The Ultra Violets,"
Harper's Bazaar, August 1958.
Photograph by Richard Avedon.

Bazaar was thrown in and out of its graphic story; a narrative that repeatedly generated experiences of surprise and then discovery.

As McFadden indicates, to achieve these sweeping compositions Brodovitch was highly dependent on the use of photocopying facilities. The influence of Xerography, invented in 1946, cannot be overestimated when assessing Brodovitch's late-forties and fifties designs. During this period, after receiving photographs for an issue of *Bazaar* Brodovitch's first task was to order multiple copies of the most stimulating images in various sizes. Once he had received these copies he would lay them out on the floor and proceed to crop them mercilessly with a pair of scissors. Finally, he would tape the photostats to the regulation-size paper used for the magazine, leaving his assistants to straighten them up. Like McFadden, those who witnessed this process were always amazed at Brodovitch's casual approach. Simply casting his eye over the copies and moving the pages around, he would produce dynamic and imaginative layouts in the space of minutes.

Prior to going to press Brodovitch's layouts would have to be personally approved by Carmel Snow and other senior *Bazaar* editors. During the final run-through, Brodovitch's relationship

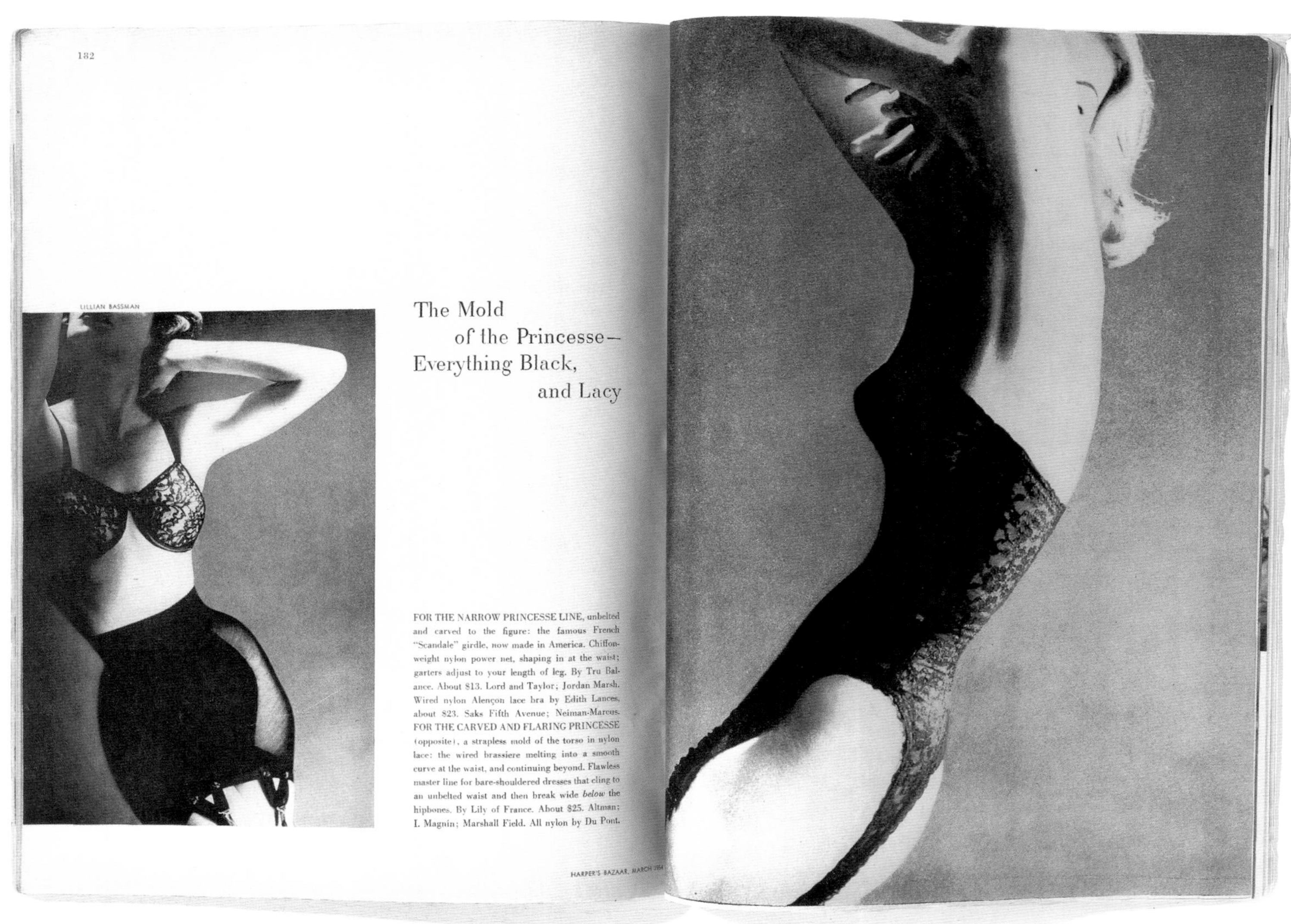
182

LILLIAN BASSMAN

The Mold of the Princesse–Everything Black, and Lacy

FOR THE NARROW PRINCESSE LINE, unbelted and carved to the figure: the famous French "Scandale" girdle, now made in America. Chiffon-weight nylon power net, shaping in at the waist; garters adjust to your length of leg. By Tru Balance. About $13. Lord and Taylor; Jordan Marsh. Wired nylon Alençon lace bra by Edith Lances, about $23. Saks Fifth Avenue; Neiman-Marcus. FOR THE CARVED AND FLARING PRINCESSE (opposite), a strapless mold of the torso in nylon lace: the wired brassiere melting into a smooth curve at the waist, and continuing beyond. Flawless master line for bare-shouldered dresses that cling to an unbelted waist and then break wide *below* the hipbones. By Lily of France. About $25. Altman; I. Magnin; Marshall Field. All nylon by Du Pont.

HARPER'S BAZAAR, MARCH 1954

with Carmel Snow was, by all accounts, characterized by frequent acts of capitulation. As art director with Brodovitch of *Bazaar*'s short-lived subsidiary *Junior Bazaar*, Lillian Bassman was often a witness to such moments. She once recalled that:

[Brodovitch] had great respect for Carmel and she was a staunch ally of his and trusted him enormously. But she always had to keep an eye on what was commercial and he wouldn't take her on over this. It was custom then to make "A" and "B" choices of the photographs for the magazine. It was uncanny, but if there were, say, four sheets of contacts, Brodovitch and I always

Opposite: "The Mold of the Princesse...," *Harper's Bazaar*, March, 1954. Photographs by Lillian Bassman.

Below: "The Line Lengthens," *Harper's Bazaar*, October, 1955. Photographs by Lillian Bassman.

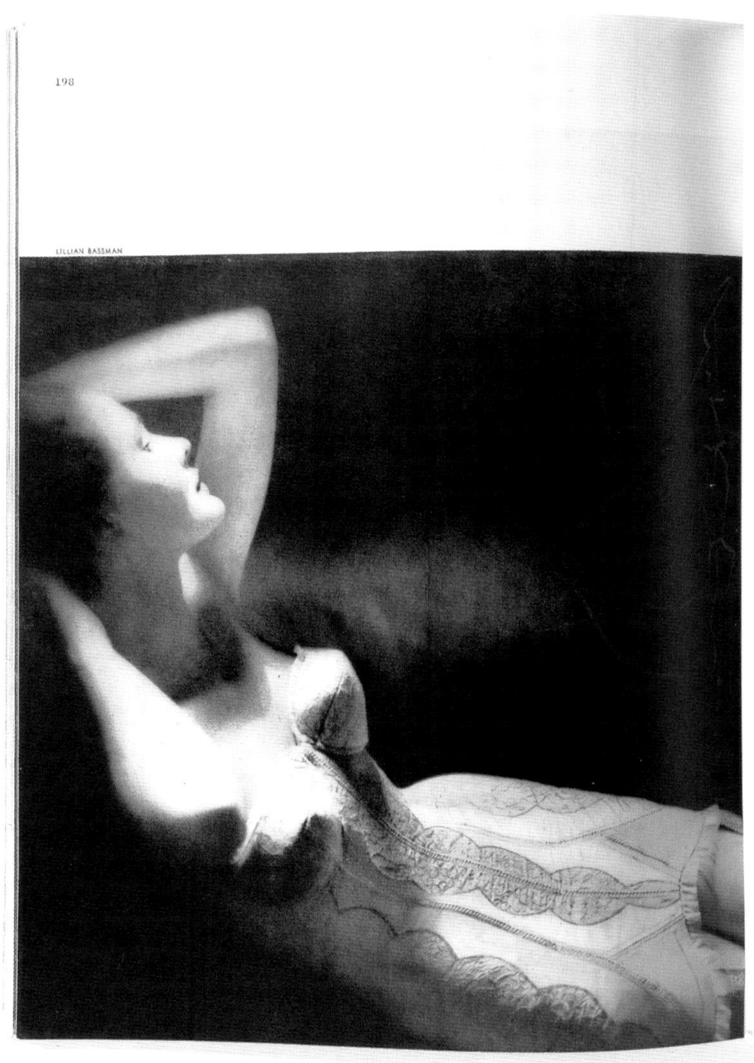

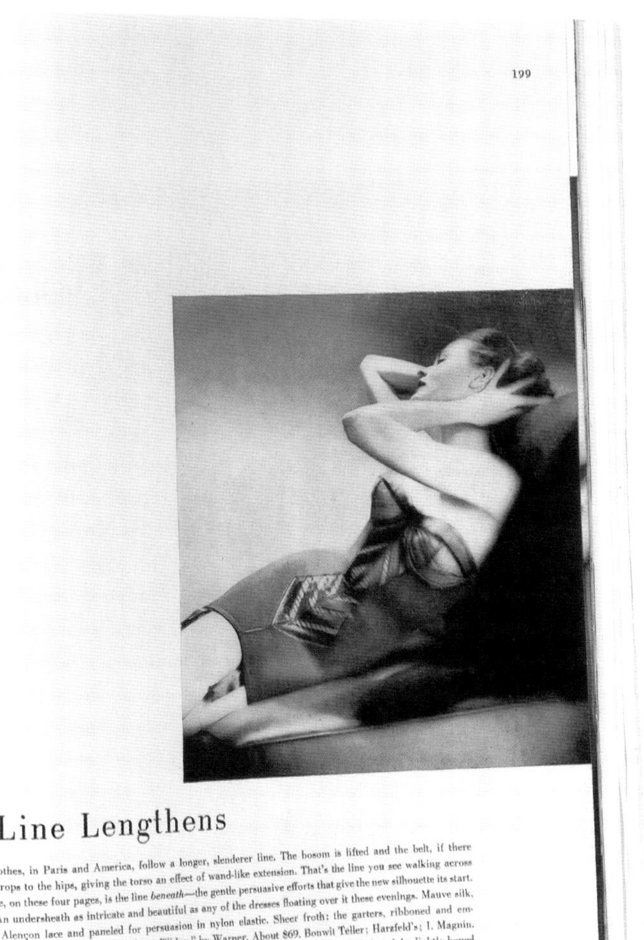

The Line Lengthens

• The new clothes, in Paris and America, follow a longer, slenderer line. The bosom is lifted and the belt, if there is one, often drops to the hips, giving the torso an effect of wand-like extension. That's the line you see walking across the room. Here, on these four pages, is the line *beneath*—the gentle persuasive efforts that give the new silhouette its start.
• Opposite: An undersheath as intricate and beautiful as any of the dresses floating over it these evenings. Mauve silk, overlaid with Alençon lace and paneled for persuasion in nylon elastic. Sheer froth: the garters, ribboned and embroidered. About $69. Bonwit Teller; Harzfeld's; I. Magnin. A new version of the famous "Merry Widow" by Warner, low-dipped in back for evening décolletés, lightweight, lightly boned
• Above: A long measure of ribboned black nylon, to shape the figure. By Lily of France, in power net, marquisette and satin. About $19. Bonwit Teller; I. Magnin.

...S BAZAAR OCTOBER 1955

marked the same first choice. If Carmel preferred the second choice, however, Brodovitch would say "Well, Mrs. Snow likes it and it's OK.[71]

Such acts of deference must have been a great surprise to those young photographers who held the legendary Alexey Brodovitch in high esteem. Ted Croner, a photographer and one-time assistant to Brodovitch, remembers the shock of seeing him humbled by Snow and Diana Vreeland:

I was in Brodovitch's office [and] in the middle of our conversation these two ladies walked in, Carmel Snow and Diana Vreeland.... They'd come in and Brodovitch is going to show them a layout, one of the layouts for the next issue. I'd retire to the other side of the room, not to be in the way. Well, in my opinion... I was an ally of Brodovitch so to speak, and these two, the way they were treating him, they were the enemy. They were making demands: "Well, you know Alexey you have to do this...that can't be that way." And he would change it around and everything. And when they left...in my own twenty-six-year-old way, I would say: "You're Alexey Brodovitch, why are you letting them take the reins?" He says: "I don't want to argue. I will do it my way in the end." And when they left, they assumed it was all going to be exactly how they wanted it. It wasn't. It was going to be Brodovitch's way.[72]

On one occasion, Snow apparently sent photocopies back to Brodovitch with the word "no" scribbled across the layout.[73] It was instances such as these that imparted a semblance of truth to the fictional character Maggie Prescott, who featured in the 1956 Stanley Donen film *Funny Face*. Prescott, the editor of *Quality* magazine – a fictionalized version of *Harper's Bazaar* – was a thinly veiled caricature of Snow and Vreeland. Throughout the film Prescott constantly berates those around her for not understanding what the modern woman wants. In one moment that echoes the Carmel Snow anecdote above, Prescott abruptly dismisses a design that does not "speak" to her by writing three D's across the layout. While doing this she says: "'D' for down, 'D' for dreary, and 'D' for dull and depressing, dismal and deadly." In two other scenes we also see an art director named Dovitch, who humbly acquiesces to Prescott's every order.

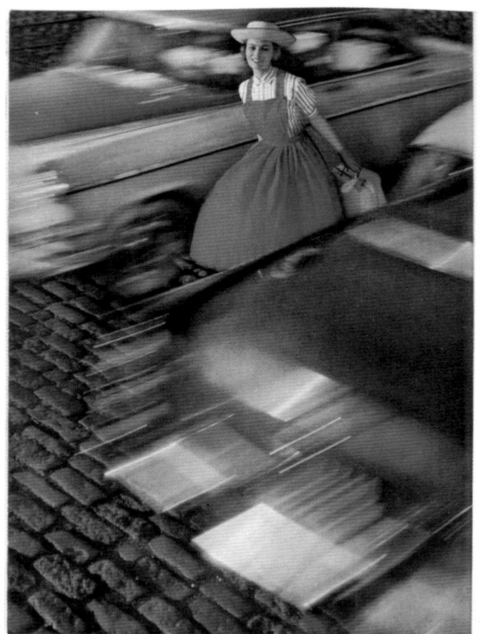

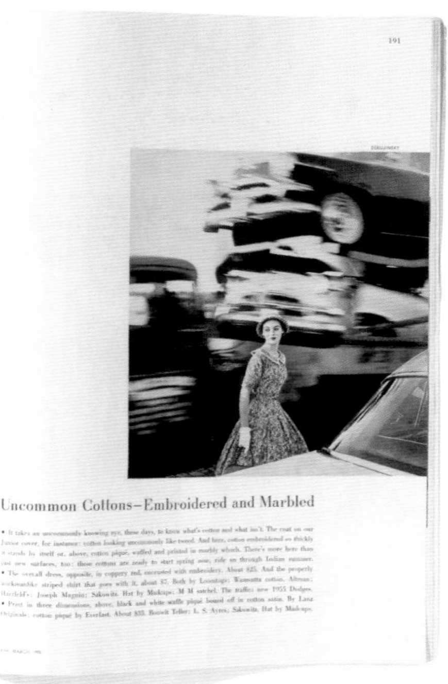
191

Uncommon Cottons–Embroidered and Marbled

FIFTH AVENUE at Rockefeller Center SAKS FIFTH

at Rockefeller Center SAKS FIFTH AVENUE at Rockefel

FIFTH AVENUE at Rockefeller Center SAKS FIFT

at Rockefeller Center SAKS FIFTH AVENUE at Rockefel

FIFTH AVENUE at Rockefeller Center SAKS FIFT

at Rockefeller Center SAKS FIFTH AVENUE at Rockefel

FIFTH AVENUE at Rockefeller Center SAKS FIFTH

at Rockefeller Center SAKS FIFTH AVENUE at Rockefel

FIFTH AVENUE at Rockefeller Center SAKS FIFTH

at Rockefeller Center SAKS FIFTH AVENUE at Rockefel

FIFTH AVENUE at Rockefeller Center SAKS FIFT

at Rockefeller Center SAKS FIFTH AVENUE at Rockefe

FIFTH AVENUE at Rockefeller Center SAKS FIFT

at Rockefeller Center SAKS FIFTH AVENUE at Rockefel

FIFTH AVENUE at Rockefeller Center SAKS FIFT

at Rockefeller Center SAKS FIFTH AVENUE at Rockefe

FIFTH AVENUE at Rockefeller Center SAKS FIFT

at Rockefeller Center SAKS FIFTH AVENUE at Rockefel

FIFTH AVENUE at Rockefeller Center SAKS FIFTH

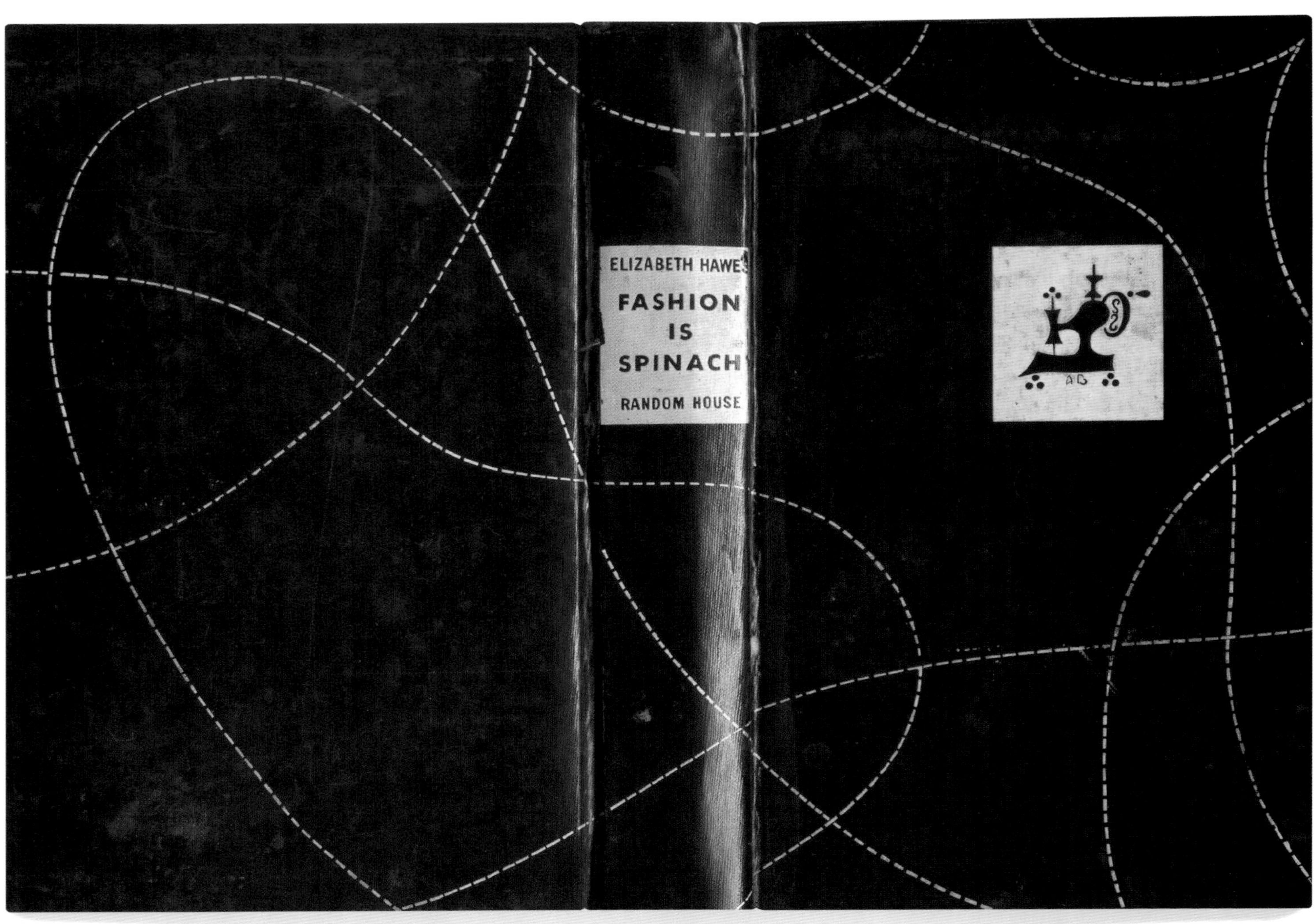
ELIZABETH HAWES
FASHION
IS
SPINACH
RANDOM HOUSE

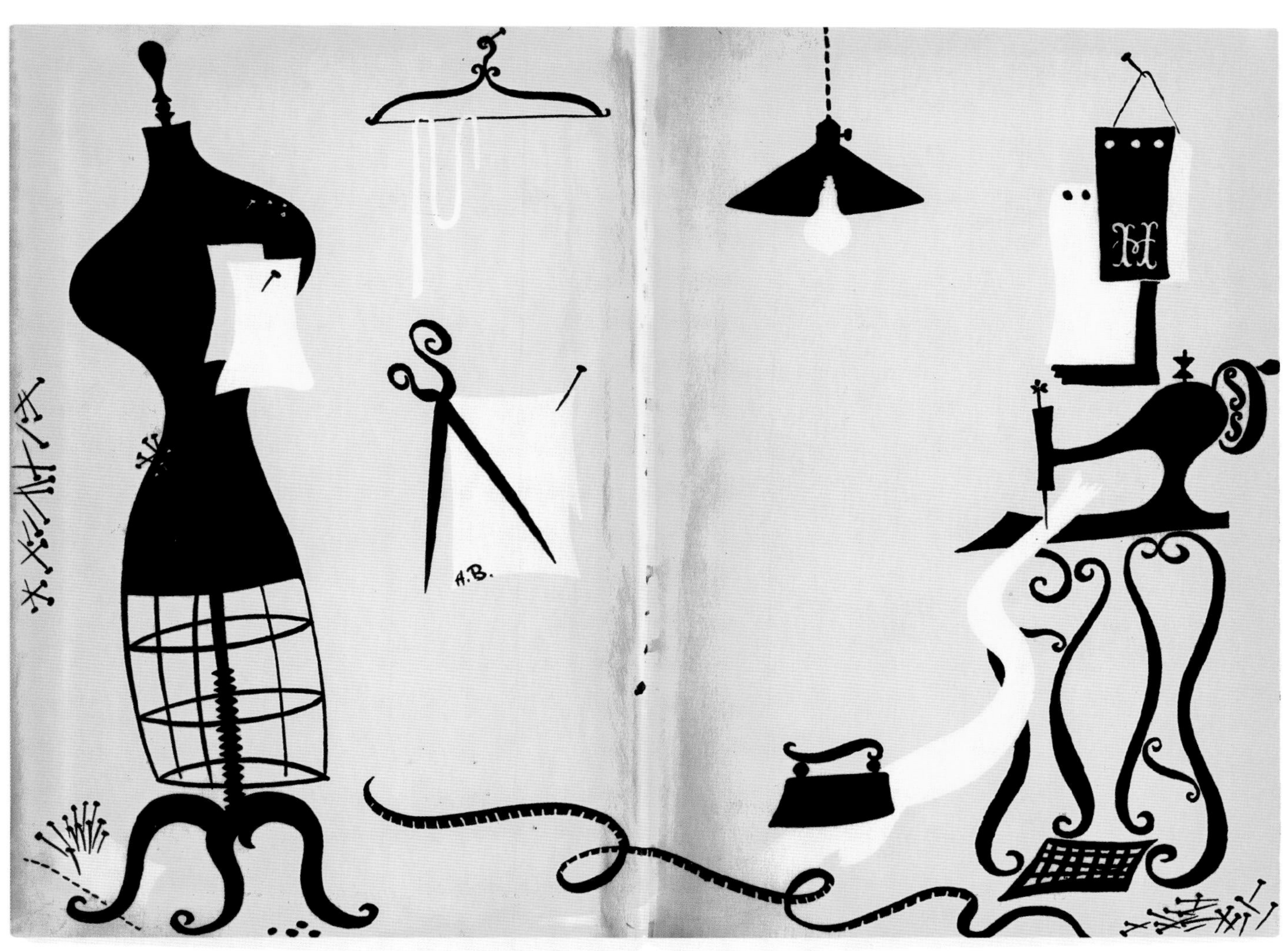

Cover and endpapers, *Fashion is Spinach* by Elizabeth Hawes. New York: McGraw-Hill, 1938. Cover design and illustrations by Brodovitch.

Advertisement for the Container Corporation of America. Produced for N.W. Ayer, 1962.
This ad, one of Brodovitch's last designs for N.W. Ayer, was part of a series called "Great Ideas of Western Man."

freelance commissions – the cover design and a series of illustrations for *Fashion is Spinach*, a 1938 book by the dress designer Elizabeth Hawes. On the slipcase the feminine silhouette of the mannequin is defined by its superimposition upon a "masculine" letter "H." Under this slipcase is an ingenious use of a stitching effect across the book's casing. The mannequin motif is repeated in the vibrant endpapers, where it is situated among illustrations of the various instruments of a designer's studio. Other notable commissions during this period include a delicate window display for Elizabeth Arden, the 1939 Sears Roebuck catalogue design, an advertising campaign for Helena Rubenstein, and a mural for the education pavilion at the 1939 New York World's Fair. In 1941, Brodovitch also volunteered his considerable design skills to the American war effort, principally through the position of design consultant at the Red Cross. Beyond this, being multilingual, he was also an obvious candidate for the production of propaganda leaflets being dropped over occupied Europe. In 1944, he designed the leaflet "Libres de Miseria" (Freedom from Want) for the Department of Inter-American Affairs, where we once again see Brodovitch's repeated use of the hand motif.

On the eve of the Vietnam War, one of Brodovitch's last designs for the N. W. Ayer agency also focused on the fragility of peace. Produced in 1962 for the Chicago-based Container Corporation of America, Brodovitch's illustration was part of the series "Great Ideas of Western Man." Novel for a large corporation, CCA had given carte blanche to N. W. Ayer to produce a series of advertisements that actually contained little information about the company – a technique commonplace in today's advertising. Published in *Fortune* magazine, Brodovitch's design was part of a long history of illustrations for the CCA by some of the leading modernist designers of the day, including Herbert Matter, Cassandre, and Herbert Bayer. The format of the design was frequently a radical illustration with a brief but well-known quote attached. Brodovitch's own contribution is a gauche sketch of a dove with a bullet hole through its center, a thin line highlights the trajectory of the bullet. Below this illustration we see written in Brodovitch's own hand the famous quote by Rousseau: "As soon as any man says of the affairs of the State, 'What does it matter to me?' the State may be given up for lost."

It was partly because of his heavy drinking as well as a perceived need to change management that Brodovitch was eventually sacked from his position at *Harper's Bazaar* in August 1958 (Carmel Snow's dismissal followed a year later). Receiving no pension after twenty-four years of service, and following the death of his wife Nina in 1959, Brodovitch's financial and physical state deteriorated. His departure from *Bazaar* signaled the end of a twenty-four-year period of continual design innovation for Brodovitch. In September 1958, Henry Wolf replaced Brodovitch as art director at *Harper's Bazaar*. Wolf later said that he suffered from Brodovitch's excellence for many months. In a posthumous celebration of Brodovitch's achievements, Wolf made a speech in 1972 that honored his lasting legacy. Questioning what it was that compelled photographers to show their work to a man so resolutely intolerant of mediocrity, Wolf points to the enigma at the heart of Brodovitch's revolutionary eye:

Alexey Brodovitch only wore one kind of suit. It was grey, rumpled and one size too large. It seemed that just sitting there, all three buttons buttoned, his hands awkwardly clutching a pencil, a Martini or the Picayune cigarettes he was fond of, or just sitting there was agony. Only his eyes were loose, observing, editing, clarifying. His voice came almost as a footnote, an afterthought, a stage whisper with a heavy Russian accent.... The truth was that you never got to know him any better than the very first time. And it was this mystery, this vacuum that he created that was the big force that generated a desire to please, to help him, to relieve his discomfort by bringing him, like an offering, the best work one was capable of producing.[75]

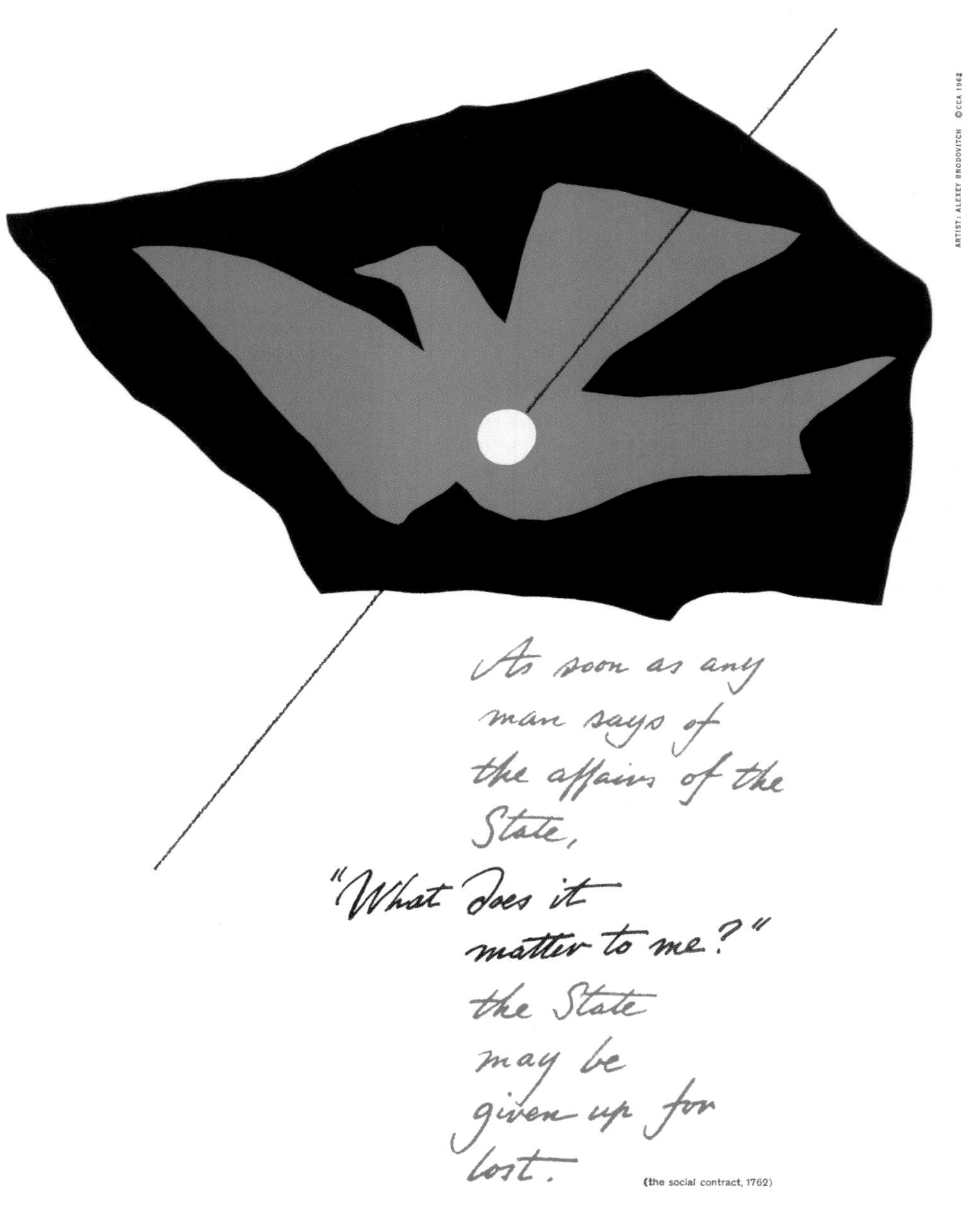

ROUSSEAU on the citizen and the state GREAT IDEAS OF WESTERN MAN . . . one of a series **Container Corporation of America** 

Design Laboratory: The Theater of Invention

in Brodovitch to reestablish the Design Lab class in New York. Thus, beginning in spring 1941, the class was held in the Thomas Hart Benton room under the auspices of the New School for Social Research. Brodovitch continued to split the lab into two sections per week, one specializing in design, the other photography, with each section running for about ten weeks. The aim of these courses was, according to the catalogue, to "help the student to discover his individuality, crystallize his taste, and develop his feeling for the contemporary trend by stimulating his sense of invention and perfecting his technical ability. The course is conducted as an experimental laboratory, inspired by the ever changing tempo of life, discovery of new techniques, new fields of operation."[13]

The photography classes met on a Tuesday or Wednesday night and ran from 7 to 10 pm. With Brodovitch's reputation preceding him, more than sixty people would sometimes arrive at his class on the first night. But, as Harvey Lloyd witnessed, "by the end of the sessions there might be three, four, or eight left. Because it was like Marine training. You either got it, or you came to understand what he was doing, or you just got disgusted

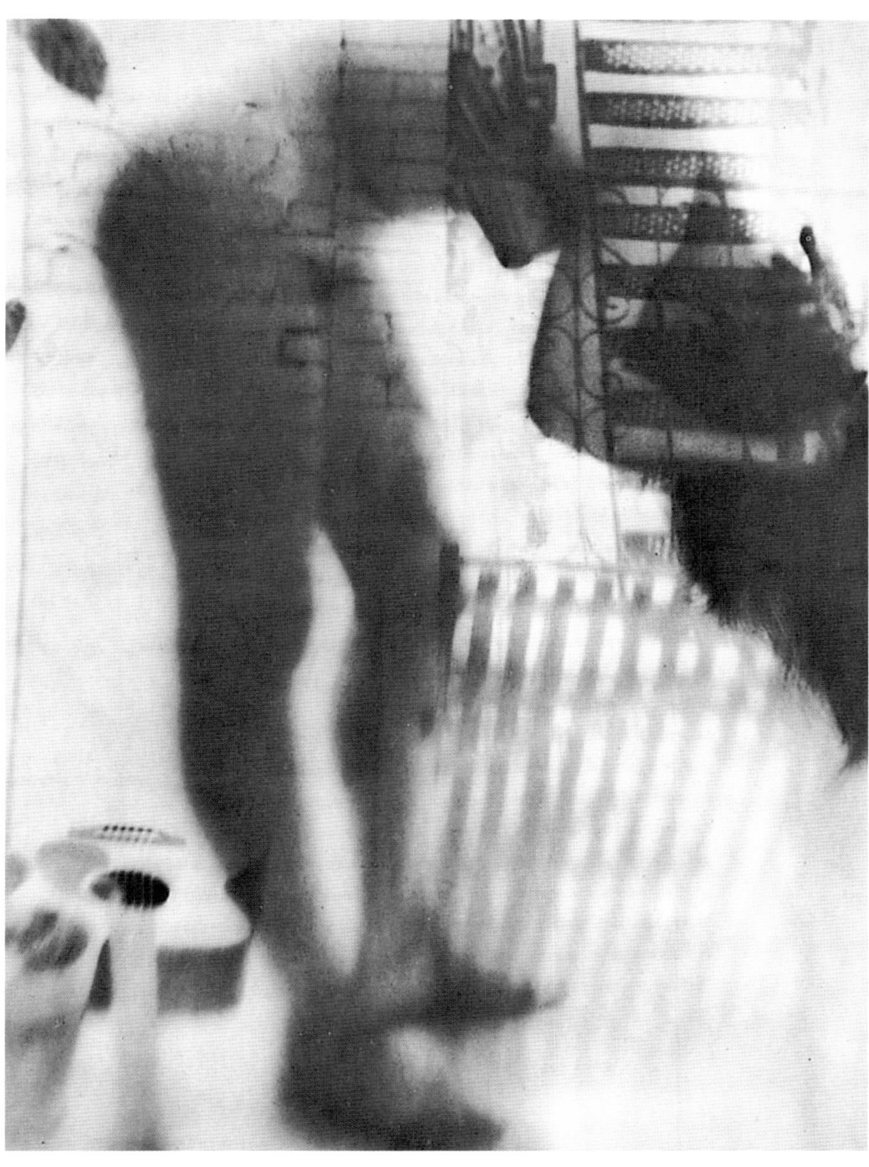

Following pages: Alexey Brodovitch (upper left, wearing glasses) and students in the Design Laboratory, early 1960s. The photographer Hiro is seated to Brodovitch's right. Photograph by David Attie.
Students in the Design Laboratory always began each session by allowing other members of the class to see their responses to the previous weeks assignment. These were then returned to Brodovitch, who would begin his critique.

Opposite and left: Photographs by David Attie, published in *Saloon Society* by Bill Manville and David Attie. New York: Duell, Sloan and Pierce, 1960.
David Attie was a student in the Design Lab and went on to become a successful commercial photographer. These photographs from his book *Saloon Society*, which chronicles the bohemian life of New York's Greenwich Village during the Beat era, display the creativity and experimentation that Brodovitch demanded of his students.

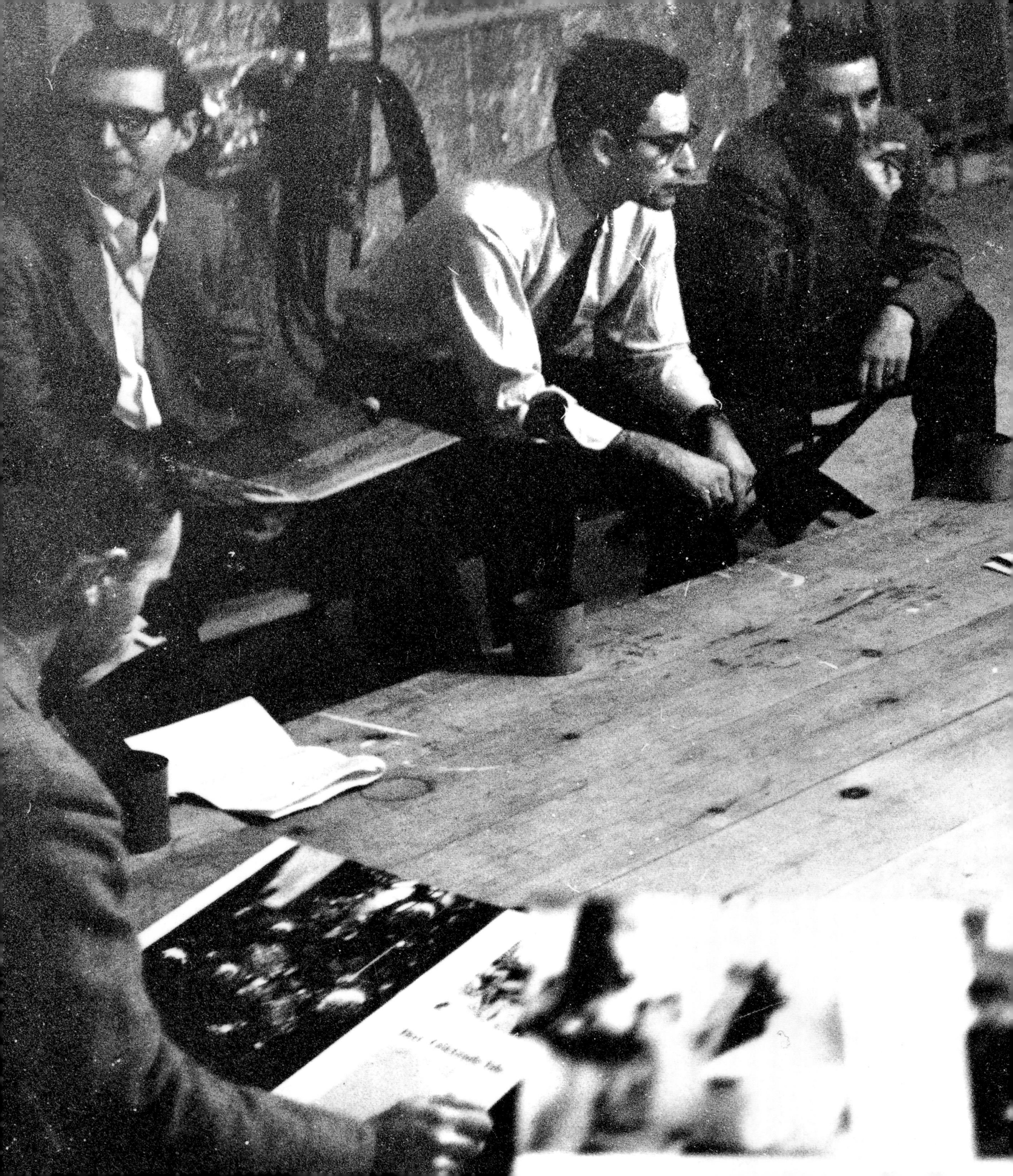

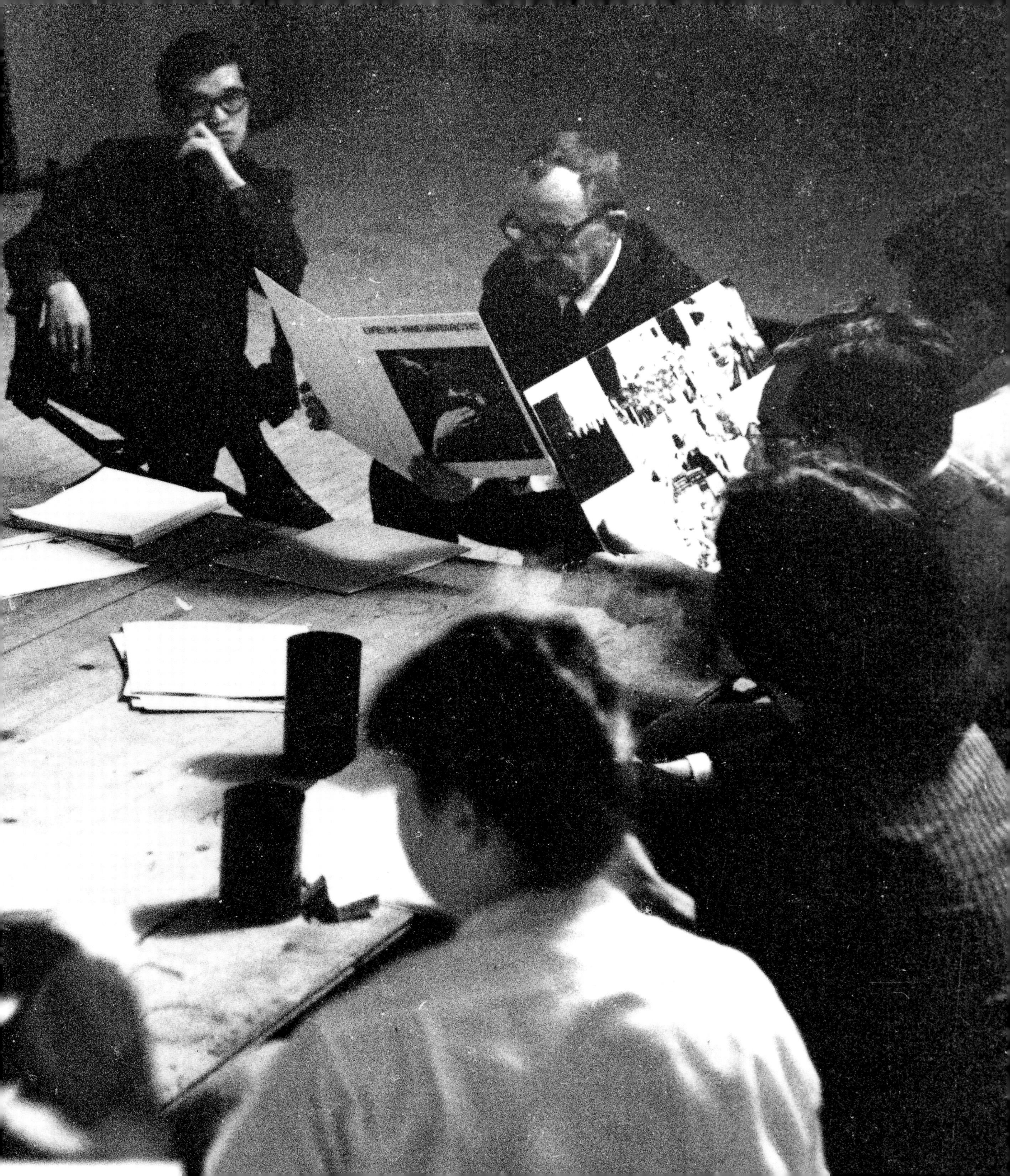

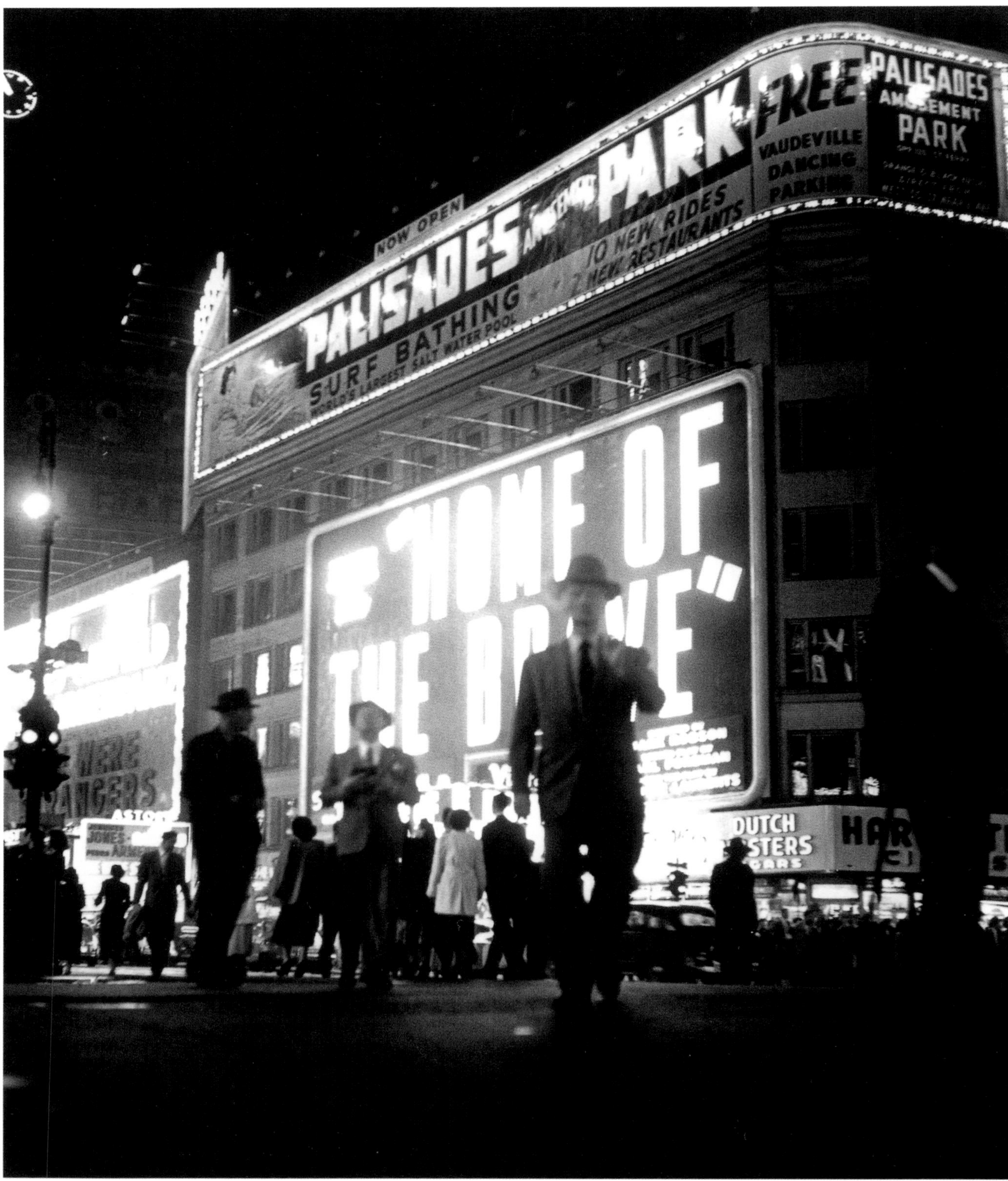
NOW OPEN
PALISADES
PARK
FREE
PALISADES
AMUSEMENT
PARK
VAUDEVILLE
DANCING
PARKING
SURF BATHING
10 NEW RIDES
"HOME OF
THE BRAVE"
DUTCH
ASTOR

Opposite: Ted Croner, *Home of the Brave*, 1947–48.
Right: Ted Croner, *Taxi, New York at Night*, 1947–48.
Ted Croner was a student in the Design Lab. His night pictures of New York were inspired by Brodovitch's demand that a photographer continually seek new and imaginative responses to familiar subjects.

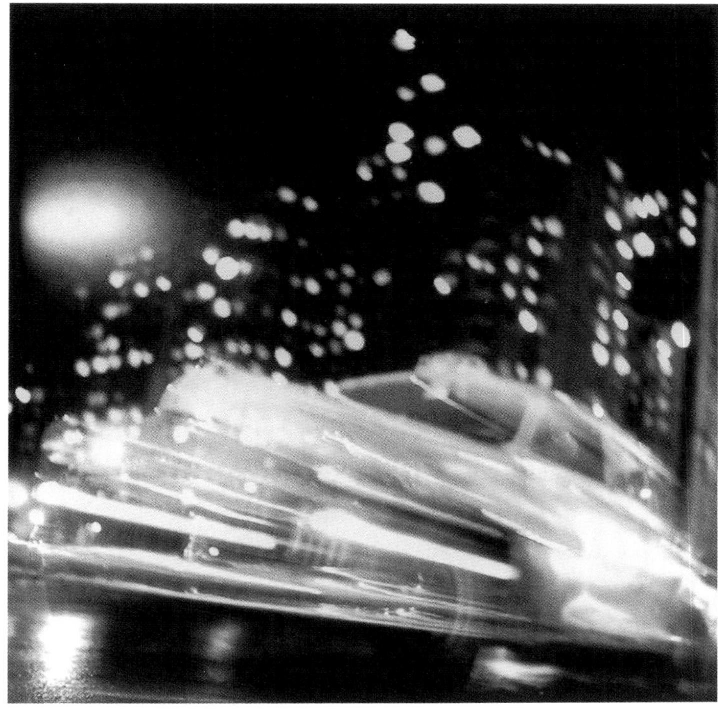

and left. Which a lot of people did."[14] After a few weeks the number of students attending would settle down. Among the photographers who attended Brodovitch's New York classes were Diane Arbus, Eve Arnold, Richard Avedon, Lisette Model, and Gary Winogrand. At one time or another there were also many architects, designers, and art directors. After everyone had got to know one another's work, Brodovitch would then set assignments. As at the PMSIA, the subject matter of these projects was intended to generate new and novel responses, not imitations. In the New York Design Lab, some of the subjects included: the United Nations, jazz, Central Park, Broadway, soft drinks, juvenile delinquency, parades, Chinatown, fantasy, atomic display, football, metals, light and shadow, contrast and scale, the Brooklyn Bridge, ballet, traffic, reflections, people and their emotions, cosmetics and perfume, hurricanes, New York markets, newspaper stands, and Halloween. Students were expected to produce three or four prints that offered a personal interpretation of these topics.

The class would usually begin with Brodovitch passing around the prints made in response to the previous week's assignment. After everyone had a chance to look at the work of other students, the prints would be returned to Brodovitch, who would then begin his critique. Peter Larson, a student in the Design Lab, recounted what usually happened next:

He generally went through the whole lot, print by print. "Rubbish," "Didn't you listen to the assignment last week?" "Why must we always talk and photograph in clichés?" "Is there no good photography today?" Then finally, one print would get his approval. "This man is using his imagination!" or "This picture really captures what the idea was about!" "You see this print – it's no good, but if you crop it here, now look!" When he got to my pile, I would feel a bit hot around the neck, wondering what he was going to say next, and hoping strongly that one or two of my efforts would receive favourable comment. Well, sometimes I was rewarded. Sometimes I felt indignant and after, when asked for comments, I would pick up a print and perhaps "stick up" for it – sometimes he even partly agreed with me, but most times he kept to his original points, and later I generally found out he was right.[15]

As he did in Philadelphia, Brodovitch would produce cuttings from magazines and newspapers to illustrate his ideas. As well as turning to the latest publication on the newsstand, Brodovitch still referred to the early influences on his visual sensibility such as *Gebrauchsgraphik* and *Arts et Métiers Graphiques*. He would display these works as good or bad examples of possible solutions to the previous week's assignment. He would offer little in the way of praise for the work his students produced. Yet, striving to attract positive comments from Brodovitch projected the creative expectations of the Design Lab members beyond the commonplace

Harvey Lloyd, *Roland Kirk, Jazz Musician*, c. 1965. Harvey Lloyd was another student in the Design Laboratory who went on to a successful career in photography. Brodovitch encouraged students to experiment and to capture the personality and impression of the picture, an approach that deviated from the fine-art and documentary style photography common when he founded the Design Lab.

and everyday. Pushing themselves to the limit, many students started to produce work they never thought they were capable of. "Once having imbued the student with a feeling for newness and exploration," the photographer Ben Rose has said, "he is able to get them to work indefatigably, through all hours of day and night. One soon learns that one cannot submit a photograph to Brodovitch if it hasn't got a new concept, a unique approach, or an interesting suggestion."[16]

Over the weeks, the work produced for the class would gradually move from straightforward and literal representations of the subject to more impressionistic imagery. After repeatedly having their work snubbed by Brodovitch, Design Lab members would begin to exceed the limits of what they thought was acceptable or possible in photography. Images would be produced that were blurred, printed through unusual objects, and cropped at strange angles, all offering new perspectives on the ordinary and mundane. A much quoted example of his inventive approach to artistic imagining is illustrated in an instance involving Richard Avedon. In one of Avedon's first classes with Brodovitch the assignment was to design a neon sign. Avedon apparently explained to him that he couldn't draw. Brodovitch told him to use spaghetti.

Brodovitch actively encouraged his students to take risks. Accidents, which in other photography courses may have been considered mistakes, were regarded as "beautiful errors" that "opened up a whole new world of picture taking."[17] One of Ted Croner's most famous images of the New York skyline, *New York at Night* (1948) was the result of just such a mistake. The class assignment for that week was "New York." Croner decided to take a photograph of Manhattan at night:

I only had about a week to do those pictures. But [with] that picture I had gone...beyond the boat lake of Fifty-ninth Street.... I didn't have a tripod with me, I had a Rolliflex. I had to take my gloves off, it was winter time, but it was February. And there was snow on the ground, a couple of inches. And I was going to take a conventional picture of Central Park South. [However], I couldn't hold my hands steady and they started to move, and totally by accident I moved [the camera] up and down. And then, because I thought I was going to be so clever, I said what if I made circles, and I made circles. Then I made "X"s...I got several versions of it moving and different shutter exposures. [But the first one] was the picture. Because I immediately recognized in the ground glass that the circles were fake and corny, not classic.... And the "X"s were corny. But somehow these streaks were the right thing. And they were more exciting and I knew Brodovitch would like them.[18]

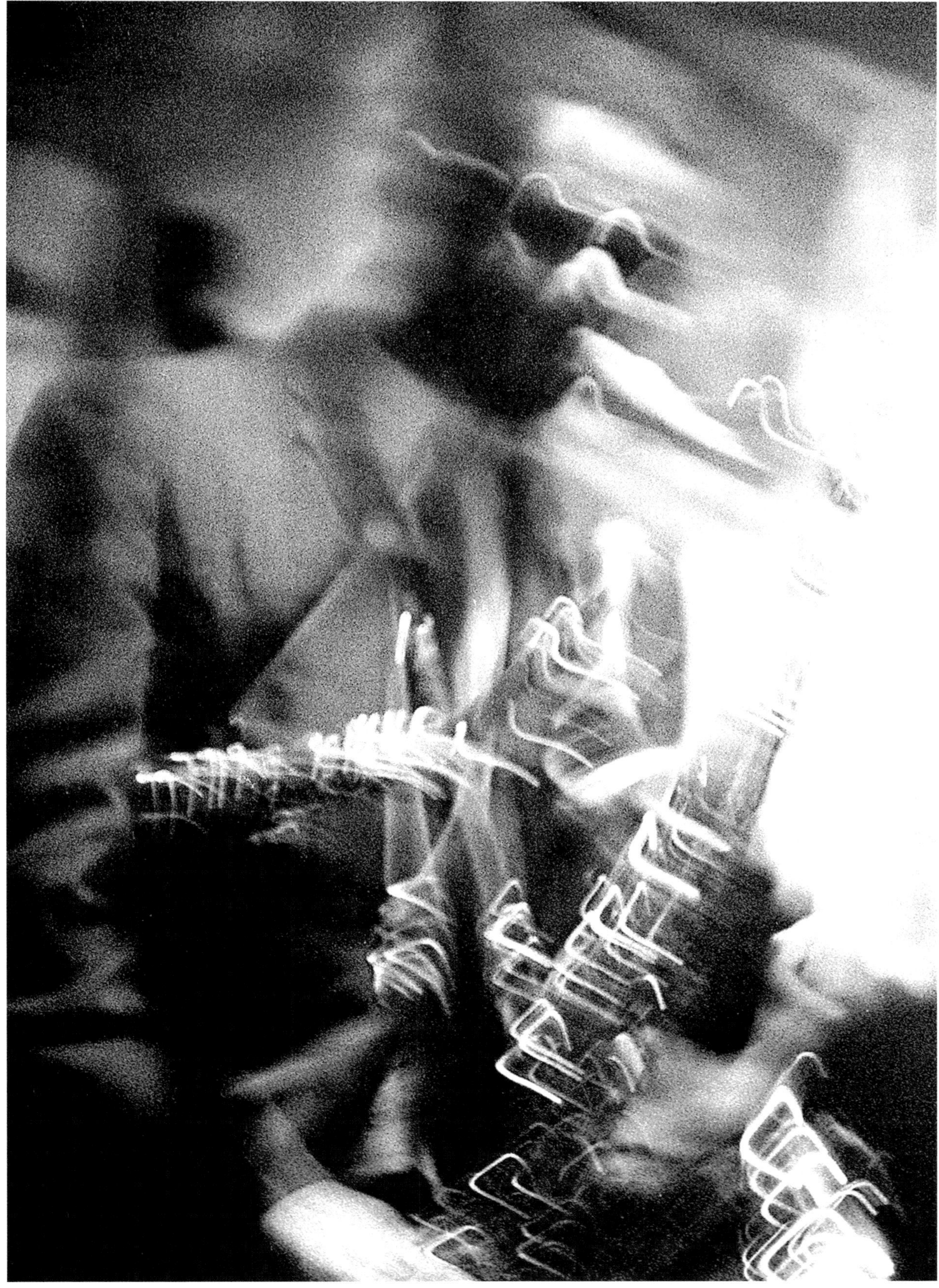

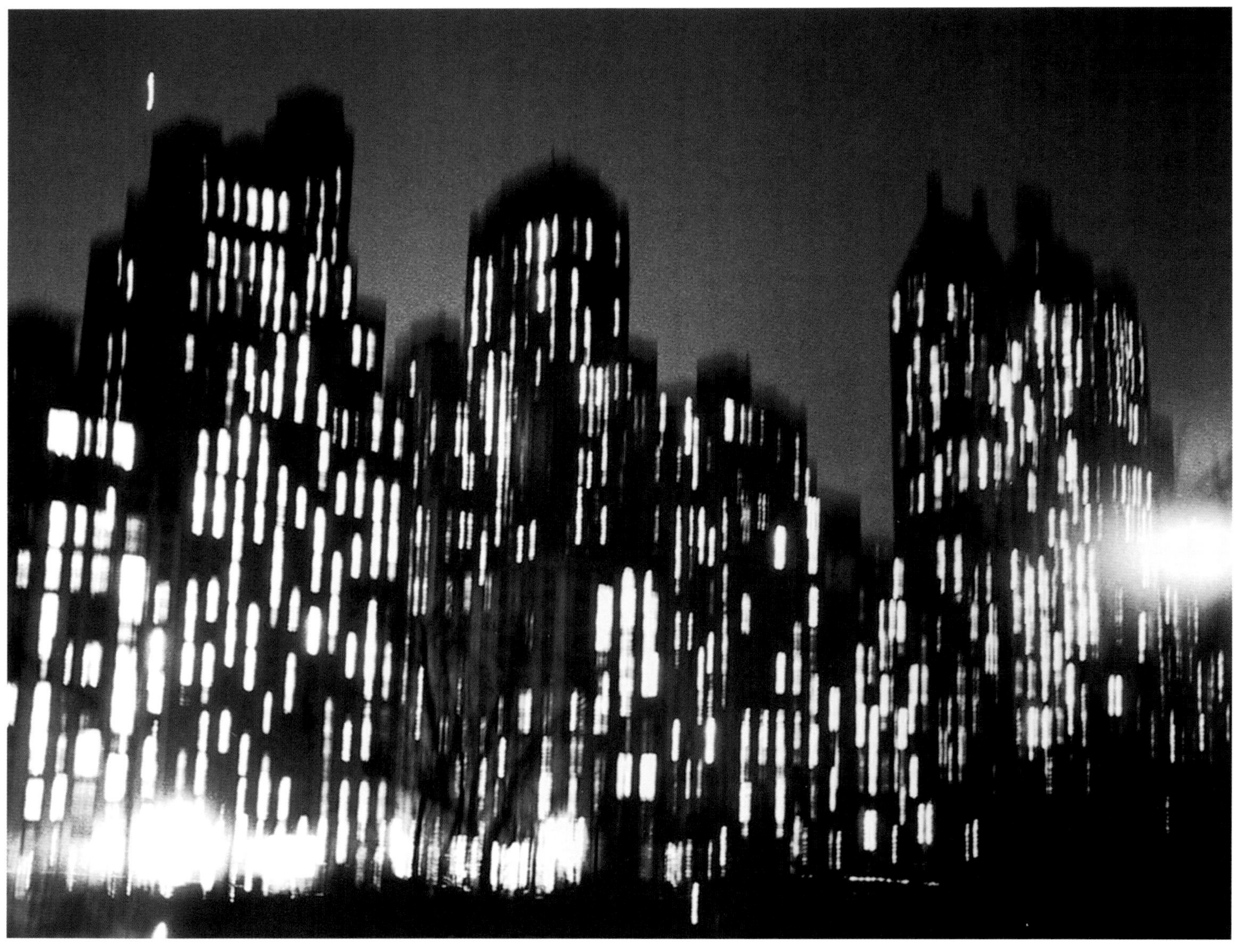

Ted Croner, *New York at Night*, 1948.
The blurry effect in Croner's famous image of the New York skyline was an accident, and in amateur photography courses would probably have been dismissed as technically substandard. However, Brodovitch always embraced the potential of photographic accidents to produced fresh and original works.

Brodovitch approved of Croner's accidental image. He recognized that with a rather straightforward subject matter Croner "brought a certain fantasy to the problem, created a strong picture, stronger than realistic attempts, which were too dry."[19] He encouraged Croner to do more, especially photographs that were produced using available light. Brodovitch constantly espoused the values of this form of photography. Obviously thinking of Munkacsi's groundbreaking images for *Harper's Bazaar*, Brodovitch had no time for images that seemed staged or created or gimmicky. He once said that "things should be used which could happen, not things which are obviously posed, obviously artificial."[20] Nevertheless, after promoting the unaffected virtues of available-light photography, he would then confound some students by going on to advocate the value of blurring, chemical reducers, or airbrushing – anything that created "surprise value" in their images. Like Croner's *New York at Night*, with subjects such as Central Park or traffic, photographers were urged to use all the techniques available to produce images that conveyed an almost corporeal interpretation of the assignment. For instance, in William Helburn's take on the assignment "fantasy," he uses both soft-focus and high-key tonality to produce a dreamlike image of a New York street. He wittily heightens the reverie of the image by adding two characters from *Alice in Wonderland*. In Ben Rose's interpretation of the project "rollercoaster" he utilizes a 360-degree circuit camera to reproduce photographically the experience and sensation of this ride.

In our age of computer manipulation, the radical nature of Brodovitch's proposals seem commonplace. It has to be remembered, however, that around the time Brodovitch began his Design Laboratory the two dominant strands of photography were the fine art work of the f.64 group and the documentary photographs of the Farm Security Administration (FSA) – both precious about the individual image, whether as a print or document. Through the work of photographers such as Ansel Adams, Imogen Cunningham, and Edward Weston, the f.64 group promoted precisionism in the photograph. Advocating the use of large-format cameras, they shot images through a very small aperture (f.64) and printed by contact rather than enlargement. The outcome of such a process was that the significance of the work lay in the purity of the final print. Subject matter being secondary, objects were chosen that would offer the greatest opportunity to express the values and tonal ranges of the print. While print quality was important with FSA photographers such as Dorothea Lange and Margaret Bourke-White, it was the subject matter that was paramount. Charting the ravages of the 1930s depression, the worth and authenticity of the image resided in its content. While Brodovitch respected the values of the print as object or document, he was, unlike many of the above, never precious about its manipulation. As we know from his work at *Harper's Bazaar*, cropping a photographic image (following the photographer's approval) was just another way of achieving the right look and feel to a layout. In fact, in the Design Lab sessions he repeatedly stressed the importance of cropping as a tool:

One of the photographer's most important tools is cropping. I know Cartier-Bresson does not approve of anyone cropping his pictures. For most photographers, however, I believe it is a mistake to refuse to crop. Photographers should make three of four prints from a negative and crop them differently. The cropping can very often create your new vision and help discover and explain your new language. I read a profile in the New Yorker *of Yehudi Menuhin's interest in Yoga, and before each concert he stands on his head. I don't care if he does this if he plays beautiful music. It is the end result which counts.*[21]

Art Kane's response to the assignment "personality" illustrates what could be achieved through cropping. A darkened image of a cab driver looking right into the lens is given added contrast by the cab's white roof. The rectangular cropping of the photograph sets up a duality between the dark and light aspects of the frame and lends an almost sinister aspect to the cab driver's gaze.

For Brodovitch, deciding which image would benefit from being cropped came with an examination of the contacts of a shoot. He always urged his students to look through their contacts and choose those images that expressed a personal point of view. He said that the picture chosen should "be a completely individual expression which intrigues the viewer and forces him to think."[22]

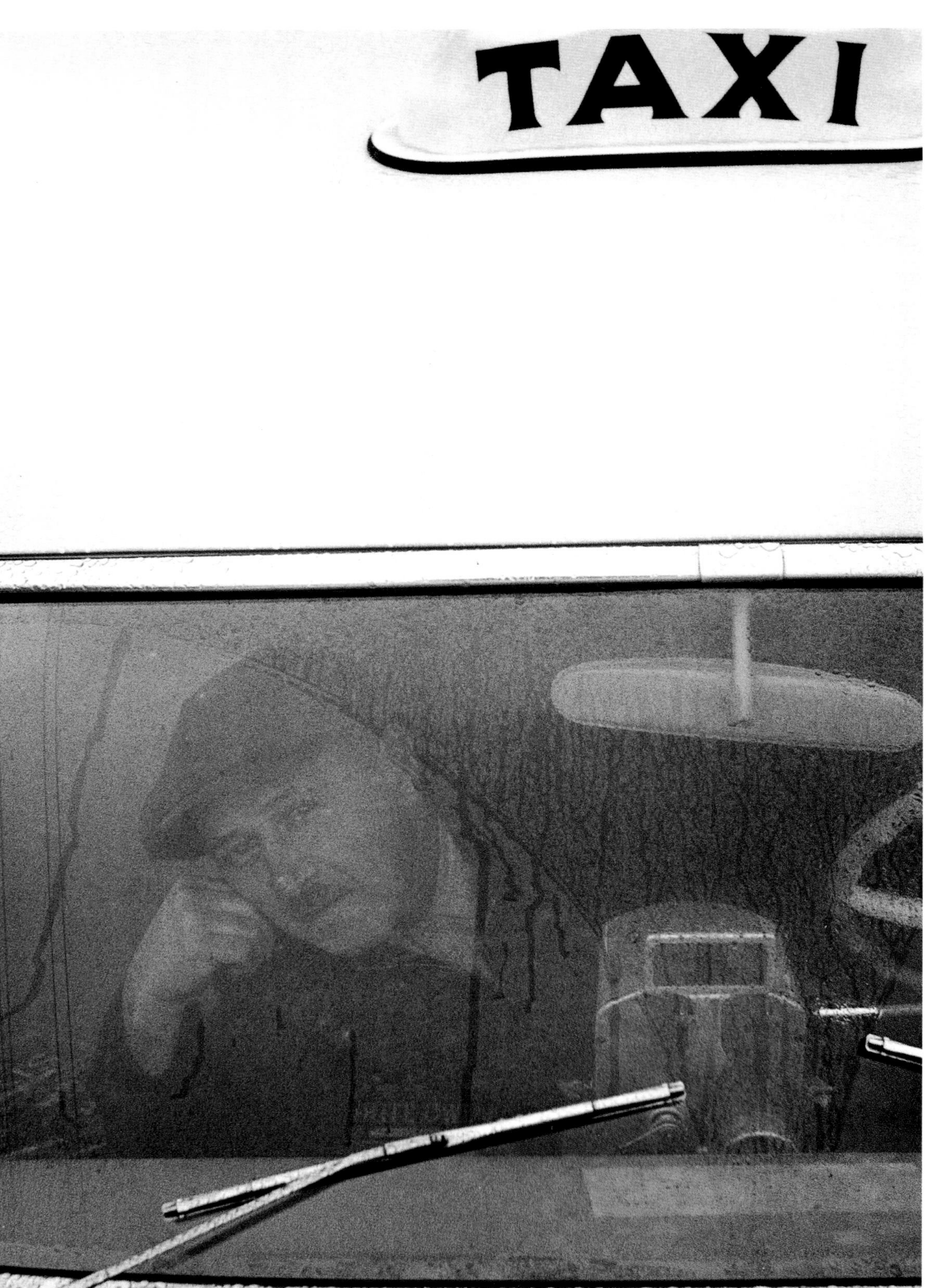
TAXI

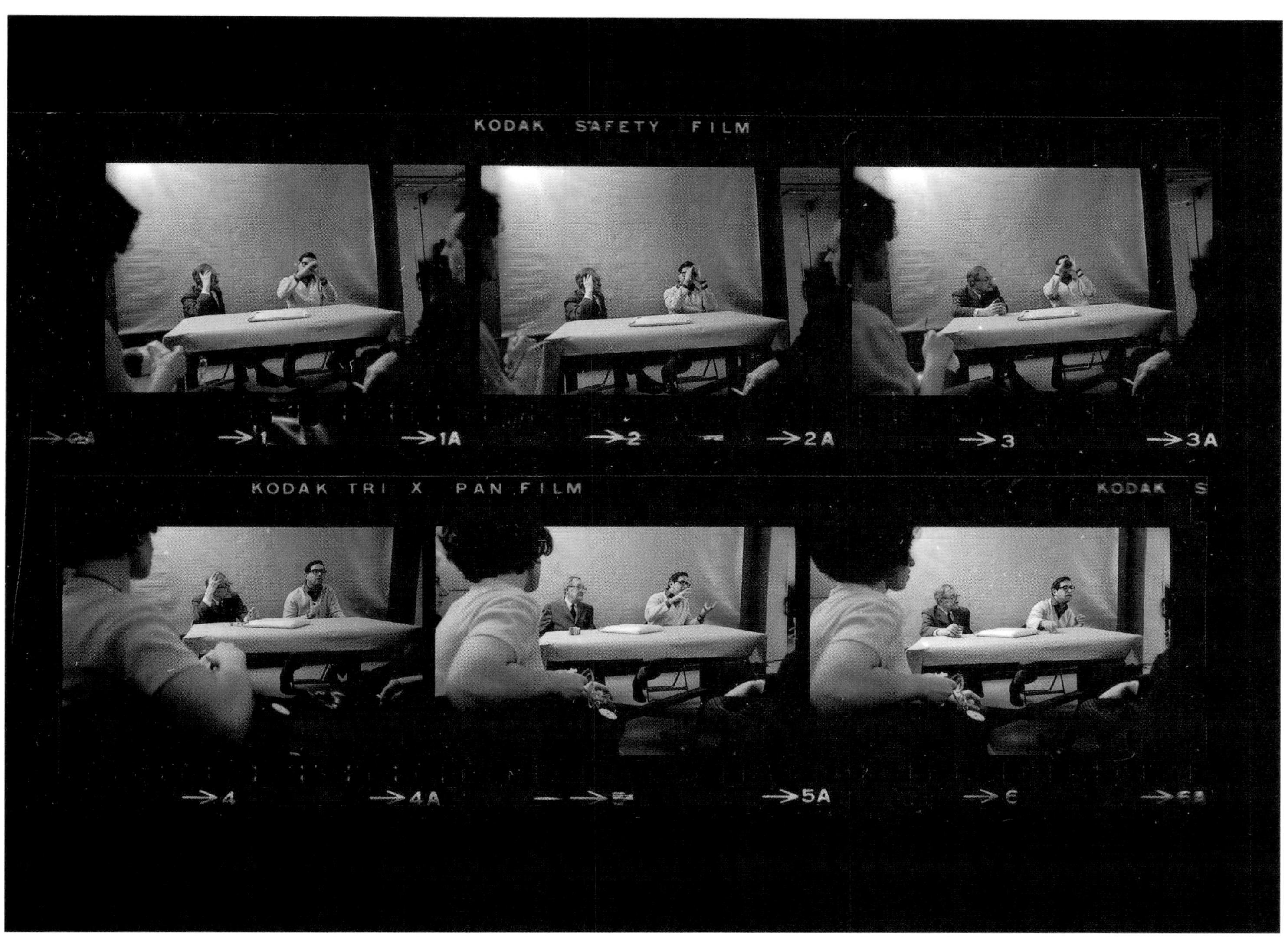

Opposite: Art Kane, *Taxi (Herman Kane)*, 1958. In this response to a Design Lab assignment on "personality," Kane's rectangular cropping creates a dramatic contrast between dark and light which emphasizes the cab driver's gaze.

Above: Alexey Brodovitch and Ben Rose lecturing in the Design Laboratory, c. 1963. Photographs by Georges Tourdjman.

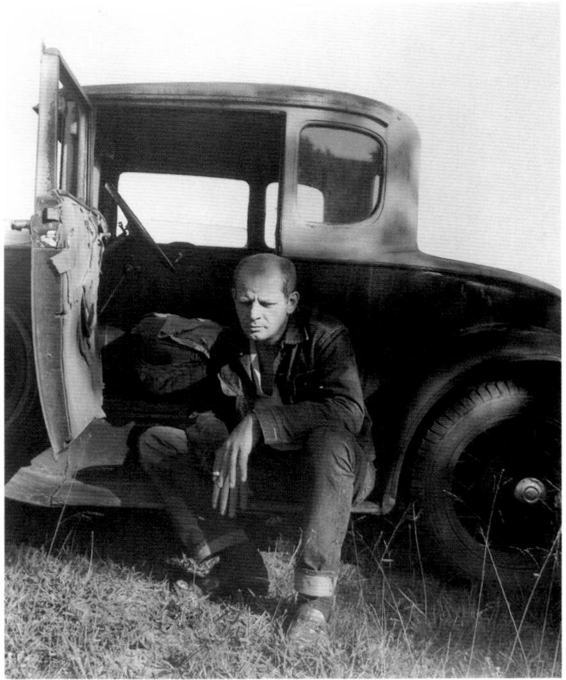

Left: Hans Namuth, *Jackson Pollock*, c. 1950.
Namuth, a student in Brodovitch's Design Lab, became well known for his iconic photographs of Pollock.

Opposite: Students in the Design Lab, c. 1945–50. Photograph by Edward Kasper.
Front row, from left: Richard Avedon, Margie Cato, Edward Kasper. Back row, from left: Unidentified man, Lillian Bassman, Paul Himmel, unidentified standing woman, Doe Avedon, Bob Cato.

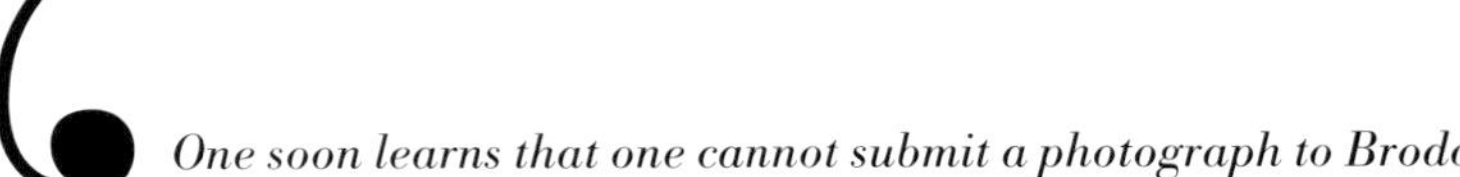

The photographer Hans Namuth acknowledged that it was Brodovitch who taught him to "read" contact prints. He recalled: "It took [Brodovitch] seconds to look at one sheet, minutes to scan the lot, making marks with his grease pencil here and there (very few) and handing them back to me.... [He] never missed – it amazed and startled me each time. With an eagle eye he could spot the exact picture frame on a given sheet containing 36 or 12 exposures which could range from medium fair to excellent."[23] Namuth is best known for his pictures of Jackson Pollock frozen in an energetic burst over the canvas. And it was Brodovitch who apparently turned him on to Pollock's work. In a 1947 Design Lab class Brodovitch asked the students if any of them had seen the current Jackson Pollock exhibition. Namuth said: "I was the only one to raise my hand. I had seen his show at the Betty Parsons gallery – and hadn't liked it at all. Brodovitch's question and the following searching remarks suddenly made me realize that I should take another look at Pollock's art. A few days later I mustered all my courage and approached Pollock at an opening at East Hampton's Guild Hall. This led to a friendship which lasted until his death."[24] The outcome of this meeting was a image produced for the class that, in retrospect, is a portentous signifier of Pollock's death several years later in an automobile accident.

Brodovitch demanded total commitment from his students. In one famous example the photographer Hiro – another of Brodovitch's numerous assistants – was required to photograph a pair of shoes. Each time Hiro brought the images back to Brodovitch, he asked him to try again. His now famous statement to Hiro was "If you look in the camera and you see something you have seen before don't click the shutter." Hiro worked for many days until he produced something that surprised Brodovitch. His reward was to see his work reproduced on the pages *Harper's Bazaar*. Such demands were an essential part of the ten-week course. Irving Penn, an early student at Philadelphia, remembered that the "climate around him was never warm and easy, there was no room for levity, a student was expected never to have a financial problem, an upset stomach, or even a private life. But within these austere and forbidding circumstances, when a student did somehow manage to push forward into new ground, Brodovitch glumly, even grudgingly left no doubt that something remarkable had been done."[25] In an interview with the Magnum agency editor Inge Bondi, Brodovitch made clear what he expected from his Design Lab members. When Bondi asked the question: "How can a photographer always discover something new?" Brodovitch responded by saying: "The photographer should put himself against the wall, crucify himself, ask himself if he wants to find a new way."[26] Such an attitude was not just spirited exaggeration. Brodovitch had no time for "Sunday photographers." Harvey Lloyd recounted a Design Lab story in which one student wished to know how he could become a full-time photographer when he had so many commitments:

There was a student in one of the Design Laboratories who said to Alexey: "Mr. Brodovitch I am very anxious to be a photographer, I want to pursue this career, I want to dedicate myself to it, you have inspired me."... He said: "However, what am I to do. I have a house, I have two cars, I have children in private schools, I have a summer house, I have an enormous amount of overheads. And from what I hear, if you go into photography, it could be years before you can make any money." Brodovitch listened and very quietly said: "You must send your children to their grandparents to live. You must divorce your wife. You must sell all your property. And you become a photographer." And the guy just stood there looking at him like he thought he was crazy. But of course he wasn't crazy at all. Because that's what it amounted to. He was not going to become a photographer under those circumstances.[27]

Few could handle such commitment. Ralph Steiner, the individual who had first introduced Brodovitch to Carmel Snow, also thought that such an approach to artistic education was

asn't got a new concept, a unique approach, or an interesting suggestion. – Ben Rose

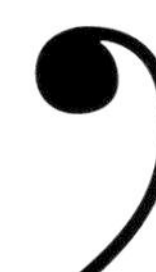

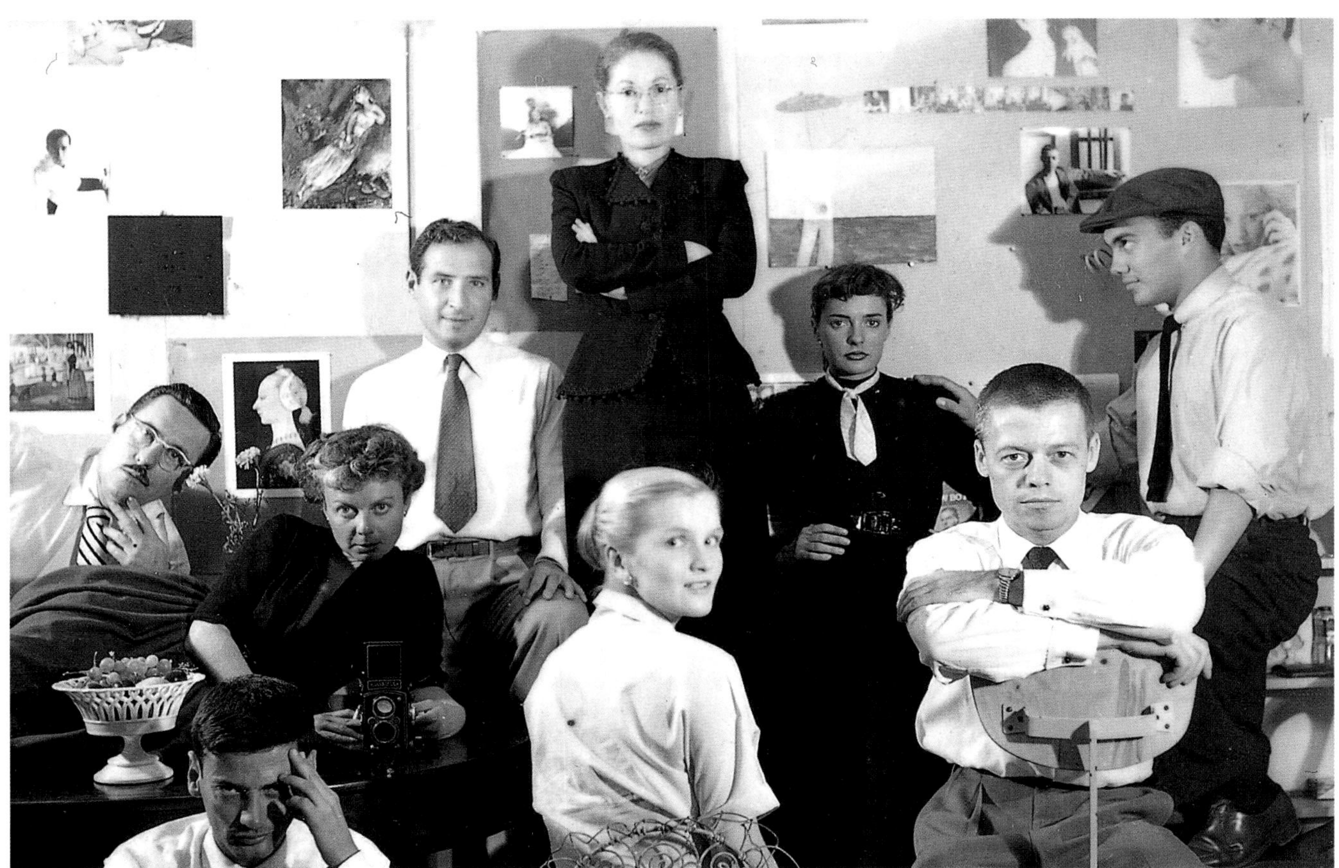

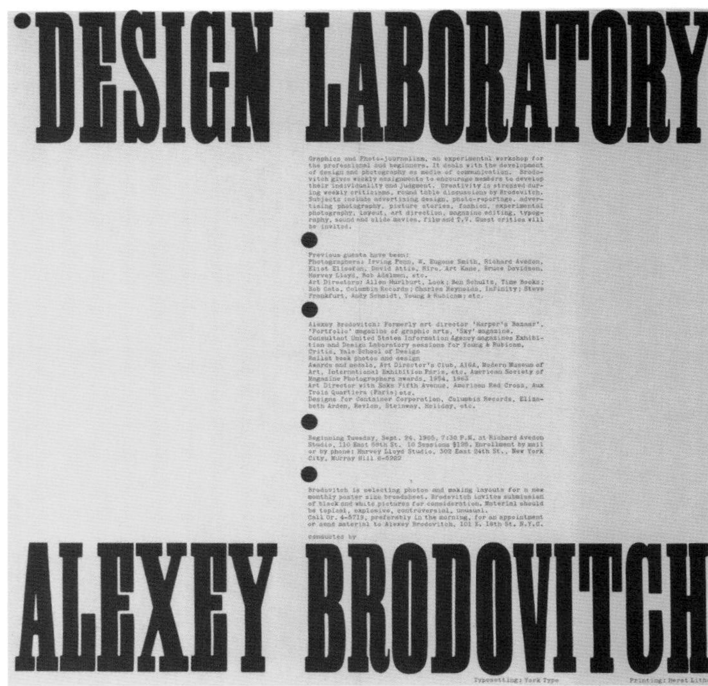

harmful. In "Photography: The Curse of Having to Be Different," an essay in his monograph *Ralph Steiner: A Point of View*, he argued that Brodovitch's desire to be constantly new and innovative was "a destructive and unhelpful concept." Obviously referring to Brodovitch's famous comment to Hiro mentioned above, Steiner asked: "How can it help a photographer to be more original if he says to himself, standing before his subject: 'Now I must be original?' Such a self-assignment would be constipating."[28] Diane Arbus, one of the many students who attended Brodovitch's class and then left soon after, seemed to agree with Steiner. After a few sessions she apparently said to a fellow photographer that "she simply didn't like the forbidding atmosphere he created around himself, didn't like the abuse he heaped on his students, [and] thought his approach too monotonous, too narrow."[29]

Many of the disagreements with Brodovitch's methods seemed to have stemmed from the belief that much of the work students produced in the lab were being judged by the capricious terms of the fashion world. Like Arbus, Robert Frank obviously considered Brodovitch's fashion agenda too narrow for the direction in which his own work was heading. He said in Martin Harrison's book *Appearances* that the Design Lab was not for him because he "felt intuitively that your best idea shouldn't be used for fashion."[30] It was certainly the case that Brodovitch sometimes set projects that would provide material for possible feature articles at *Harper's Bazaar*. But, the truth was, with the majority of students this appropriation of work was actively reciprocated. For many photographers the main reason for attending Brodovitch's class was the vague hope that he would recognize their talent and commission them to work for *Bazaar*.

There was a more historically specific reason why Brodovitch's educational methods may have seemed alien to many students at the time. Although he taught in 1950s America, Brodovitch's expectations of student scholarship and performance had been formed in Russia and Europe of the early twentieth century. As an ex-Russian officer of the White Army, the strict formality of the classroom and need to respect authority was obviously something he valued. "He wasn't the kind of person you would slap on the back," Harvey Lloyd said, "you just didn't do it."[31] For example, one time in his early teachings at Philadelphia Brodovitch apparently berated a student for having his shirt sleeves rolled up, perceiving his behavior as "crude and undignified."[32] The photographer Peter Basch was himself a European émigré and familiar with such attitudes. He has said of Brodovitch's classes:

I felt that he was in his disciplines – and in the discipline he imposed on those that he influenced – willing to exert the kind of strictures that are identified with Europe. Because, basically the world he sprang from – and I assume he was born around the turn of the century – both in Russia and in Germany involved the

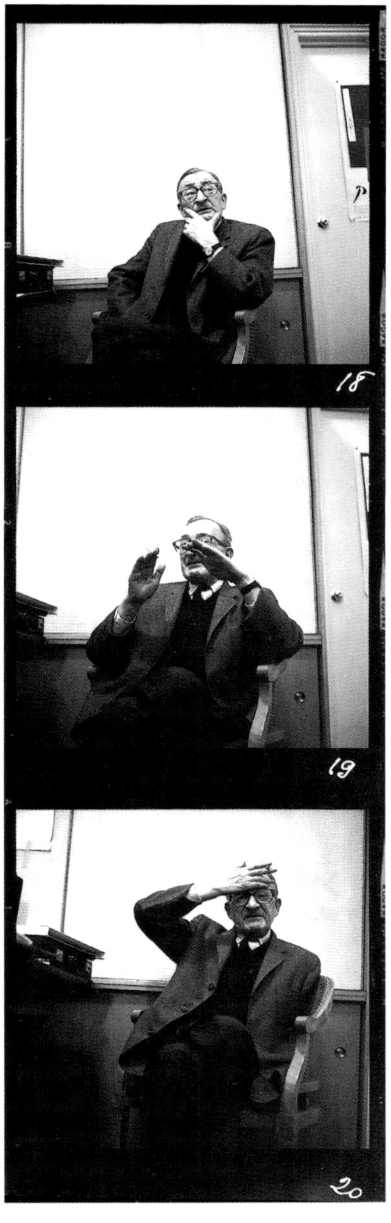

kind of intolerance of laissez-faire, intolerance of slipshod work. He wanted perfection and he was willing to drive people in order to get it. And I think that is very valuable, because Americans by and large are more casual in the pressures they're willing to exert, not that they don't achieve perfection. But the personal disciplines, and the personal goals in Europe I think were different, and he brought many of those to his work.[33]

With such methods, students were never detached when assessing the worth of the Design Lab to their careers. They either hated it or perceived it as the moment their unique photographic vision was born. For those students who endured Brodovitch's needling, it was usually during the last few weeks of the course that they would begin to discover something new about themselves. Endeavoring to avoid clichés, the class engendered in the students a palpable enthusiasm to produce, in Brodovitch's words, "surprise quality" in each new photograph they printed. Richard Avedon believed the drive for something new and exciting that Brodovitch demanded of Design Lab members stayed with them for many years after the course had finished. As he has said, "[t]here is nothing you can take away from him but the essence. Like an inherited quality, there is something of him in you for the rest of your life and it keeps

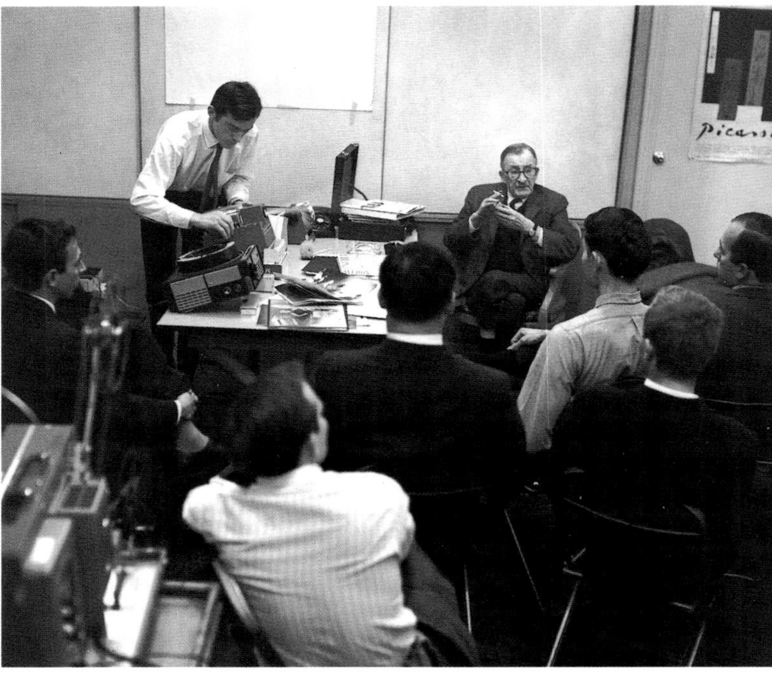

Opposite: Poster for the Design Laboratory. Design by Brodovitch.

Above and right: Brodovitch teaching the Design Laboratory, c. 1963. Photographs by Georges Tourdjman.
According to the photographer and Design Laboratory student Ben Rose, Brodovitch "needed little language to communicate, for his mastery of English was like a charming disaster. His ideas communicated themselves in some ultra-mysterious fashion, no doubt by radiations or vibrations of some kind."

growing.... You never learn anything the day he says it. He gets you irritated and angry. Then, one or two months later it happens."[34]

Brodovitch's Design Lab was run under the aegis of the New School until 1949. In 1947, while still attached to this institution, he decided to teach the class from Avedon's studio. It remained there until 1949 when, after injuring his hip when he was hit by a Hearst truck on 57th Street, it was temporarily abandoned. Held in such high esteem, the far-reaching acclamation for the Design Lab presented Brodovitch with many other teaching opportunities during the forties and fifties. From 1946 to 1948 he held the position of instructor of design at the Print Club of Philadelphia. In 1954 he was offered and accepted the position of visiting critic at the Yale School of Design and Architecture, teaching publication design until 1957. As far as we know, beyond a handful of classes, it wasn't until 1961 that the Design Lab was reestablished on a permanent basis. From that year until 1966 it was conducted at various locations around New York City. The venues during this period tended to be photographic studios. At one time or another the studios of Paul and Karen Radkai, and Steve Colhoun were used to teach the class. In 1964 it was taught under the auspices of the American Institute of Graphic Arts. And in 1965 Brodovitch apparently taught the class for a short period of time at the Corcoran Gallery of Art, in Washington, D.C. It finally returned, for a short period of time, to Avedon's studio in 1966. As many of Brodovitch's students had gone on to work as photographers or art directors in agencies and corporations around New York, Brodovitch was frequently asked to give a Design Lab master class. As far as we know a one-off session was held at the *National Geographic* office, and from 1964 to 1965 Brodovitch gave a series of classes at the advertising agency Young and Rubicam. After he left *Harper's Bazaar* in 1958, all of this work offered Brodovitch the chance to earn some much needed income.

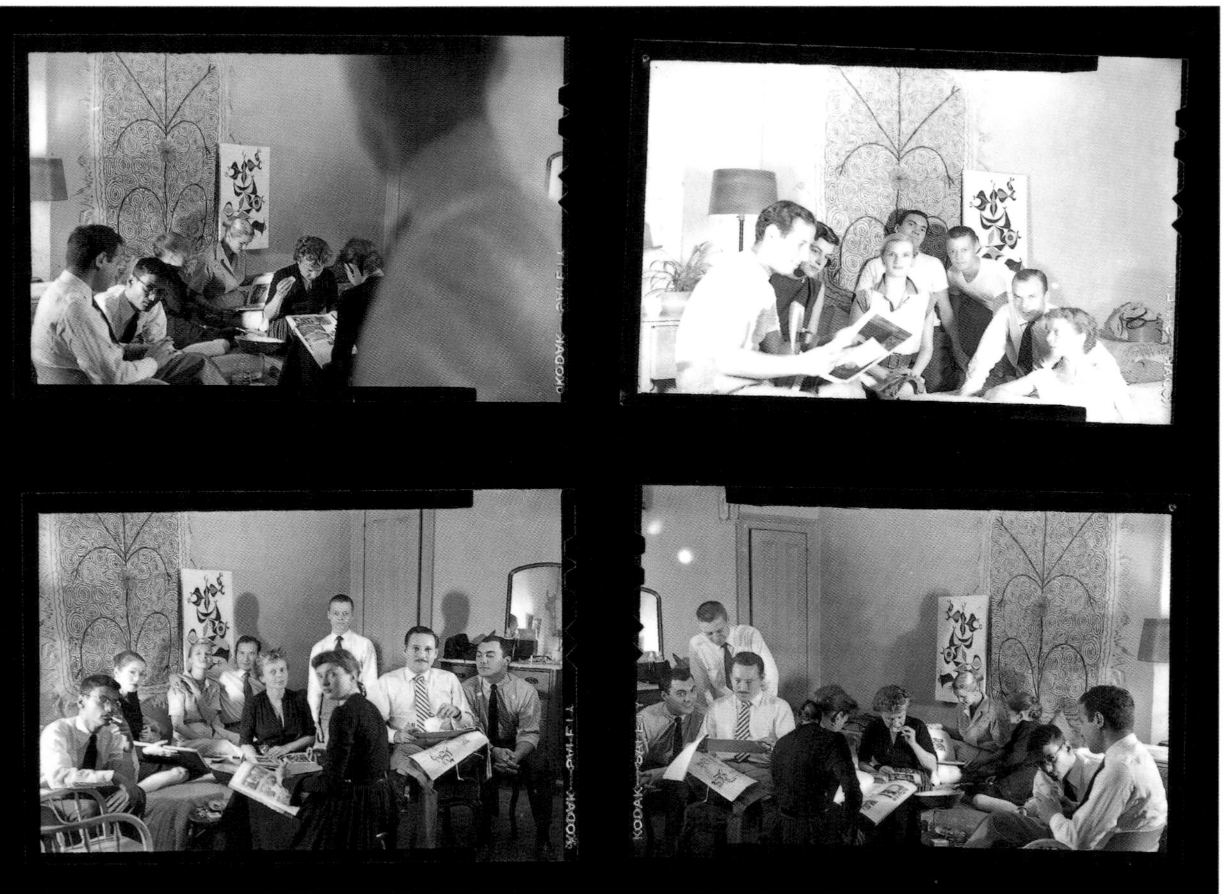

Left: Students in the Design Lab, c. 1945–50. Photographs by Edward Kasper.
Students pictured include Doe Avedon, Richard Avedon, Lillian Bassman, Bob Cato, Margie Cato, Paul Himmel, Edward Kasper (see p. 125).

Opposite: Design Laboratory, c. 1963. Photographs by Georges Tourdjman.

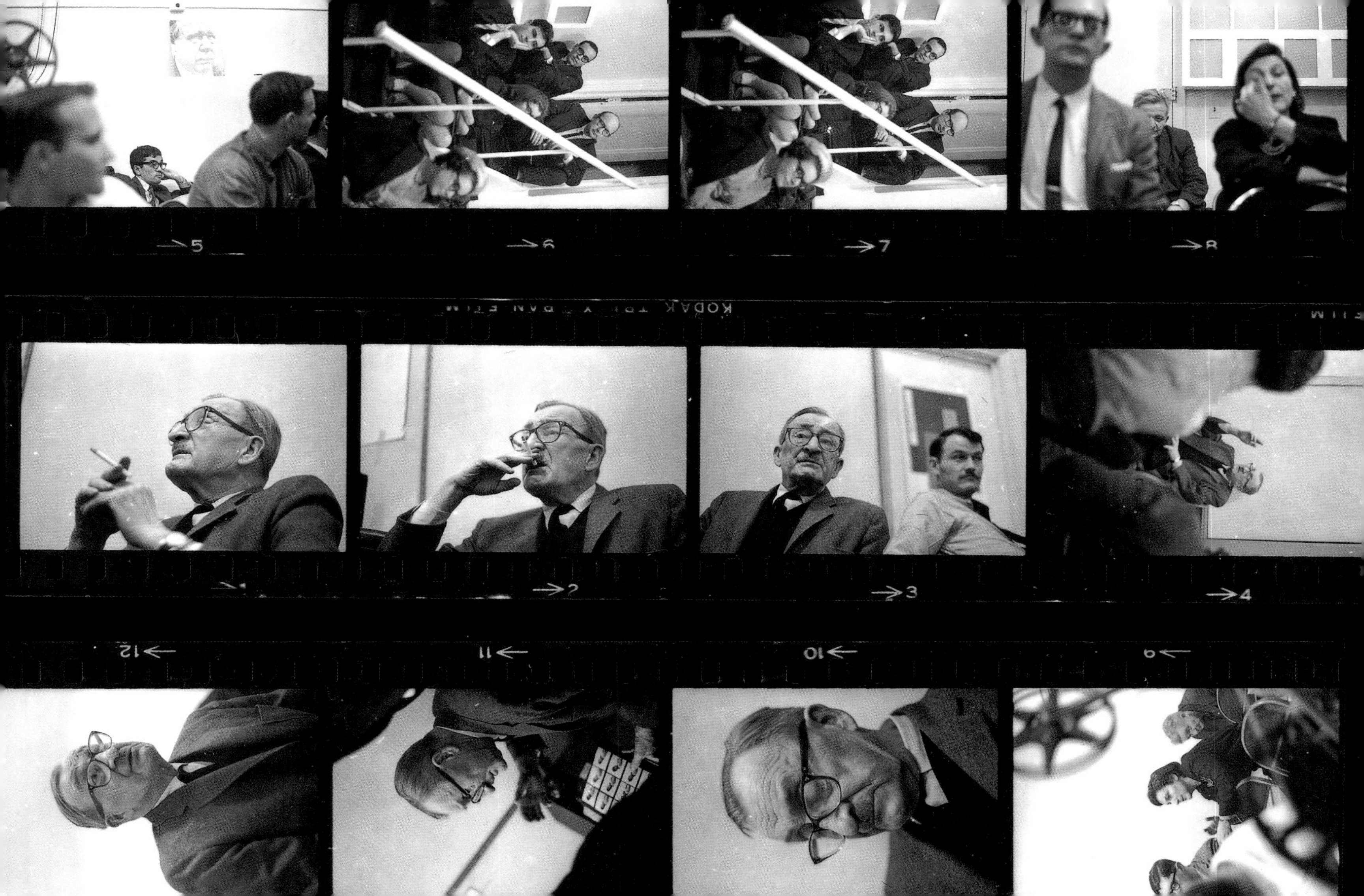

Photography: The Revolutionary Eye

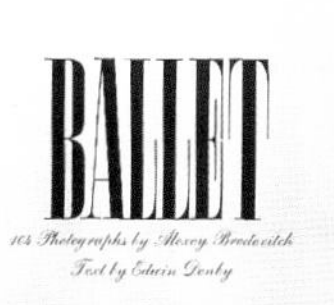

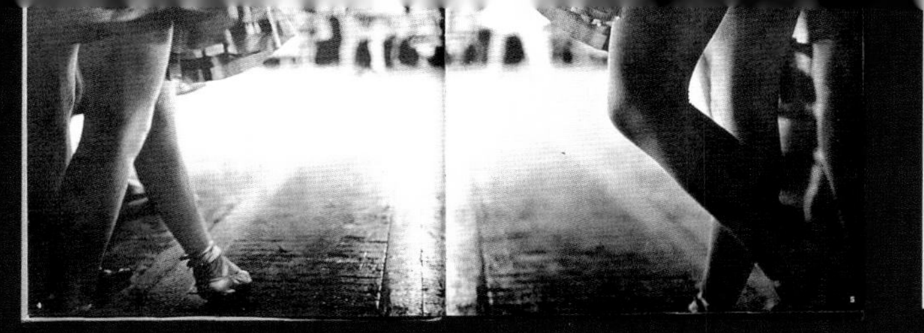

LES NOCES
LES CENT BAISERS
SYMPHONIE FANTASTIQUE
LE TRICORNE
BOUTIQUE FANTASQUE
COTILLION
CHOREARTIUM
SEPTIÈME
SYMPHONIE
LE LAC DES CYGNES
LES SYLPHIDES
CONCURRENCE

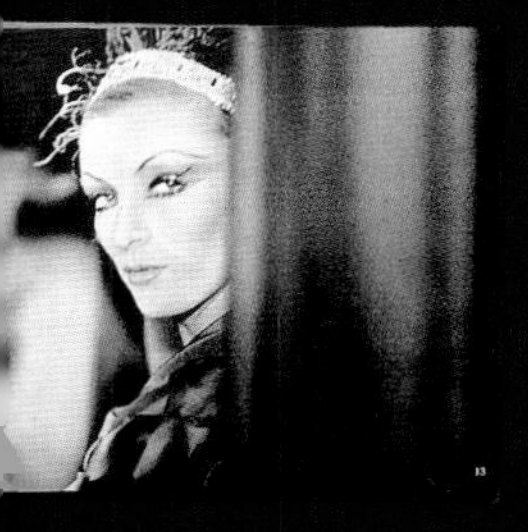

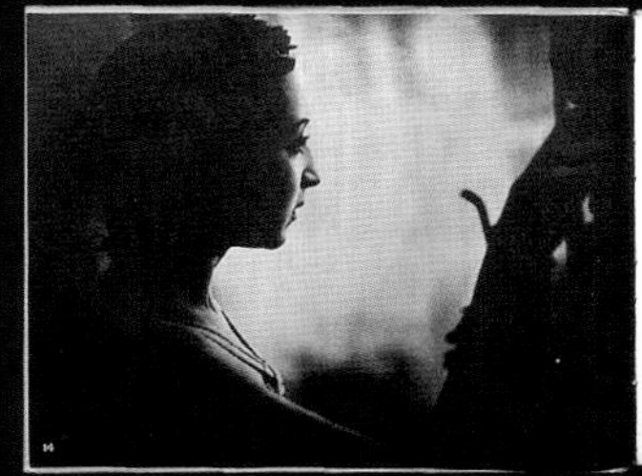

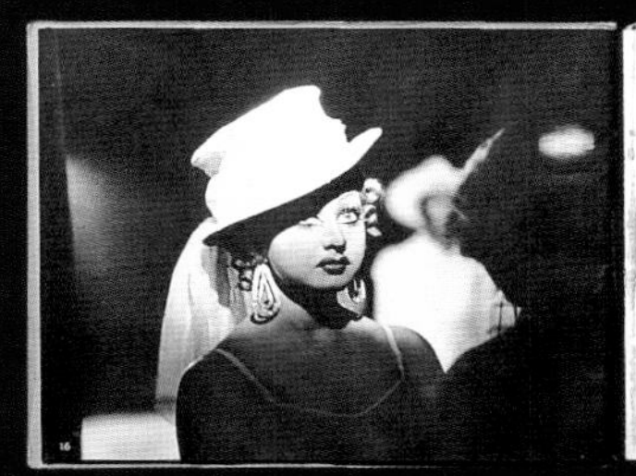

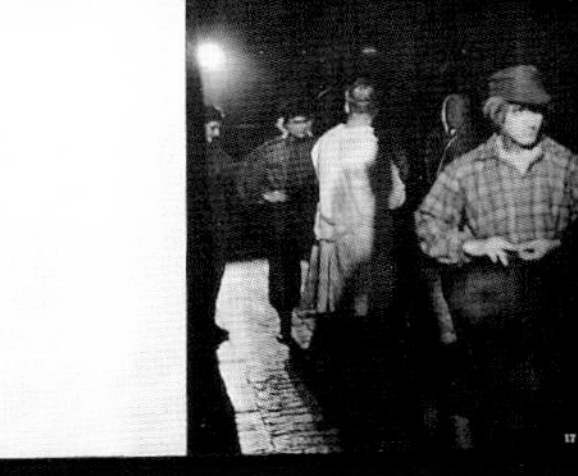

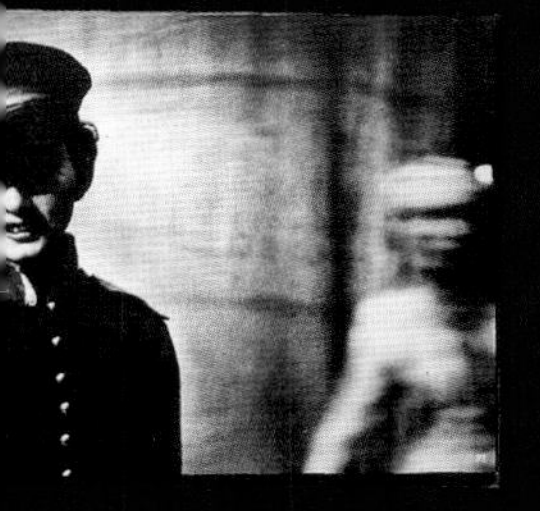

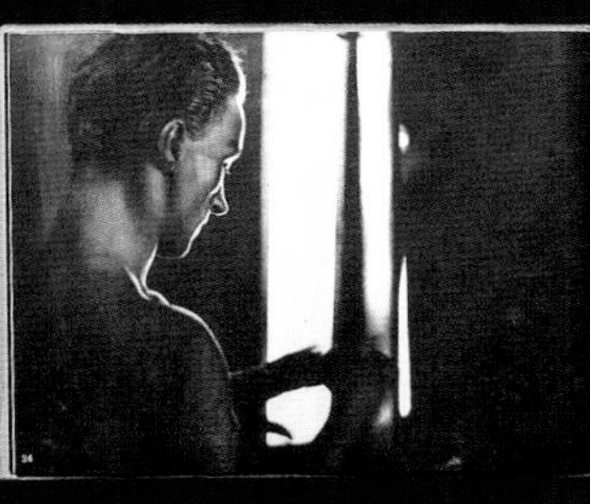

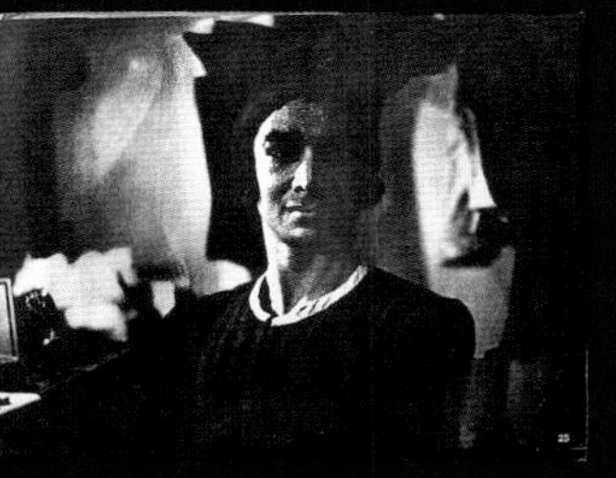

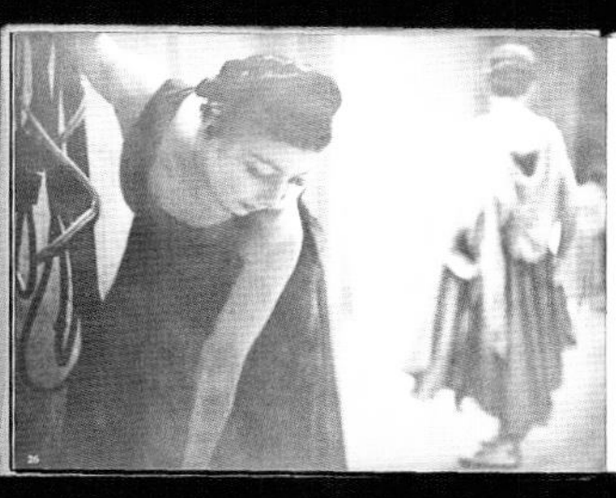

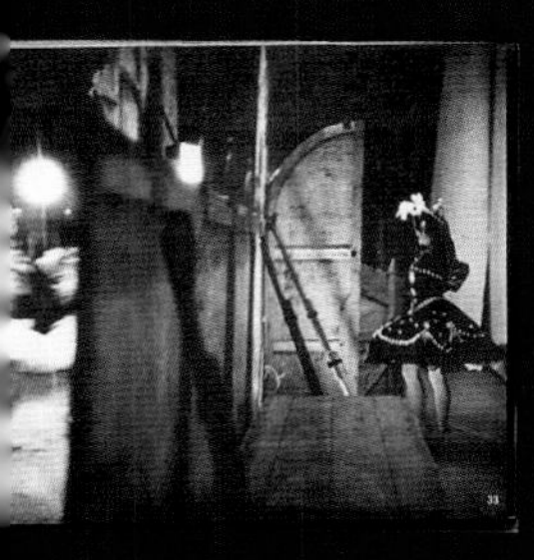

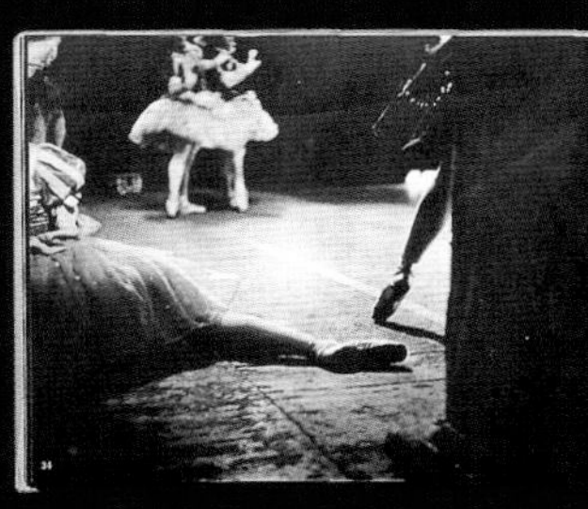

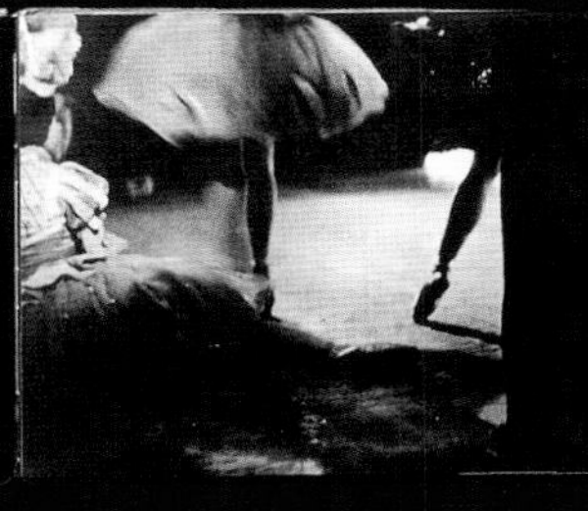

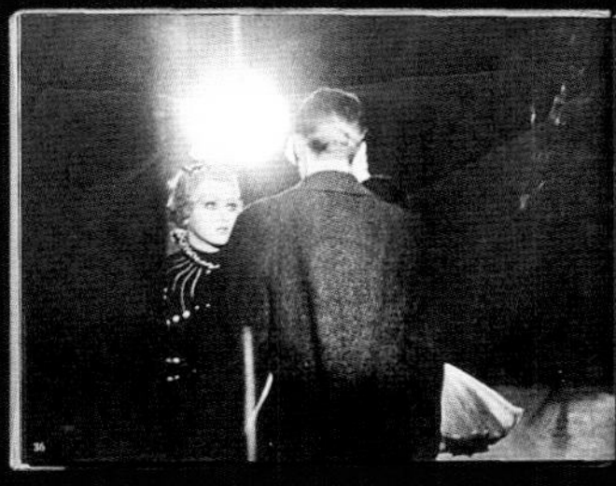

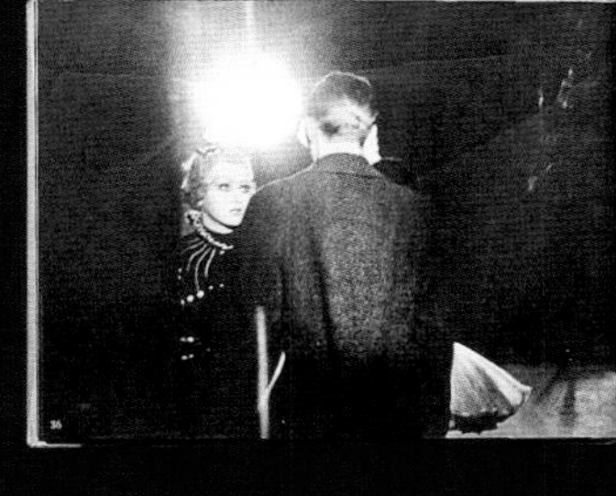

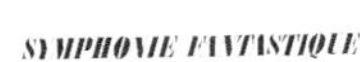

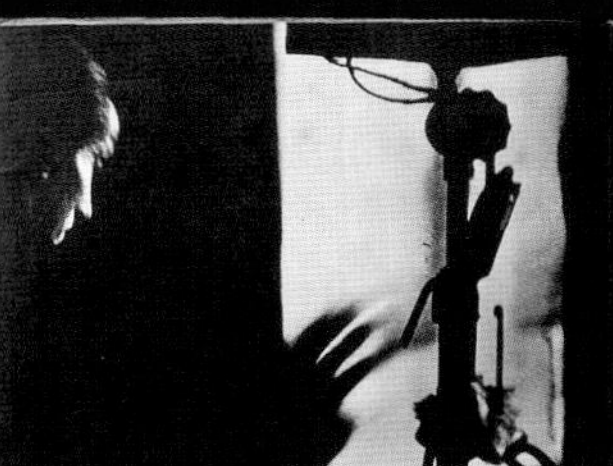

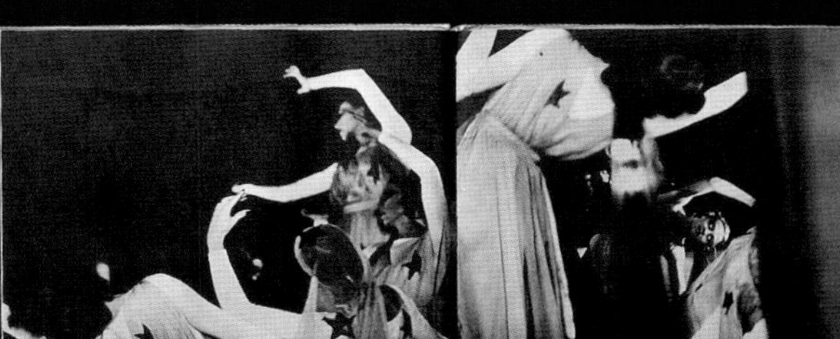

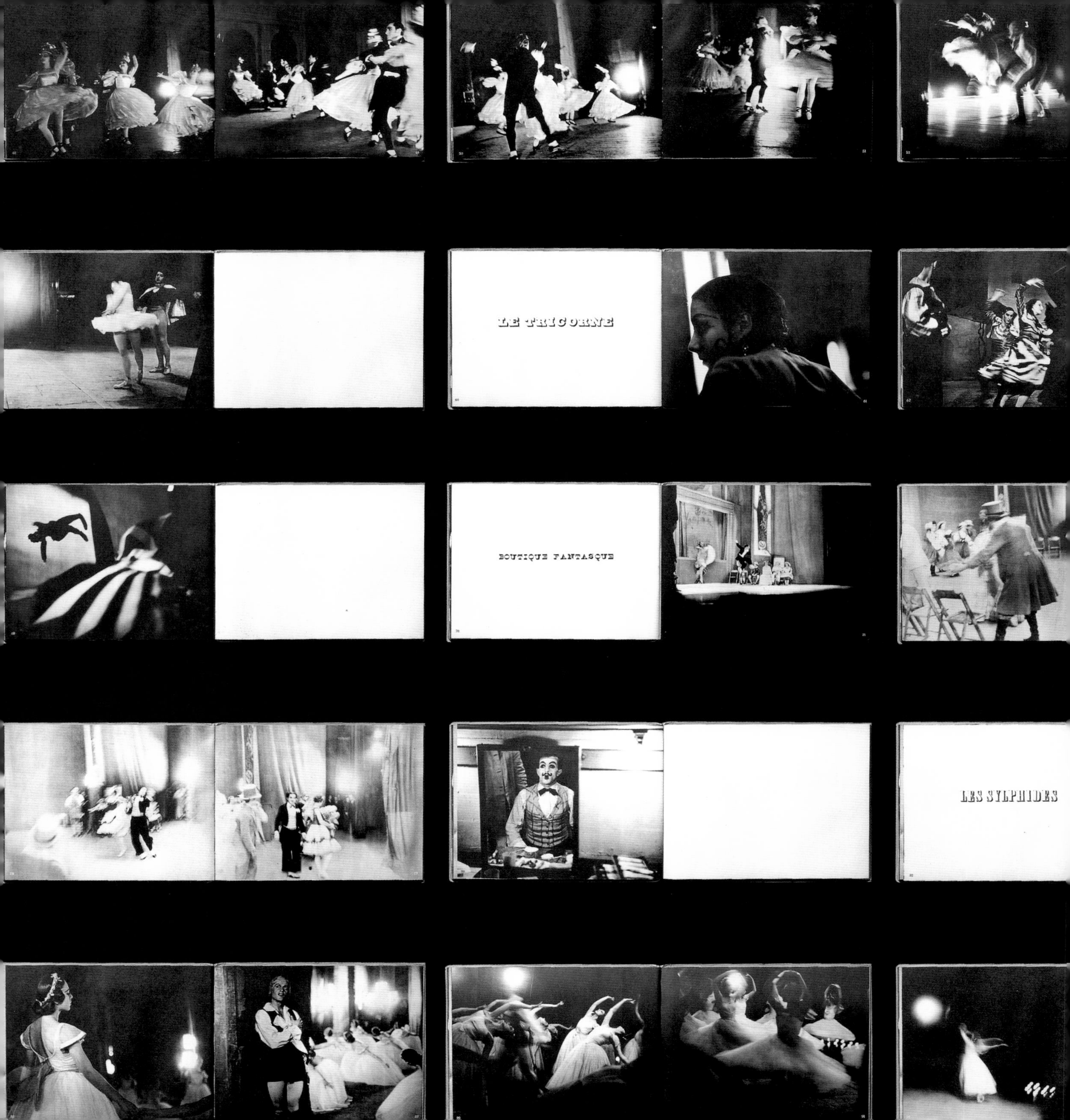
LE TRICORNE
BOUTIQUE FANTASQUE
LES SYLPHIDES

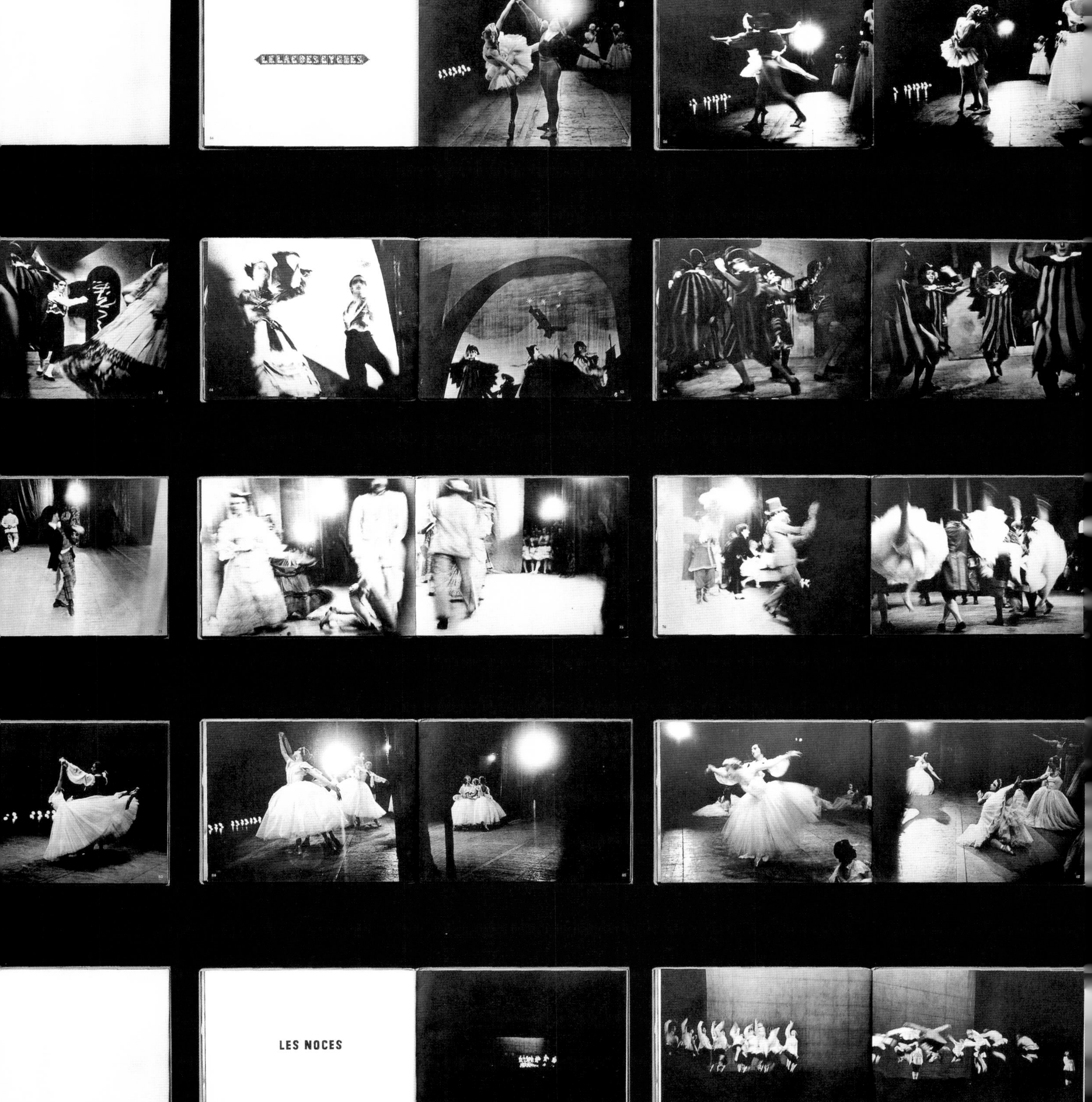
LE LAC DES CYGNES
LES NOCES

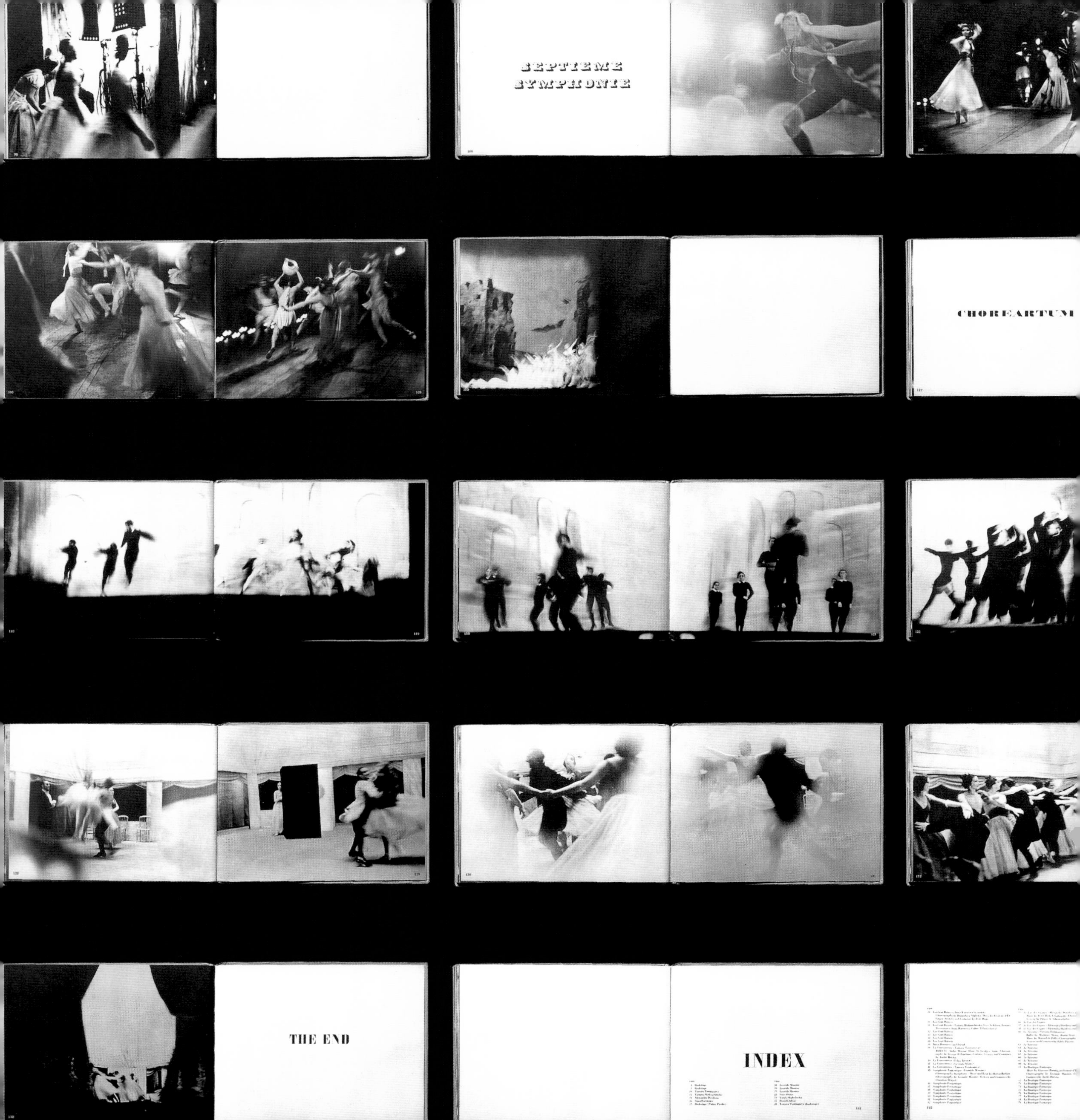
SEPTIEME
SYMPHONIE
CHOREARTUM
THE END
INDEX

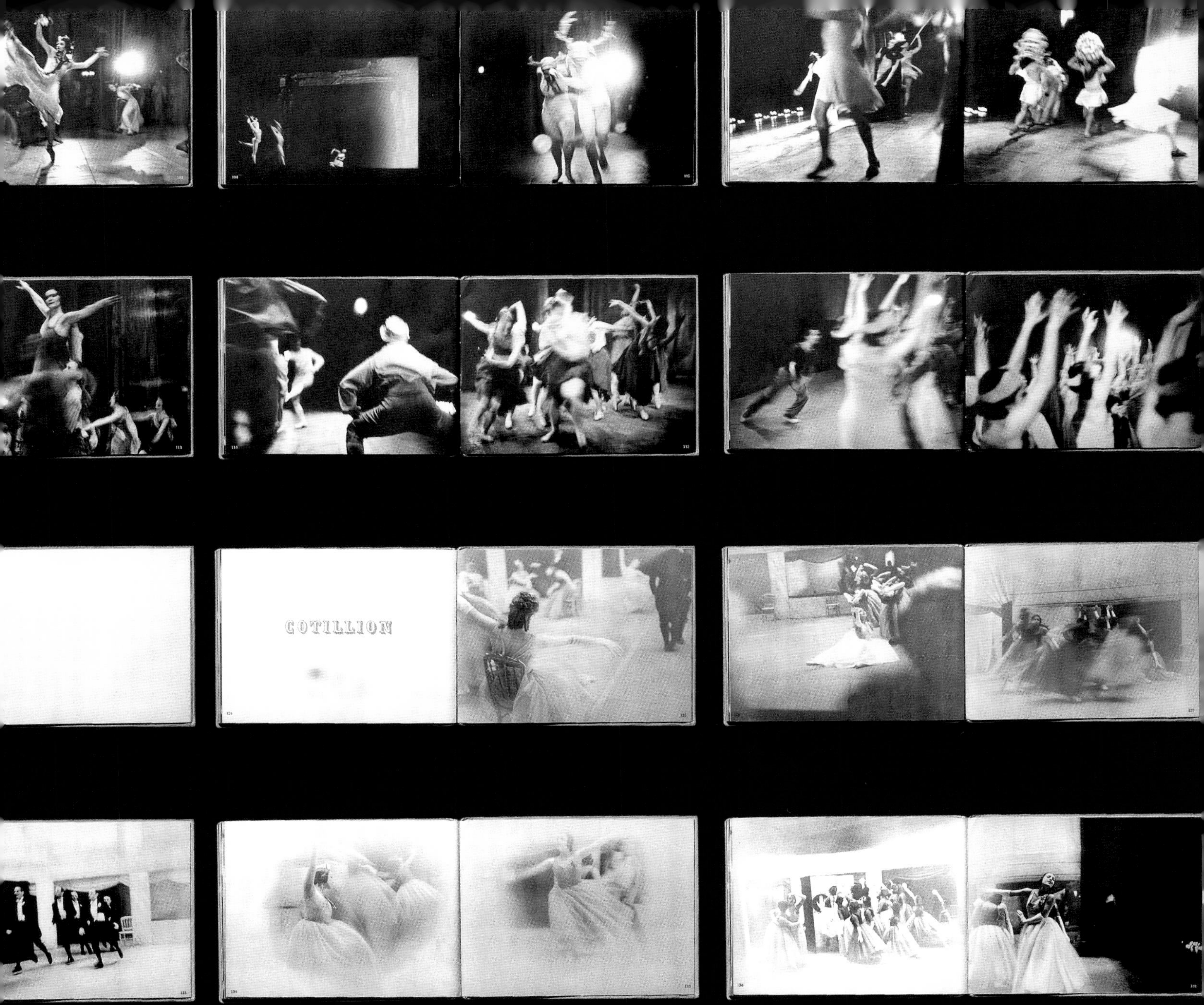

Pages 134–139: Cover and complete sequence of spreads from *Ballet* by Alexey Brodovitch. New York: J. J. Augustin, 1945.

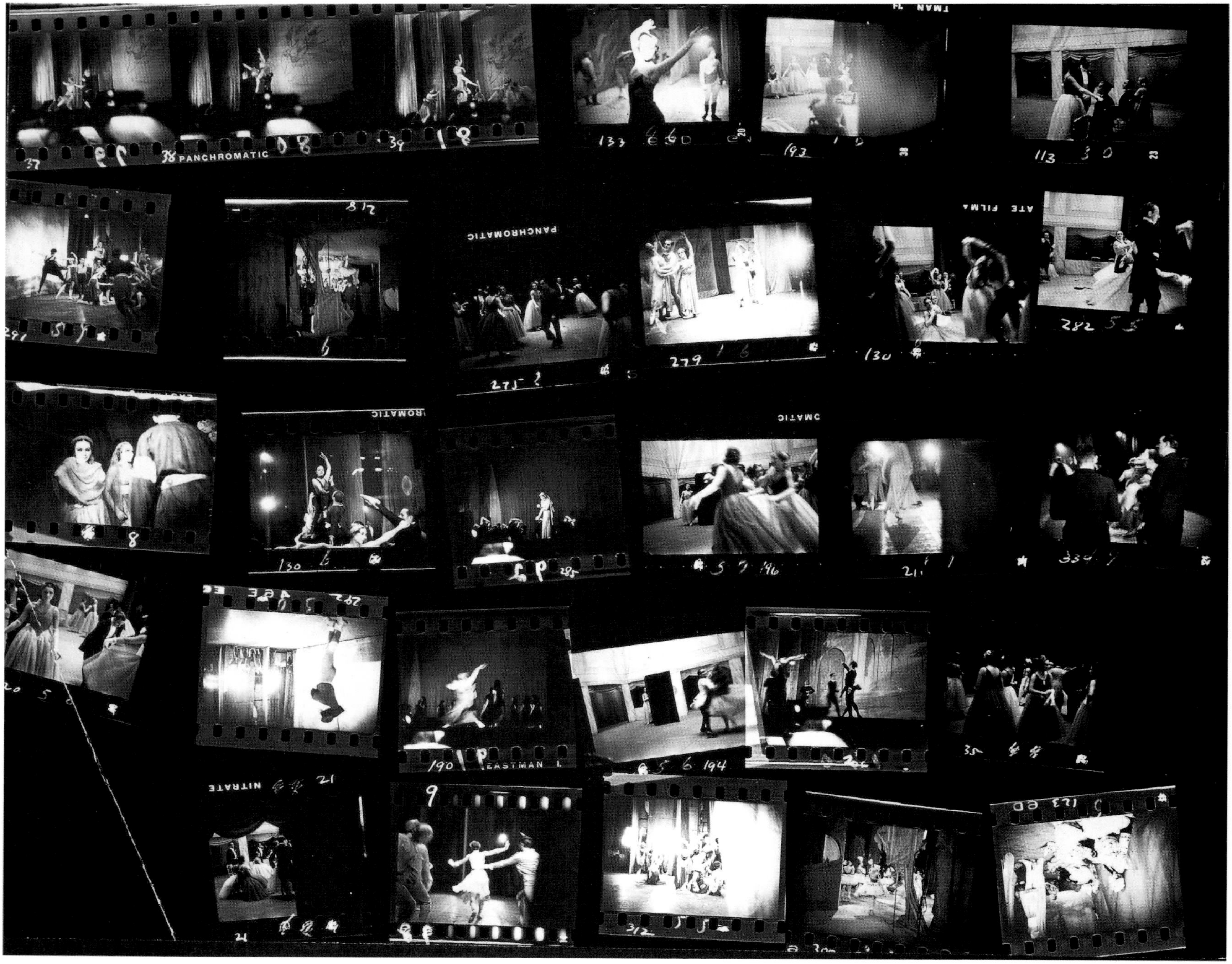

Contact sheets of negatives for *Ballet* by Alexey Brodovitch.
Fire in Brodovitch's house in Pennsylvania in 1956 and later in his house in East Hampton, New York, destroyed much of Brodovitch's original work and library. Only a few negatives and eight contact sheets of the original *Ballet* photographs survived the fires.

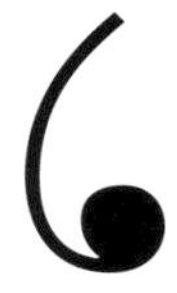

Obviously thinking about his years in Paris with Diagh

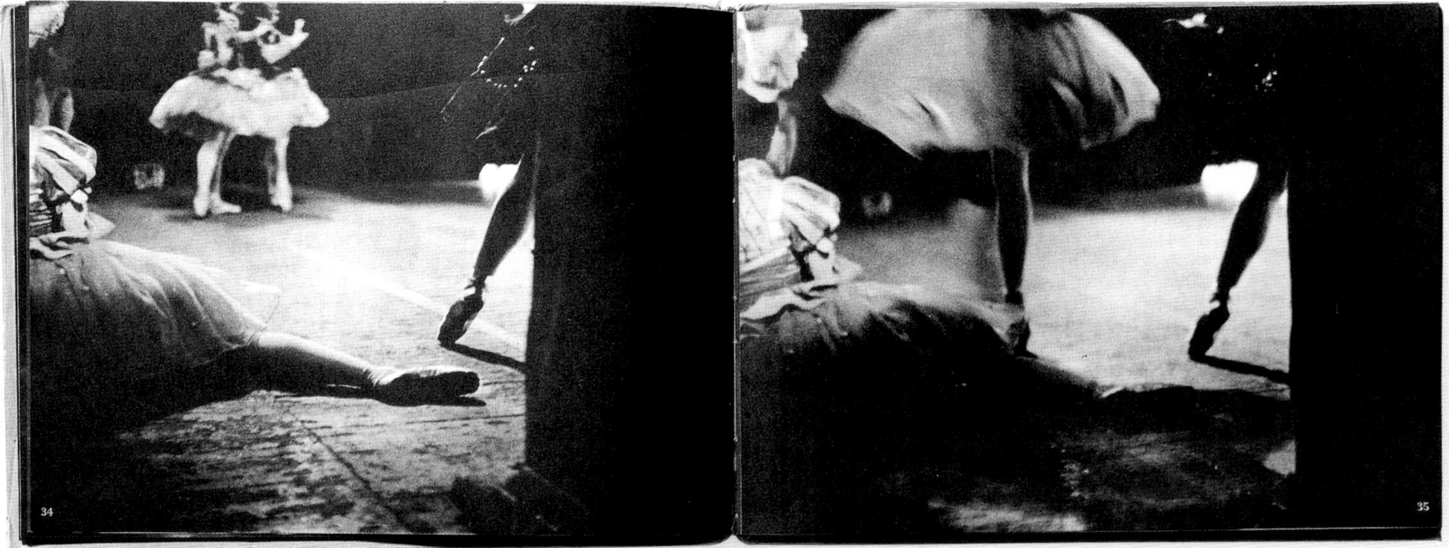

Unlike the glacial reproduction of reality seen in the work of the f.64 group, Brodovitch's images express the interior essence of the subject through the photographer's ability to capture pure movement. Setting the shutter speed at one-fifth of a second enabled Brodovitch to trace the fluidity and gracefulness of the ballet dancers around the stage and amplify their movements by painting with light. Allowing the stage lights to flare and cause halation in the lens, he echoes the flashes and outbursts of music that would have accompanied these elegantly vivacious performances. Listening to Stravinsky's irregular four-minute piece *Feu d'Artifice* (written specifically for Diaghilev's Ballets Russes in 1908) while reading *Ballet*, we can almost see how Brodovitch's own movements with the camera are choreographed to the music. Shifting from staccato to adagio and then to andante, Brodovitch's photographs are harmonized with the score of the ballet. Obviously thinking about his years in Paris with Diaghilev, Brodovitch's camera fizzes, erupts, leaps, and dives with the action of the performers. His "own performance as a photographer," Phillips observed, "is equally exhilarating and at the same time haunting. In these transient figures which swirl, swoop, spring and spin through the pictures we can catch a fleeting glimpse of Brodovitch's own memories stirring. Indeed, what these fugitive shapes and unexpected transformations ultimately suggest is the phantasmagoria of memory itself."[3]

Viewed at the time, *Ballet* must have offered the reader an astonishing new vision. By bleeding the blurred images into the gutter of the book, Brodovitch mirrors the sensation and experiences of the dance. In the chapter that depicts the performance of *Les Cent Baisers* we can see how he joins two pages together to produce a unique graphic flow across the spread. The rhythm of images rises with the lyrical and vertiginous expression of the music, then descends to moments of quietude and softness. Page by page the orchestrated panorama compels our eye to follow the ethereal ballerinas of the *Les Sylphides* or the rush of the ghostlike characters of *Cotillion*. As with *Harper's Bazaar* the analogy with film is unavoidable. In *Les Cent Baisers* we see jump cuts from one page to the next. For instance, in one spread a slight movement of the ballerina's leg, a change of perspective, and the appearance of a new figure all combine to engage the viewer's imagination. In his introduction to *Ballet*, the critic Edwin Denby appreciated the audacious nature of Brodovitch's imagery:

When you first glance at them Alexey Brodovitch's photographs look strangely unconventional. Brodovitch, who knows as well as any of us the standardized Fifth Avenue kind of flawless prints, offers us as his own some that are blurred, distorted, too black and spectral, or too light and faded looking, and he has even intensified these qualities in the darkroom.... What he took, what

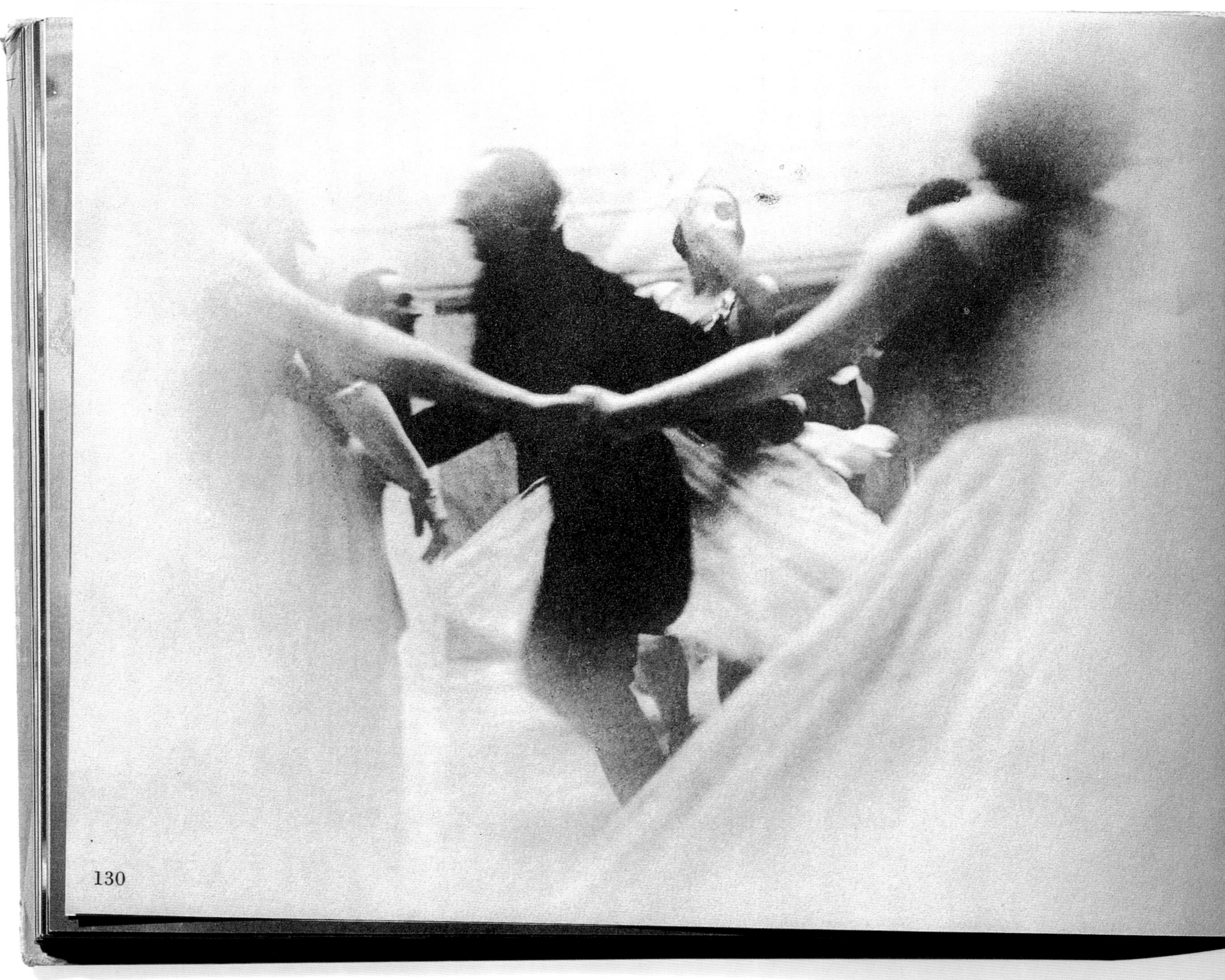
130

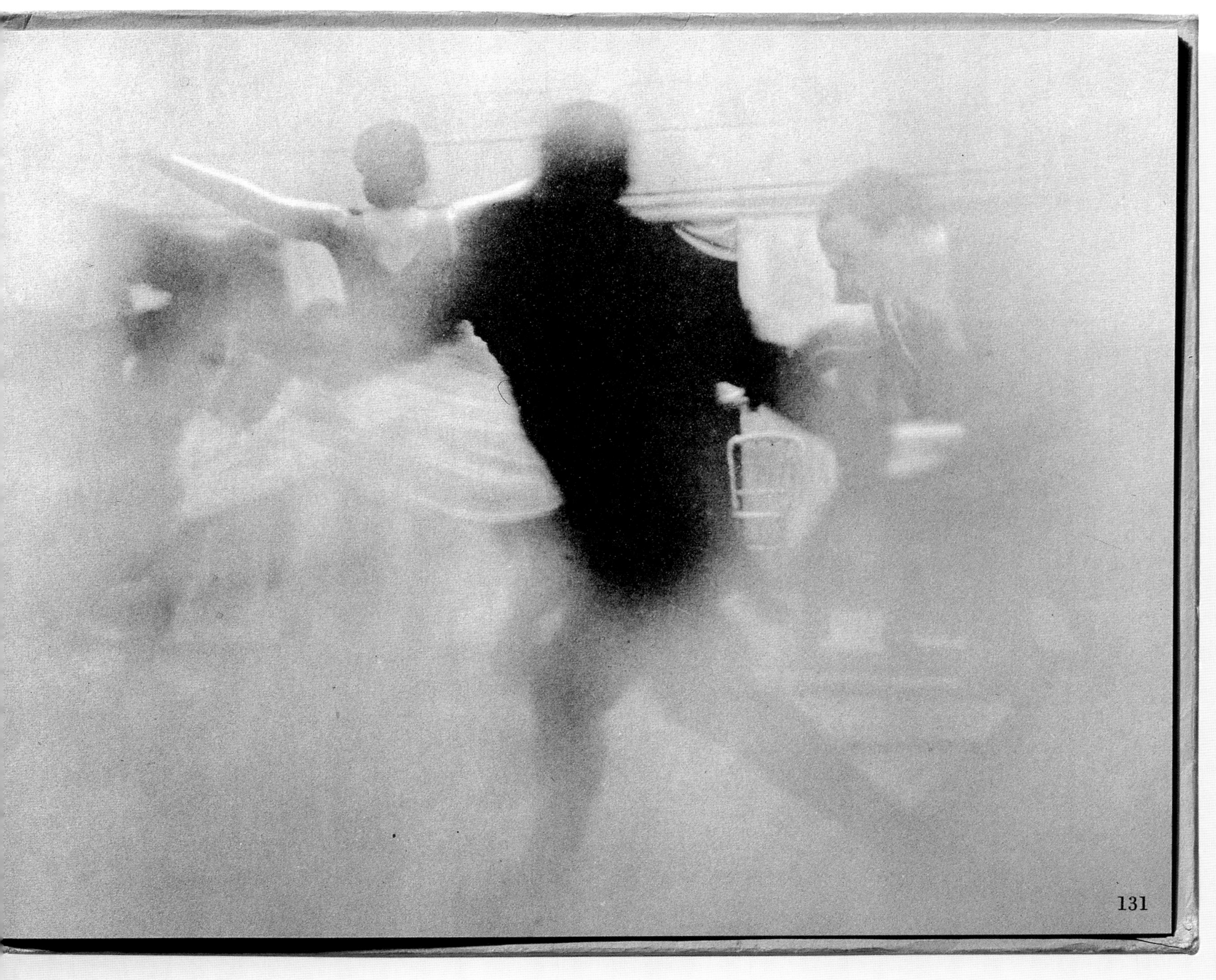

Ballet by Alexey Brodovitch. New York: J. J. Augustin, 1945. Pages 130–31.
Through his manipulation of the negative, Brodovitch portrays the dancers of the ballet *Cotillion* in a ghostly mist.

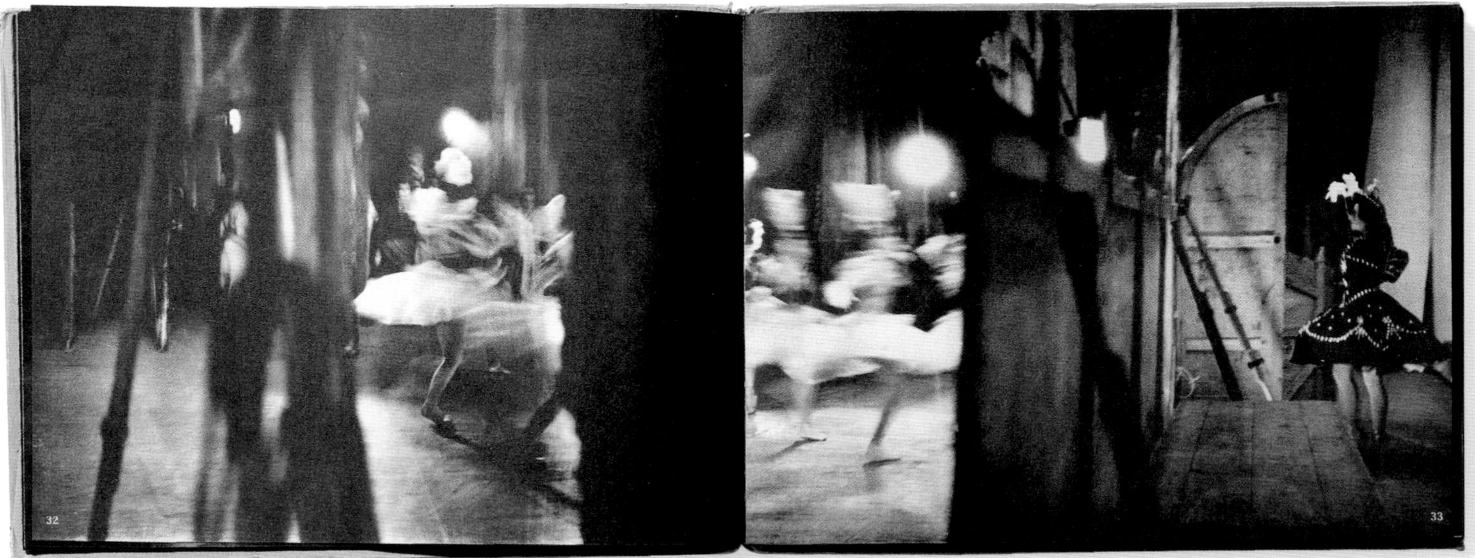

Above: *Ballet* by Alexey Brodovitch. New York: J. J. Augustin, 1945. Pages 32–33.

Opposite: *Ballet*, pages 120–21. *Ballet* is a collection of photographs Brodovitch took of performances in New York by international ballet companies from 1935 to 1939. As seen in these pictures, he was permitted access to all parts of the theater.

he watched for, it seems, were the unemphatic moments, the ones the audience does not applaud but establish the spell of the evening.[4]

Brodovitch sought to intensify the impression of movement in *Ballet* by manipulating the negatives in the darkroom. He bleached out areas of negative to heighten the solarization of the footlights and stage lights. He enlarged just tiny fragments of the 35-mm negative to stress the grainy and distorted properties of the image. He even covered the lens of the enlarger with cellophane to produce a fade-out effect at the edges of the frame. As with the reverie of the blurred dancers, Brodovitch actively seized on the outcome of any beautiful "accidents" in the darkroom. When the photographer Herman Landshoff was asked by Brodovitch to make the *Ballet* prints to be used for the book, he accidentally dropped a negative on the studio floor and stood on it. As Richard Avedon remembers, Landshoff "was horrified and called Brodovitch and said a terrible thing had happened, one of the negatives fell and I stepped on it. And Brodovitch on the phone said, 'Print it exactly as it is. It's part of the medium, things like that.'"[5]

In the history of photography there are only a handful of images that capture movement with the same level of intensity as Brodovitch does in *Ballet*. Munkacsi's images obviously had some influence on Brodovitch, as we have already witnessed in chapter 2. A collection of Edward Steichen's images may also have inspired Brodovitch's decision to push the visual potential of movement in his work. Steichen's flowing images of Lillian Gish and the dancer Thérèse Duncan on the Acropolis, especially the photograph *Wind Fire* (1921), contain many of the aspects we see in Brodovitch's *Ballet* work. However, in Steichen's oeuvre these are just isolated examples, more a legacy from the soft-focus pictorialism of his turn-of-the-century work than a radical departure to something new. One of the earliest photographers who did make a conscious attempt to examine the question of movement in his work, and whose compositions Brodovitch may have come across during his time in Paris, is the Futurist photographer Anton Giulio Bragaglia. As part of Futurism's philosophy, which proclaimed the death of all artistic forms of the past, Bragaglia coined the phrase "Photodynamism" to identify his novel approach to the photographic image. Bragaglia took photographs of various individuals in action that stressed the movement of the subject by allowing a blurring of the image. With titles such as *Image in Motion* (1913) and *The Carpenter* (1913), Bragaglia's work documents the physicality of movement rather than, as in the work of Eadweard Muybridge and Etienne Jules Marey, frozen moments. In his 1911 manifesto "Futurist Photodynamism," Bragaglia's words have a resonance when viewing Brodovitch's *Ballet:*

[A]s things are dematerialized in motion they become idealised, while still retaining, deep down, a strong skeleton of truth....

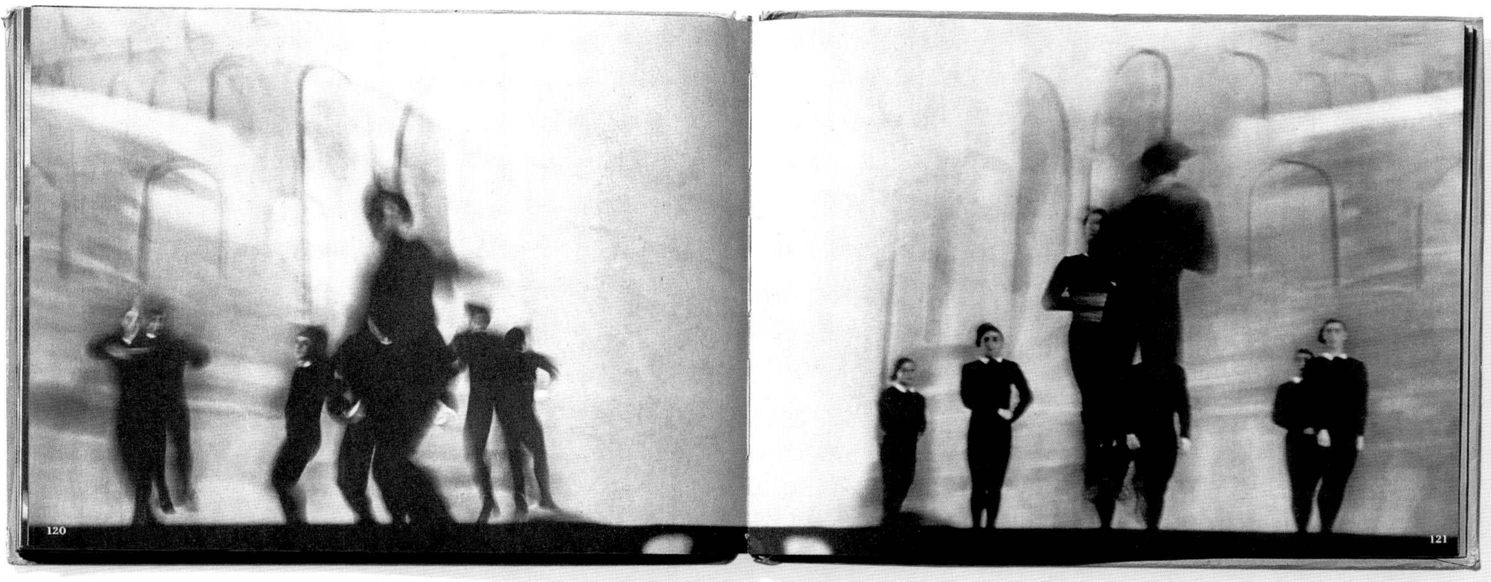

In this way, if we repeat the principal states of the action, the figure of a dancer – moving a foot, in mid-air, pirouetting – will, even when not possessing its own trajectory or offering a dynamic sensation, be much more like a dancer, and much more like dancing, than would a single figure frozen in just one of the states that build up a movement.... [These images] endeavour to extract not only the aesthetic expression of the motives, but also the inner sensorial, cerebral and psychic emotions that we feel when an action leaves its superb, unbroken trace.[6]

Bragaglia once said that "when a person gets up the chair is still full of his soul." For Irving Penn, the traces of light left by the dancers in *Ballet* represented, for the first time, the mystical value in photography.

Ballet was not given a widespread release by J. J. Augustin. The monograph had a print run of only a few hundred copies and it seems to have never been sold through any major bookstores. In fact, the only way that his colleagues and friends acquired copies of this rare book was through Brodovitch himself giving them away as gifts. The scarcity of the monograph was only exacerbated when, in 1956, a fire at Brodovitch's farmhouse in Phoenixville, Pennsylvania, destroyed the majority of the *Ballet* negatives. This fire also destroyed the bulk of his library and his collection of signed lithographs by Picasso and Matisse. Brodovitch suffered another fire, apparently started by his son Nikita (who, sadly, had learning disabilities), in his next house in East Hampton, Long Island. Compounding the tragedy, this second fire occurred during an extreme winter and, because of the hazardous conditions, the fire service was unable to make it to his house. Only a small number of *Ballet* negatives still survive. In the end, Brodovitch was left with only a few copies of the book itself. Ted Croner remembered visiting Brodovitch's farm after the fire, and when Brodovitch tried to give him a copy of *Ballet*, his wife Nina said: "You can't give him that Alexey, you only have three copies left." Even in the face of such misfortune Brodovitch was always generous with his close friends and colleagues – Croner got the book.[7]

In 1945, *Ballet* received the Book of the Year Award from the American Institute of Graphic Arts. For many photographers it remains a treasured touchstone of photographic expression. Its influence can be seen in everything from Avedon's *Observations* to the expressionistic color photography of Ernst Haas. *Ballet* inspired many photographers to explore the theme of dance in their own projects. Among the works clearly affected by Brodovitch's book are Ted Croner's circus pictures (1947 – 52) and Paul Himmel's book *Ballet in Action* (1954). Brodovitch himself returned to the subject of the ballet on two more occasions. In 1949, in his first collaboration with Richard Avedon away from the pages of *Harper's Bazaar*, he designed the *Ninth Ballet*

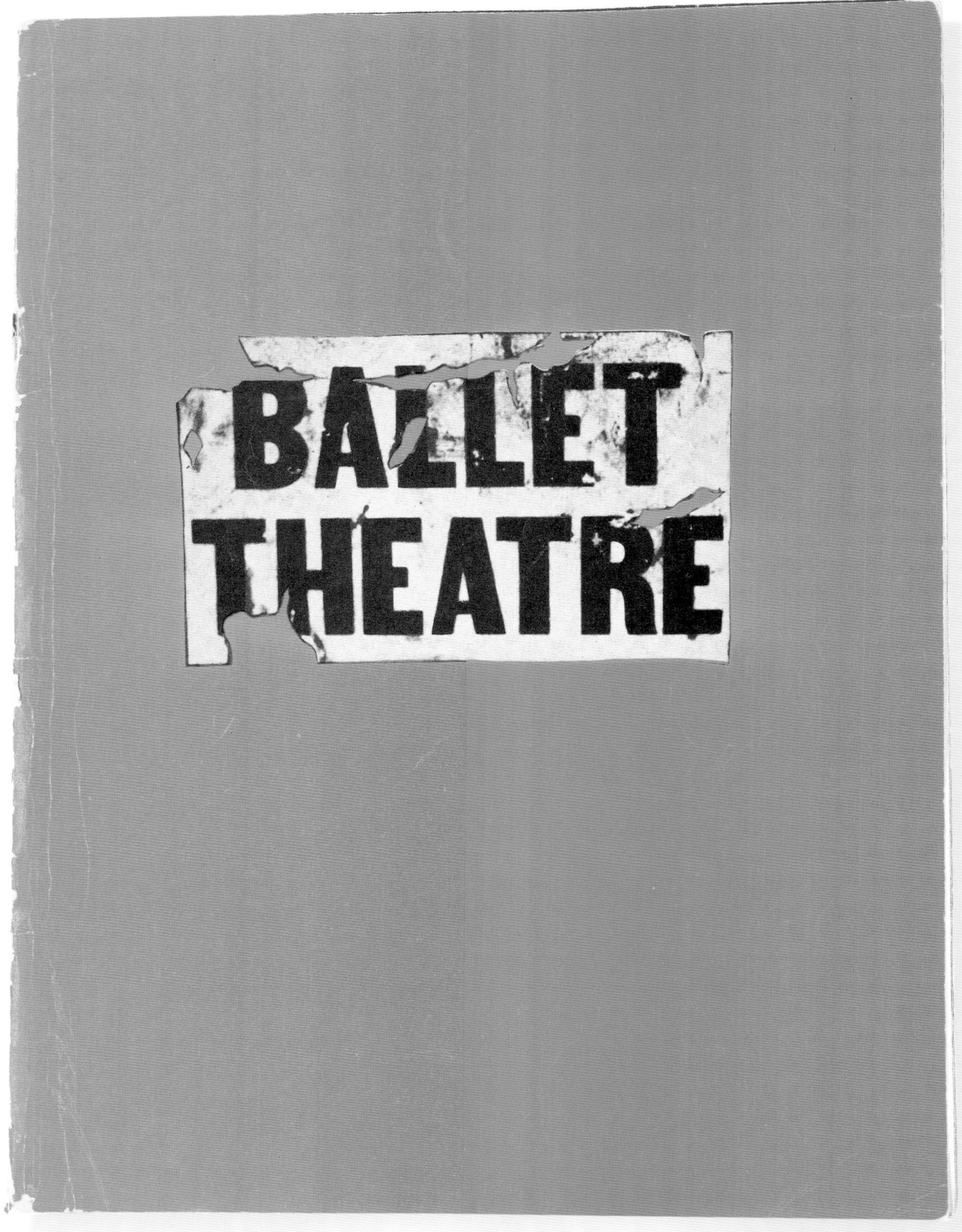
BALLET
THEATRE

Theatre Annual, which includes Avedon's black-and-white photographs of Igor Youskevitch, Maria Tallchief, and Hugh Lang. His synthetically aged design anticipates the fragility we now witness in the remaining rare copies of his own *Ballet* monograph. Between 1953 and 1955, he also designed several posters for the Ballet Russe de Monte Carlo. In one of these works we see a figure cropped at the shoulders wearing an extravagant mask. The name of the company is placed discreetly in the top right-hand corner of the poster. The ballet undoubtedly held a lifelong fascination for Brodovitch. These poster designs came more than forty years after he had first worked with Diaghilev in Paris. Together with *Ballet*, this work clearly indicates that throughout his life Brodovitch maintained an enduring regard for those formative years.

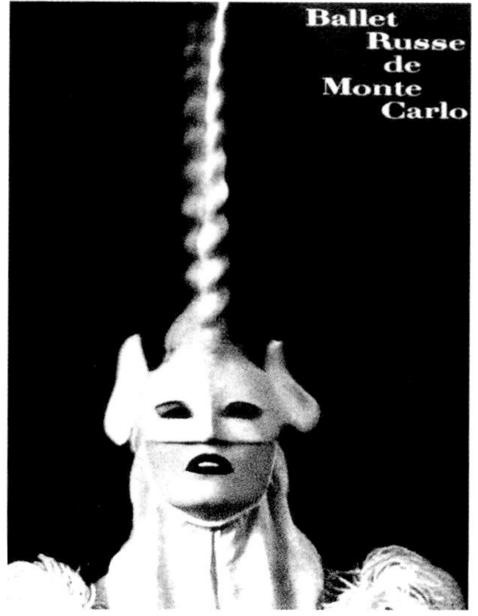

REPERTORY OF THE BALLET THEATRE

APOLLO	1943	GEORGE BALANCHINE	IGOR STRAVINSKY	DUNKEL-KARINSKA
BILLY THE KID	1941	EUGENE LORING	AARON COPLAND	JARED FRENCH
BLUEBEARD	1941	MICHEL FOKINE	OFFENBACH-DORATI	MARCEL VERTES
DARK ELEGIES	1940	ANTONY TUDOR	GUSTAV MAHLER	NADIA BENOIS
DIM LUSTRE	1943	ANTONY TUDOR	RICHARD STRAUSS	MOTLEY
FACSIMILE	1947	JEROME ROBBINS	LEONARD BERNSTEIN	OLIVER SMITH - IRENE SHARAFF
FALL RIVER LEGEND	1948	AGNES DEMILLE	MORTON GOULD	OLIVER SMITH - MILES WHITE
FANCY FREE	1944	JEROME ROBBINS	LEONARD BERNSTEIN	OLIVER SMITH - KERMIT LOVE
FILLE MAL GARDEE	1940	DIMITRI ROMANOFF	WILHELM HERTEL	SERGEI SOUDEIKINE
GALA PERFORMANCE	1941	ANTONY TUDOR	SERGE PROKOFIEFF	NICOLAS DE MOLAS
GISELLE	1940	DOLIN AFTER CORALLI	ADOLPHE ADAM	EUGENE BERMAN
HELEN OF TROY	1942	DAVID LICHINE	OFFENBACH-DORATI	MARCEL VERTES
INTERPLAY	1945	JEROME ROBBINS	MORTON GOULD	OLIVER SMITH - IRENE SHARAFF
JARDIN AUX LILAS	1940	ANTONY TUDOR	ERNEST CHAUSSON	HUGH STEVENSON
LES PATINEURS	1947	FREDERICK ASHTON	MEYERBEER	CECIL BEATON
LES SYLPHIDES	1940	MICHEL FOKINE	CHOPIN	DUNKEL AFTER COROT
ON STAGE	1945	MICHAEL KIDD	NORMAN DELLO JOIO	OLIVER SMITH - ALVIN COLT
PAS DE QUATRE	1946	KEITH LESTER	PUGNI	
PETER AND THE WOLF	1940	ADOLPH BOLM	SERGE PROKOFIEFF	LUCINDA BALLARD
PETROUCHKA	1942	MICHEL FOKINE	IGOR STRAVINSKY	ALEXANDRE BENOIS
PILLAR OF FIRE	1942	ANTONY TUDOR	ARNOLD SCHOENBERG	JO MIELZINER
PRINCESS AURORA	1941	PETIPA	TCHAIKOWSKY	LEON BAKST
ROMEO AND JULIET	1943	ANTONY TUDOR	FREDERICK DELIUS	EUGENE BERMAN
SHADOW OF THE WIND	1948	ANTONY TUDOR	GUSTAV MAHLER	JO MIELZINER
SWAN LAKE	1940	DOLIN AFTER PETIPA	TCHAIKOWSKY	LEE SIMONSON
TALLY HO	1944	AGNES DEMILLE	GLUCK	MOTLEY
THEME AND VARIATIONS	1947	GEORGE BALANCHINE	TCHAIKOWSKY	WOODMAN THOMPSON
UNDERTOW	1945	ANTONY TUDOR	WILLIAM SCHUMAN	RAYMOND BREININ

All ballets by MICHEL FOKINE were staged under his personal supervision.

Opposite: Cover from *Ninth Ballet Theatre Annual*. New York: Charles Payne, 1949. Design by Brodovitch, photographs by Richard Avedon.

Above: Ballet Russe de Monte Carlo poster, c.1953–55.

Left: Interior spread from *Ninth Ballet Theatre Annual*.

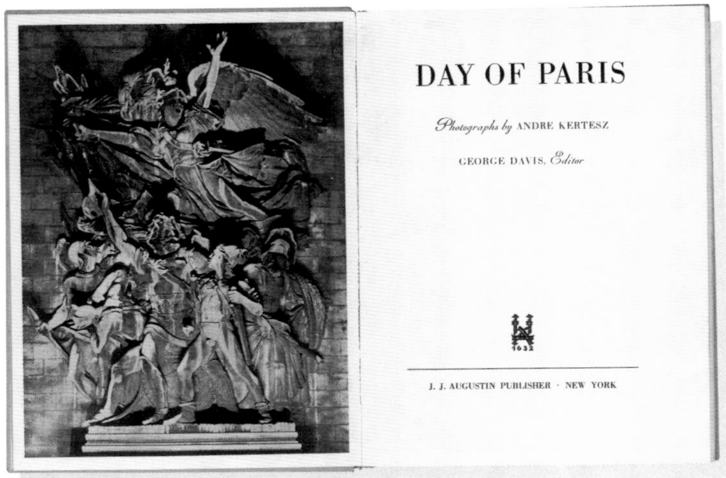

Above: Title page from *Day of Paris* by André Kertész. New York: J. J. Augustin, 1945.

Opposite: Cover, *Day of Paris*.
Rather than manipulating Kertész's work to fit his own design agenda, the central feature of Brodovitch's layout of *Day of Paris* is its unison with Kertész's photographs. The clever incorporation of the book's title into the cover photograph of a street corner, together with the delicate placement of Kertész's name below, communicates Brodovitch's intention from the outset.

Day of Paris

Ballet was not the only book Brodovitch designed for J. J. Augustin. As we saw in chapter 2, Brodovitch provided the Hungarian-born photographer André Kertész with some of his first commissions after Kertész's arrival in New York in 1936. Prior to coming to America, Kertész spent eleven years in Paris documenting the everyday events and happenings of the city. Working with Kertész, Brodovitch was obviously aware of his Parisian work and most likely informed J. J. Augustin of their possible value for publication. At this time, photographic monographs were still relatively rare, and for such a small publisher as J. J. Augustin they were a major financial risk. However, the time was ripe for this subject matter. There was much nostalgia for Paris among the soldiers of the armed forces returning home from Europe following the end of World War II. Cinemas showed films with titles such as *Paris Underground*, *Paris After Dark*, and *An American in Paris*, all incorporating (mythical) aspects of Parisian life in its prewar days. Recognizing this pent-up demand for imagery of Paris, J. J. Augustin identified a willing market for Kertész's first publication in America.

Designed in partnership with Peter Pollock, *Day of Paris* is one of Brodovitch's more quiet works. Kertész's subtle images are free from the exuberant swirls of movement and intense action witnessed in *Ballet*. The 147 deceptively simple

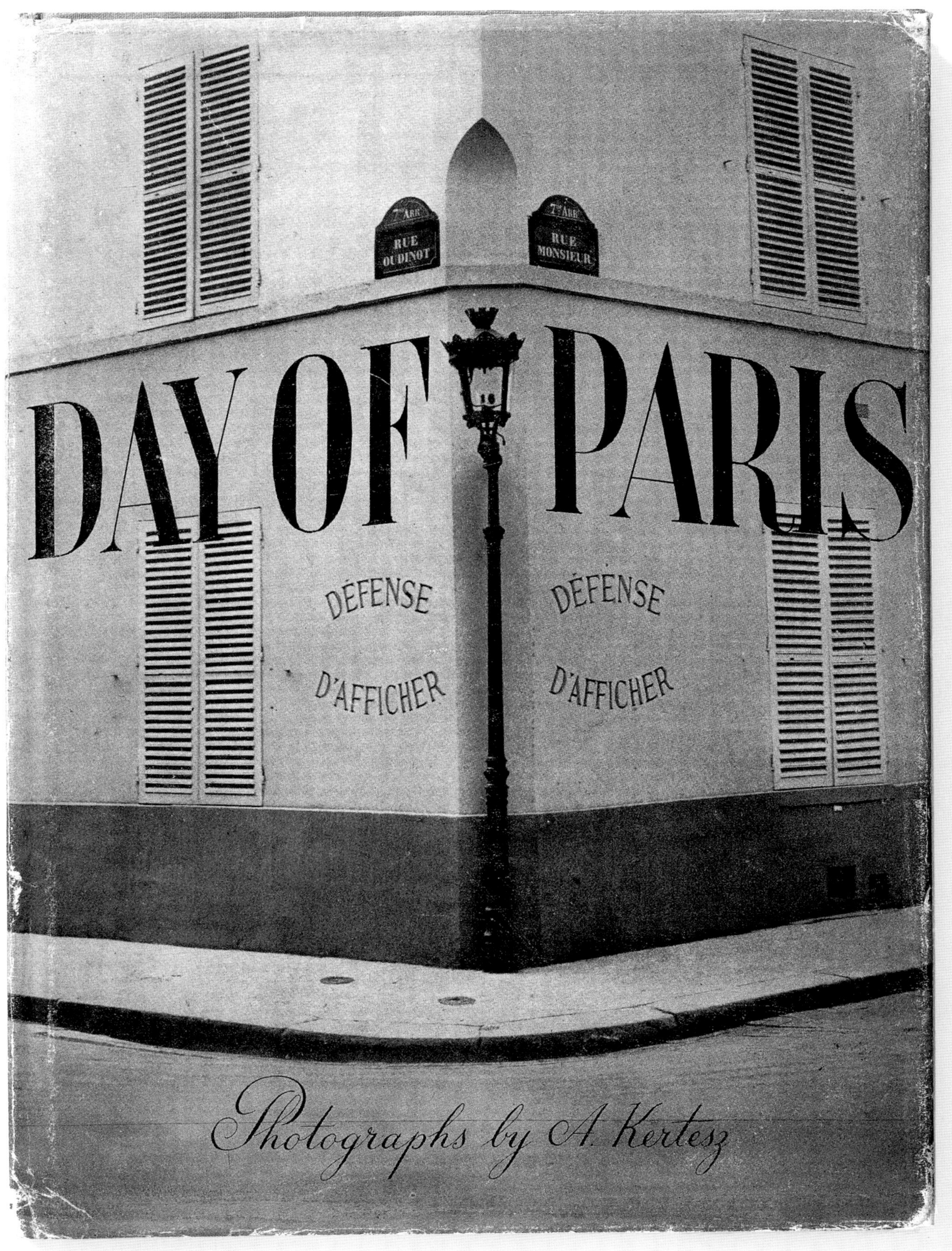
7e ARR
RUE
OUDINOT
7e ARR
RUE
MONSIEUR
DAY OF PARIS
DÉFENSE
D'AFFICHER
DÉFENSE
D'AFFICHER
Photographs by A. Kertesz

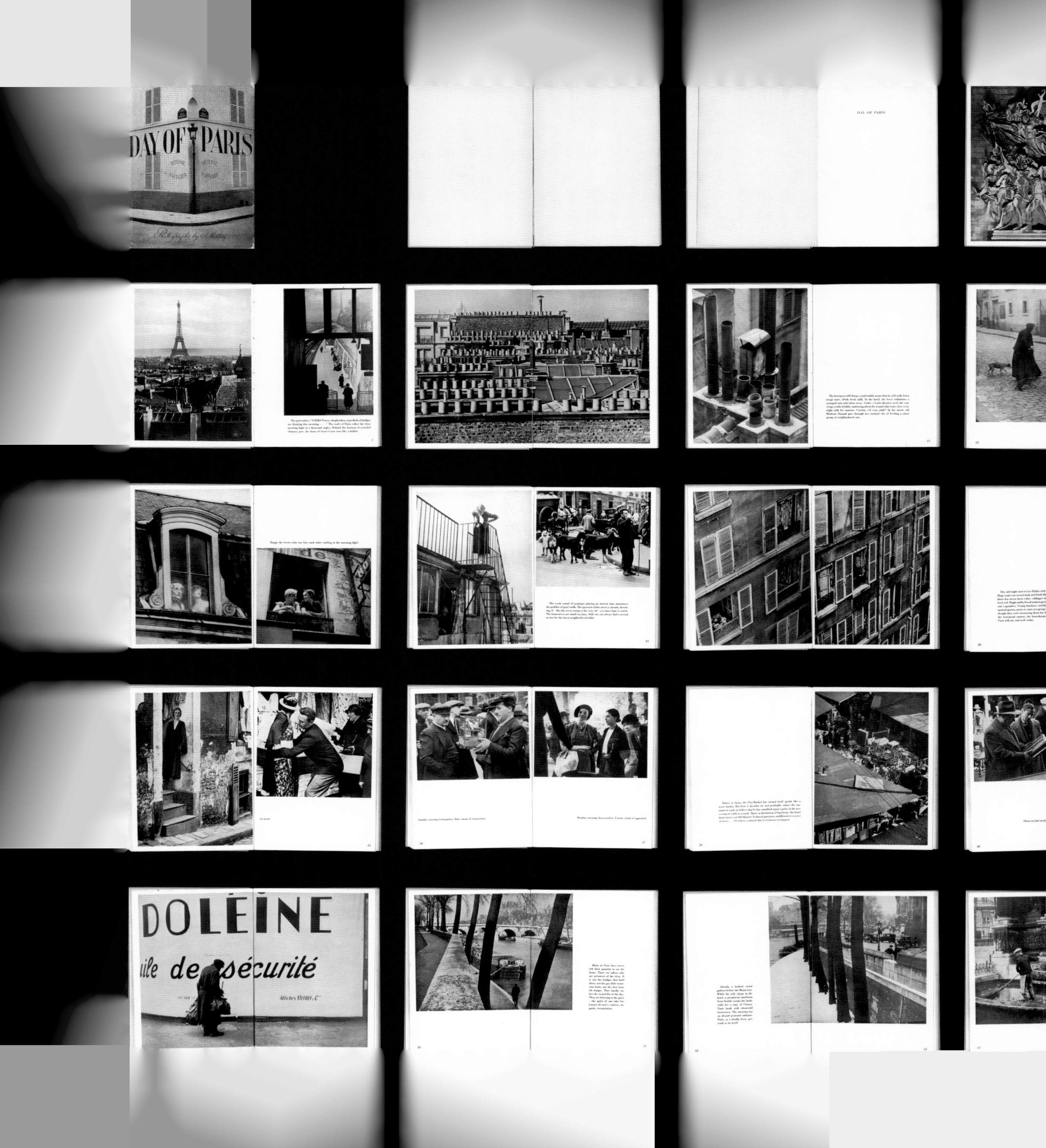
DAY OF PARIS
DOLÉINE
ile de sécurité

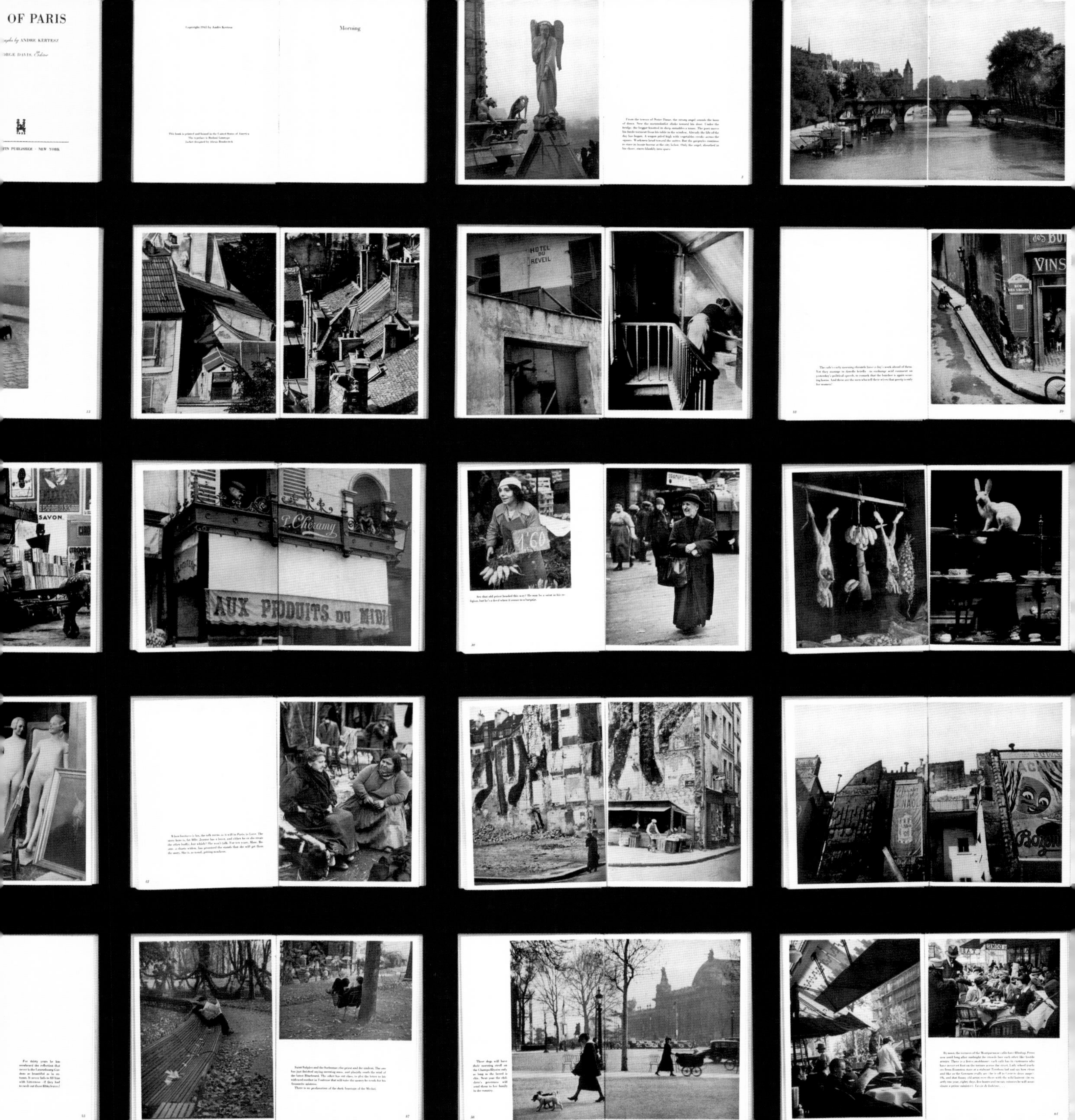
OF PARIS
Morning
HOTEL DU REVEIL
VINS
SAVON
L. Chéramy
AUX PRODUITS DU MIDI
1'60

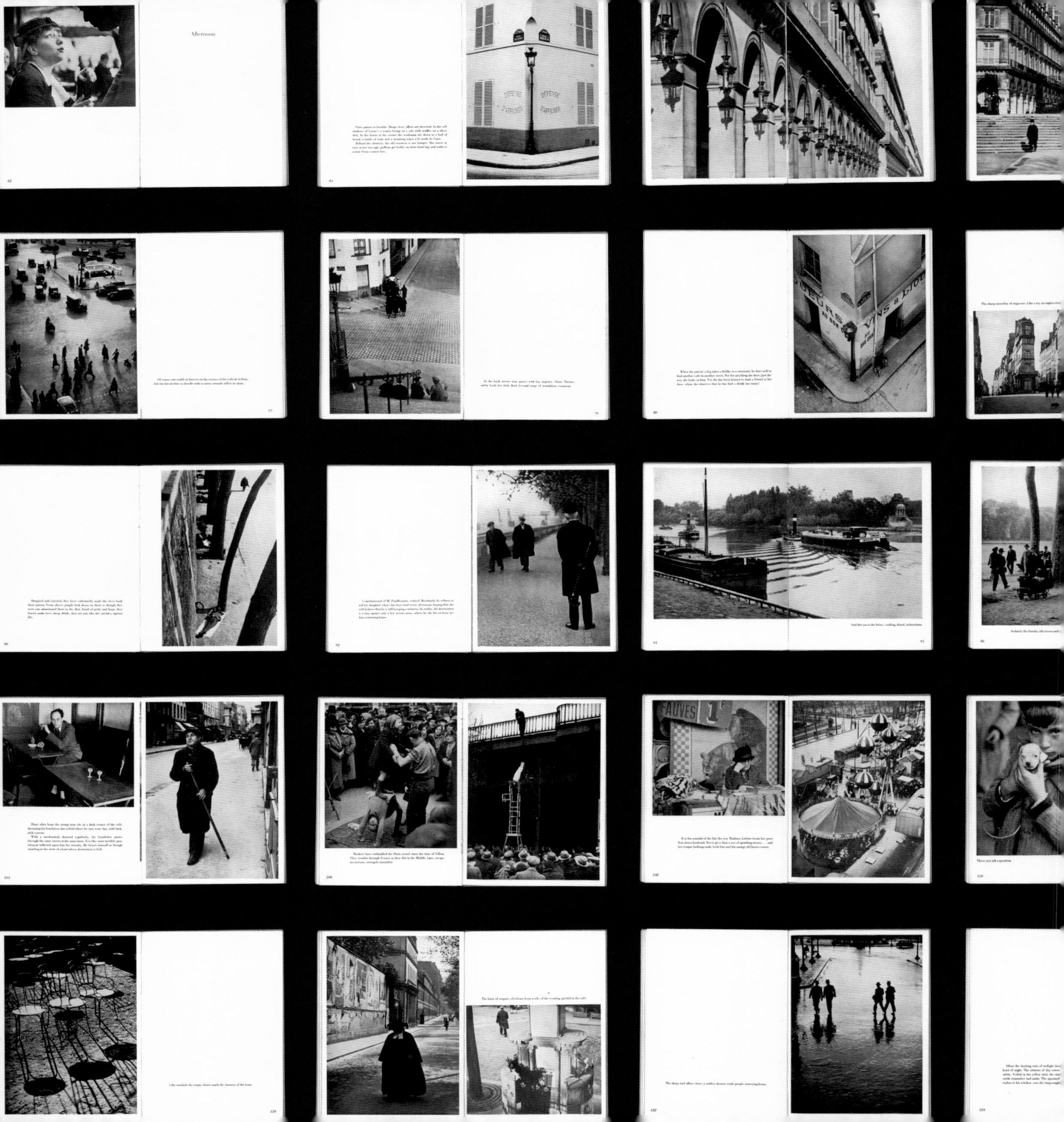

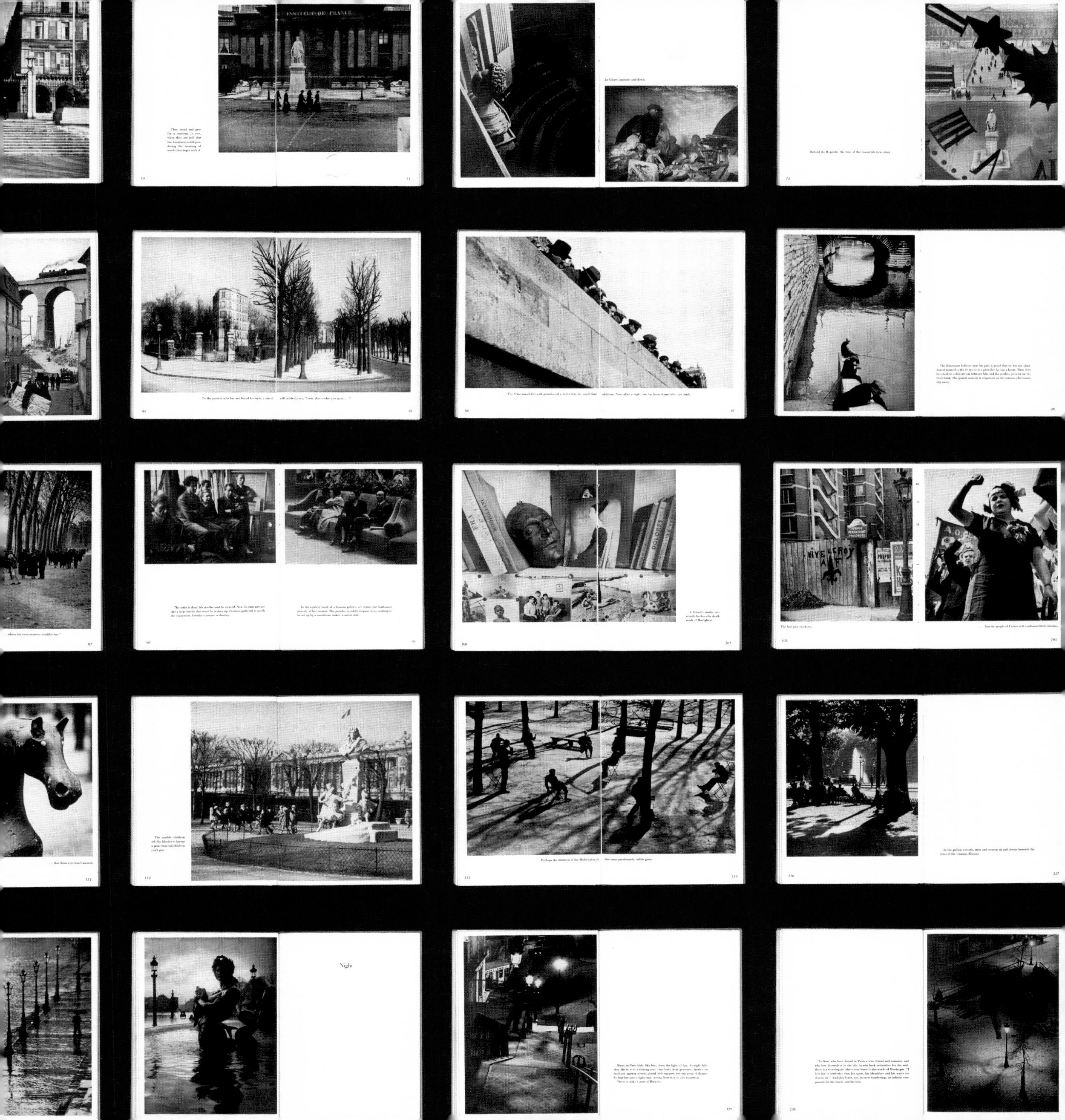
INSTITUT DE FRANCE
Night

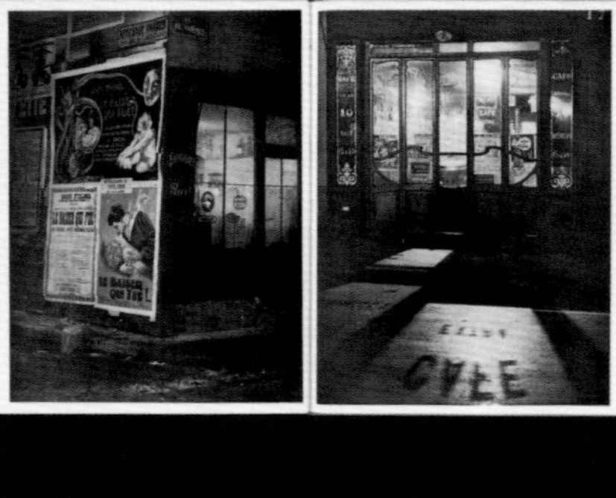

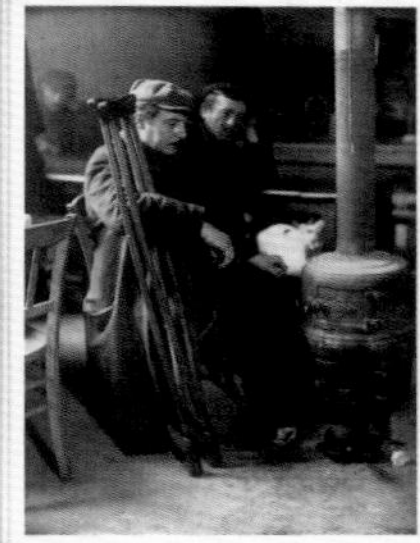

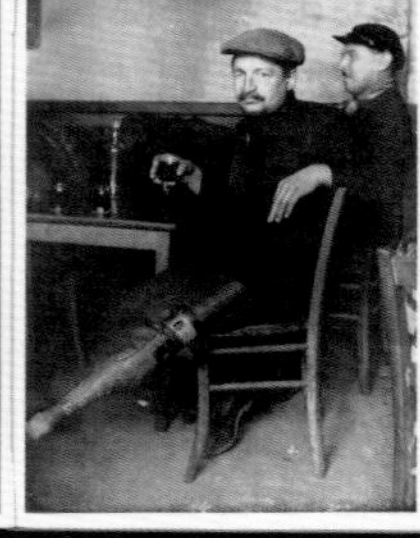

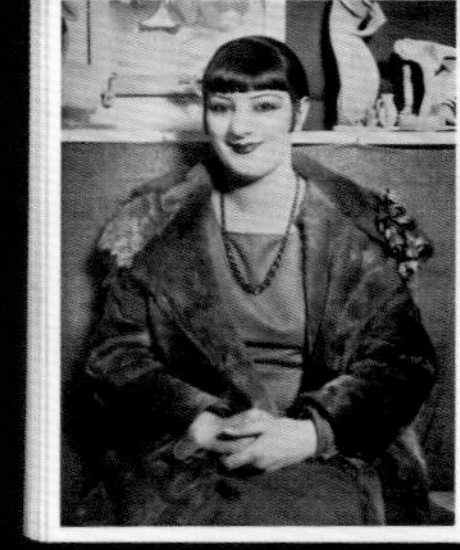

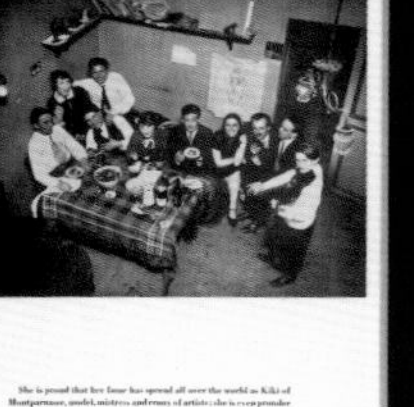

She is proud that her fame has spread all over the world as Kiki of Montparnasse, model, mistress and crony of artists; she is even prouder that she has never grown pubic hair. She has, like the celebrants above, the innocence of the classic bohemian.

The day of the wanderer has ended. Like the strong angel of Notre Dame, he looks over the city. Out of his aloneness, he has spoken to no one, he has implored no glance. He has followed no guide book, he has seen nothing on which a tourist would scrawl "Wish you were here." And so, because he is willing to lose himself, to become patiently and tenderly nobody, Paris has revealed her most precious secrets: a woman's hand at a window, the eyes of a carrousel horse, the violence of a deserted street. . . .

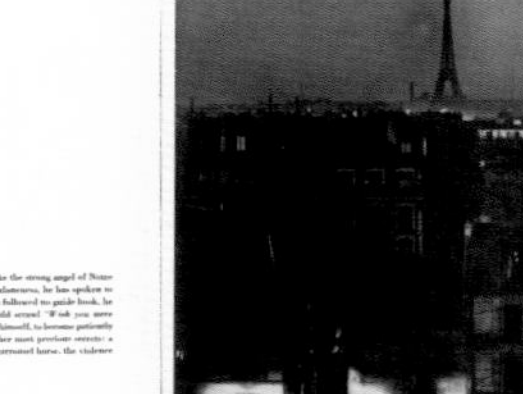

INDEX TO PHOTOGRAPHS

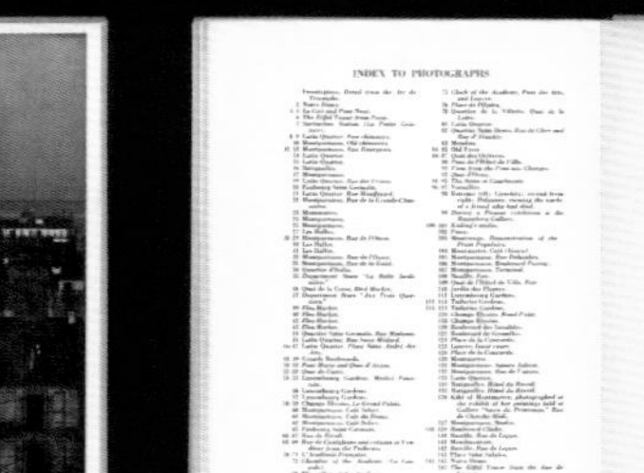

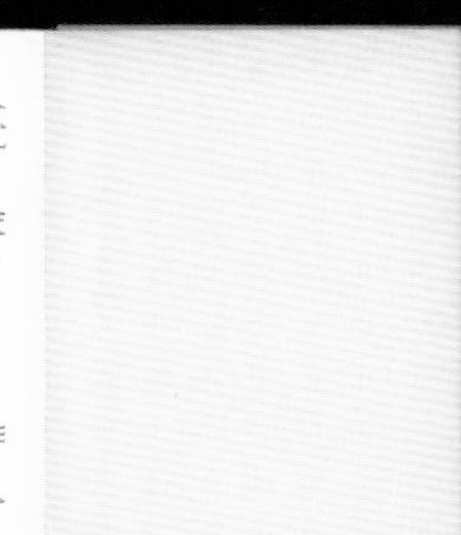

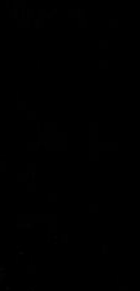

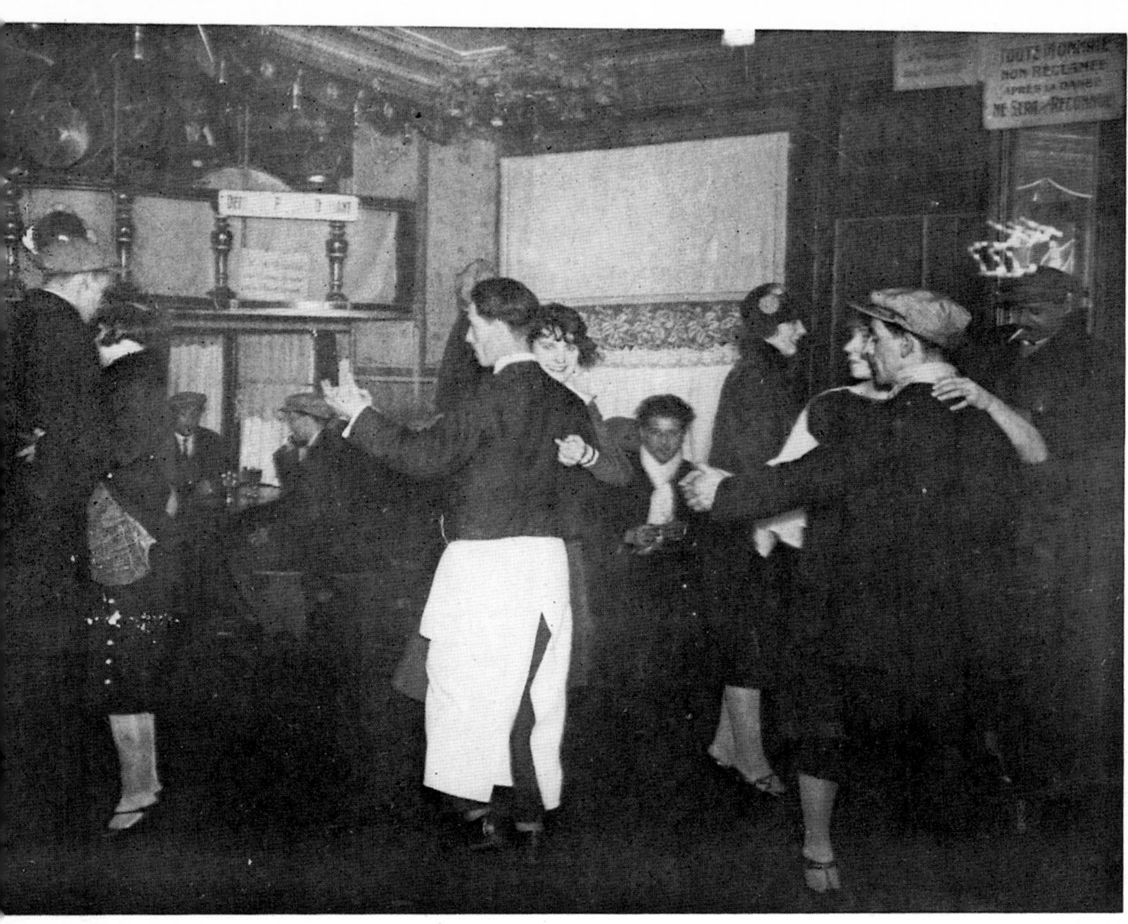

A street honorably ancient in vice becomes its own Hollywood replica, and its inhabitants twirl and grimace like movie extras before the camera.

141

Day of Paris by André Kertész.
New York: J. J. Augustin, 1945.
Pages 140–41.
Brodovitch used quarter-inch borders to "display" the photographs on the page, allowing the pictures to breathe.

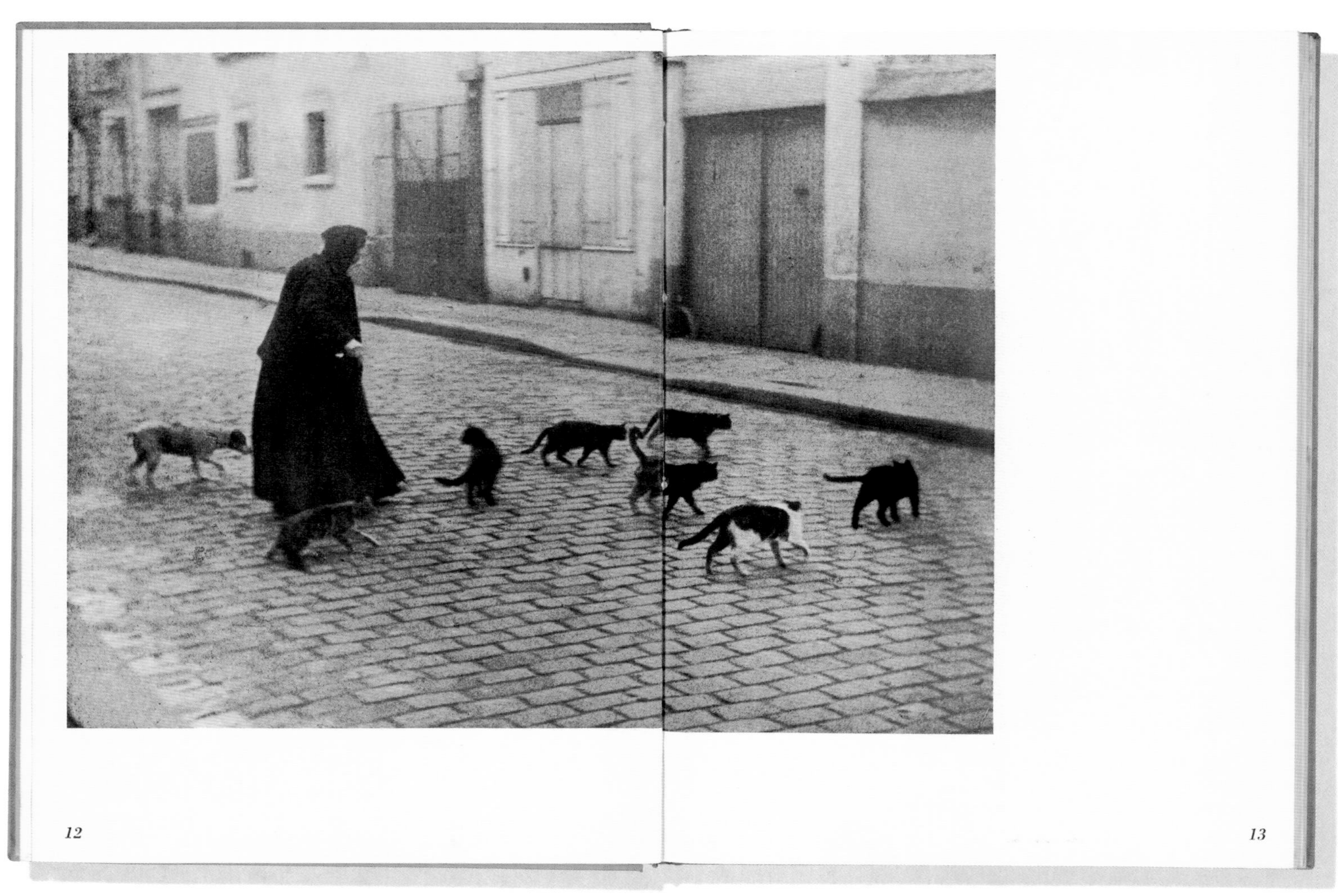

***Day of Paris* by André Kertész. New York: J. J. Augustin, 1945. Pages 12–13.**
As witnessed in *Harper's Bazaar,* Brodovitch had an ability to treat layouts like storyboards of a film. This approach was perfectly suited to Kertész's journey through a *Day of Paris* and later in David Attie's *Saloon Society.*

awareness of the interaction of two isolated photographs is experienced throughout the book. Individual portraits of people in cafés, bars, and restaurants are made to "converse" across the spread with inanimate objects and other unrelated characters. Even when a single photograph by Kertész is bled across the gutter of the book, it is still done in such a way as to establish a dialogue between the reader and the image. For instance, on pages 12 and 13 we are initially drawn to the layout by the single figure on the left-hand page. Accentuating the movement of the woman and her cats, Brodovitch directs our gaze by allowing a third of the image to flow on to the right-hand side of the page. Following the woman we feel compelled to turn the page and continue with the story.

In 1985, just months before his death, André Kertész still thought *Day of Paris* one of his most successful books. Commending Brodovitch's treatment of his work, he believed that it could still be reissued in the same format.[8] According to Pierre Borhan in his introduction to *André Kertész: His Life and Work*, Kertész "used this book to remind himself of good memories of old friends and to present himself to the decision-makers in the world of publishing."[9] *Day of Paris* was a book that offered Kertész a nostalgic vision of Paris, one that predated the disturbance of war. Even in 1945, critics focused on the highly romantic picture that *Day of Paris* painted of the city. In a review of the book, "A Mood from the Dim Past," Elliot Paul said that the book represented "not Paris, the political capital of France, not Paris at work, or Paris at play.... The figures that arrest his eye are walking. No one is doing anything useful, there are no large crowds."[10] Even though he lived in Paris for over a decade, Kertész was still an outsider there. For those American soldiers returning from Europe his vision struck a cord, resonating with emotional memories of their time abroad.

Clearly appealing to his own recollections of Paris, Brodovitch returned to this subject in another photographic monograph two years later. In 1947, almost as a response to his criticisms of Kertész's work, Elliot Paul produced his own book on the life of the city with the photographer Fritz Henle. Published in Chicago by Ziff Davis, *Paris* was another title that attempted to capture the postwar enthusiasm for all things Parisian. Similar to Kertész, the German photographer Fritz Henle had spent some time in Paris during the thirties, before emigrating to America. For many years after arriving in New York, Henle neglected the large body of work he had produced in Europe. It was not until 1945 when he received a call from the *New York Times* asking him if he had "ever been to Paris" that Henle decided to print up all 150 of his negatives.[11] The resulting images featured in the *New York Times* Sunday supplement were deemed such a success that they were collated and published as a monograph a year later. Henle, who worked at *Harper's Bazaar* from 1945 to 1950, greatly admired Brodovitch. The "combination of his fine vision and my creativity resulted in some of the finest pages in *Harper's Bazaar*," he once said. "This great artist accepted my approach without question, and I well remember how proud I felt when I visited his art department and saw large photostats of my pictures, some of which have since become well known."[12] Since Henle was working with him at the time, Brodovitch was the natural choice when it came to selecting a designer for *Paris*. Stressing the creative partnership between the photographer and designer, Henle considered the book "our greatest accomplishment."[13]

Hellas and *Egypt*

Prior to the success of *Ballet* and *Day of Paris*, Brodovitch had worked on several other titles for J. J. Augustin. In 1943 he designed two books by the photographer George Hoyningen-Huene. A fellow Russian aristocrat born just two years after Brodovitch, Huene had worked for *Harper's Bazaar* for eleven years from 1935 to 1946. Unlike many of the other photographers Brodovitch hired during this period, such as Erwin Blumenfeld and Leslie Gill, Huene's images were rather formal and self-contained. Similar to the work of de Meyer, it was a style of photography totally at odds with Brodovitch's desire to bleed images off the page and crop them at surprising angles. One can only assume that, as opposed to the highly impressionistic imagery of these other photographers, Huene's straightforward style at *Bazaar* placated the large fashion houses who clearly thought they had paid to see every stitch and button on their garments. It does seem, however, that Huene's association with Brodovitch did over time lessen the strict formality of his photographs. And Brodovitch responded to this by creating elegant designs that worked *with* his images, rather than against them. His treatment of Huene's work evidently impressed J. J. Augustin when it came to publishing two of his monographs.

The first of Huene's books that Brodovitch designed was *Hellas: A Tribute to Classical Greece*. Produced to support the Greek War Relief Committee, *Hellas* is similar to *Day of Paris* in its understated arrangement of text and image. The book consists of various images of the Acropolis, the temples and theaters of Agrolis and Attica, and numerous other photographs of Greek sculpture and the natural landscape. Huene's images in *Hellas* incorporate the uncluttered and clean geometric lines that can be seen in his fashion spreads. "These would never please the architects, who want blueprints," Huene said of the work, "but I wanted to interpret ancient buildings and ancient sites and glamorize them, just as I have done with beautiful women."[14] Set in Brodovitch's favorite type, Bodoni, the text consists of individual quotations from Aeschylus, Aristophanes, Byron, Emerson, Milton, and Sophocles among others by twentieth-century writers. Once again, the text was edited, alongside Huene and Hugh Chisholm, by *Bazaar's* George Davies.

The book begins with an image of a barren rock; facing this is a quote from Aeschylus's *Prometheus Bound*. From this we are taken on a tour of ancient Greece that asks us to value the ruins of a once noble and heroic culture. Throughout the monograph Brodovitch places most of Huene's images one to a double-page. On most occasions the images do not fill the whole page, but are gently balanced with the paragraphs of text that are set in extravagant amounts of white space. As with *Day of Paris* Brodovitch occasionally places two contrasting images opposite each other to achieve surprising graphic contrasts. The overall outcome of Brodovitch's sparse design is that it lends an imposing, if delicate, weight to the monumental and historic subject matter.

The second book Brodovitch designed in 1943 for J. J. Augustin and Hoyningen-Huene was another thesis on ancient civilization, *Egypt*. As with *Hellas*, Egypt charts this ancient culture through a collection of photographs of Egyptian temples, statues, and works of art. Unlike *Hellas*, however, *Egypt* is a more conventional photographic monograph. While we still see striking full-page enlargements of Huene's work, smaller photographs are frequently integrated into the main body of text. We don't see any of the mirroring of text and image witnessed in the previous book. In the traditional sense of illustrations, the content of Huene's images serve as simple appendages to George Steindorf's essay. Brodovitch's design echoes this.

To what extent Brodovitch was actively involved in other book designs at J. J. Augustin is unknown. Looking at a collection of photographic titles issued by this small publishing house in the mid-forties, it does seem that Brodovitch had an uncredited hand in their visual conception. Two more Huene titles, *Mexican Heritage* (1946) and *Baalbeck/Palmyra* (1946), contain several graphic elements that point to Brodovitch's involvement, including a synthesis of image and text, a generous use of white space, and a favoring of Bodoni over any other typeface.

Jacket design and interior spread from *Hellas: A Tribute to Classical Greece* by George Hoyningen-Huene. New York: J. J. Augustin, 1943.

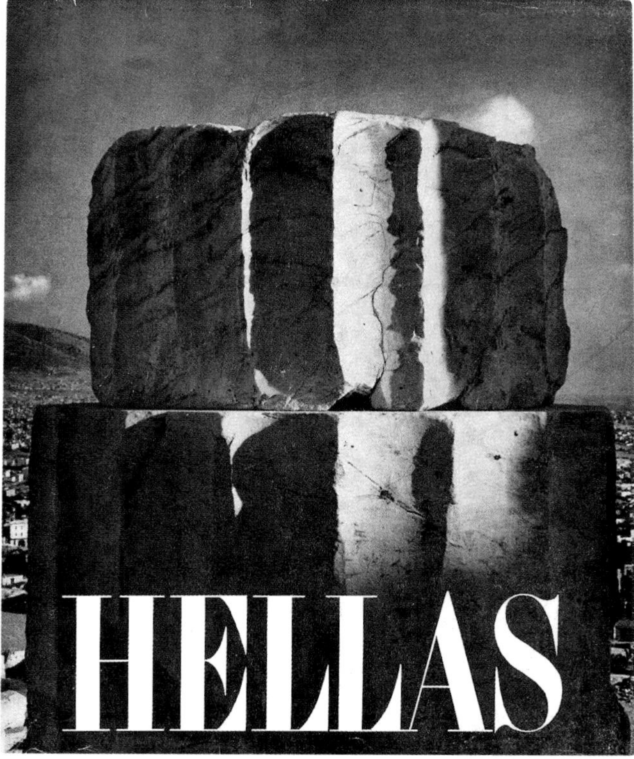

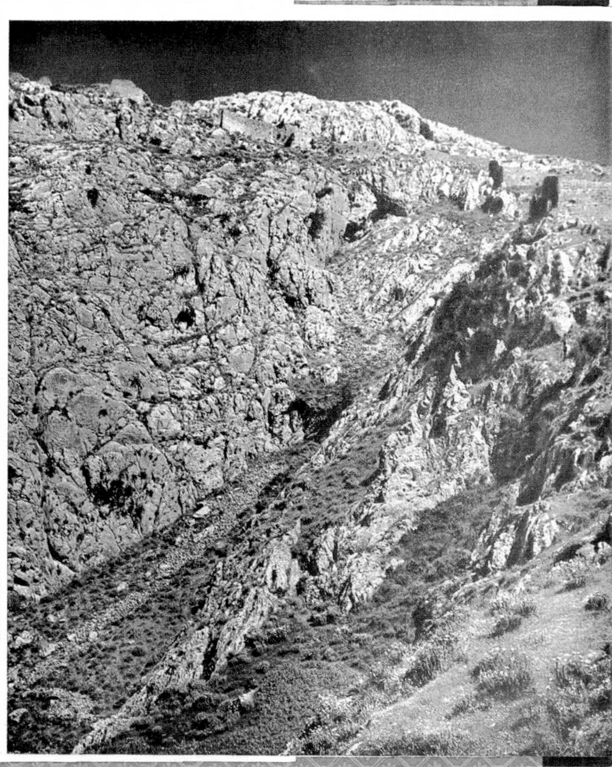

in confusion. No houses of brick raised in the warmth of the sun they had, nor fabrics of wood, but like the little ants they dwelt underground in the sunless depth of caverns. No certain sign of approaching winter they knew, no harbinger of flowering spring or fruitful summer; ever they labored at random, till I taught them to discern the seasons by the rising and the obscure setting of the stars. Numbers I invented for them, the chiefest of all discoveries; I taught them the grouping of letters, to be a memorial and record of the past, the mistress of the arts and mother of the Muses. I first brought under the yoke beasts of burden, who by draft and carrying relieved men of their hardest labors; I yoked the proud horse to the chariot, teaching him obedience to the reins, to be the adornment of wealth and luxury. I too contrived for sailors sea-faring vessels with their flaxen wings. Alas for me! such inventions I devised for mankind, but for myself I have no cunning to escape disaster.

LEADER OF THE CHORUS

Sorrow and humiliation are your portion: you have failed in understanding and gone astray; and like a poor physician falling into sickness you despond and know not the remedies for your own disease.

PROMETHEUS

Hear but the rest, and you will wonder more at my inventions and many arts. If sickness visited them, they had no healing drug, no salve or soothing potion, but wasted away for want of remedies, and this was my greatest boon; for I revealed to them the mingling of bland medicaments for the banishing of all diseases. And many modes of divination I appointed: from dreams I first taught them to judge what should befall in waking state; I found the subtle interpretation of words half heard or heard by chance, and of meetings by the way; and the flight of taloned birds with their promise of fortune or failure I clearly denoted, their various modes of life, their mutual feuds, their friendships and consortings; I taught men to observe the smooth plumpness of entrails, and the color of the gall pleasing to the gods, and the mottled symmetry of liver-lobe. Burning the thigh-bones wrapt in fat and the long chine, I guided mankind to a hidden art, and read to them the intimations of the altar-flames that before were meaningless. So much then for these inventions. And the secret treasures of the earth, all benefits to men, copper, iron, silver, gold,—who but I could boast their discovery? No one, I ween, unless in idle vaunting. Nay, hear the whole matter in a word,—all human arts are from Prometheus.

Aeschylus

9

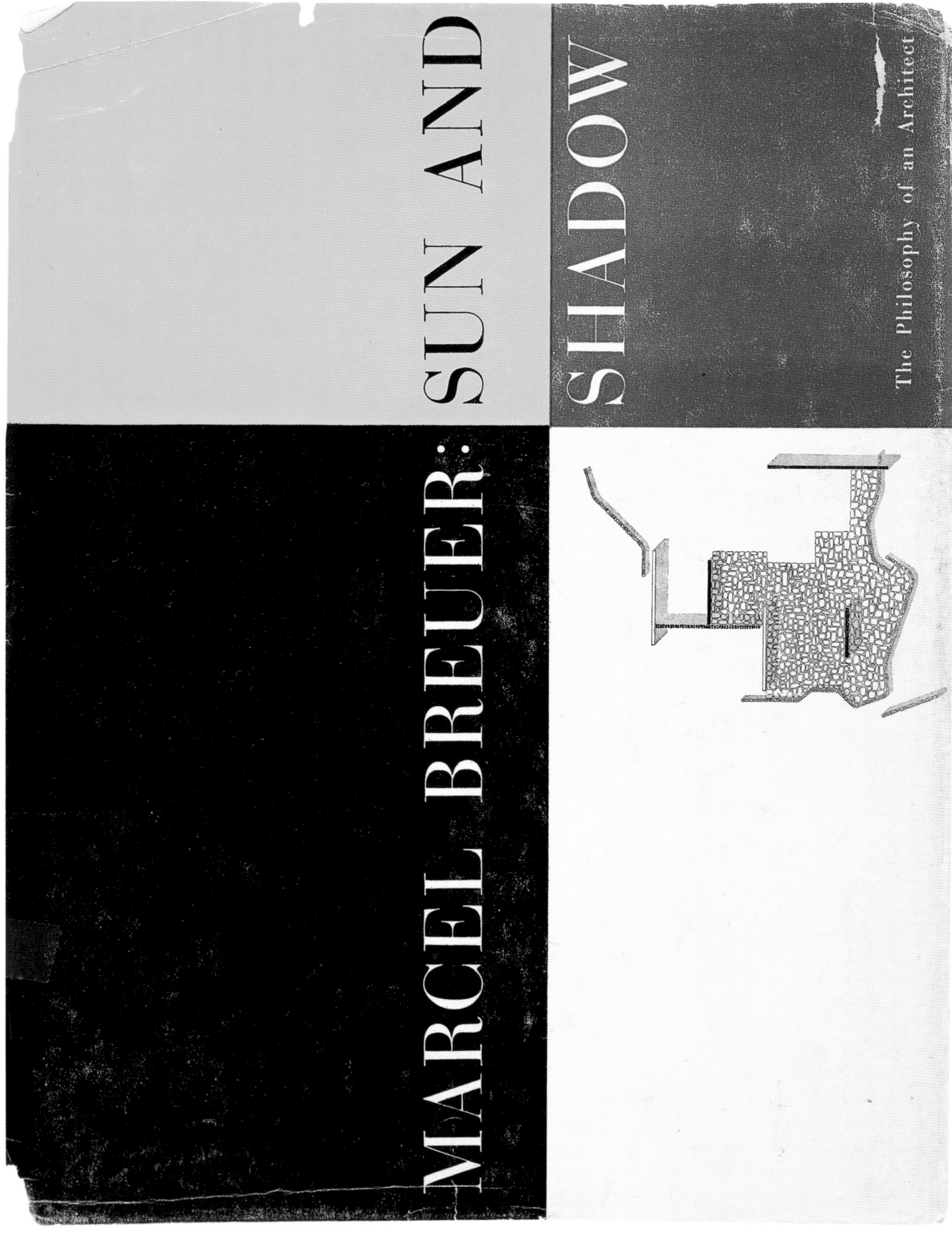
MARCEL BREUER: SUN AND
SHADOW
The Philosophy of an Architect

Sun and Shadow

It was nearly a decade before Brodovitch would design another artist's monograph. In 1956, he was commissioned by the publishers Longmans, Green and Company to design *Marcel Breuer: Sun and Shadow*. Brodovitch possibly came to the attention of the publishing company through the editor of *Sun and Shadow*, Peter Blake. Blake, managing editor of *Architectural Forum*, attended Brodovitch's Design Lab and was an enthusiastic admirer of Brodovitch's work. He said in 1961: "It seems to me that Brodovitch possesses two qualities that raise him above the level of all other graphic artists whose work I know: first, he has an unfailing, discriminating eye and is able to grasp the visual essentials of any picture or page and translate understanding into some of the most beautiful layouts I have ever seen; and secondly, he is a perfectionist craftsman of such extraordinary high standards that he is probably fast becoming an anachronism."[15] Blake's creative relationship with Brodovitch was cemented in 1961, when Brodovitch designed the cover of Blake's book *The Master Builders*.

Brodovitch opens the book with a closely cropped image of Breuer himself. What is surprising about the image is that it is turned on its side, presented in a landscape format. Brodovitch proceeds to use this technique throughout the book. The opening chapter design is a featureless photograph of Breuer's iconic tubular steel cantilever chair. Obviously familiar with Breuer's Bauhaus work, Brodovitch recognizes the centrality of this design to his oeuvre – it is the only illustration in a chapter heading that receives a whole page. All the other sections display a design or a small feature of Breuer's work horizontally cropped by the title of the chapter. On the whole *Sun and Shadow* is not one of Brodovitch's most inspired works. The most interesting feature of the book is the secondary application of three primary colors to images of Breuer's architectural designs. In a monochrome book these blocks of color printed onto the photographs of Breuer's buildings bring the page alive. They are highly reminiscent of the de Stijl aesthetic and specifically bring to mind the famous modernist house of Schröder-Schrader designed by Gerrit Rietveld in 1924.

Opposite and below: Jacket and interior spreads from *Marcel Breuer: Sun & Shadow*, edited by Peter Blake. New York: Longmans, Green and Company, 1956.
The work of Marcel Breuer held a life-long fascination for Brodovitch. He enlivened the pages of Breuer's book by surprinting blocks of primary colors on selected areas of the photographs.

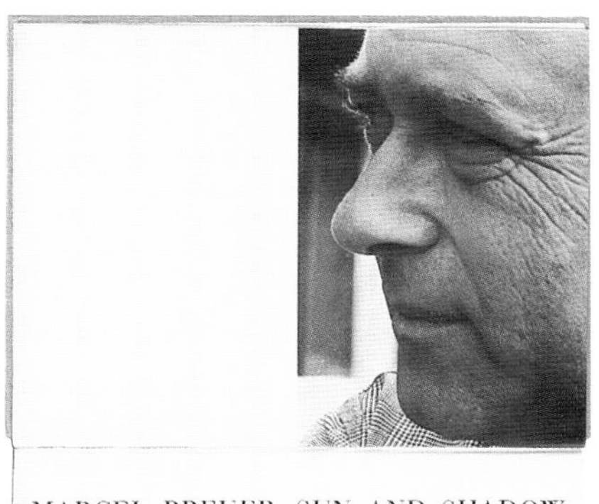

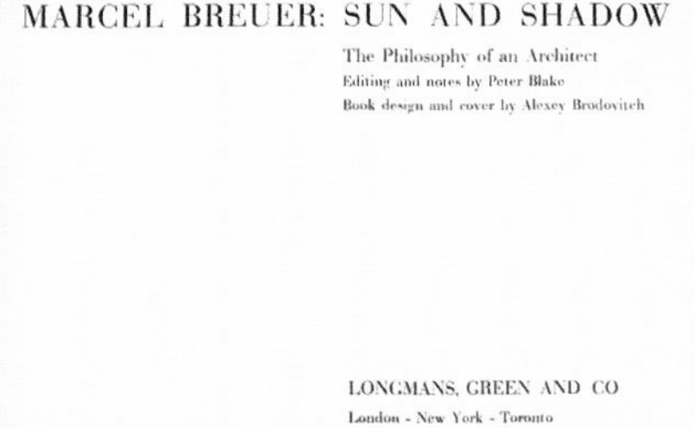

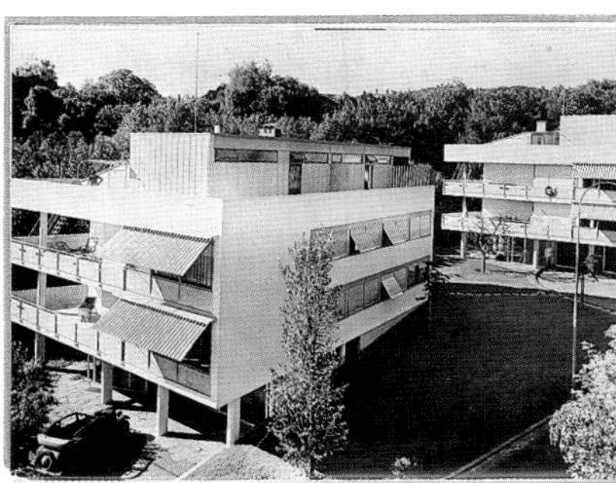

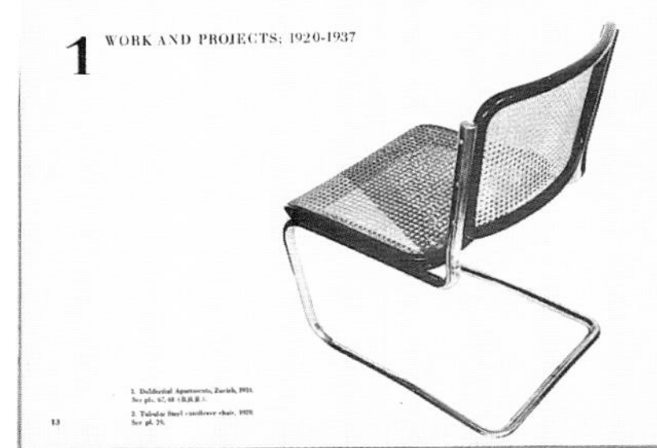

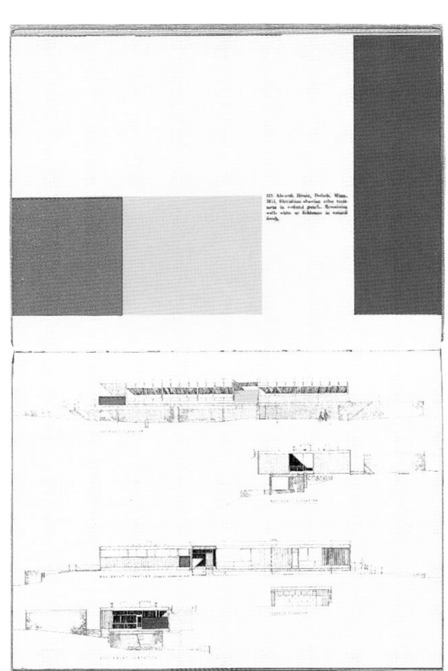

Slipcase for *Observations*. Photographs by Richard Avedon, text by Truman Capote. New York: Simon & Schuster, 1959.

Observations

Observations is the zenith of Brodovitch's book designs. Representing a pinnacle in the world of photographic publishing, it marks the synthesis of three individuals at the height of their creative powers. Richard Avedon's images, Truman Capote's text, and Brodovitch's design all came together to produce a visual experience that was a tour de force of graphic invention. Published in 1959 by the prestigious Swiss publishers of *Camera* magazine, C. J. Bucher, *Observations* signaled a turning point in the expectations and possibilities of what could be done with a photographic monograph. Presented in a slipcase, the dimensions of the book are a considerable 11 by 14 inches. Printed in the sheet-fed gravure method, which lends an almost corporeal sensation to the images, it is an object of exceptional opulence. Throughout the book we see all the familiar leitmotifs of Brodovitch's *Harper's Bazaar* designs. However, free from the limitations of advertising that frequently curtailed Brodovitch's layouts to two- or four-page spreads, Avedon's images are allowed to flow. In a true sense of the phrase, *Observations* is a "cinematic book."

Succeeding the bold lettering of the book's cover, set in red, blue, and gray uppercase Bodoni, the title page provides a dramatic opening to the monograph. What we see above the word "Avedon" located at the bottom of page 1, is an extended light-gray photograph that captures three costumed figures jumping into the air. In Jane Livingston's essay "The Art of Richard Avedon," featured in the 1995 catalogue *Evidence*, Avedon recounted the creation of this opening image:

> *That page is an example of a perfect collaboration. Those figures are the three crooks from a ballet by Jerome Robbins in the musical* High Button Shoes. *I thought the picture was a failure. So in the darkroom I tipped the easel both up and down, which elongated the image and gave it some of the elation I was looking for. I brought the results to Brodovitch as a square picture. He turned it into a column, which intensified everything.*[16]

By "stretching" the print, Avedon accentuated the upward stress of the dancers. Brodovitch further emphasizes the internal dynamics of the image by placing the photograph along the vertical axis of the page. This is the only photograph in *Observations* to be treated in this way. As the introductory image, it seems to function as a visual dedication. To whom it was intended would have been abundantly clear to the initiated admirers of Brodovitch's *Ballet*.

Following this opening, we then have three virtually blank pages with very little text apart from the announcement "Comments by Capote." This is succeeded by Capote's eloquent introduction of Avedon's work. Beyond these words the book then proceeds to advance a combination of experiences that are at times facetious, extravagant, reflective, and somber. Photographs that are barely contained by the edges of the book accost the viewer, precipitating moments of shock, surprise, and humor; the use of multiple portraits of the same individual compels us to question any claim for a "decisive moment"; connections are made across the layout on the basis of profession, emotion, or expression; sometimes a figure's performance is clarified by Capote's text, other times figures are left gesticulating to themselves in the empty white space. Aside from their disposition on the page the one thing that unites all these images is Avedon's apparent fascination with the human face. Though not just any human face. As Capote comments in the introduction, Avedon seems to have a fascination with "the elderly; and, even among the just middle-aged, [he] unrelentingly tracks down every hard-earned crow's-foot."

Observations is the culmination of Avedon's postwar work. In this respect it represents the two areas that held most fascination for him during this period. The early images are primarily portraits of stars of the stage and screen. These photographs, as the critic Janet Malcolm recognized, are "characterised by their aliveness and (often exaggerated) expressiveness, and the photographer's conception of the subject as the embodiment of what he does: comedians are shown mugging, singers singing, actors acting, professional beauties being beautiful. At this point, the fashion work and the portraiture are stylistically and emotionally of a piece; both are animated by an innovator's spirit of experiment and risk-taking, and a young man's wish to please and dazzle."[17] Avedon's desire to "please and dazzle" is obviously due to the fact that many of these images first appeared in

OBSERVA
-TIONS

PHOTOGRAPHS BY

RICHARD
AVEDON

COMMENTS BY

TRUMAN
CAPOTE

The only front-rank artists that have been exclusively developed by the movie medium are, all too obviously, Garbo, Chaplin, a couple of cameramen, several directors, and the Italian screen-writer Cesare Zavattini.

An amiable hysteric with jutting chipmunk teeth, left-minded and a would-be hermit, Zavattini is the single original literary figure for which films can assume credit: if the form had gone uninvented, it is not likely that his writing would have amounted to much—pictorial plays are his true means of expression and, living in the hills beyond Rome far from the Via Veneto parade, he works on them with that isolated intensity one associates with the more dedicated poets; in result, he is in good measure responsible for the successes of De Sica, for whom he composed, among others, The Bicycle Thief, Shoe Shine, Miracle in Milan, Umberto D., *and, lately,* The Roof. *It is interesting that De Sica has never made a first-rate film not derived from Zavattini's work; after reading a half dozen of his scripts, the reason would seem to be:*

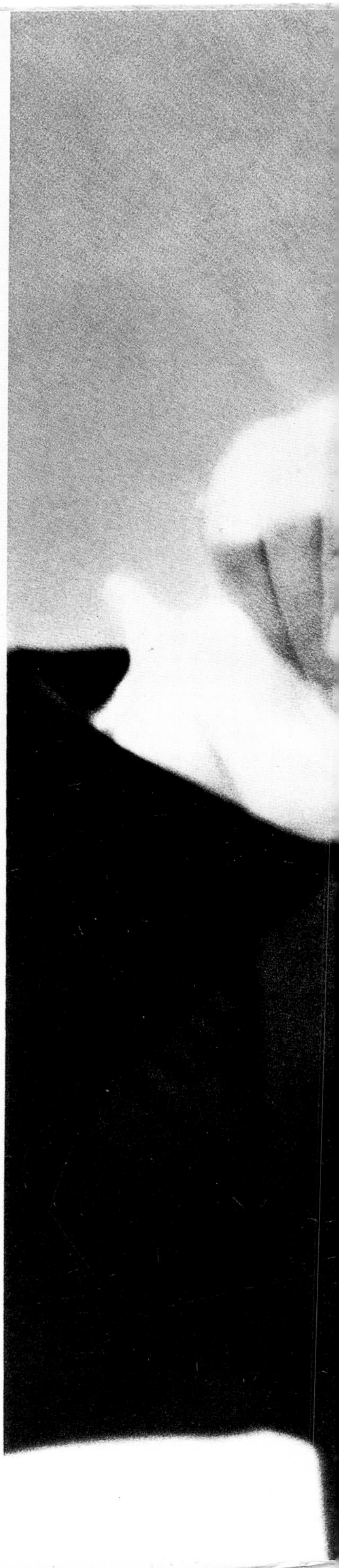

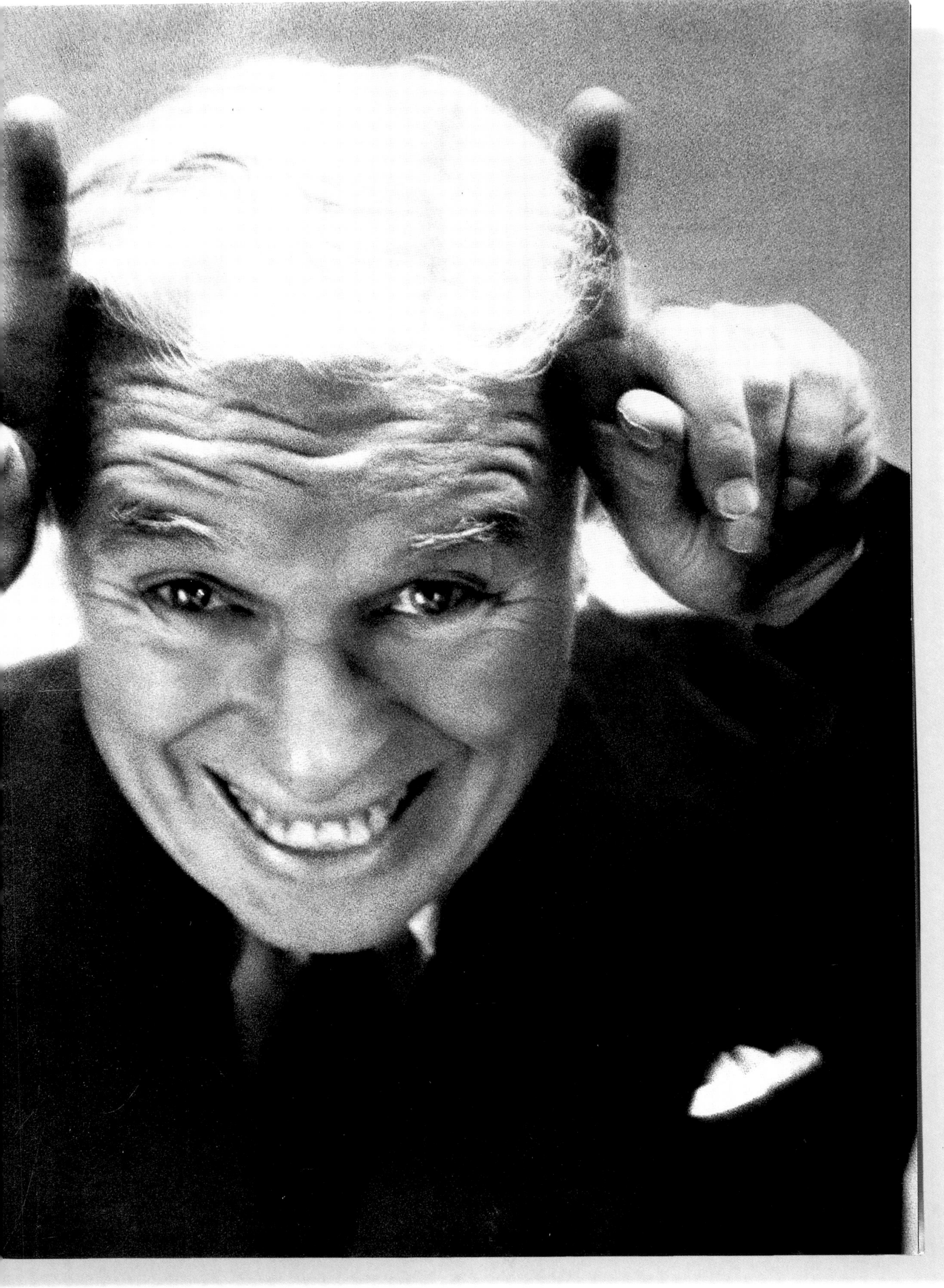

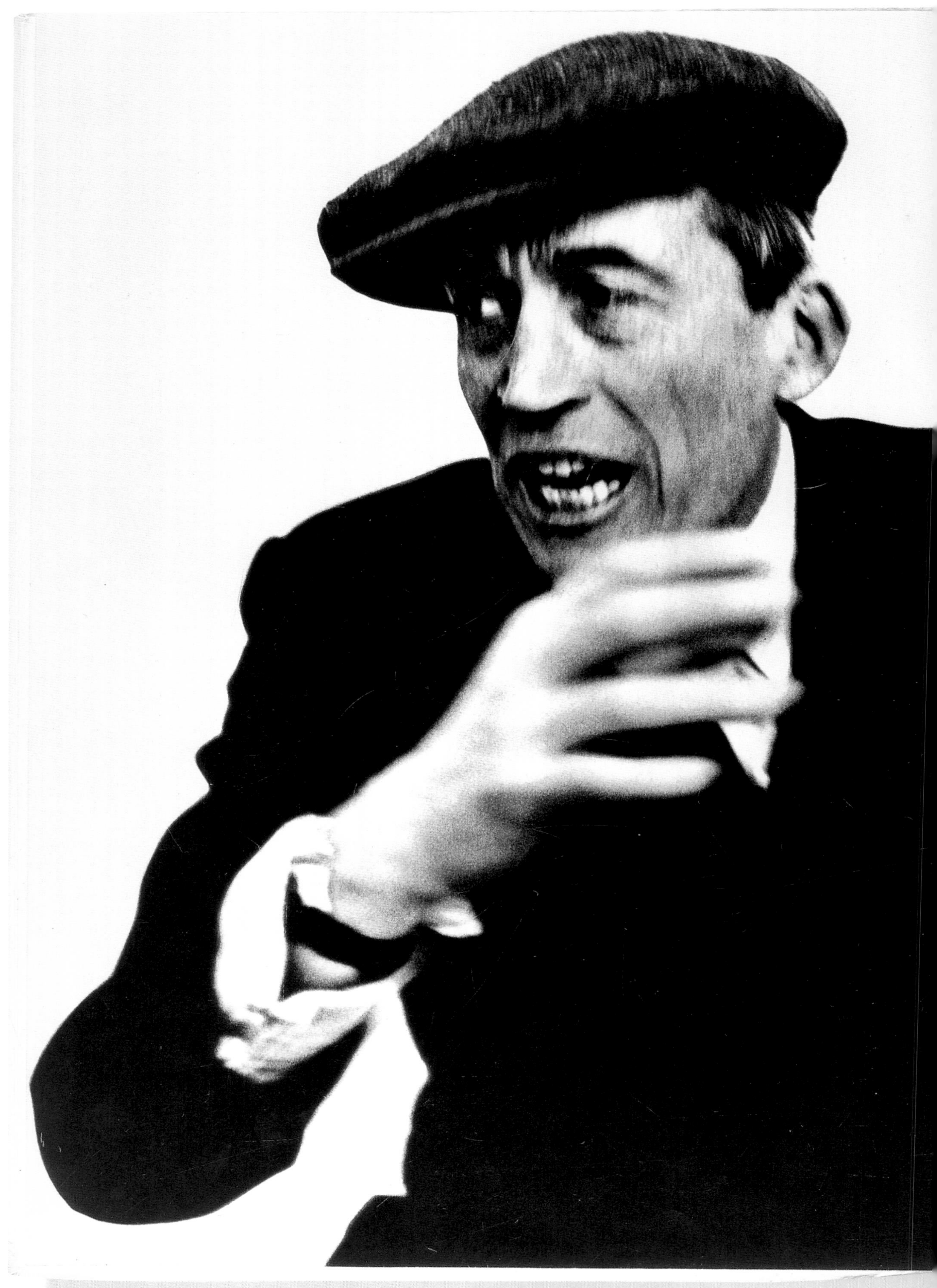

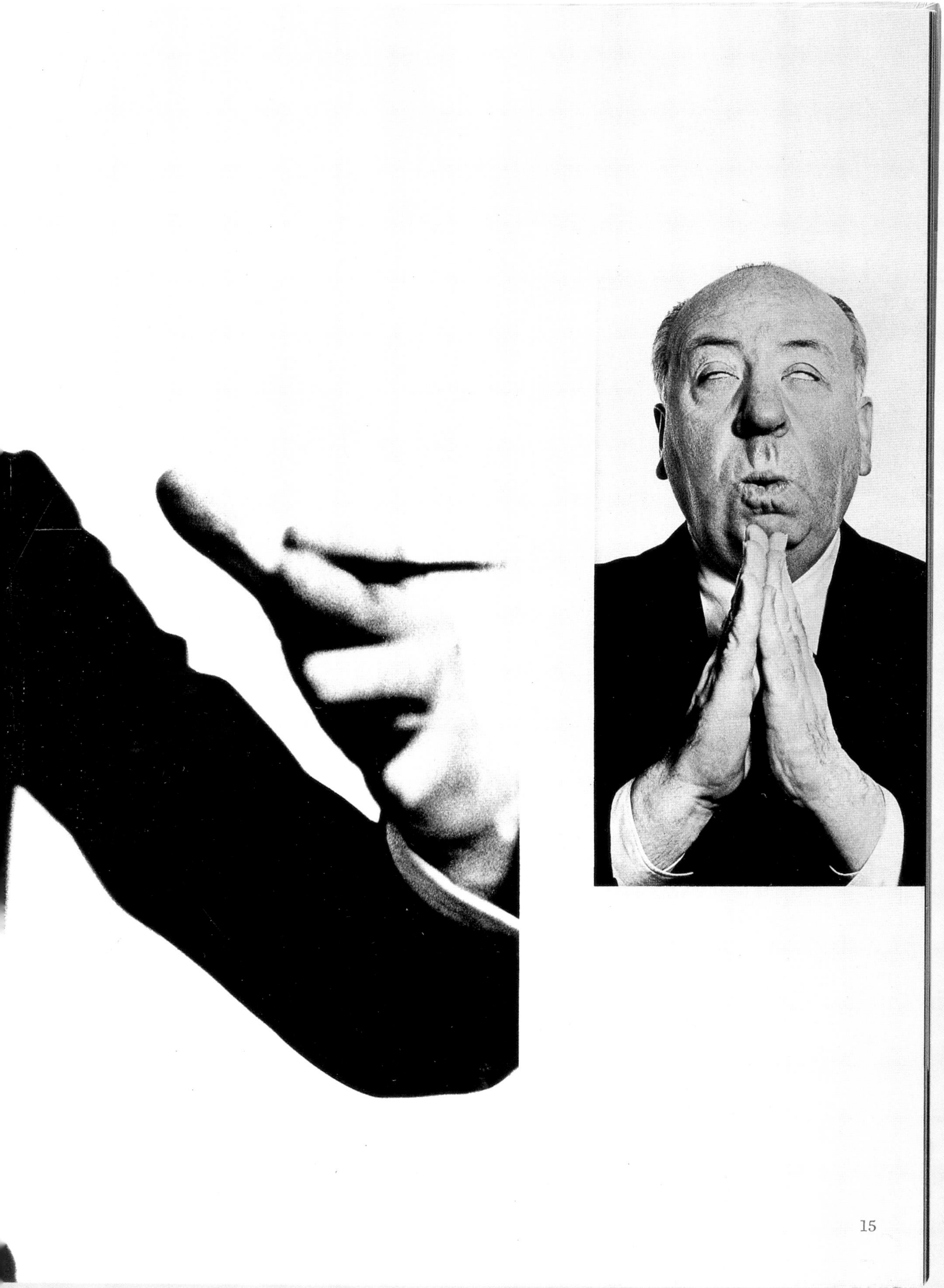

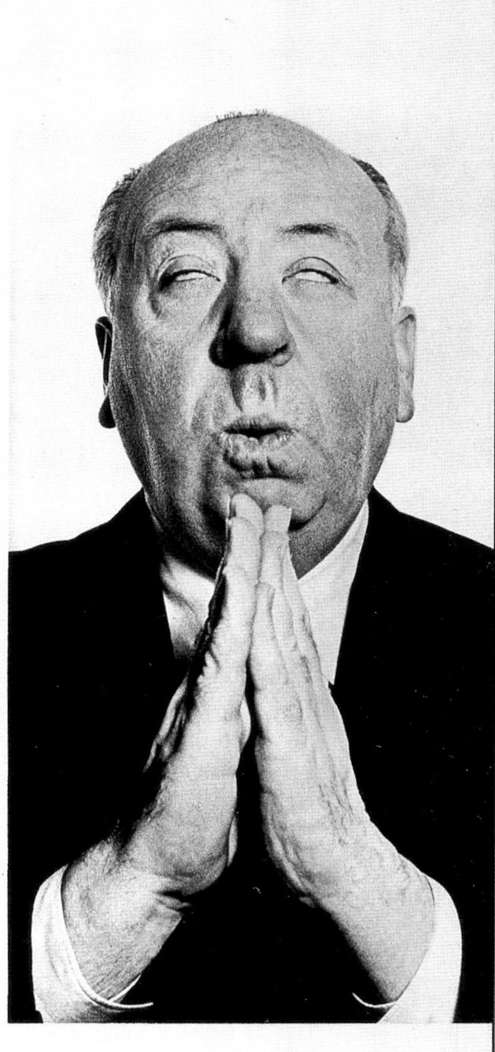
15

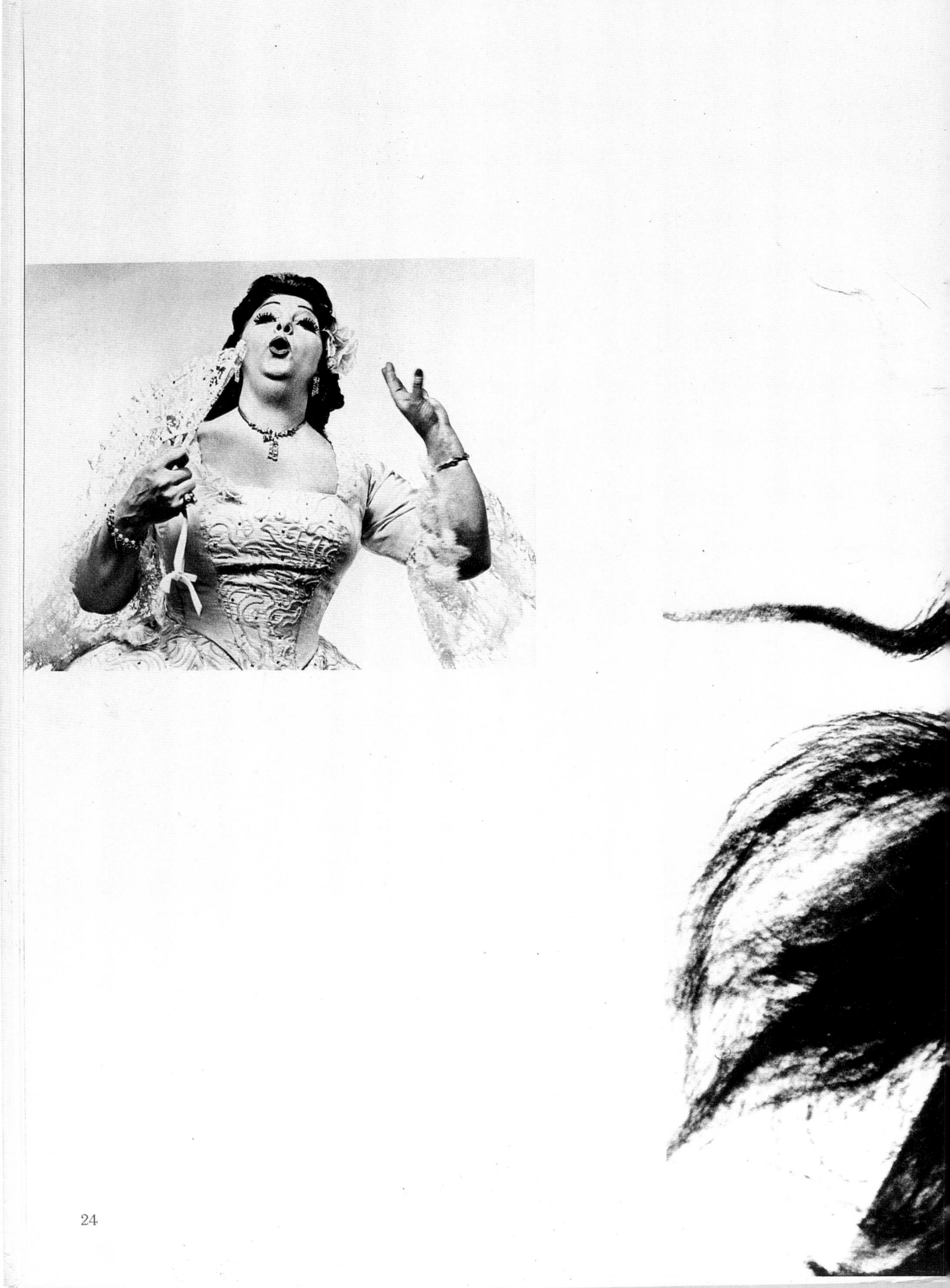

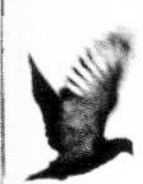

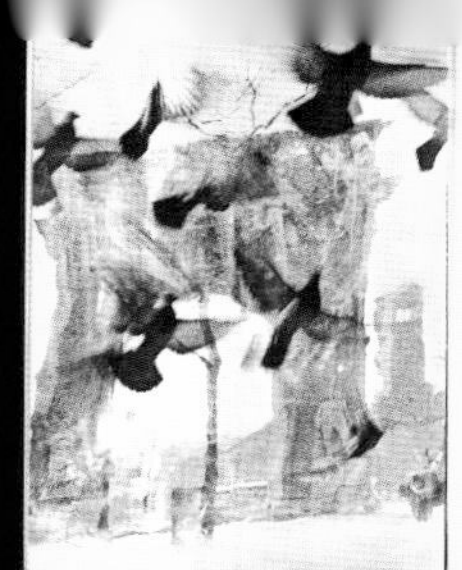

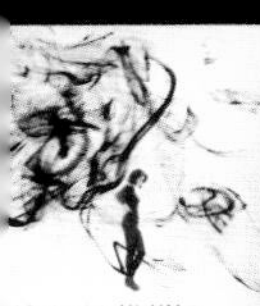

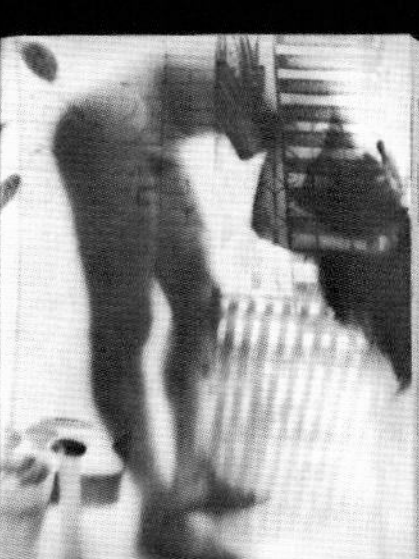

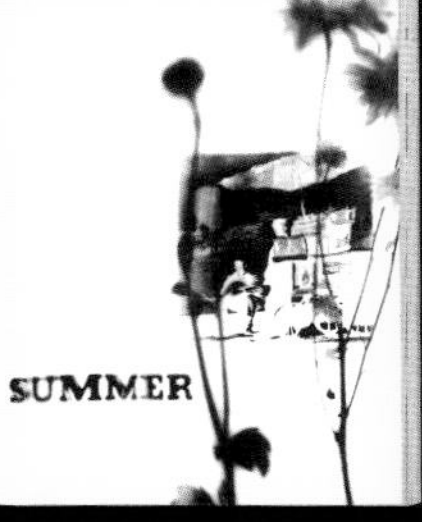

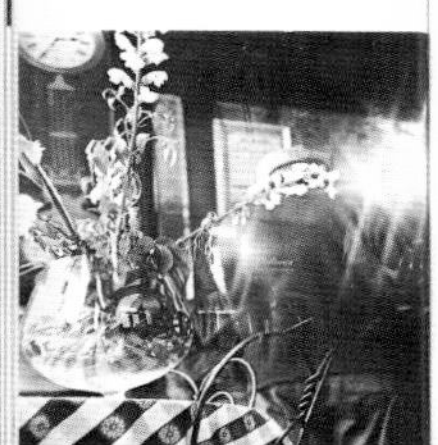

FALL

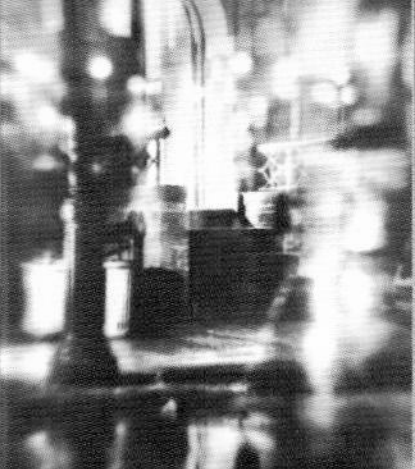

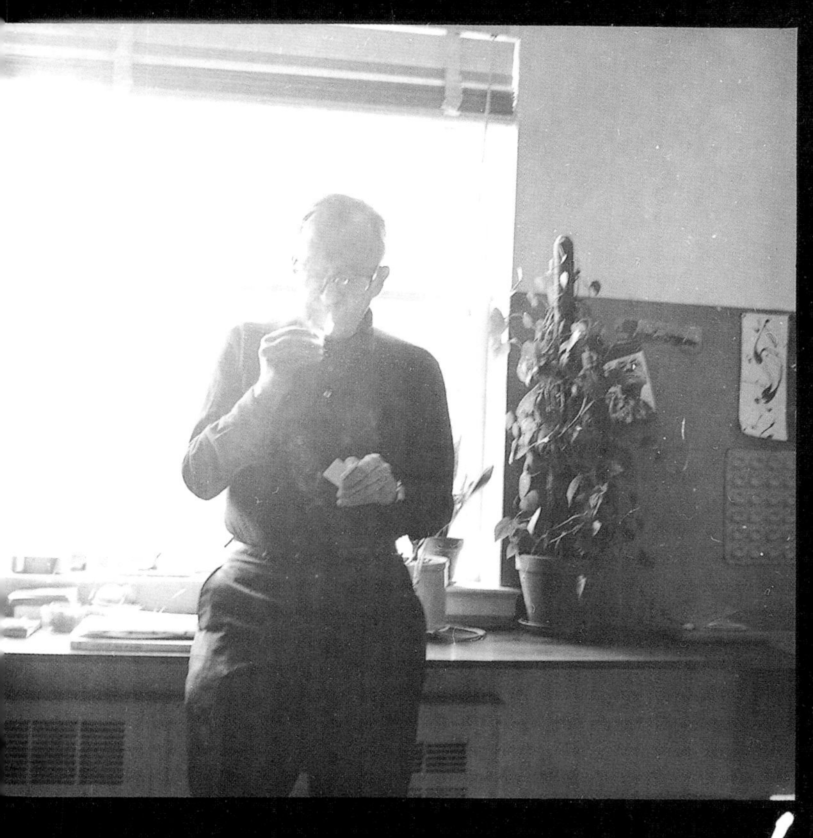
1

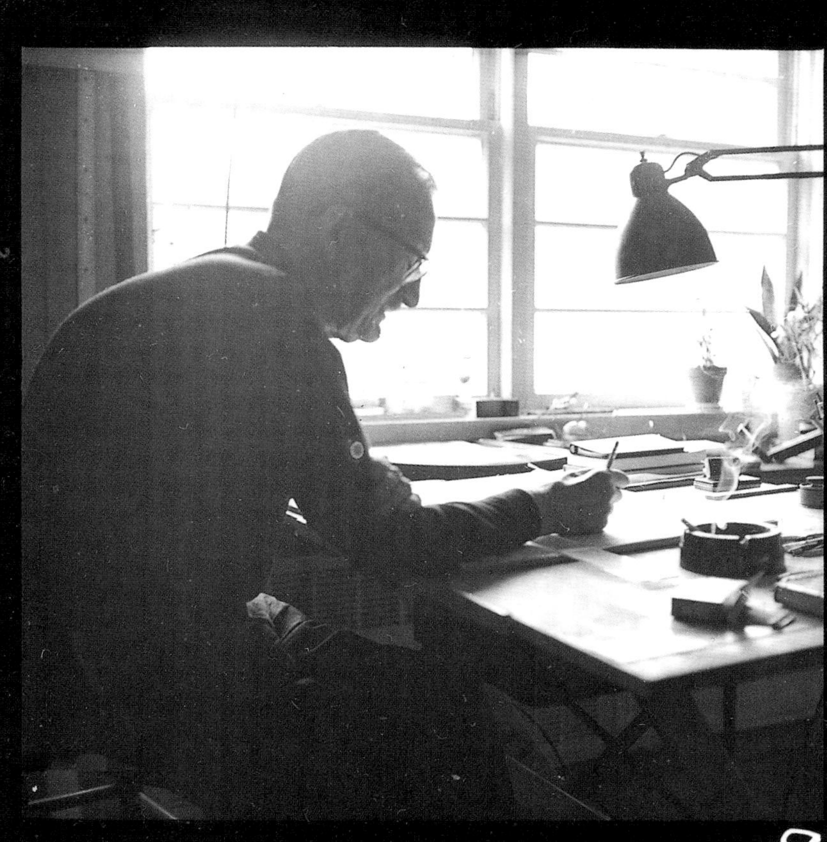
9

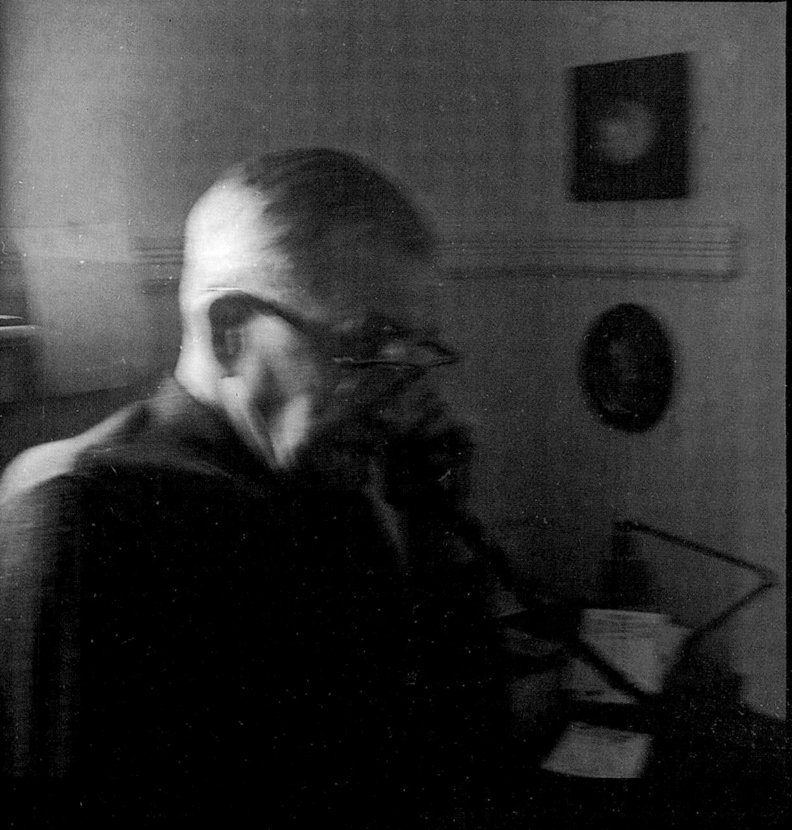
2

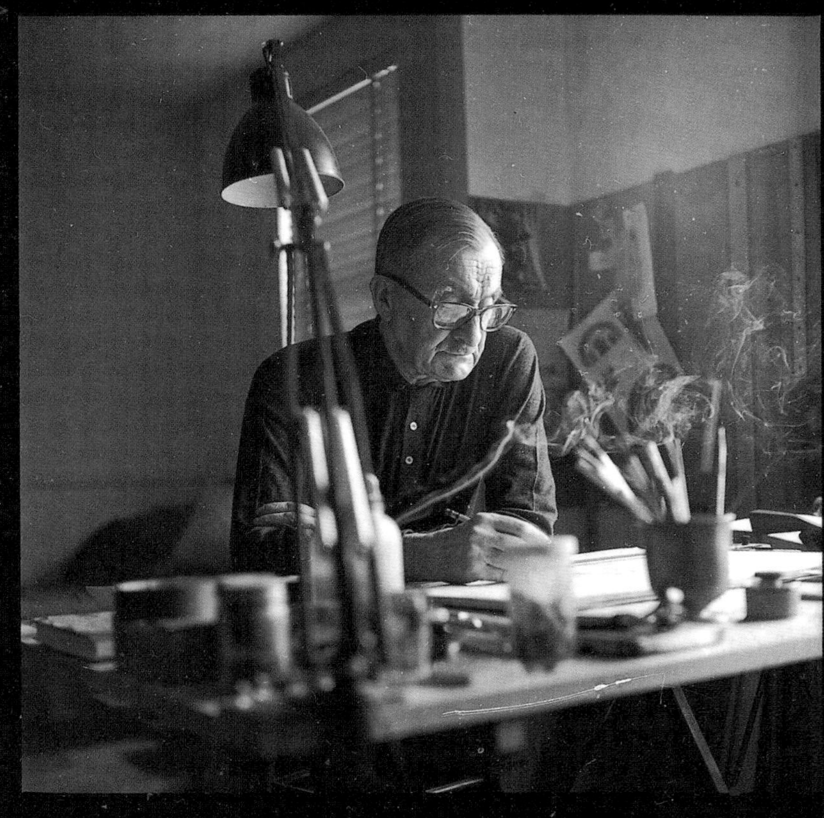
10

Brod had a... particular vision, you know, and we thought we could really do this with grace and elegance, which he did. – Frank Zachary

Portfolio

ALEXEY Brodovitch frequently referred to *Harper's Bazaar* as the "catalogue." For him, having to limit his considerable design skills to the repetitious illustration of the latest "must have" dress or "this season's" new shoe designs was obviously frustrating. Moreover, as *Bazaar* sought a large percentage of its revenue through advertising, the meager amount of editorial space allotted to Brodovitch placed an additional limitation on his desire to develop and advance new design ideas. It was probably the inherent constraints of the fashion magazine that partly accounted for his burgeoning interest in projects beyond the confines of *Bazaar* throughout the forties and fifties. Aside from the numerous book designs surveyed in the previous chapter, in 1949 Brodovitch also collaborated in the production of a new publication. Free from the restrictive obligations of the commercial world, *Portfolio* was Brodovitch's graphic sensibility unfettered. It has been widely acknowledged as the archetypal graphic design magazine of the twentieth century.

The idea for a publication that focused entirely on art and design, and would itself be an outstanding example of art and design, came from the imagination of art director Frank Zachary. "It was in 1948," recalled Zachary, "I was between jobs, and I thought to myself, my God I'd better get myself something permanent, my own operation, you know. So... I had a good friend in Cincinnati, George Rosenthal, who was a graduate of

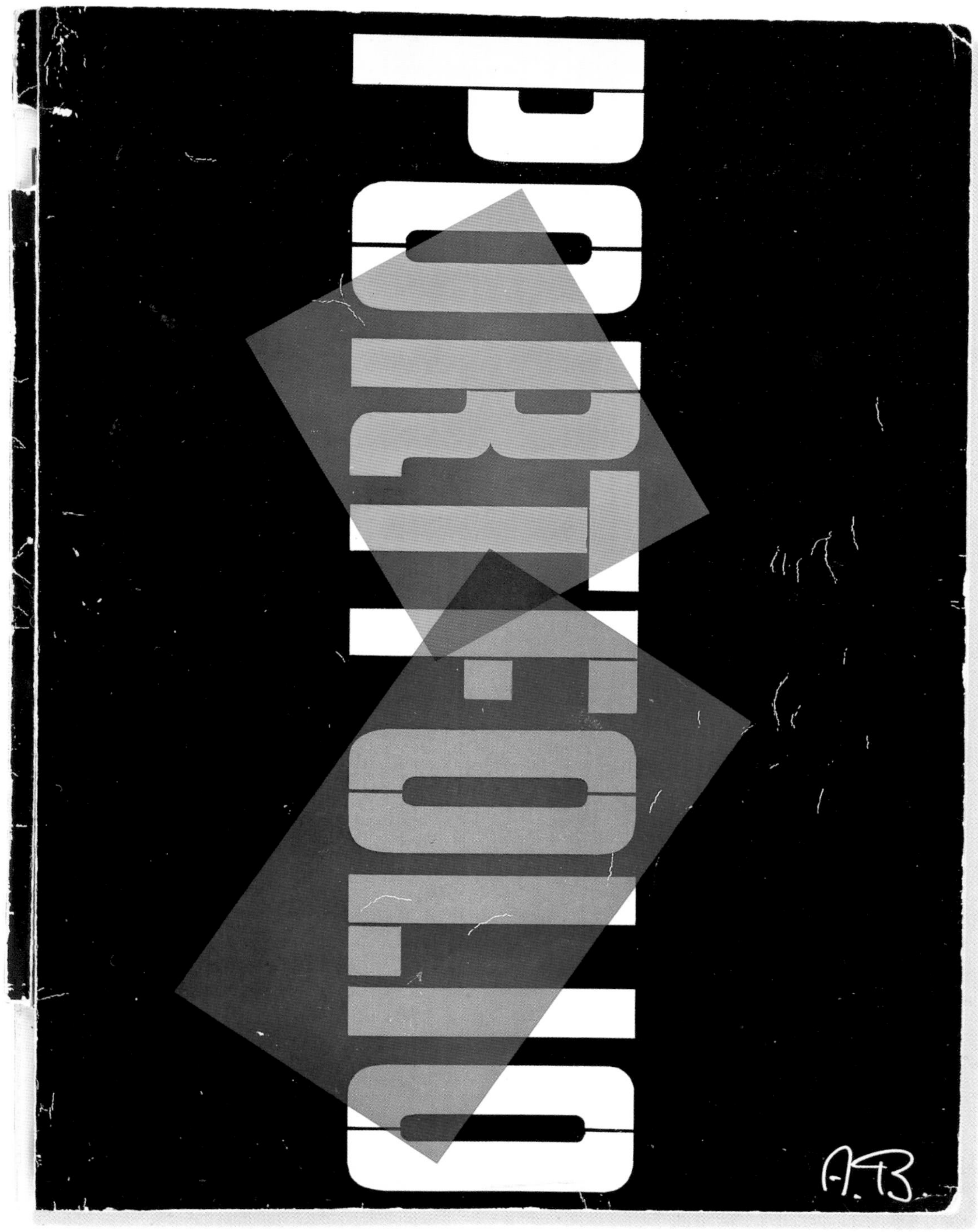

Page 195: Brodovitch at work in his studio, New York, c.1960. Photographs by Georges Tourdjman.

Left: Cover of *Portfolio* #1, winter 1950. Editors George S. Rosenthal and Frank Zachary. Cincinnati: Zebra Press.
By using only type on the cover – a practice unheard of in American magazines at the time – and placing two color filters over the *Portfolio* logo, Brodovitch announced his intention to produce a publication unlike any other.

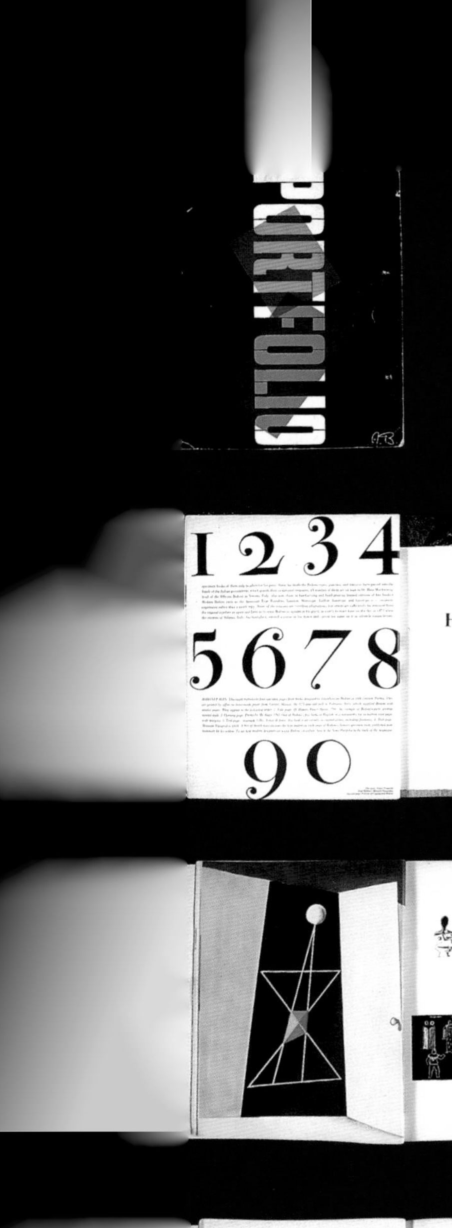
PORTFOLIO
1 2 3 4
5 6 7 8
9 0
Q. HORATII FLACCI OPERA
PARMAE
XENOGRAPHY

PORTFOLIO 1

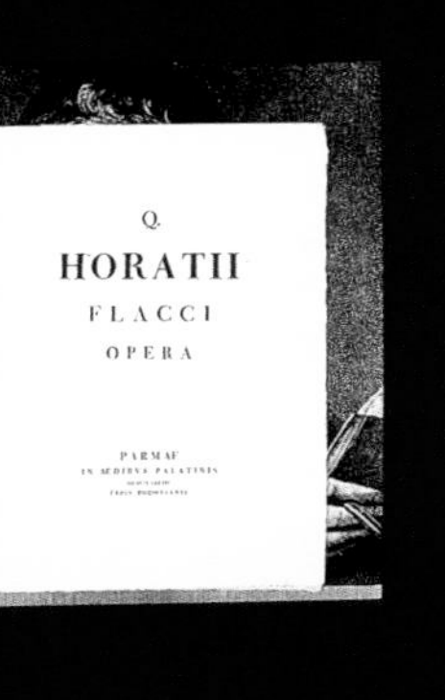

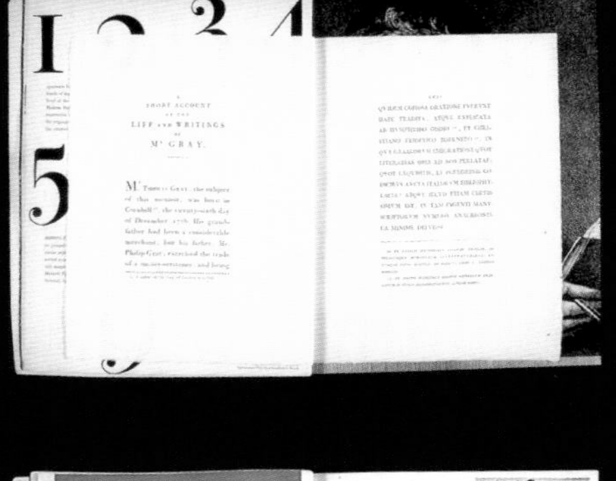

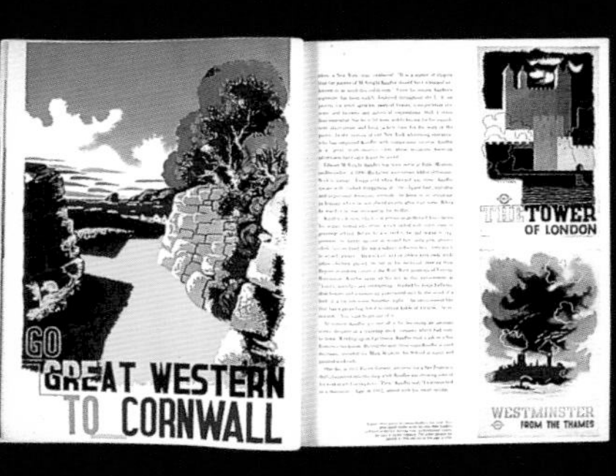
GO
GREAT WESTERN
TO CORNWALL
TOWER OF LONDON
WESTMINSTER
FROM THE THAMES

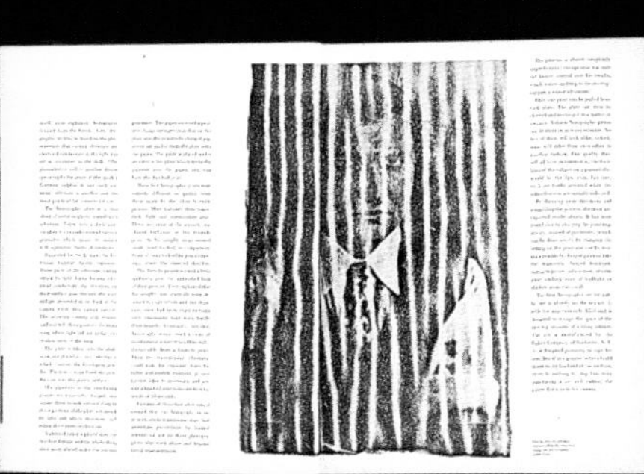

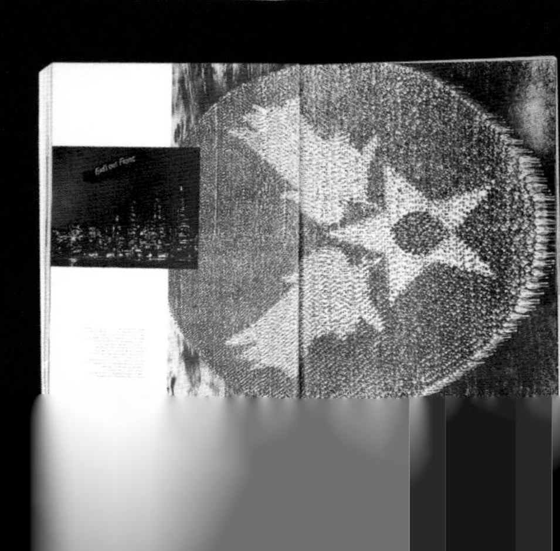

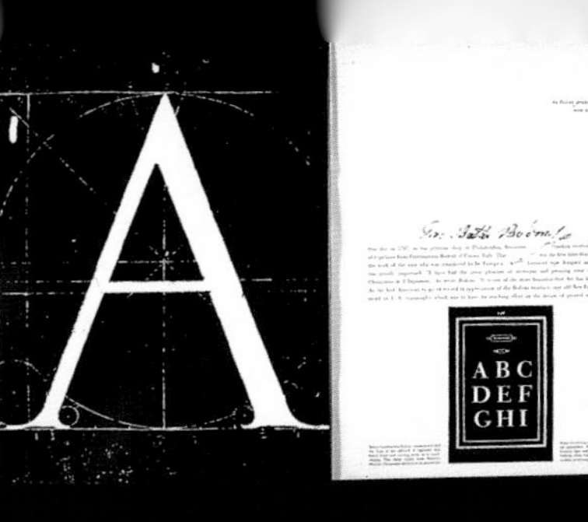
A
ABC
DEF
GHI

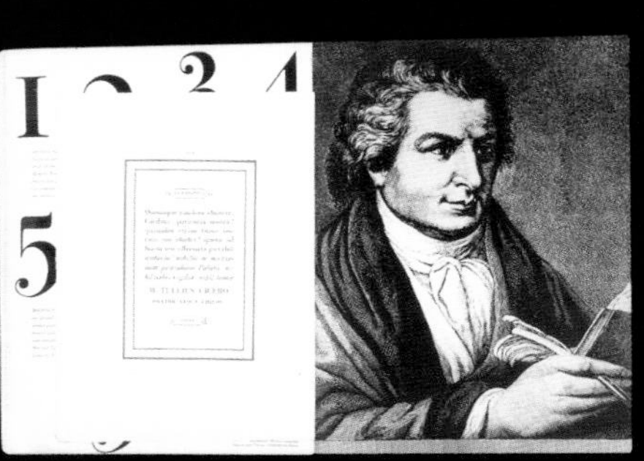

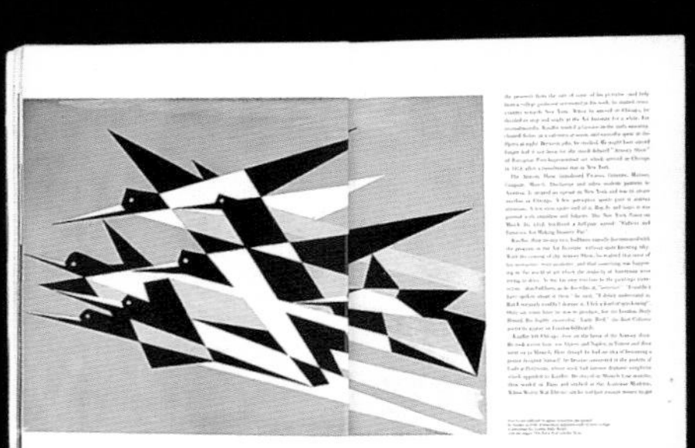

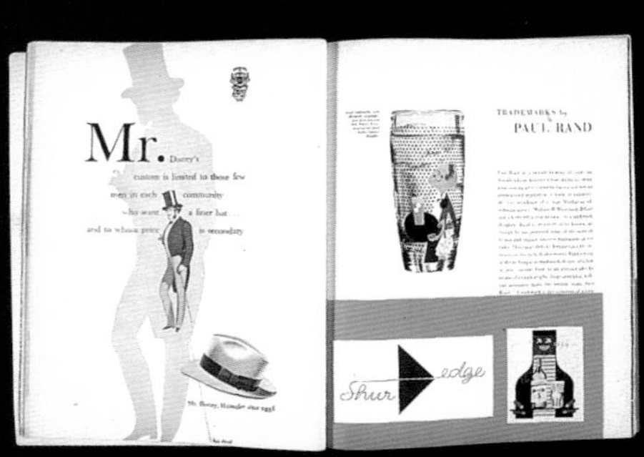
Mr.
TRADEMARKS by
PAUL RAND

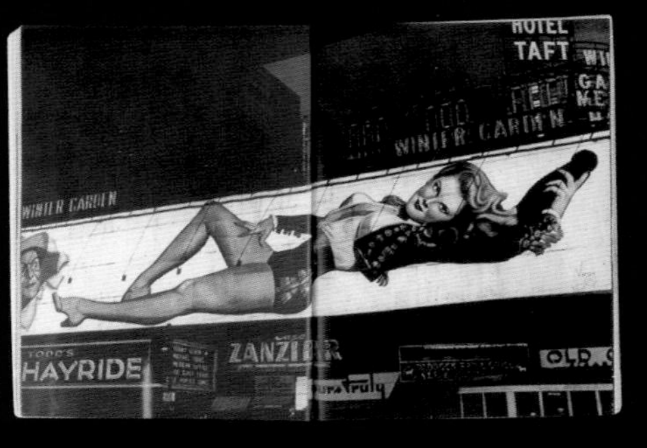
HOTEL
TAFT
WINTER GARDEN
HAYRIDE
ZANZIBAR

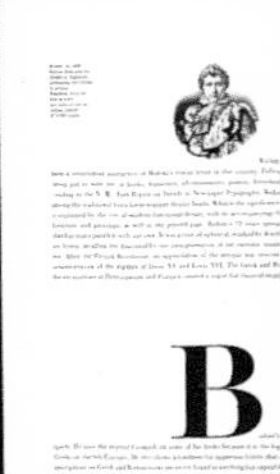
B

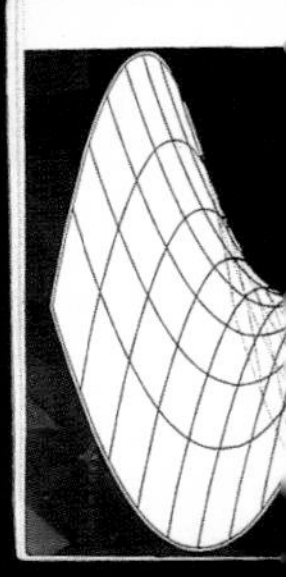

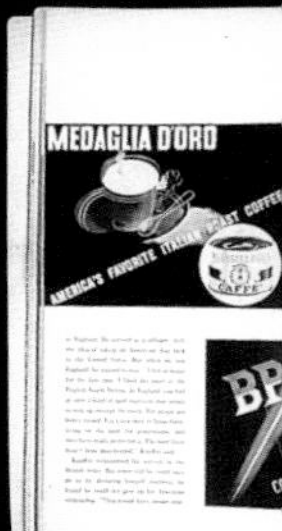
MEDAGLIA D'ORO

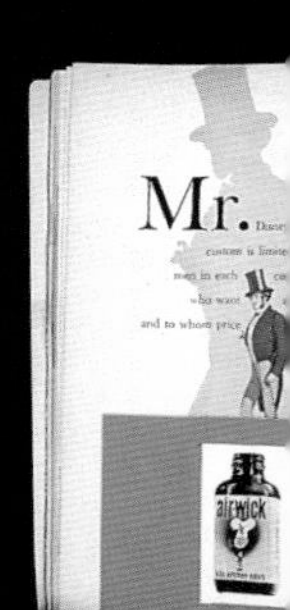
Mr.

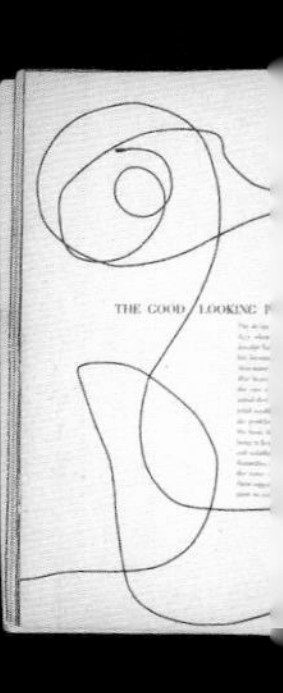

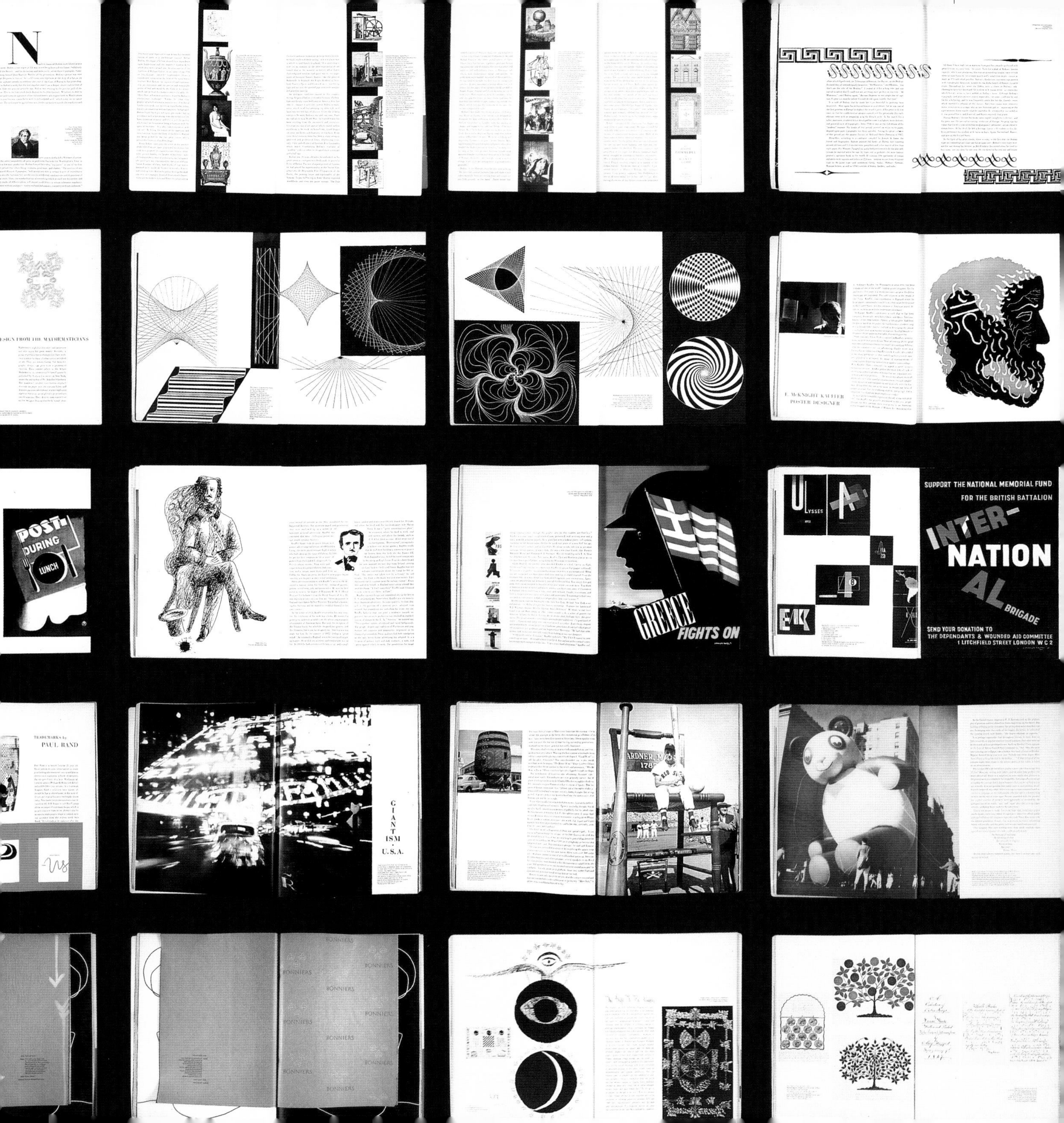

E. McKNIGHT KAUFFER
POSTER DESIGNER
POST DURING LUNCH
GREECE
FIGHTS ON
SUPPORT THE NATIONAL MEMORIAL FUND
FOR THE BRITISH BATTALION
INTER-
NATION
AL
BRIGADE
SEND YOUR DONATION TO
THE DEPENDANTS & WOUNDED AID COMMITTEE
1 LITCHFIELD STREET LONDON W C 2
TRADEMARKS by
PAUL RAND
GIANT
ISM
U.S.A.
BONNIERS

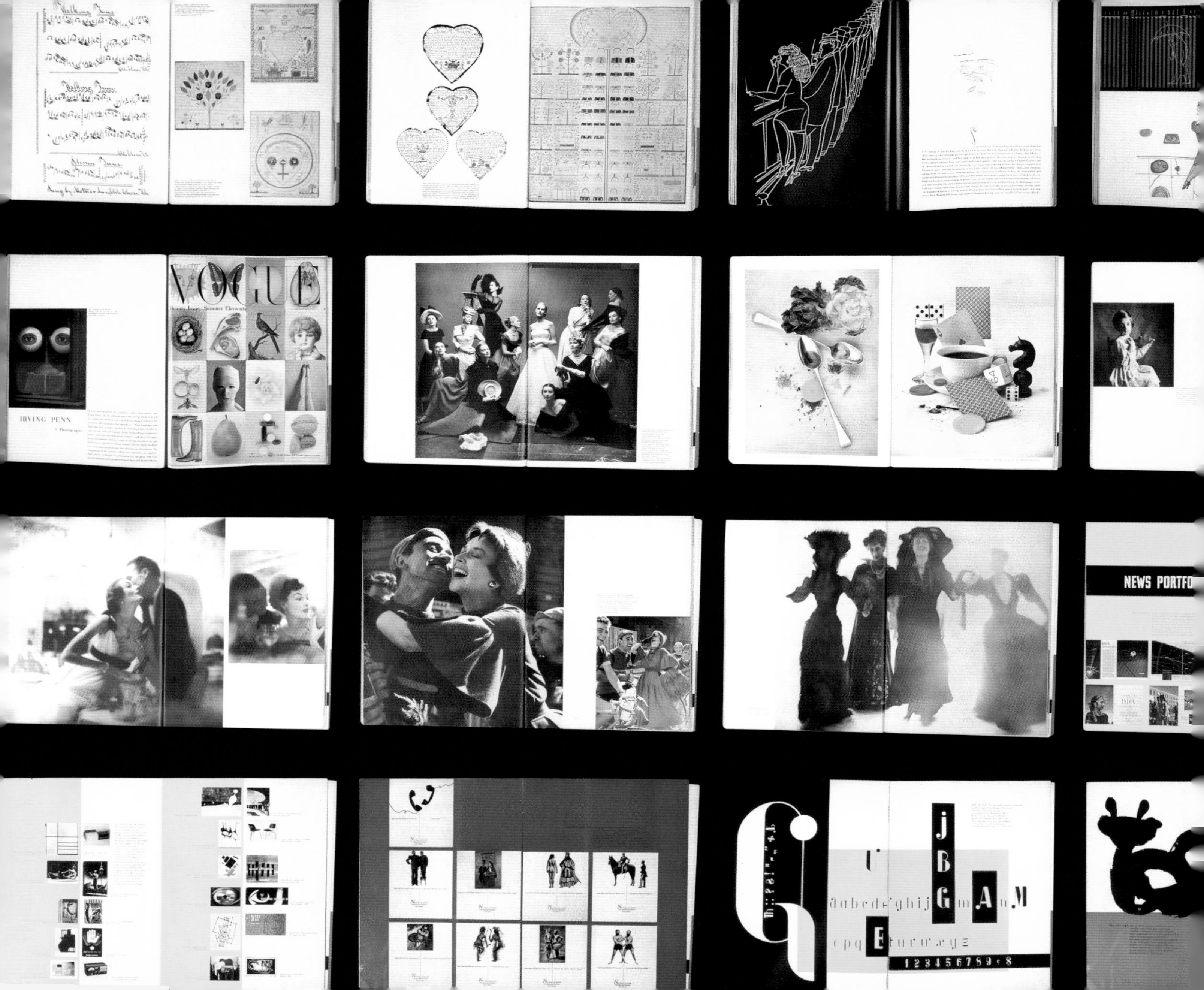

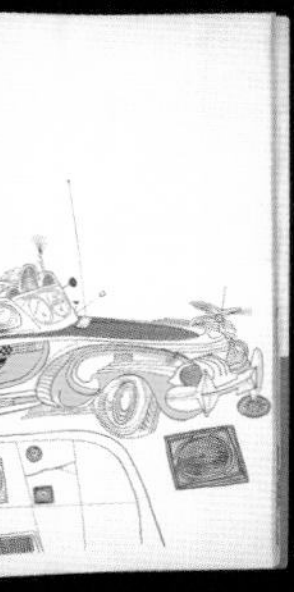
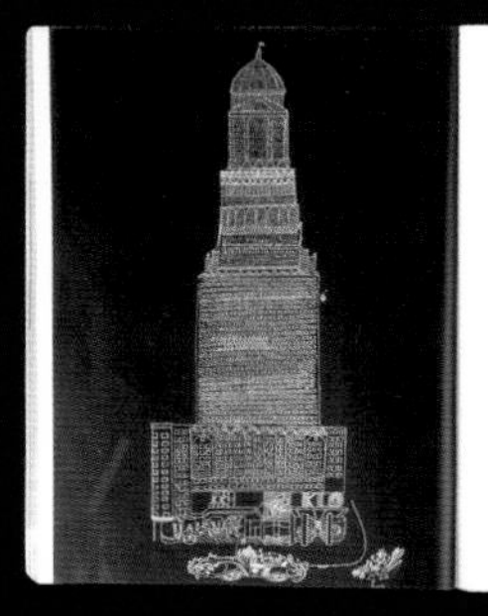

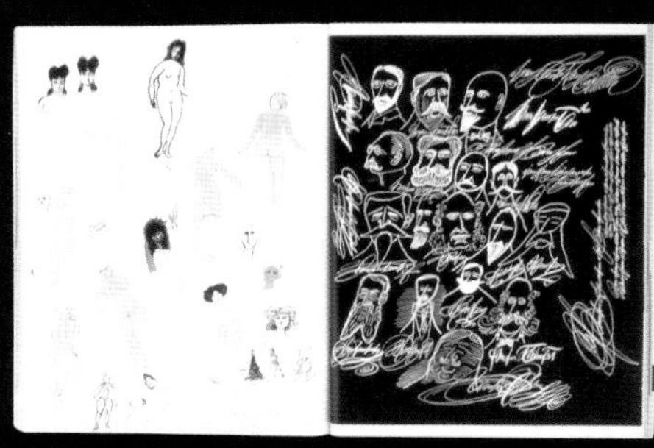
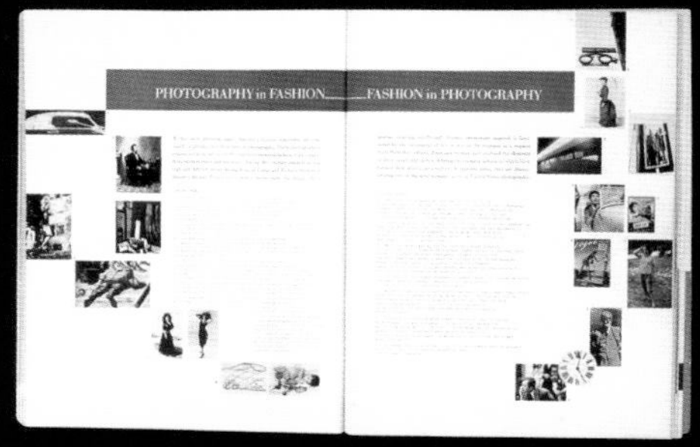

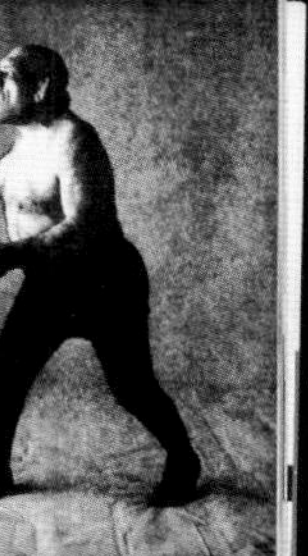
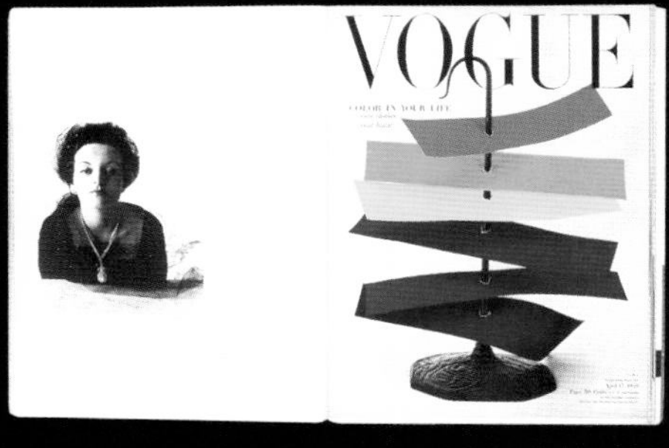

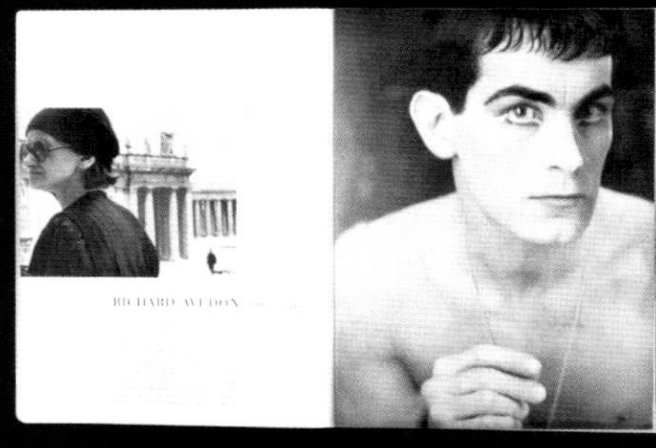

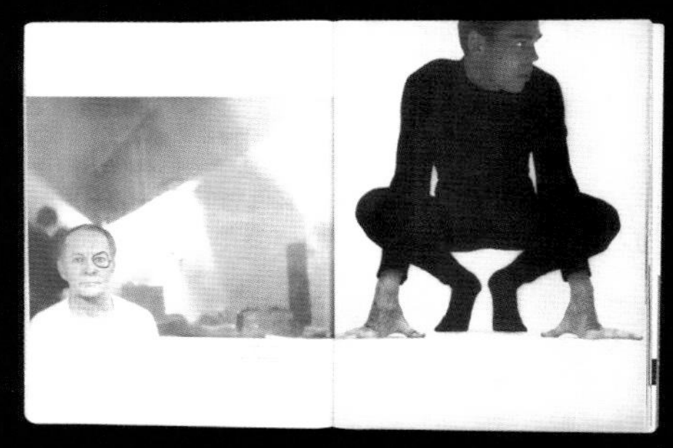
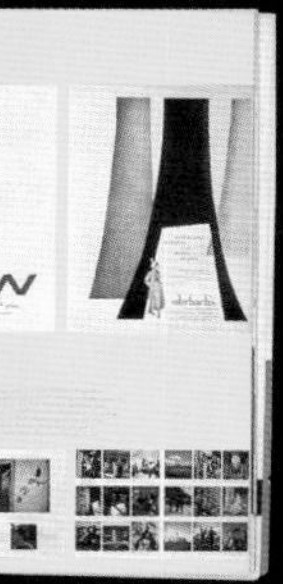
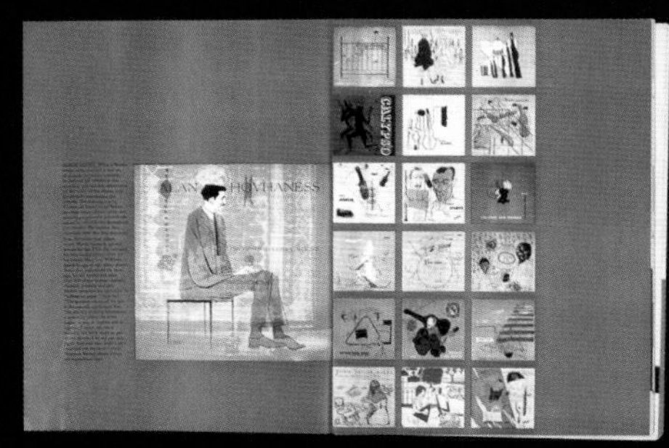
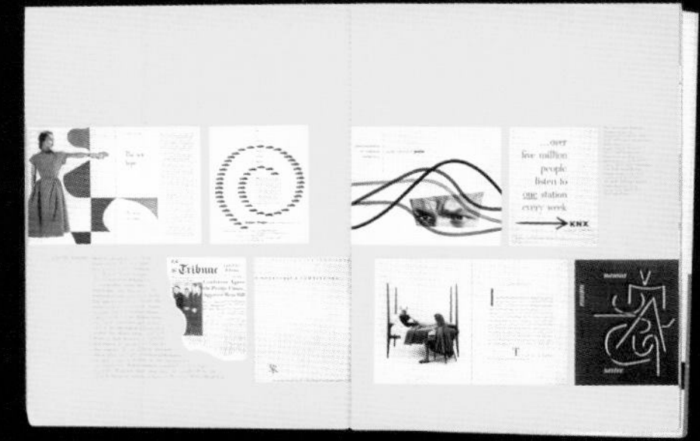
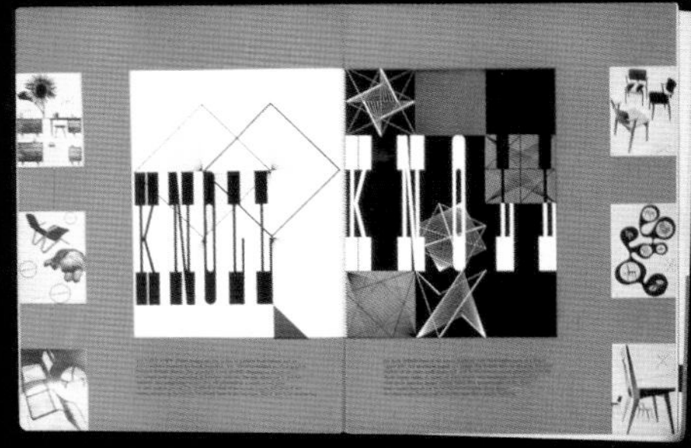
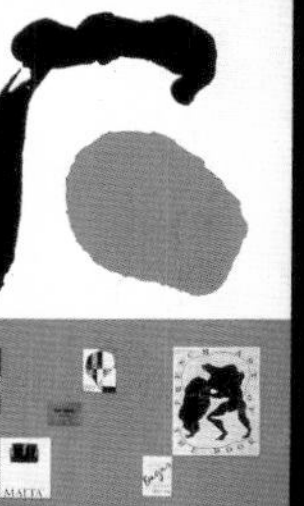
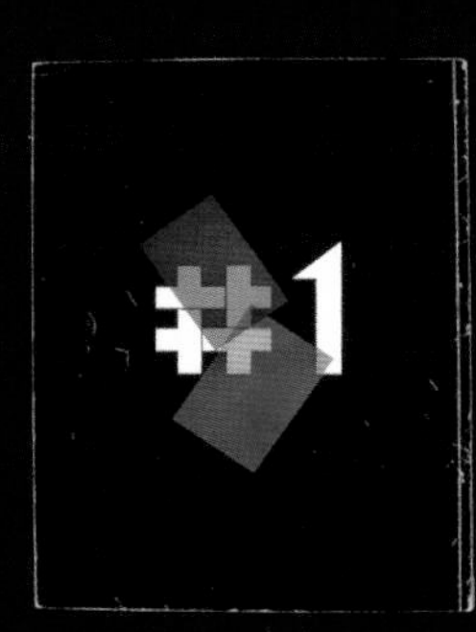

Pages 198 – 201: Cover and complete sequence of spreads from *Portfolio* #1, winter 1950. Editors George S. Rosenthal and Frank Zachary. Cincinnati: Zebra Press, 1949.
Striving to produce not just a magazine but a "graphic experience," *Portfolio* lasted for just three issues. Yet, even with such a short life span, it is still widely recognized today as one of the most significant publications in design history.

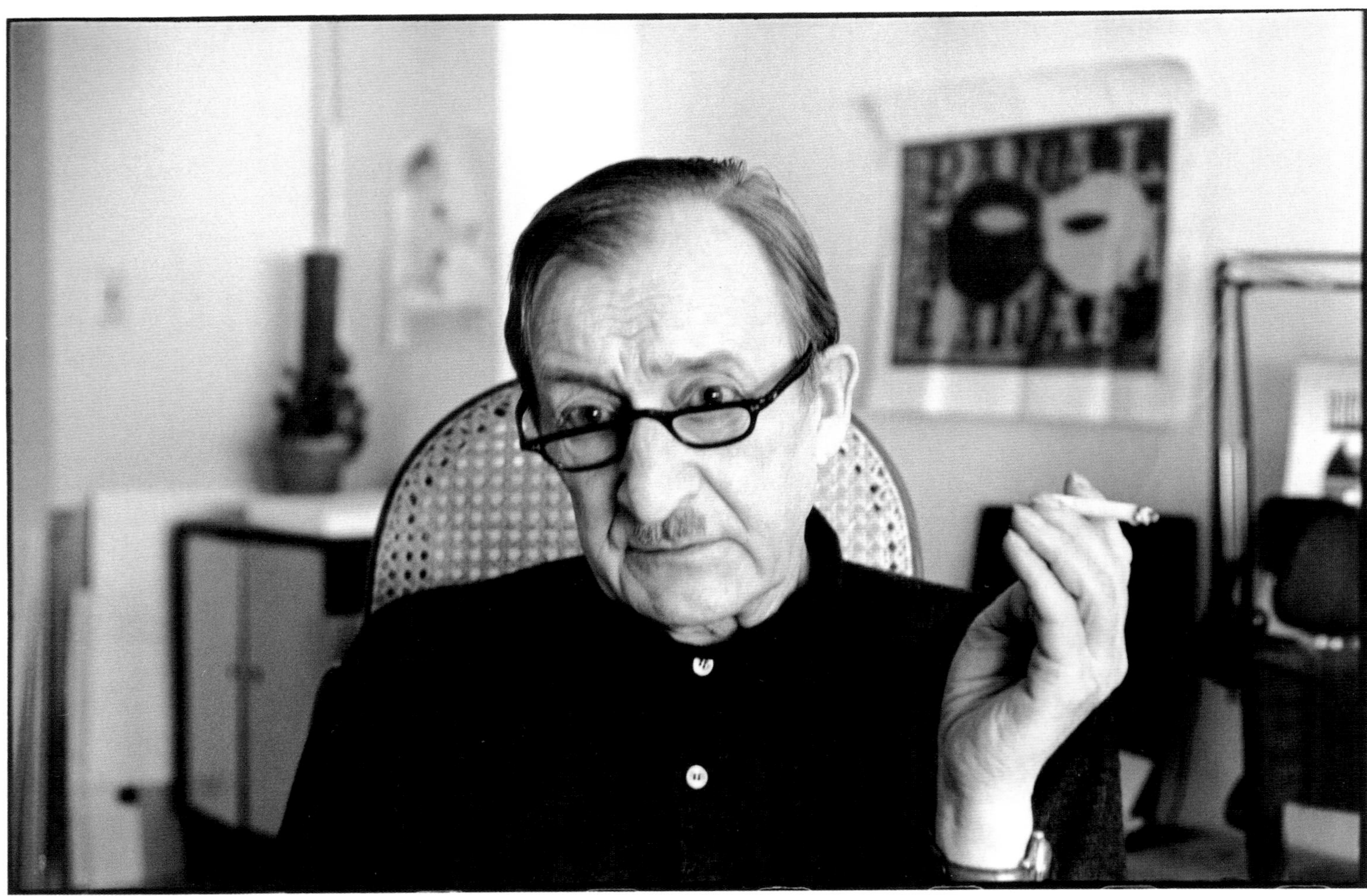

Brodovitch in New York, c. 1960. Photograph by Henri Cartier-Bresson.

the Moholy-Nagy School, a fine photographer, but his principal commercial interests were running his family printing company. George was considerably younger than I, we were close friends, and I wrote George and told him I thought there was room for, how will I describe it, an American *Graphis*."[1]

George S. Rosenthal's family owned Zebra Press, a printing company whose stock-in-trade publications were mass-market pictorial paperbacks. In the field of photographic publishing Zebra Press was at the forefront of producing affordable photojournalist books. *Naked City*, one of the first monographs on Weegee's work, was on their list of twenty-five-cent titles. Rosenthal, recently affected by the radical ideas of the New Bauhaus, probably saw producing *Portfolio* as an excellent opportunity to create a luxurious flagship publication for the company. To achieve this end Rosenthal spared no expense. He bought the finest paper and permitted Zachary to include special inserts such as shopping bags and wallpaper. When it came to choosing an art director to give birth to their shared vision, both Zachary and Rosenthal could only think of one suitable candidate. As Zachary recounted:

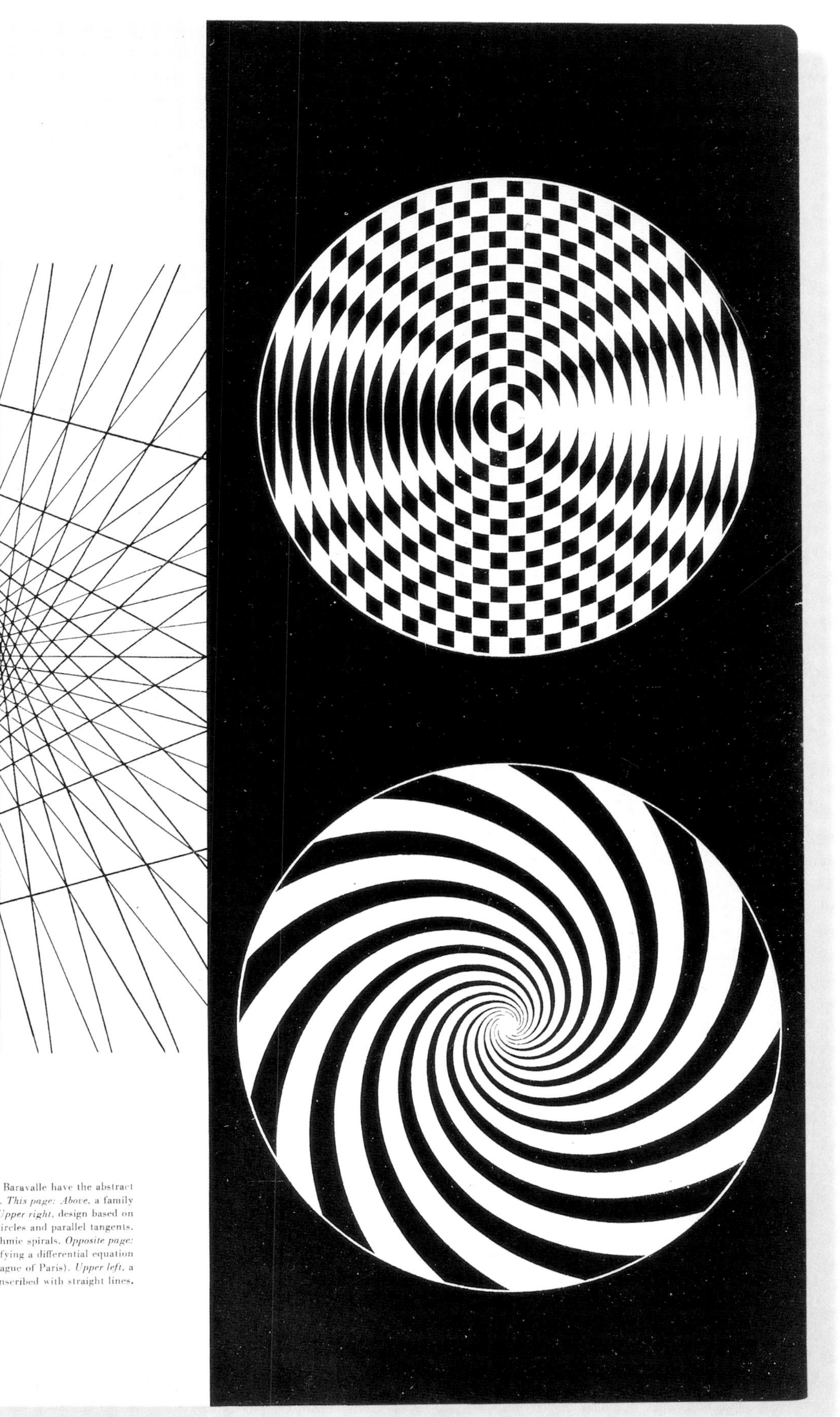

Mathematical drawings by Dr. Baravalle have the abstract quality of modern art. *This page: Above*, a family of lines tangent to a parabola. *Upper right*, design based on series of concentric circles and parallel tangents. *Lower right*, a family of logarithmic spirals. *Opposite page: Lower left*, a family of curves satisfying a differential equation (by Professor Andre Saint-Lague of Paris). *Upper left*, a triangle inscribed with straight lines.

"Design from Mathematicians," *Portfolio* #1, winter 1950.

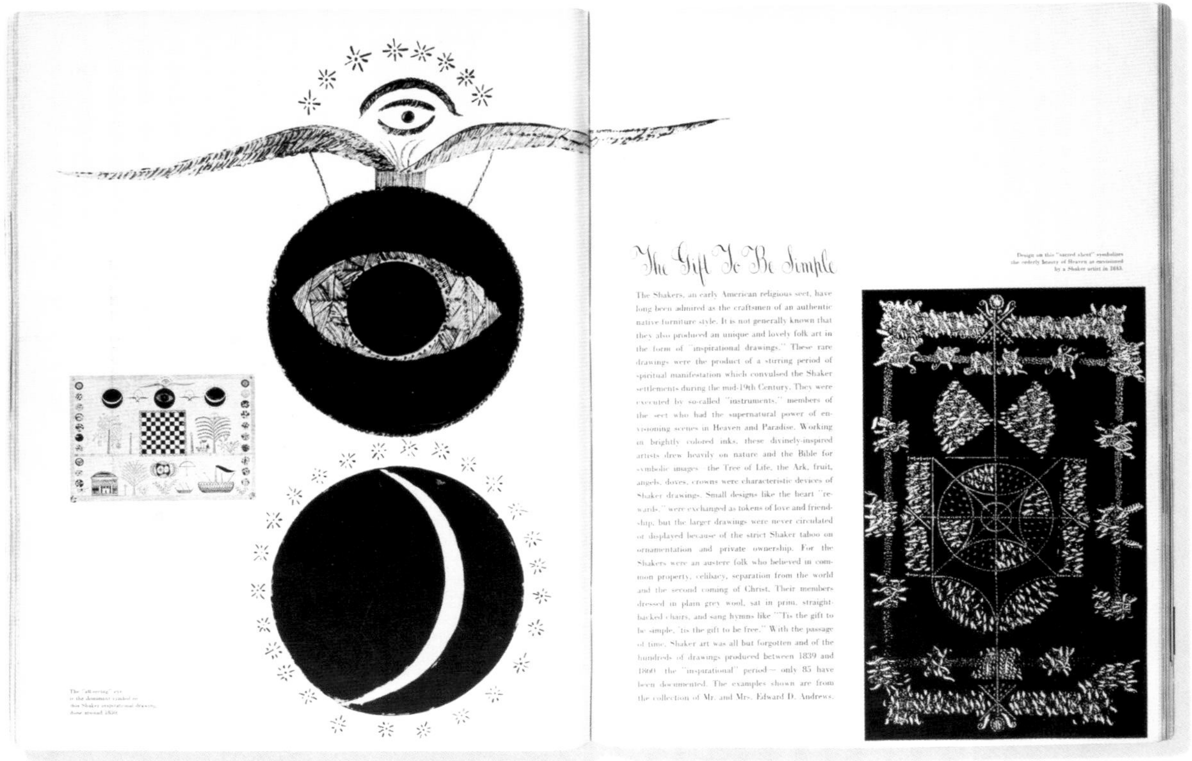

The "all-seeing" eye is the dominant symbol in this Shaker inspirational drawing, done around 1850.

The Gift To Be Simple

The Shakers, an early American religious sect, have long been admired as the craftsmen of an authentic native furniture style. It is not generally known that they also produced an unique and lovely folk art in the form of "inspirational drawings." These rare drawings were the product of a stirring period of spiritual manifestation which convulsed the Shaker settlements during the mid-19th Century. They were executed by so-called "instruments," members of the sect who had the supernatural power of envisioning scenes in Heaven and Paradise. Working in brightly colored inks, these divinely-inspired artists drew heavily on nature and the Bible for symbolic images—the Tree of Life, the Ark, fruit, angels, doves, crowns were characteristic devices of Shaker drawings. Small designs like the heart "rewards," were exchanged as tokens of love and friendship, but the larger drawings were never circulated or displayed because of the strict Shaker taboo on ornamentation and private ownership. For the Shakers were an austere folk who believed in common property, celibacy, separation from the world and the second coming of Christ. Their members dressed in plain grey wool, sat in prim, straight-backed chairs, and sang hymns like "'Tis the gift to be simple, 'tis the gift to be free." With the passage of time, Shaker art was all but forgotten and of the hundreds of drawings produced between 1839 and 1860—the "inspirational" period—only 85 have been documented. The examples shown are from the collection of Mr. and Mrs. Edward D. Andrews.

Design on this "sacred sheet" symbolizes the orderly beauty of Heaven as envisioned by a Shaker artist in 1843.

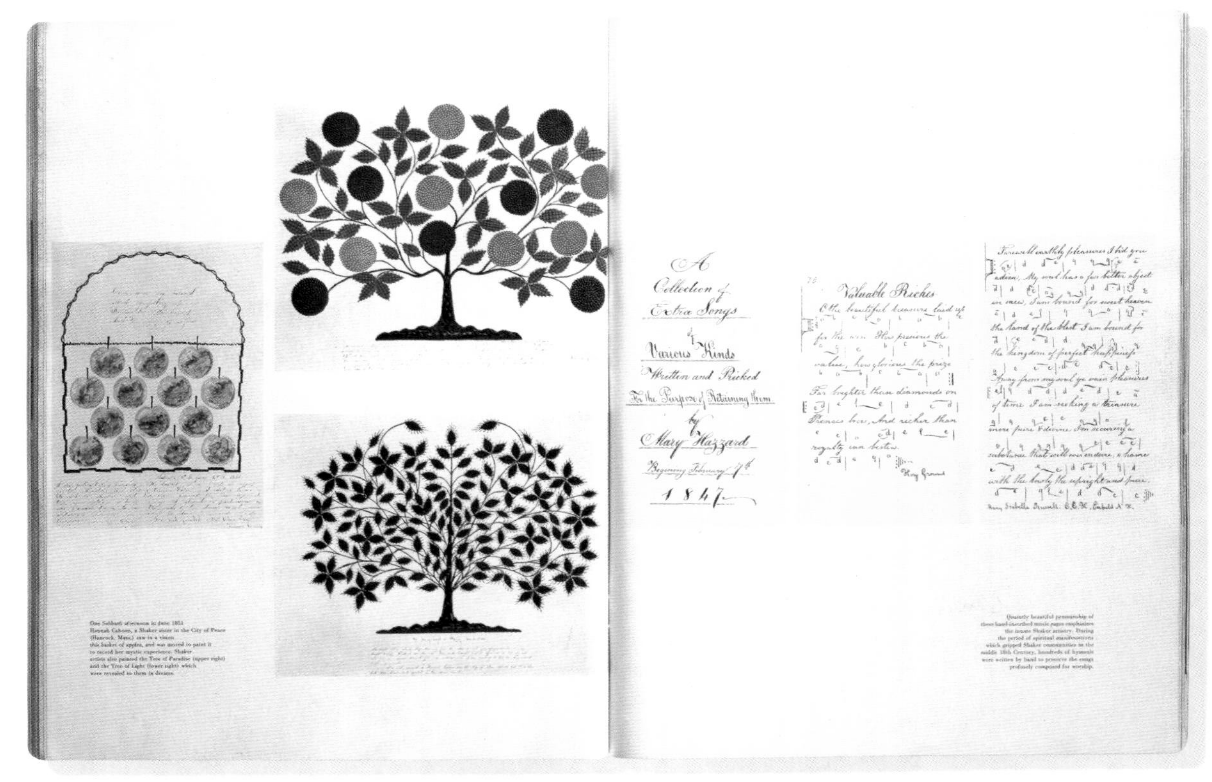

One Sabbath afternoon in June 1851 Hannah Cahoon, a Shaker sister in the City of Peace (Hancock, Mass.) saw in a vision this basket of apples, and was moved to paint it to record her mystic experience. Shaker artists also painted the Tree of Paradise (upper right) and the Tree of Light (lower right) which were revealed to them in dreams.

Quaintly beautiful penmanship of these hand-inscribed music pages emphasizes the innate Shaker artistry. During the period of spiritual manifestations which gripped Shaker communities in the middle 19th Century, hundreds of hymnals were written by hand to preserve the songs profusely composed for worship.

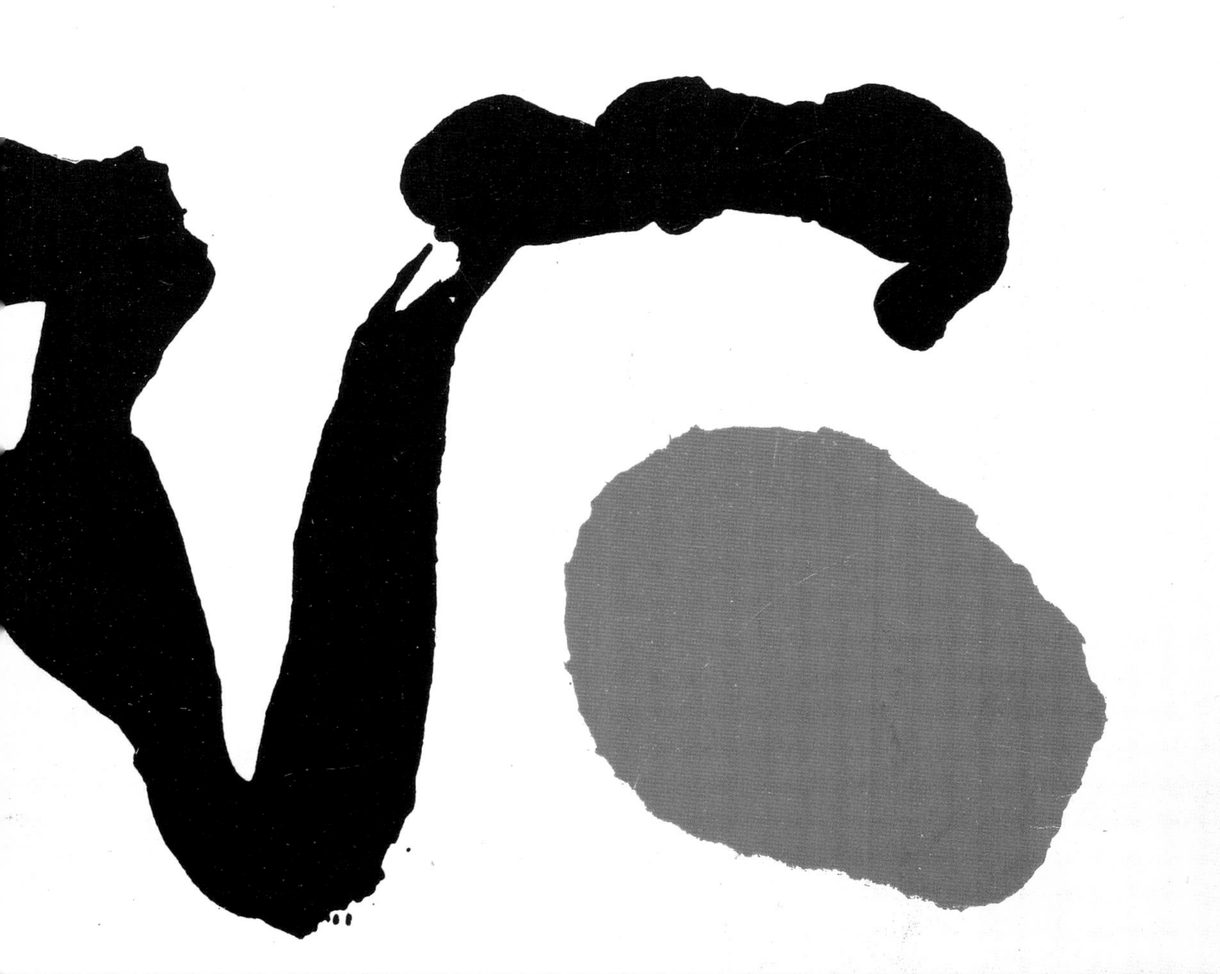

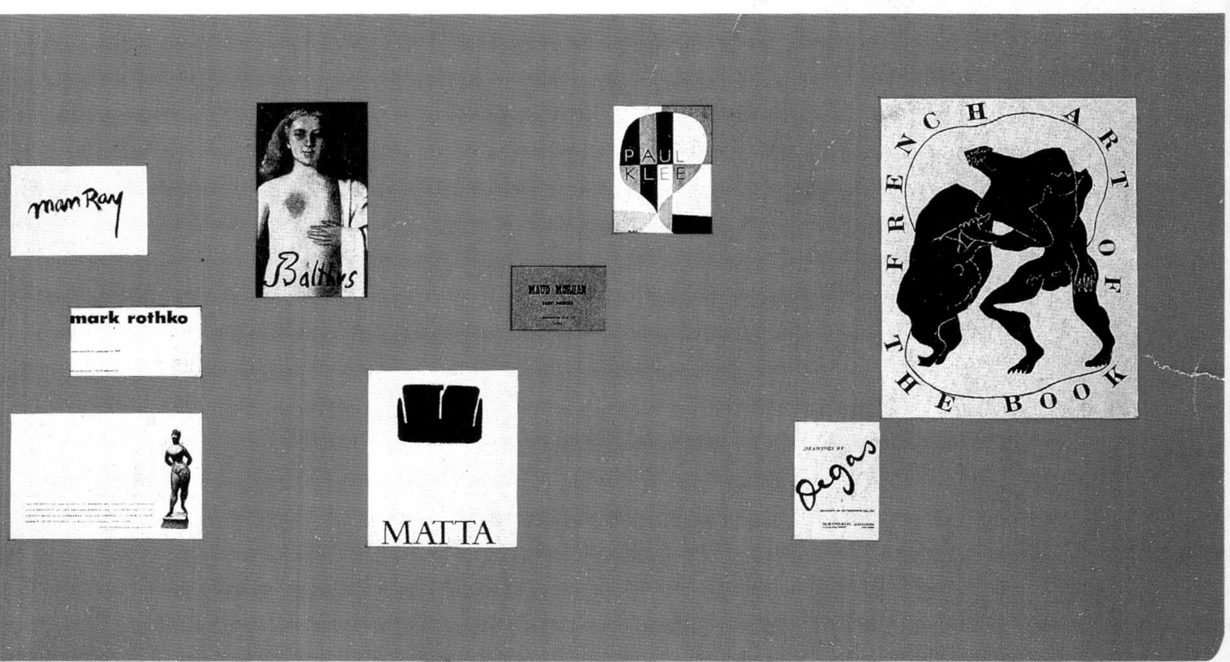

"For Art's Sake," *Portfolio* #1, winter 1950.
The enlarged signature of Spanish painter Joan Miró anchors a feature on recent cover designs for art exhibition catalogues produced by New York galleries.

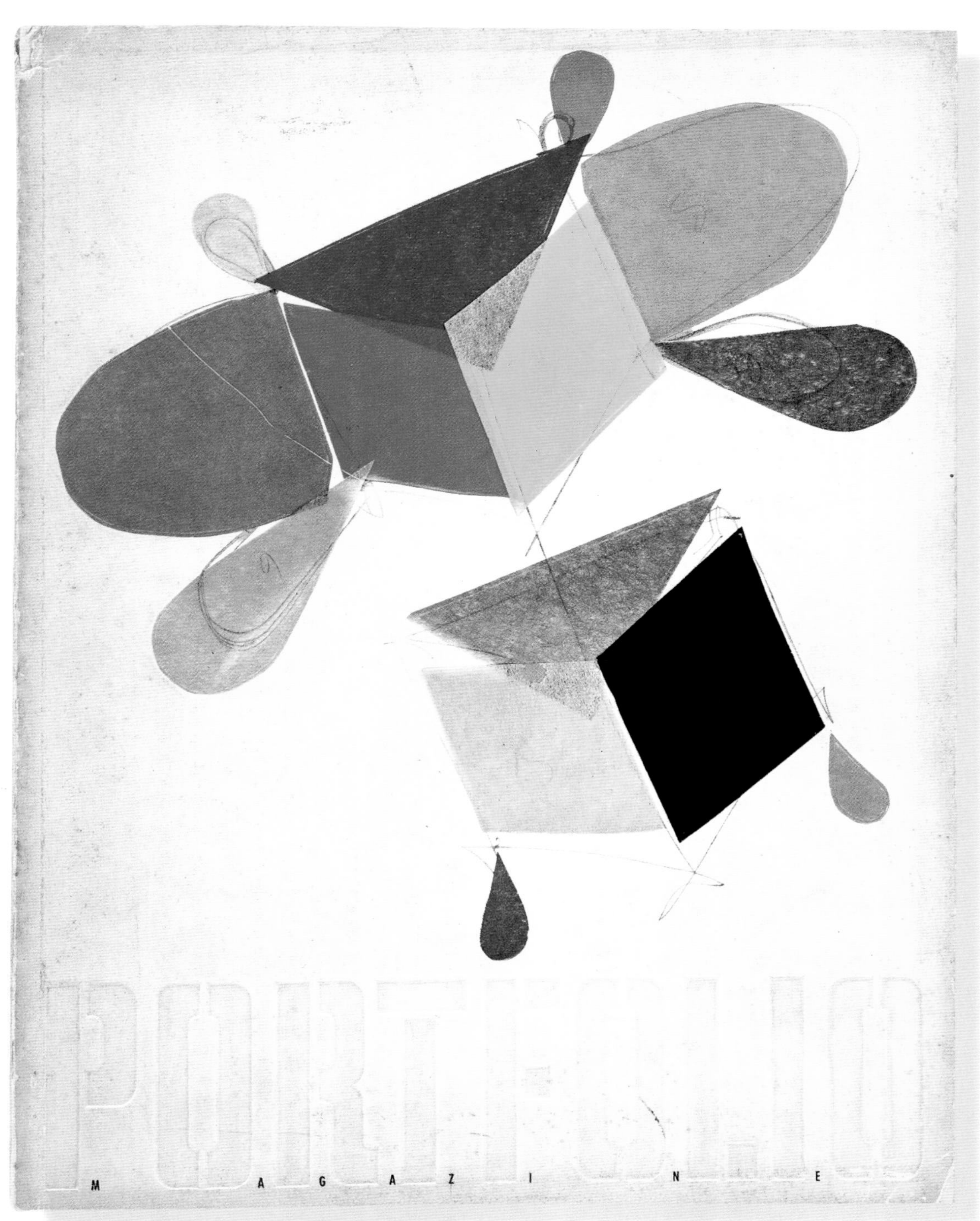

Cover of *Portfolio* #2, summer 1950. Editors George S. Rosenthal and Frank Zachary. Cincinnati: Zebra Press.
Portfolio #2 contains a feature on the furniture and interior designs of Charles Eames. For the cover, Brodovitch reproduced Eames's tissue-paper design for a kite, combining it with an embossed reproduction of the *Portfolio* logo.

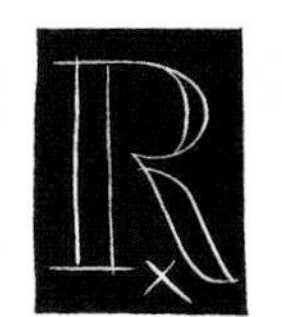

arely is the printed page considered a medium of plastic invention. Its design has become standardized, a machine-like element devoid of feeling and esthetic significance. This is cause for regret, for the variety of forms possible when typography and calligraphy are creatively used approaches that of abstract painting. On the following seven pages, Portfolio reproduces in facsimile a number of unusual pages which possess real visual charm and excitement. First is the modern French poet Guillaume Apollinaire's sensitive arrangement of his poem Il Pleut (It Rains), trickling down through the clean white air of the page opposite like a gentle spring shower. It is followed in turn by two curious pages from an early Christian panegyric, printed in 16th Century Germany and stenciled with mysterious religious symbols—a superb example of that now extinct form of literary expression known as "carmen figurato" (figured poem). Next is a contemporary spread from Pierre Reverdy's poem Le Chant des Morts (Song of the Dead Ones), with the text in the poet's script and illustrated with lithographs by Pablo Picasso, who derived the abstract form of his designs from the skull, the bone and the straight line. Last is a poem by Wu Chang-Shih, one of the greatest of modern Chinese calligraphers, written in the calligraphic style known as Ts'ao-Shu, or "grass" style, because of the impromptu nature of the strokes with which the characters are formed. For designers chafing under the conventional discipline of the printed page and seeking new directions, these pages should bring both pleasure and inspiration.

Guillaume Apollinaire, Il Pleut, from Arts et Metier Graphiques, Paris, France, 1930.

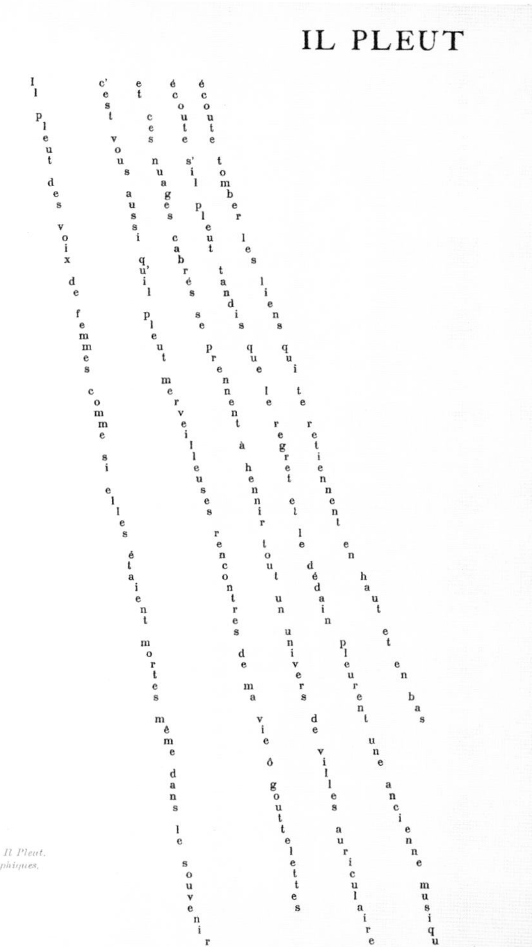

Above: "Il Pleut," *Portfolio* # 2, summer 1950. Guillaume Apollinaire's 1918 book of poems *Calligrammes* fascinated Brodovitch. He reproduced Apollinaire's poem "Il Pleut" as it was printed in the 1930 issue of *Arts et Métiers Graphiques* from France. While more restrained in his use of type, Brodovitch's designs for *Harper's Bazaar* and *Portfolio* echo the way Apollinaire used type to communicate the spirit of his poems.

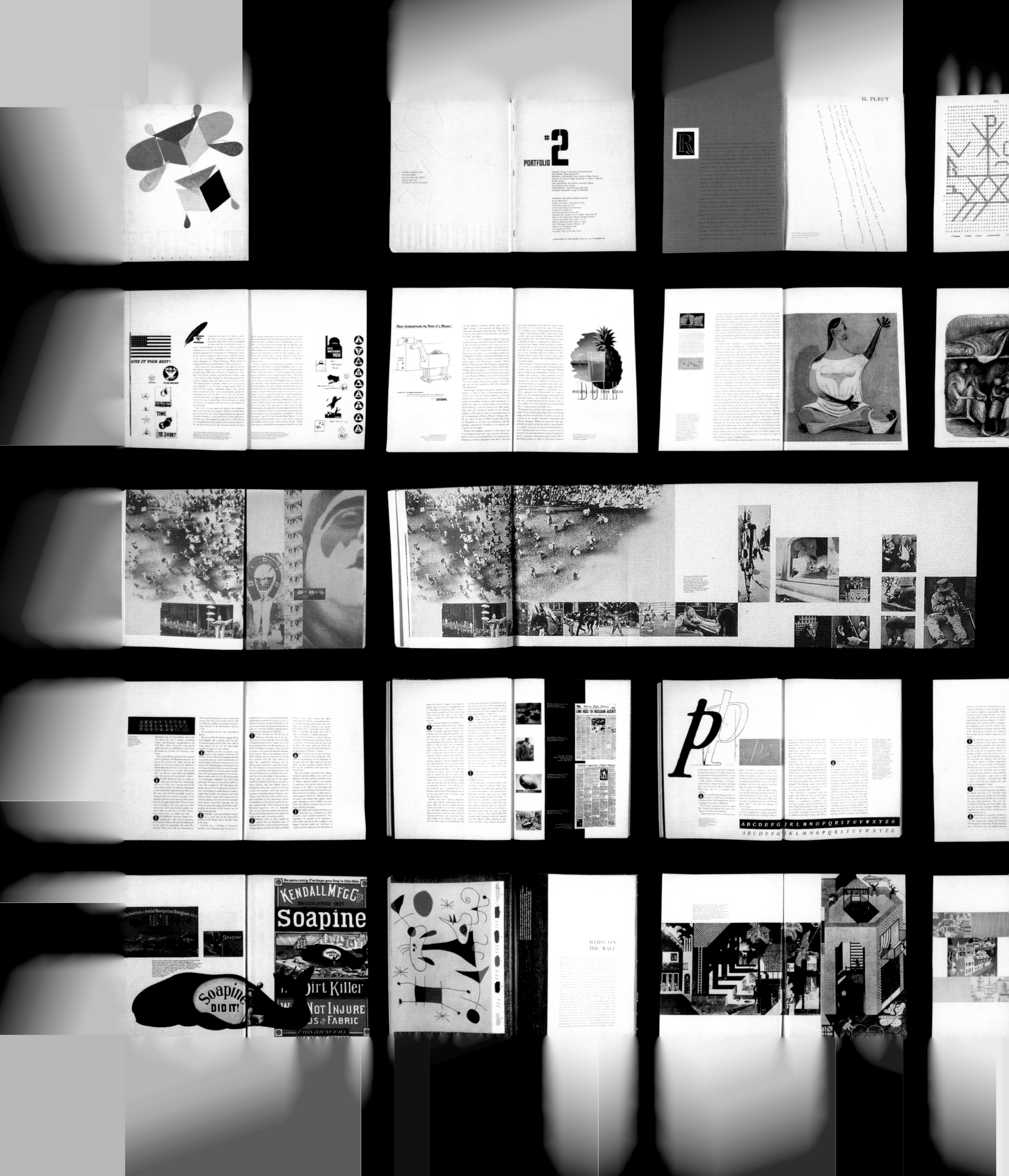

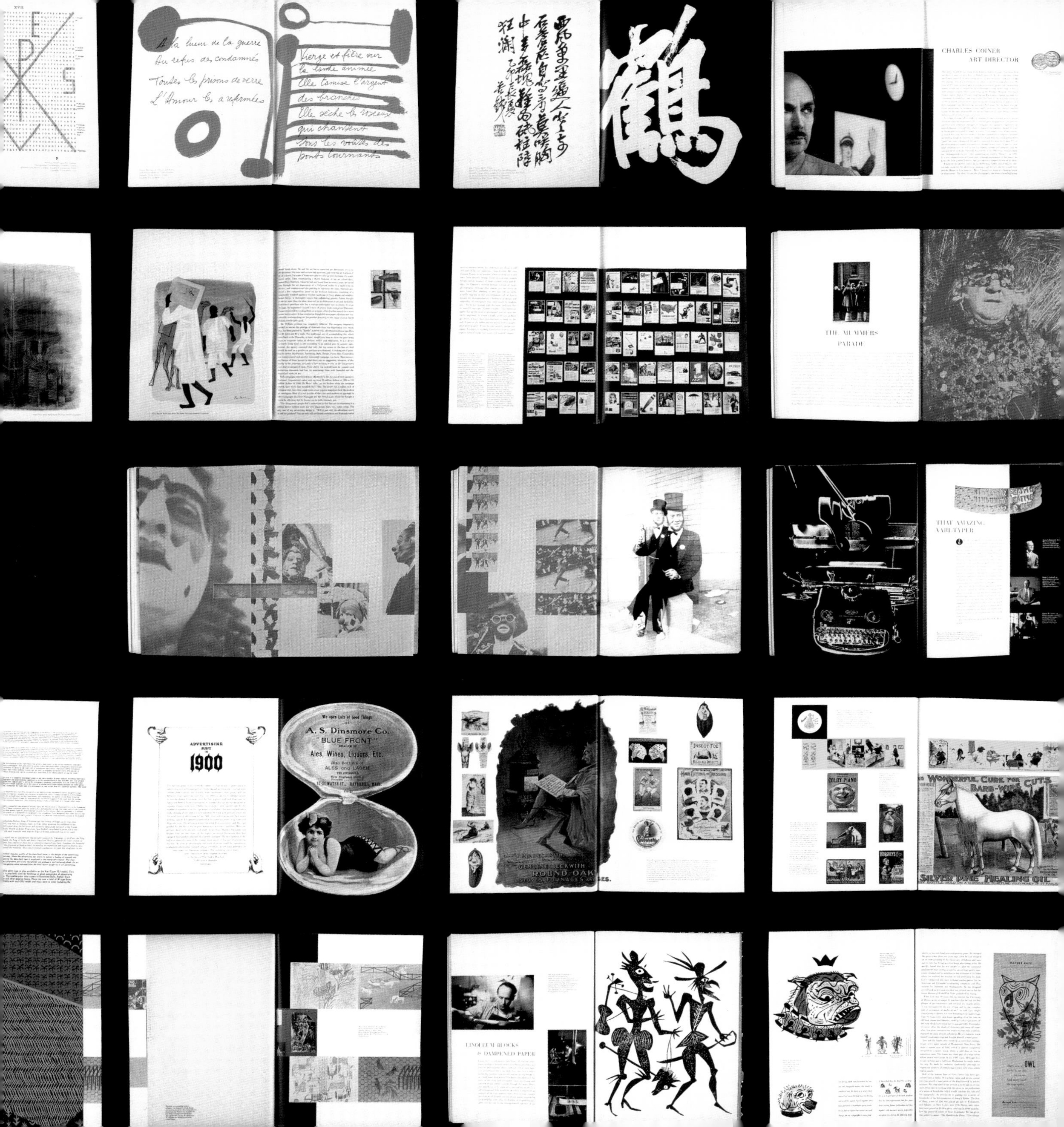
A la lueur de la guerre
Au refus des condamnés
Toutes les prisons de verre
L'Amour les a refermées
Vierge et fière sur
la lande animée
Elle tamise l'argent
des branches
Elle sèche les oiseaux
qui chantent
sous les voûtes des
ponts tournants
CHARLES COINER
ART DIRECTOR
THE MUMMERS
PARADE
THAT AMAZING
VARI-TYPER
ADVERTISING
1900
We open Lots of Good Things
A. S. Dinsmore Co.
"BLUE FRONT"
Ales, Wines, Liquors, Etc.
ALES and LAGER
GENUINE BECKWITH
ROUND OAK
INSECT FOE
COLBY PIANO
WONDERFUL CURE FOR BARB-WIRE CUTS
SILVER PINE HEALING OIL
LINOLEUM BLOCKS
& DAMPENED PAPER
OWL

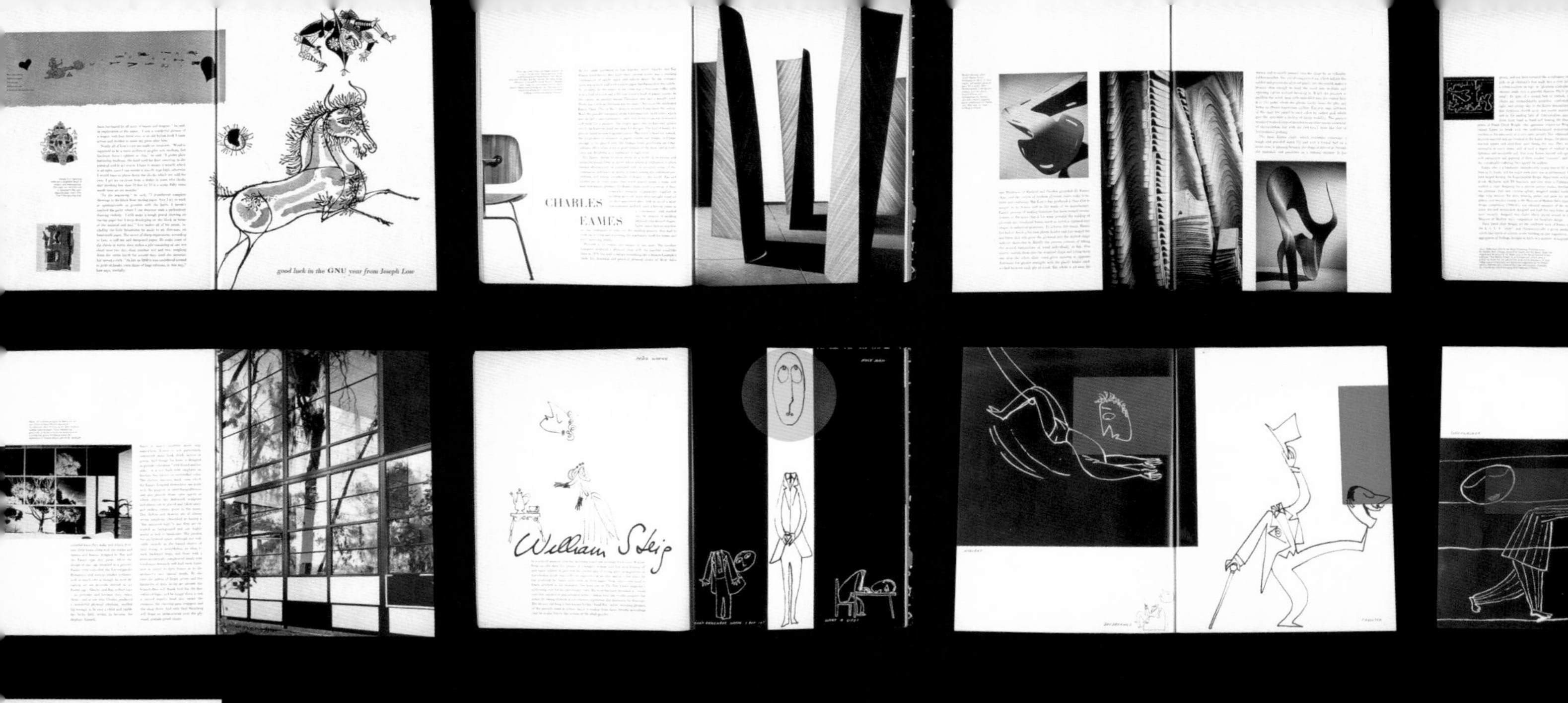

He always "started with a big picture" — then modulated to a smaller picture and then kind of an interval, and then bam-boom again. He p

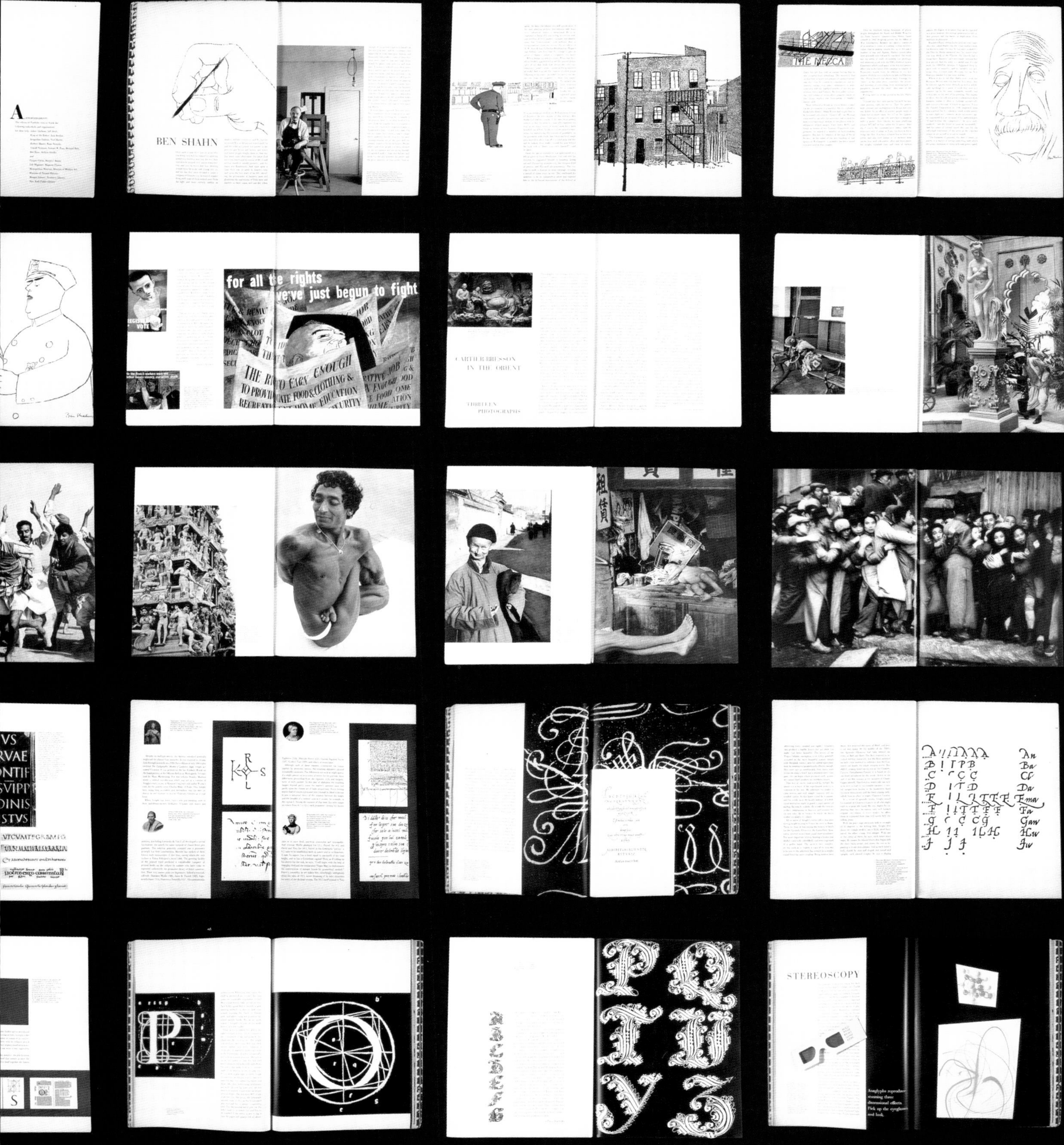
BEN SHAHN
for all the rights
we've just begun to fight
CARTIER-BRESSON
IN THE ORIENT
THIRTEEN
PHOTOGRAPHS
STEREOSCOPY

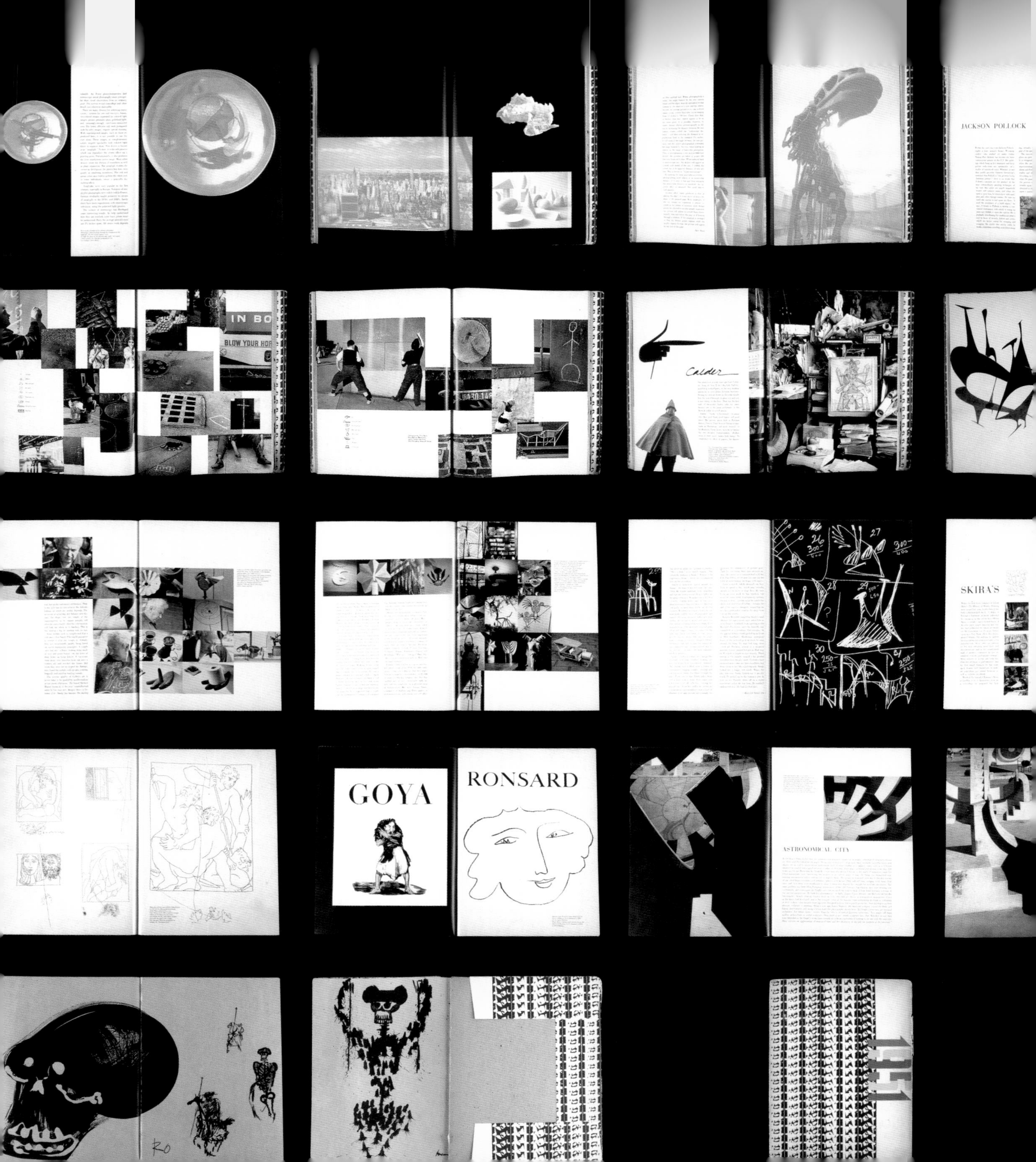
JACKSON POLLOCK
IN BO
BLOW YOUR HOR
Calder
SKIRA'S
GOYA
RONSARD
ASTRONOMICAL CITY

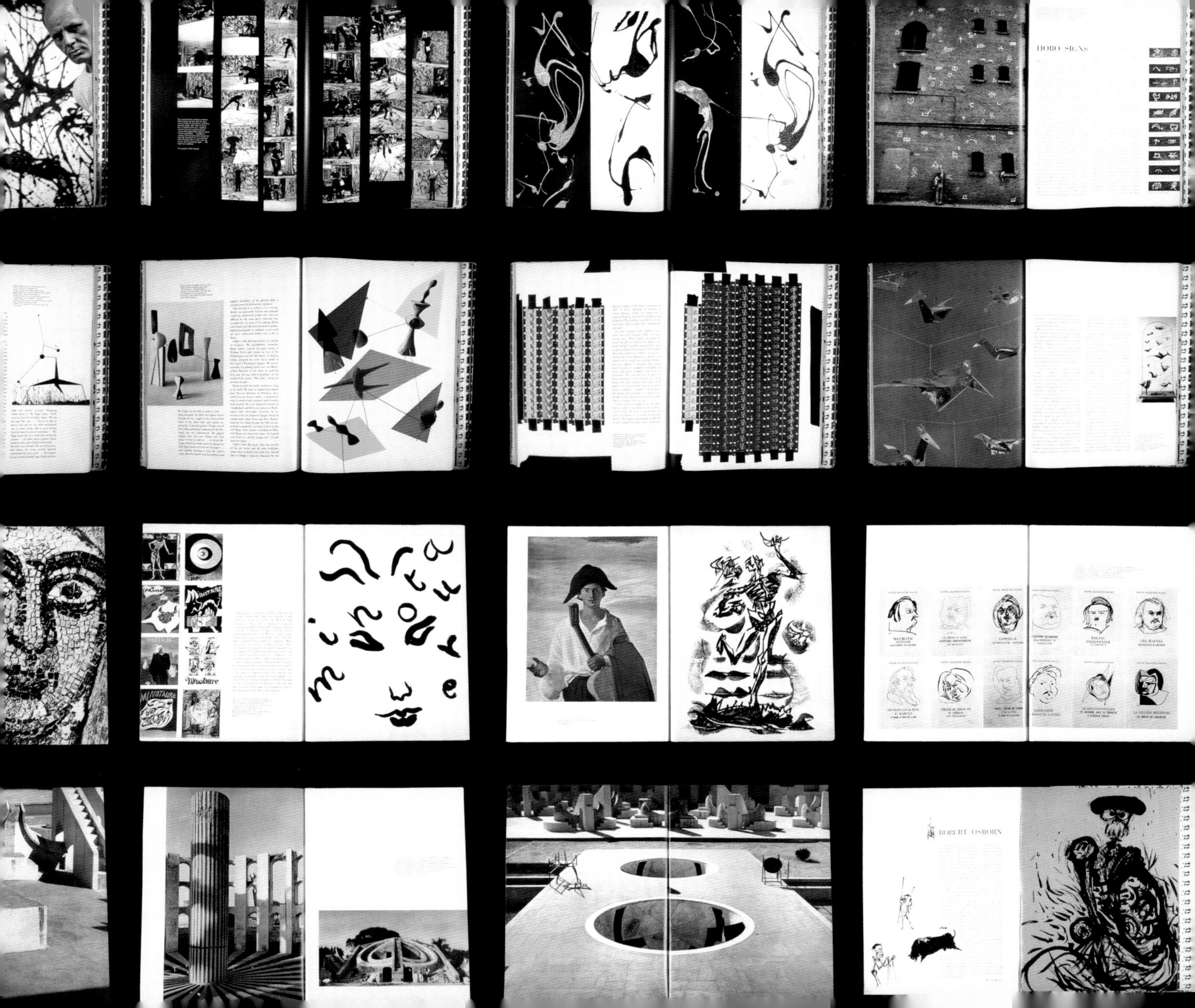

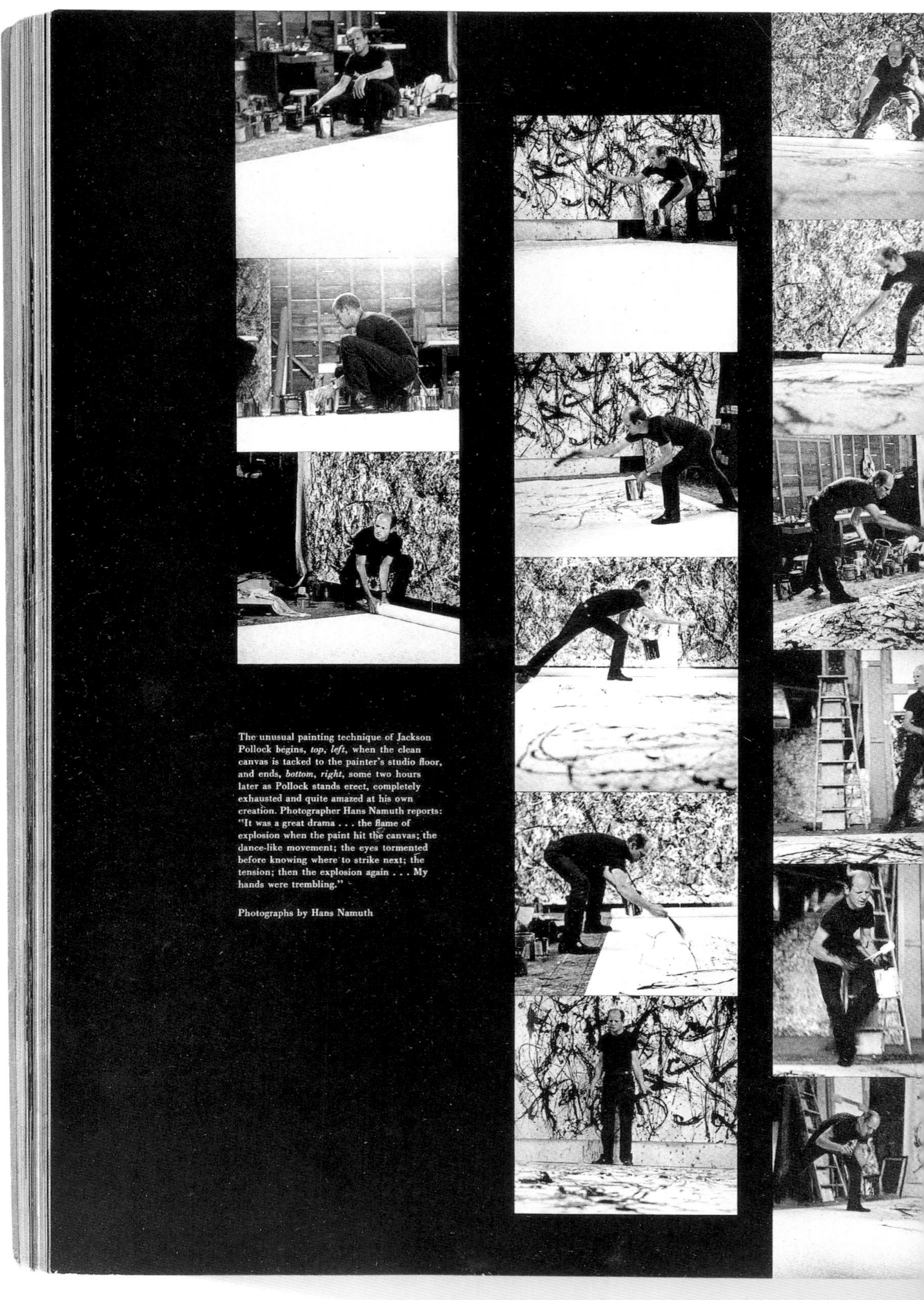

The unusual painting technique of Jackson Pollock begins, *top, left,* when the clean canvas is tacked to the painter's studio floor, and ends, *bottom, right,* some two hours later as Pollock stands erect, completely exhausted and quite amazed at his own creation. Photographer Hans Namuth reports: "It was a great drama . . . the flame of explosion when the paint hit the canvas; the dance-like movement; the eyes tormented before knowing where to strike next; the tension; then the explosion again . . . My hands were trembling."

Photographs by Hans Namuth

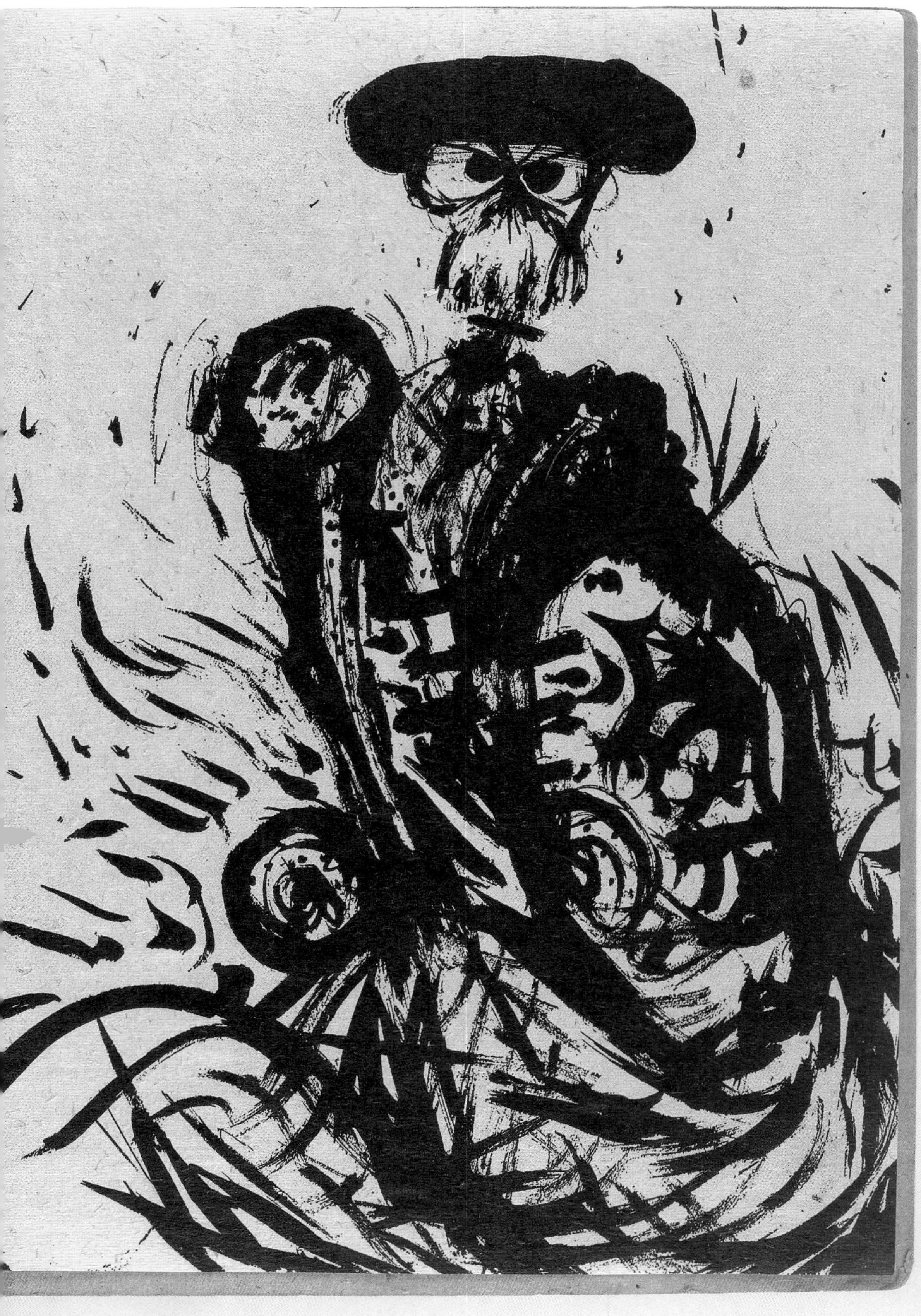

Alexey Brodovitch: Postscript

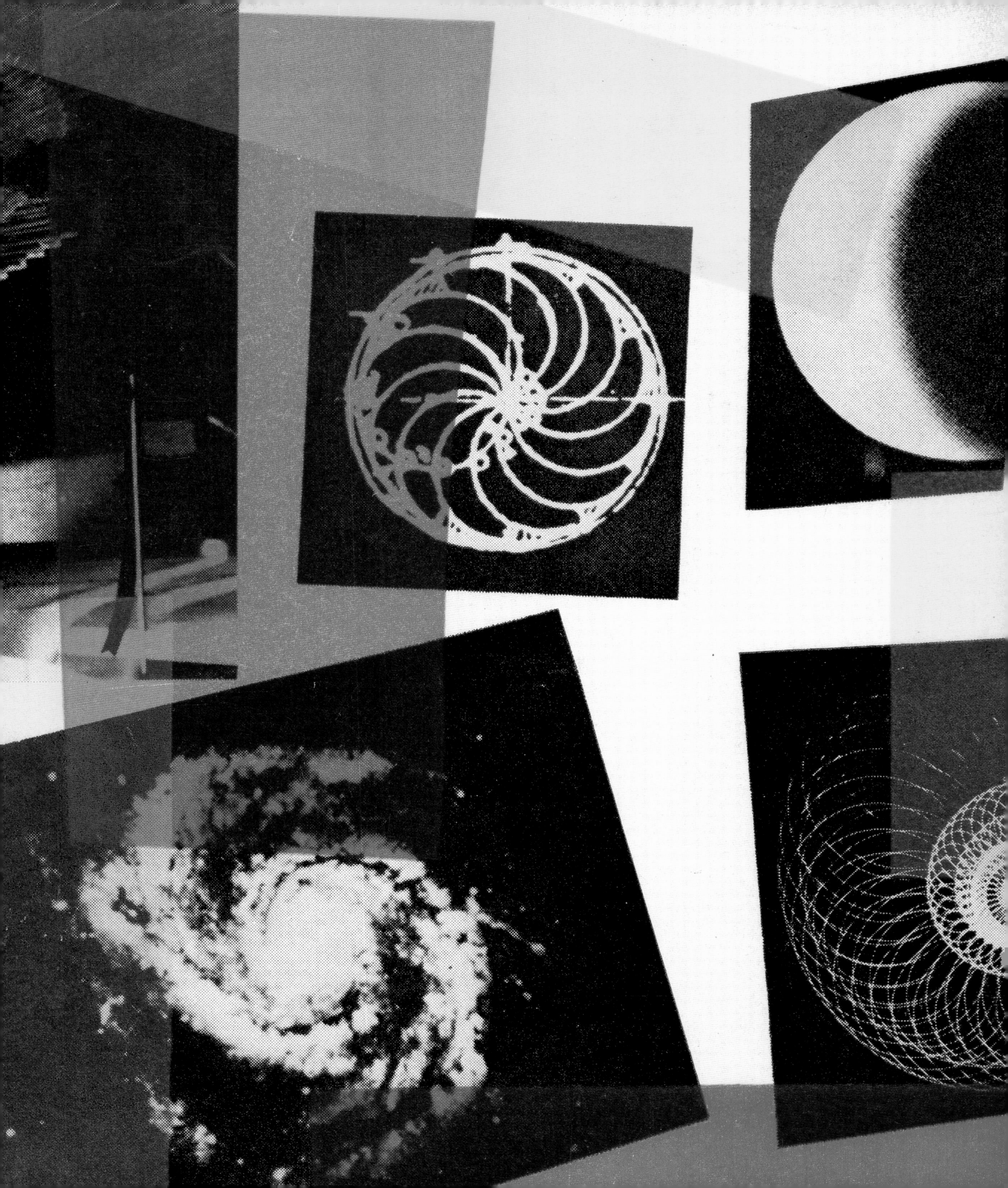

Yesterday – temptation. Today – activity. Tomorrow – challenge. – Alexey Brodovitch in "Focus on Alexey Brodovitch," *Popular Photography*, 1961

Throughout the early part of the 1960s, Alexey Brodovitch's increasingly lengthy hospital stays gave him time to ruminate on his considerable achievements in the graphic arts. It was during these recuperative spells that he began to assemble his life's work in the hope of producing an autobiography. In 1962, seeking a potential publisher for this project, he contacted R. E. Martinez. At the time Martinez was editor-in-chief of the Swiss photography magazine *Camera* and held the position of advisor to both *Du* magazine and C. J. Bucher Publishers. Obviously aware of Brodovitch's collaboration with C. J. Bucher on *Observations*, Martinez recommended this proposal to the company. It seems that Martinez, C. J. Bucher, and Brodovitch came to an agreement on the publication, which included its distribution throughout Europe and Japan. In Brodovitch's own words the aim of the publication was to create a "scrapebook [*sic*] arranged in a historical order including articles about me from different magazines, newspaper clippings, etc., etc."[1] Brodovitch's plan was to divide the book into the five areas he considered pivotal to his creative legacy: graphic design, photography, furniture design, education, and art direction. Acting as overall editor, Martinez suggested to Brodovitch that it would be worthwhile commissioning several key individuals who had collaborated with him on projects throughout his life to write a preface for each of these sections. Brodovitch wrote to

Henri Cartier-Bresson, Peter Blake, Monroe Wheeler, and Charles Coiner, all of whom agreed to produce a short essay-introduction on a significant aspect of Brodovitch's oeuvre. As these individuals only amount to four, it can be assumed that Brodovitch would be writing an introduction himself. Naturally, as regards the layout and selection of material, Martinez gave Brodovitch carte blanche.[2]

That book was never completed. Brodovitch did, apparently, produce a dummy copy, yet as with much of his legacy, this has been misplaced or destroyed.[3] As far as we know the only individual who actually wrote a preface for a chapter was Charles Coiner. His essay "Revolution on Pine Street" deals primarily with his teaching at the Pennsylvania Museum School of Industrial Art. From the letters of correspondence between Brodovitch and Coiner over the 1962–63 period, it is clear that because of Brodovitch's extended stays at various hospitals the book had no chance of ever getting off the ground. For example, a year after he had made the original request for essays, Brodovitch was hospitalized for six months from January to mid-June 1963. This long-term confinement was not known to most of the essayists and, as initially happened with the Coiner contribution, any works mailed to him during this time were either misdirected or lost.[4] If anything, it was the fragmented nature of Brodovitch's life that extinguished any hope of the book being completed – it simply destroyed the momentum essential to any book's evolution from conception to publication.

Page 245: Detail from cover of *Art in America*, No. 3, 1962.

Below: Brodovitch and one of his bull terriers at his house in Le Thor, France, 1971. Photograph by Georges Tourdjman.

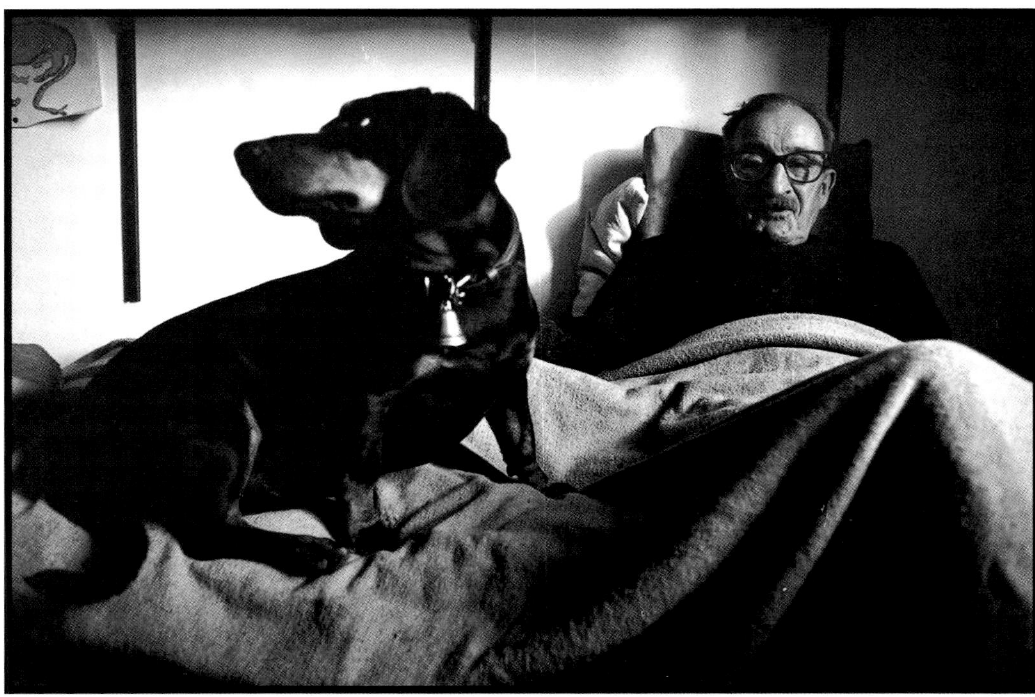

Ward's Island

By the early sixties, Brodovitch's drinking had reached such extremes that it was seen fit among his friends to send him to a sanatorium to "dry out." Throughout this decade he would be sent to various hospitals on numerous occasions. His visits would last from a few weeks to many months. However, during this time, when he was clearly supposed to be resting, he was still planning new projects and involving his students in them. Such enthusiasm can be observed in a letter he sent to Charles Coiner, dated October 5, 1962, when he was under observation for two to three weeks at Trafalgar Hospital in New York:

After this I would like to go to Bellevue Hospital New York for as long as possible. Nothing is dangerous...just me with a wonderful study (close-up) of human emotional state of suffering and behaviour. There is a new crop of students with me, with cameras to make a record of this.[5]

It was this incessant desire to seize on any personal experience as possible material for new projects that resulted in a series of pictures that came out of his time on Ward's Island (now Randall's Island). The Manhattan State Hospital, a mental institution, had opened on the island in 1954. Its occupants ranged from those with severe mental illness to individuals, such as Brodovitch, with acute alcoholism and depression. Committing himself to the hospital in 1961, Brodovitch spent several weeks under observation. During the lulls of a routine that would have included strict medication and group counseling, Brodovitch had many visitors. At some point he was visited by his former student Ben Rose, who gave him a small Minox camera. Brodovitch placed this camera in an empty packet of Pall Mall cigarettes and discretely began to take photographs of his fellow patients.

The results are raw but ethereal images that have a similar feel and look to his *Ballet* pictures. In various frames we see spectral figures caught shuffling across the canteen floor; or a solitary man sitting, staring into nothingness, the nebulous image mirroring his confused state of mind. At one point, he seems to place the camera/cigarette packet on the table in front of him. Slowly turning the camera as he takes pictures, he utilizes the table top to produce starkly cropped images of his otherworldly surroundings. Furtive and capricious, Brodovitch walks past rooms capturing images of men dozing on their beds or wardens taking individuals for treatment. As with the flare and halation of footlights in *Ballet*, he frequently uses the harsh sunlight streaming through the windows to cast his fellow patients in an ethereal light, transforming them into ghostly apparitions. In one such instance, looking into a mirror, the light from a window casting his face into a darkness, we behold a brief but poignant image of Brodovitch himself.

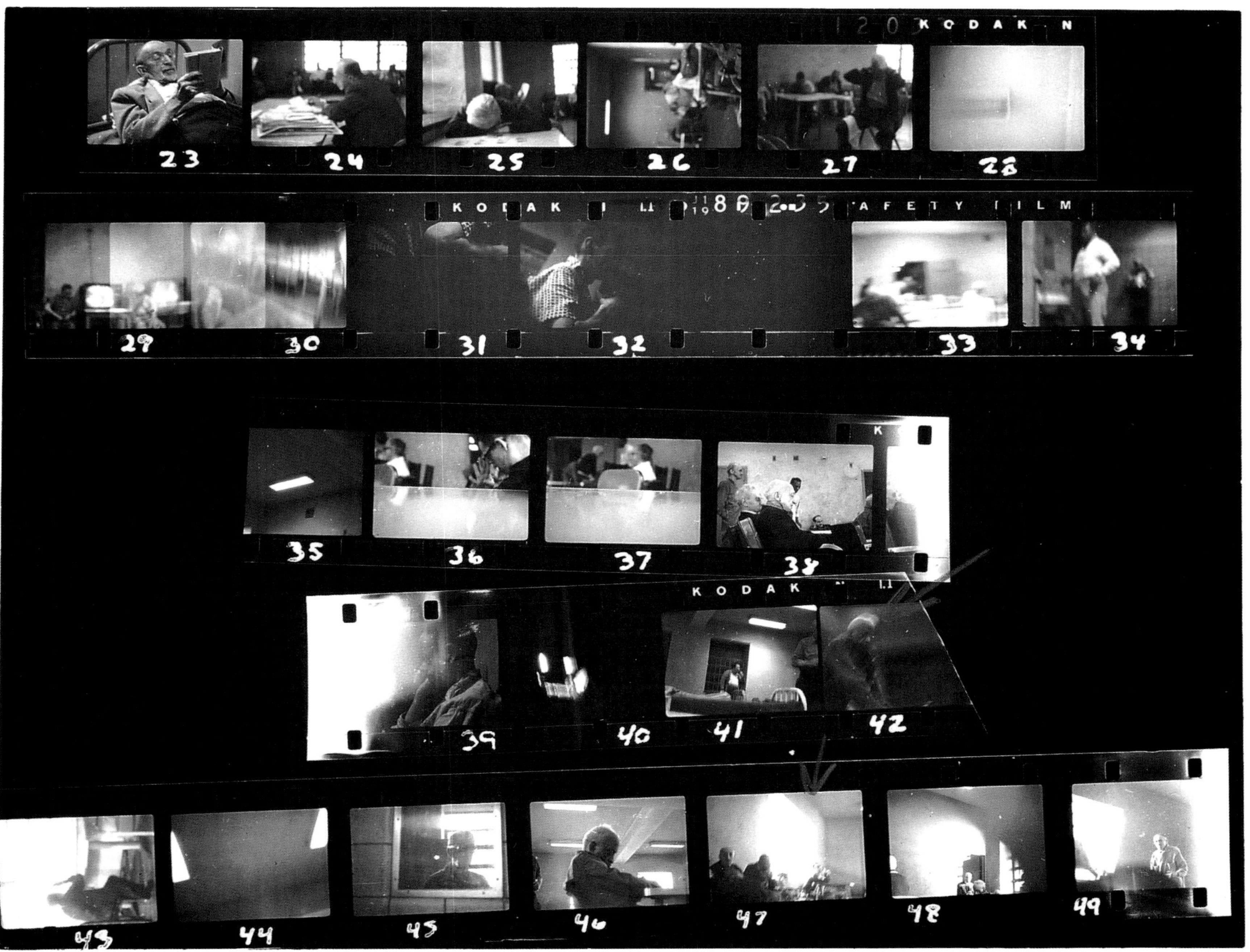

Contact sheet of photographs taken by Brodovitch at Manhattan State Hospital, Ward's Island, New York, 1961.
In 1961 Brodovitch spent several weeks at the Manhattan State Hospital, a mental institution on Ward's Island (now Randall's Island), undergoing treatment for depression and alcoholism. Using a small Minox camera smuggled in by an ex-student, Brodovitch took hundreds of photographs of his fellow patients during his stay.

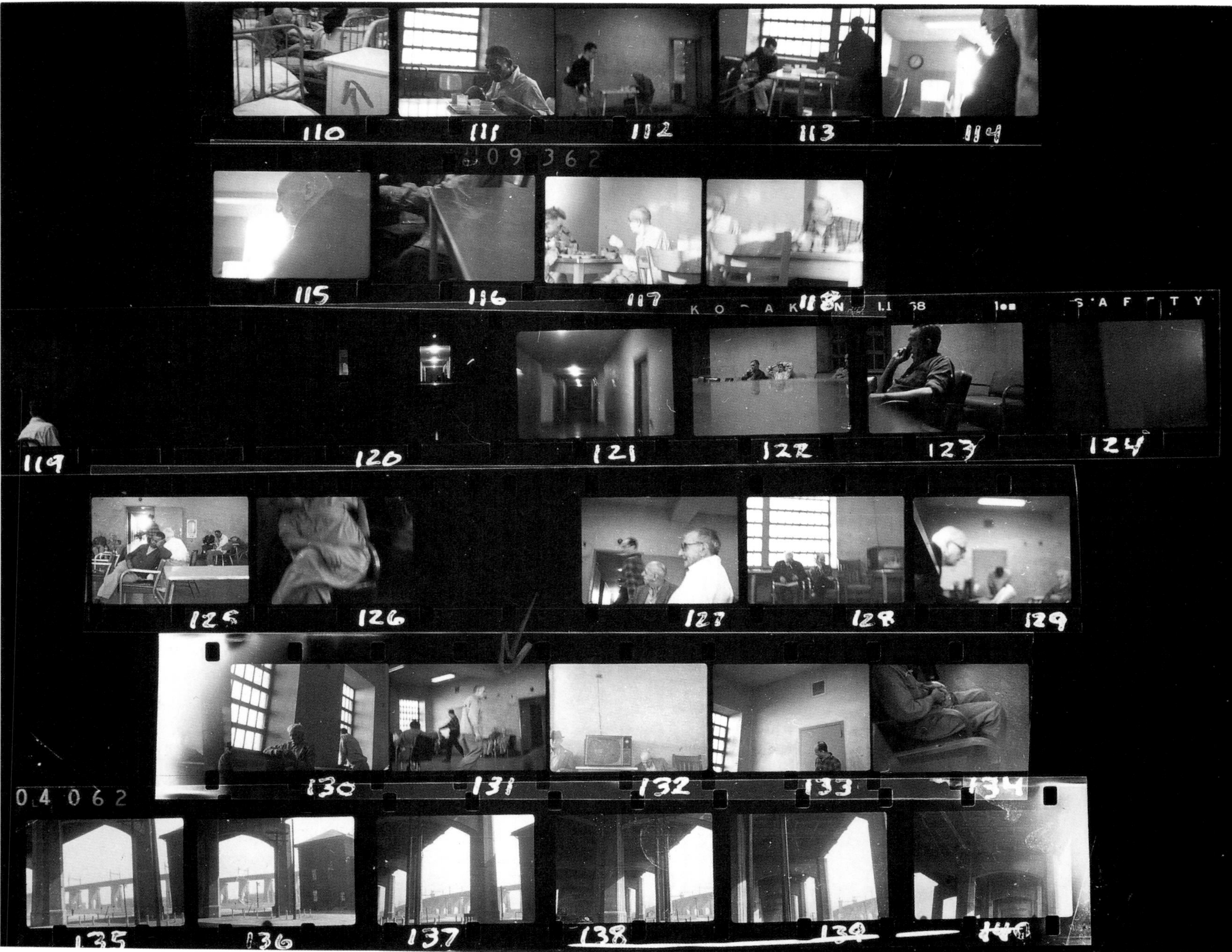

Contact sheet of photographs taken by Brodovitch at Manhattan State Hospital, Ward's Island, New York, 1961.
Far from revealing documentary objectivity, in Brodovitch's clandestine pictures of patients at this mental hospital, the line between the photographer and his subject matter – the patients themselves – is sadly indistinguishable.

On many occasions, before his treatments had run their course, Brodovitch decided to leave the hospitals. At times, he did not last even a full day. Harvey Lloyd, who cared for Brodovitch during this period, remembered one such instance in 1965:

At one point I told him: "Alexey, you have to go to a sanatorium and dry out." And he said: "No." So I said: "OK, I'll have you picked up." And I had people come and take him in the morning. He said: "OK." He didn't make any fuss. I said: "They're here Alexey, you're going to the sanatorium." That afternoon I get a phone call, it's Alexey. I said: "Where are you?" He said: "I'm back in my apartment." I said: "What!" He said: "Yeah, I checked myself out." [6]

In one strip of film from the Ward's Island contacts, we see that Brodovitch has gone outside the hospital. He captures several men looking out over the industrial landscape of the island. Toward the end of the photographs it appears that Brodovitch is simply wandering the streets. At first we see empty roads and bridges. Then we begin to catch sight of silhouetted figures walking underneath flyovers and down the side of disused buildings, seemingly detached from both each other and their environment.

It is not known if any Ward's Island negatives still exist. All that remains available are the contact sheets reproduced here. While in that hospital Brodovitch also made several drawings of the patients. They are similar in style to the work of George Grosz, an artist Brodovitch greatly admired. For many years, any knowledge about these photographs or drawings was limited to a small group of his closest friends and colleagues. Thus, unlike *Ballet*, their influence has remained rather limited. Among those entrusted with Brodovitch's legacy, the only photographer who seems to have utilized these photographs as a template in his own work is Richard Avedon. In 1963, he produced a photographic essay on the life of an asylum in Jackson, Louisiana. These images are both unforgettable and unrelenting. However, the clarity of vision witnessed in Avedon's photographs signifies a distinction between this work and Brodovitch's. In the Ward's Island contacts, the tormented gestures and activity of Brodovitch's fellow patients find a parallel in his imprecise imagery. While Avedon's images of the insane imply a level of control from behind the camera, the line between Brodovitch and his subject matter is indistinguishable. Sadly, they were one and the same thing.

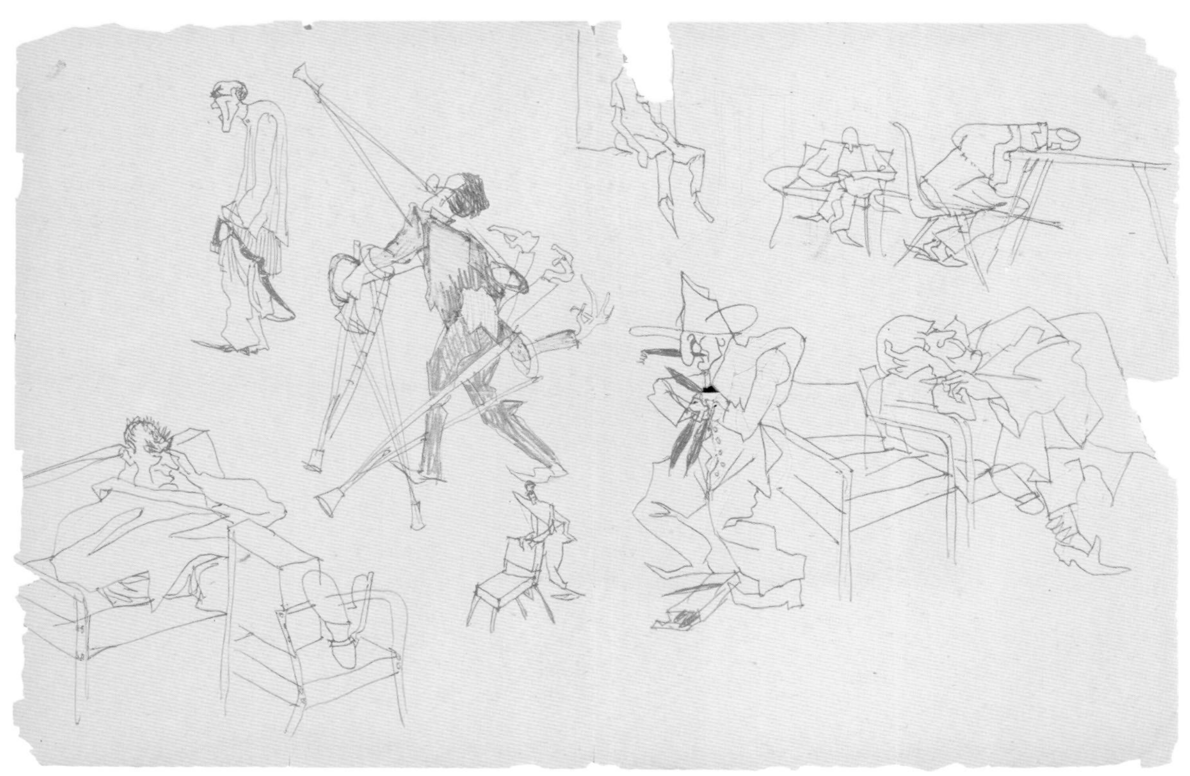

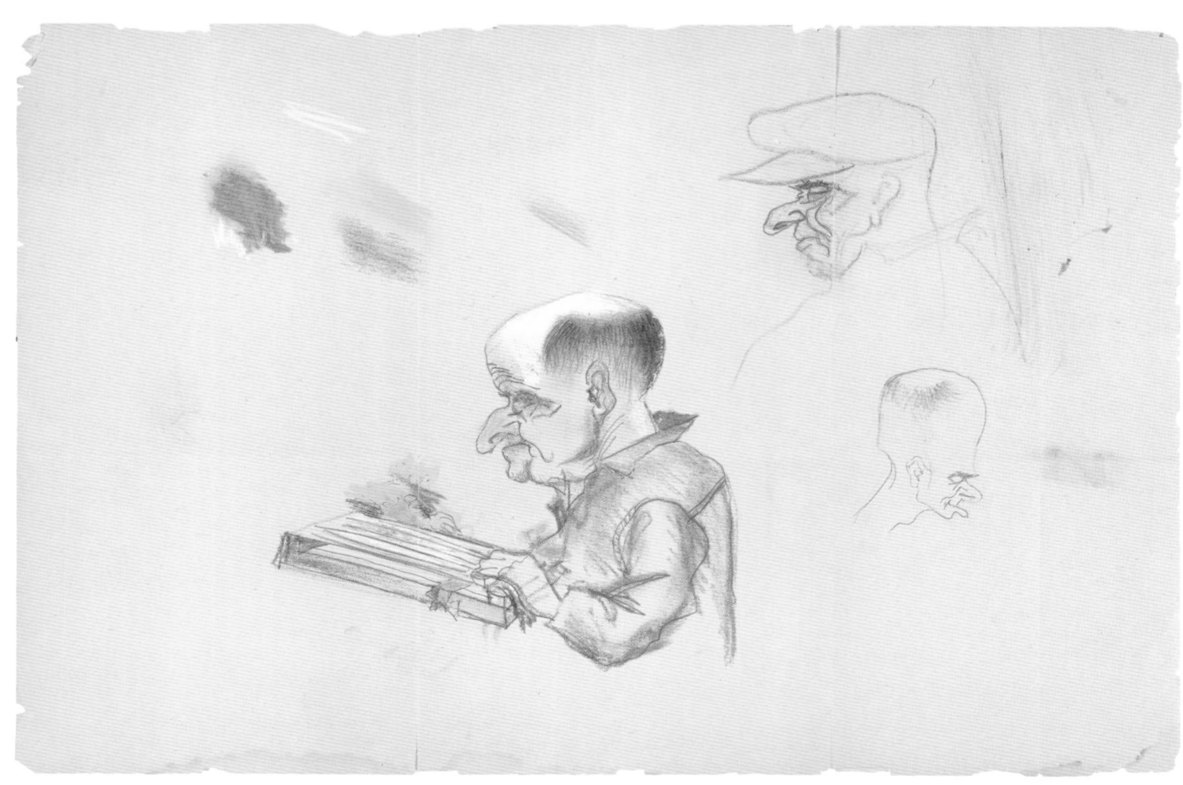

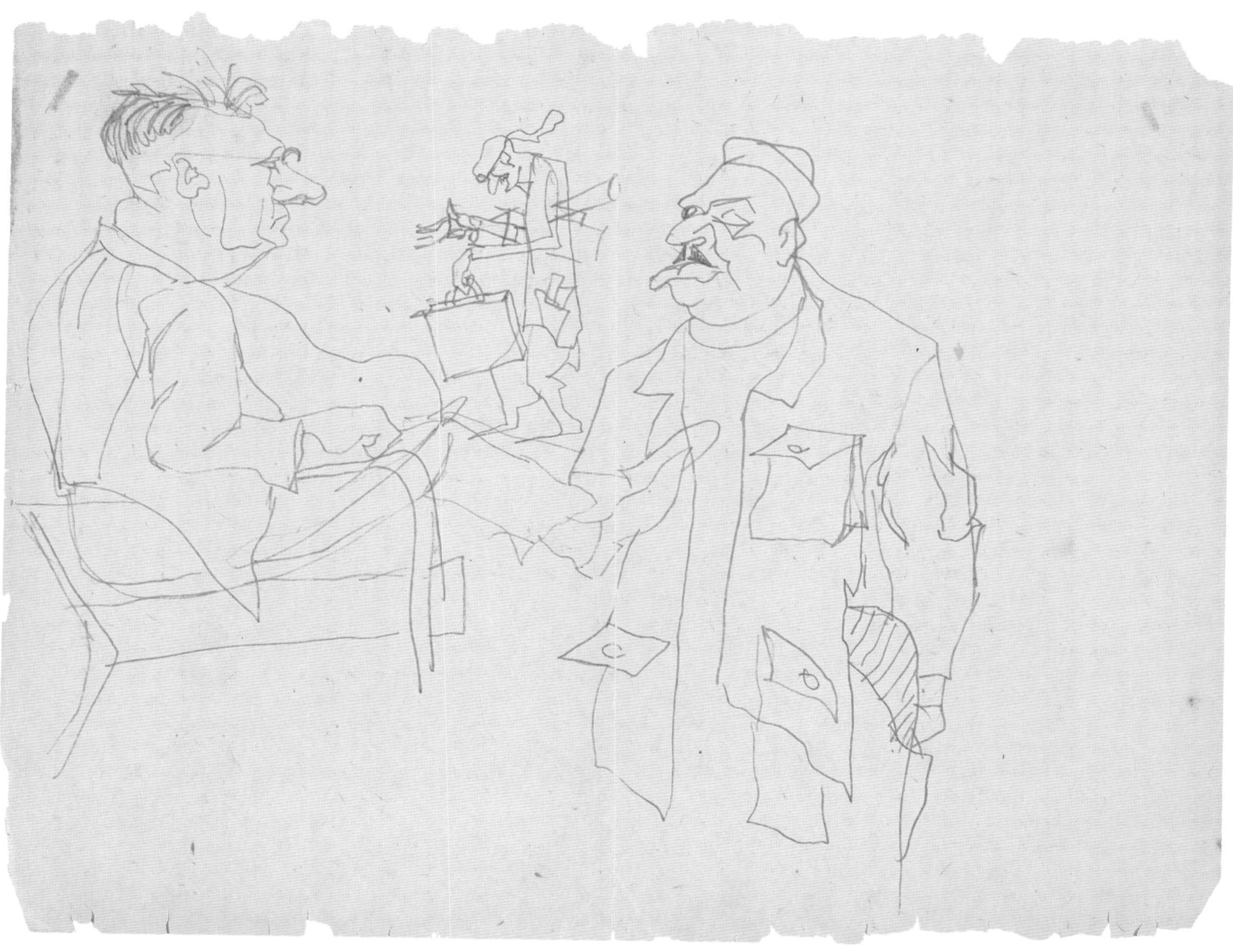

Sketches by Brodovitch of patients at Manhattan State Hospital, Ward's Island, New York, 1961.

The Ward's Island photographs are just a single instance that exemplifies Brodovitch's lifelong fascination with photography and the visual world. As a teacher his only way of conveying this ocular obsession was by enforcing his students to discover new ways of seeing. Always incorruptible, his only desire was to challenge those around him to produce something original, to surprise even themselves. For many years after the end of the Design Lab his revolutionary eye remained as an unconscious creative tic in many photographers' minds – always there, goading them to reject the banal and ordinary in favor of the novel and imaginative. As a designer, his ability to recognize when a photographer *had* discovered something unique, or to perceive the potential in the most mundane image, was remarkable. Seen as a body of work, the books he designed have a page-to-page elegance that has rarely been equaled. And finally, as a photographer himself, he set free the expressive capacity of this medium with a single book, *Ballet*, a work that today, over fifty years after of its original conception, still reminds us that photographic expression can never be fixed or formulated, that the links that bind photography with life must constantly be renewed.

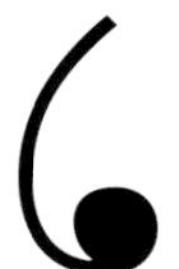

The photograph is not only a pictorial report; it is also a psychological report. – Alexey Brodovitch

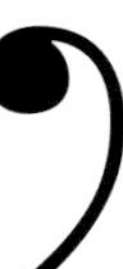

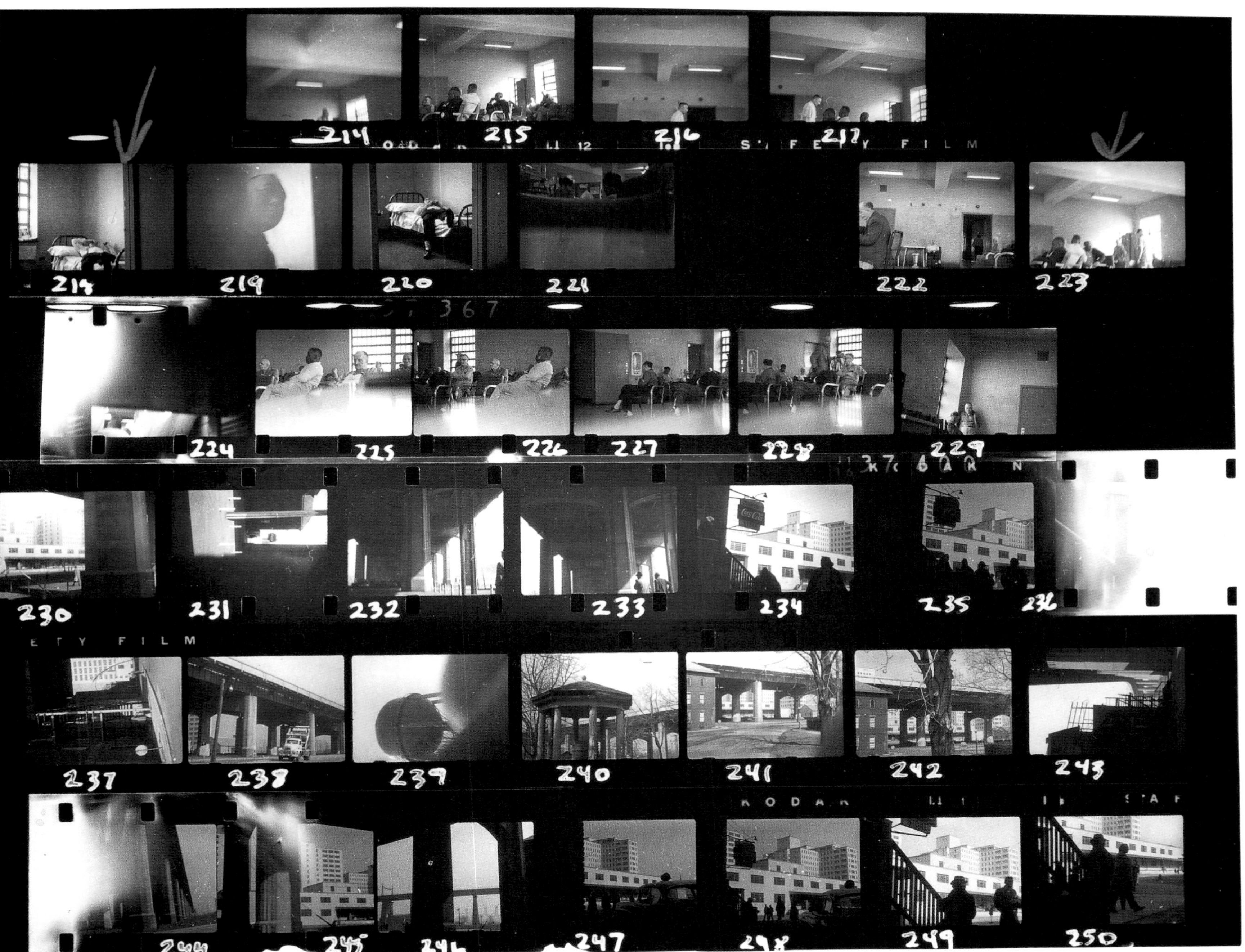

Contact sheet of photographs taken by Brodovitch at Manhattan State Hospital, Ward's Island, New York, 1961.
Some of Brodovitch's contact sheets from Ward's Island reveal that he left the confines of the hospital at some point, wandering the area and capturing the island's industrial landscape.

By this time, with no pension and mounting hospital bills, Brodovitch was financially impoverished. No longer protected by the cushion of a regular salary from *Harper's Bazaar*, his only income came via the freelance commissions he was occasionally offered. With this work, Brodovitch always held firm to his convictions of originality and innovation in design – sometimes to the detriment of his already dire situation. An example of this comes from Harvey Lloyd. Caring for Brodovitch as his health worsened, Lloyd was witness to the fact that when Brodovitch was commissioned by a company he was resolute in the belief that his idea was always the right idea, even if this meant losing the contract. "It was impossible for him to work with clients because he was dogmatic," Lloyd recalled. "He would be given an assignment, the client would come back and say 'I don't exactly want it that way, change it.' The client would come back and it would be the same way. He wouldn't change it. So, very quickly people who had heard of him – he had this towering reputation – the word got out you can't work with him."[7] Reflecting on this turn of events, Irving Penn commented, "It is painful and cruel when a giant like Brodovitch is cast out. But it is common in our time for a client to choose a secondary talent just because he is easier to deal with and easier to bend to commercial ends. You can't bend Brodovitch. He will only retreat."[8]

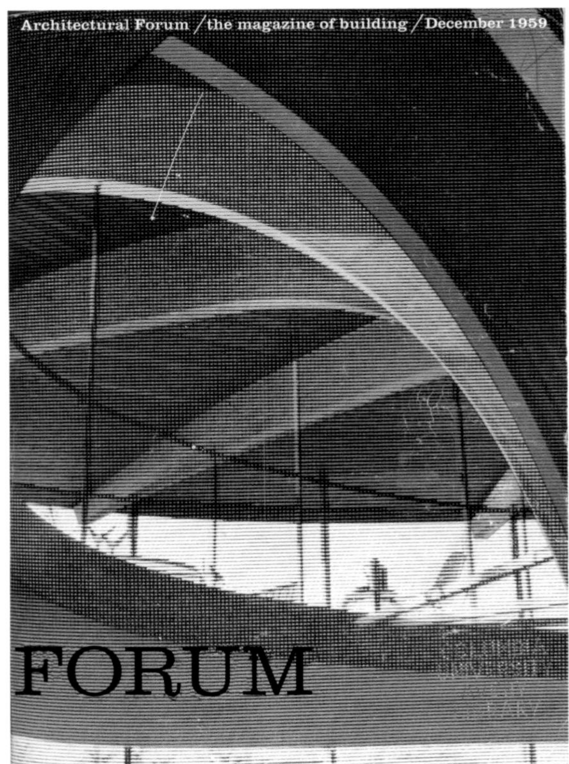

To raise much needed funds for Brodovitch, Lloyd kindly organized an evening where many of his old students – such as Ted Croner and Richard Avedon – came to celebrate his work and contribute to a collection for his welfare. While Brodovitch enjoyed seeing all his old friends, the evening did not affect his economic status in any significant way. During this period the Design Lab also began to falter. "Some weeks Brodovitch made it to class. Some weeks he didn't," Charles Reynolds remembered. "Sometimes he seemed so exhausted (distracted? bored?) that little was said about the pictures. Chain-smoking cigarettes with a shaky hand, he would leaf through students' work, occasionally pointing out a picture he found interesting or original, more frequently reviling those he felt were cliché."[9] When Brodovitch could no longer make it to the class some students kept it going in his honor. These classes without Brodovitch lasted only a short

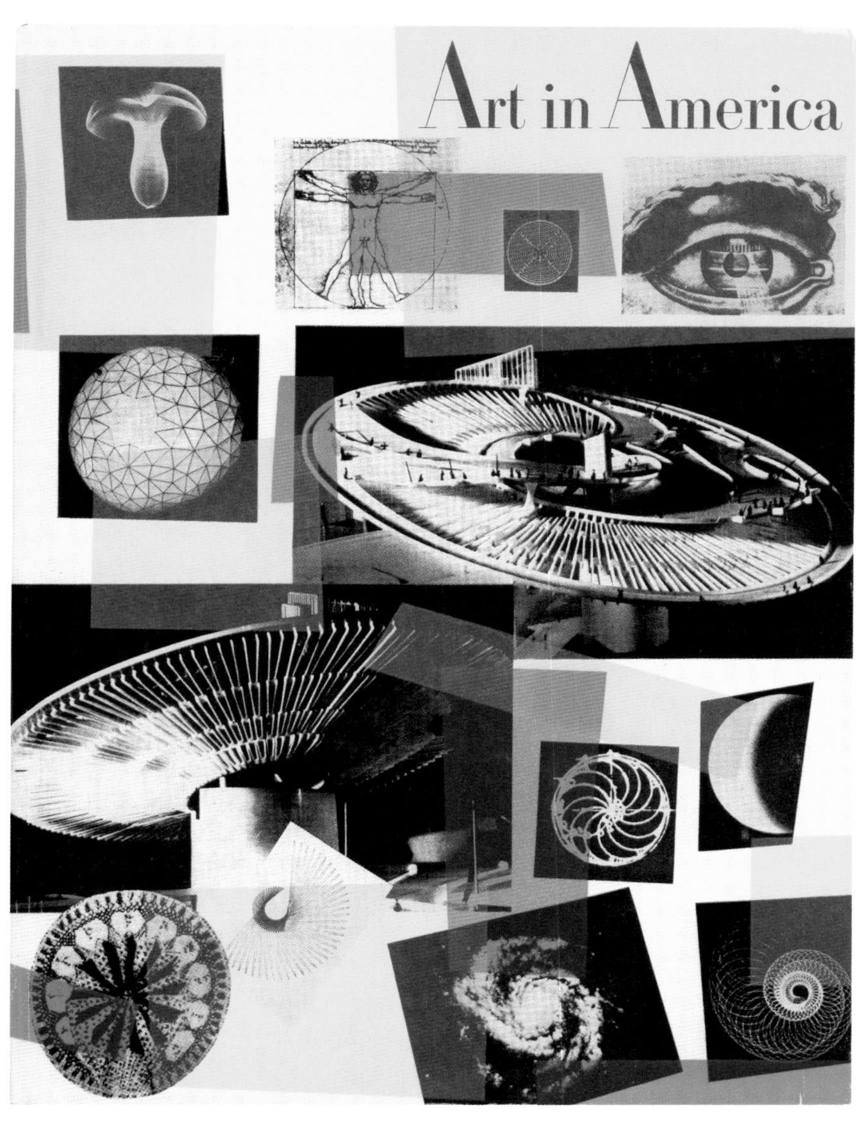

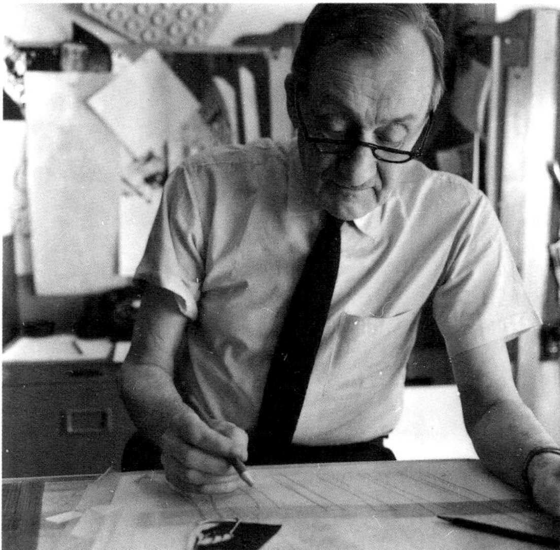

Opposite: Cover of *Architectural Forum*, December 1952.

Above: Cover of *Art in America* No. 3, 1962.

Right: Alexey Brodovitch in his New York studio, 1961. Photograph by Lida Moser.
During the early and mid-1960s, facing ill health and mounting bills, Brodovitch relied on sporadic freelance commissions and the support of his friends and former students.

while. It seemed that deprived of the man himself, the Design Lab could no longer exist. Looking for ways to improve his situation, Brodovitch did continue to hold Design Lab sessions at his home. In the end they were only partially successful and failed to make any real difference to his depleted resources. In 1966 Brodovitch fell and broke his hip. As his financial and physical state deteriorated, he reluctantly decided to return to his family in France.

In the 1930s, on one of his many return visits to France for *Harper's Bazaar*, Brodovitch had purchased an old farmhouse in Oppède-le-Vieux, a small village in southern France. Close to Avignon, where he had many relatives, Oppède-le-Vieux is located on the northern flank of the Luberon mountains. Situated high on the rocks, the village offers magnificent views of Mont Ventoux, the Cévennes, and the lower Alps. His intention when buying this property was to organize a European branch of the Design Laboratory. Unfortunately, with the arrival of World War II this project was never realized. Arriving there in 1966, it seems that Brodovitch still held hopes that the venture could be reestablished and that from this location he could also coordinate traveling classes throughout Europe.[10] When Allan Porter, a friend and former student of Brodovitch, visited him in Oppède-le-Vieux in September 1967, it seems that Brodovitch was making many plans, one of which continued to be the possibility of an autobiography. "Alexey sat on the edge of his bed and discussed recent events, his broken hip and resulting immobility and the artistic happenings of the day," Porter recalled. "All around him were books, journals, papers and souvenirs relating to his long and productive life.... He thought a lot about his past, and it was his aim to assemble it in the present; the future to him meant his book."[11]

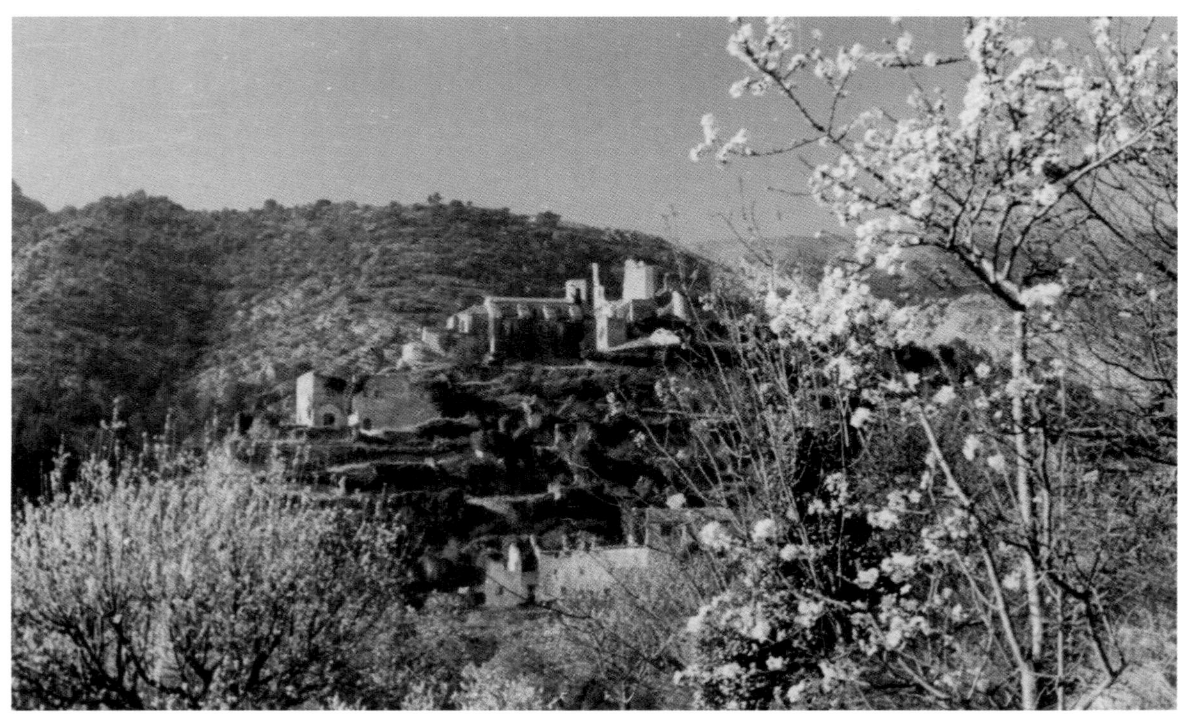

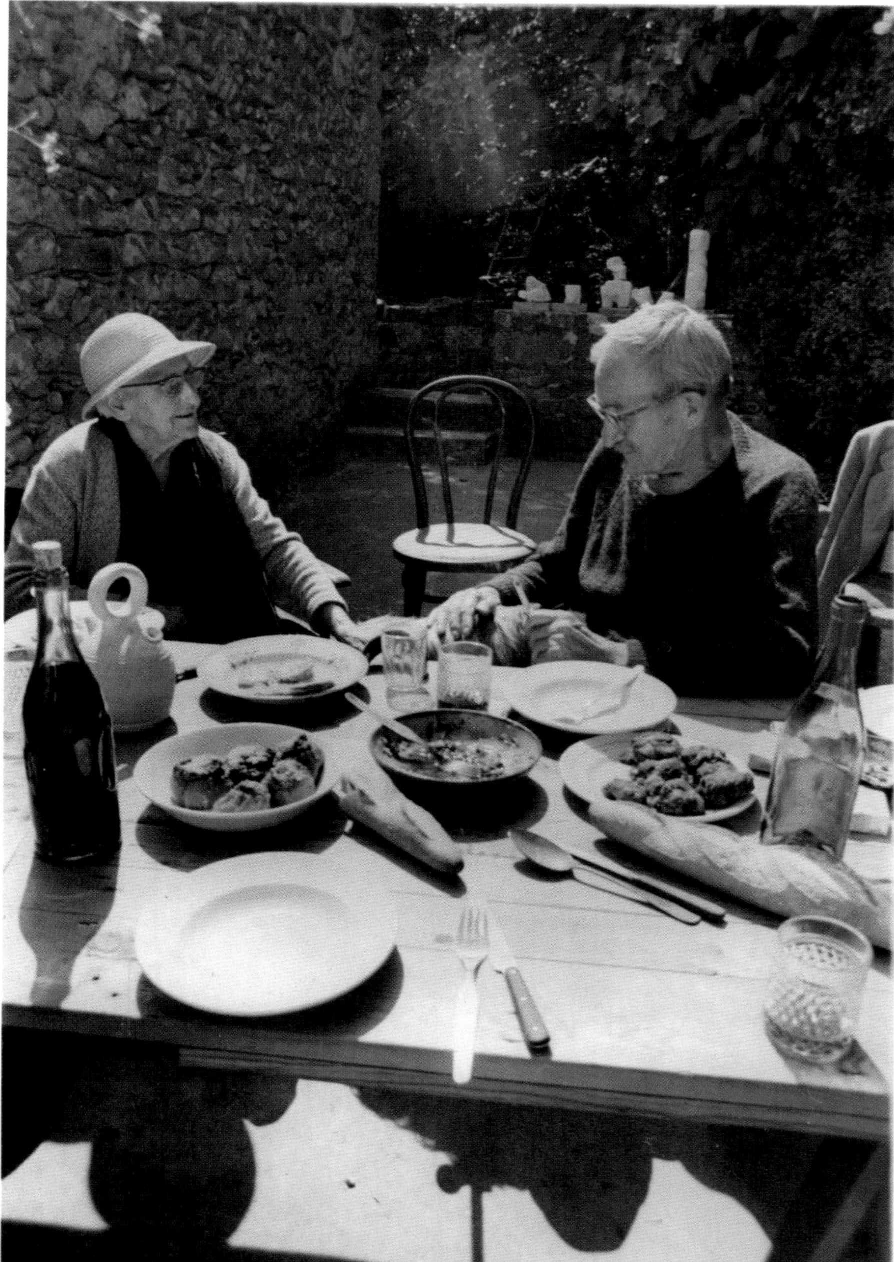

Opposite: Oppède-le-Vieux, a small village in southern France where Brodovitch had purchased an old farmhouse and olive mill, "Le Moulin," in the 1930s and where he lived from 1966 to 1968.

Right: Brodovitch and a relative, Pauline Bonnet, at Le Moulin, Brodovitch's farmhouse in Oppède-le-Vieux, France, 1968.
Brodovitch was visited by numerous former students and old colleagues at his farmhouse in France in the late 1960s. While he was in poor physical condition, he continued to plan new projects, in particular an autobiography.

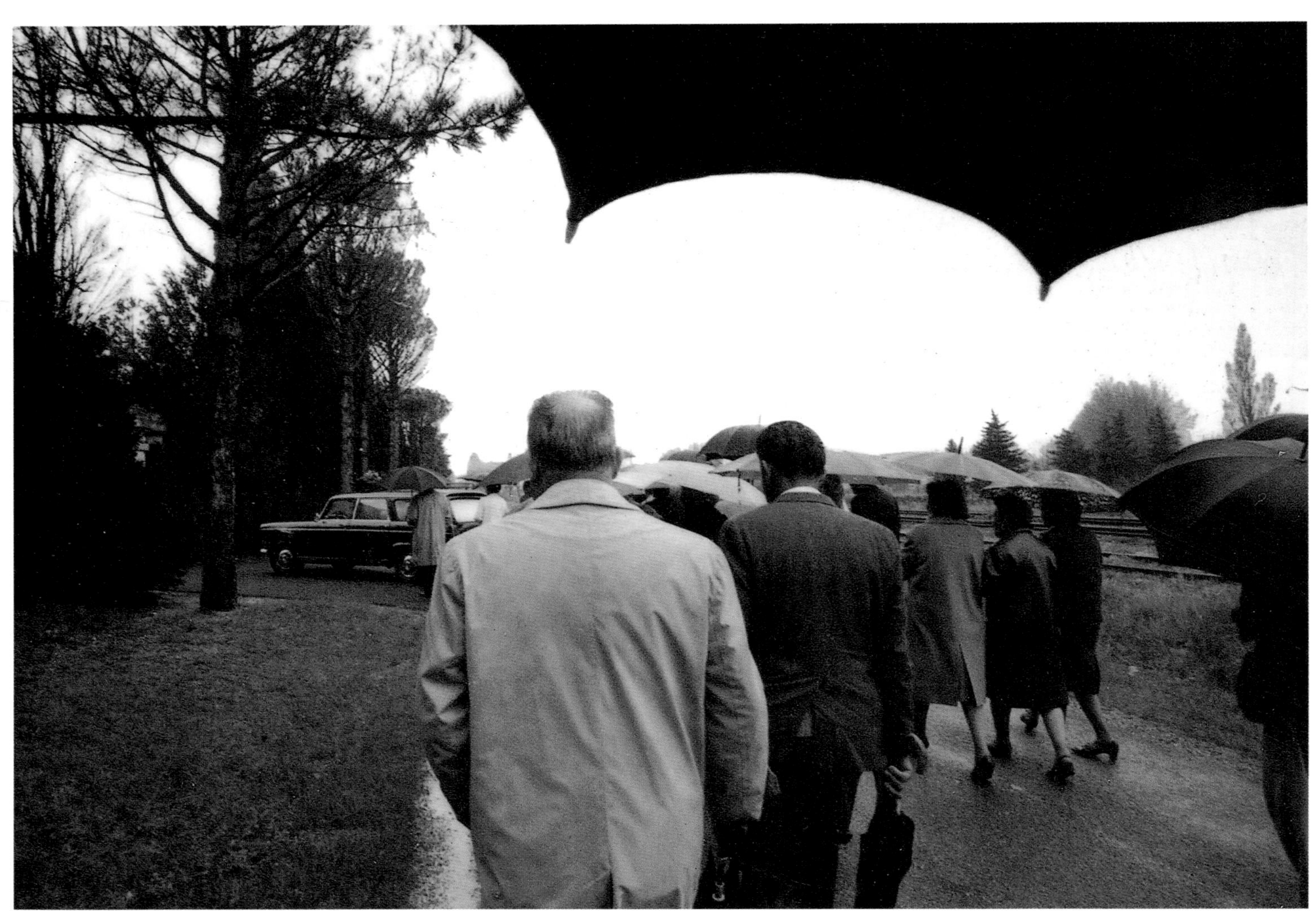

Alexey Brodovitch's funeral, France, 1971. Photographer unknown.

Because of the hilly terrain of Oppède-le-Vieux and his now limited mobility, Brodovitch decided to sell the farmhouse in 1968 and move to Le Thor, a small village just 18 km from his family in Avignon. It was here in 1969 that Brodovitch was visited by his longtime friend and student, Richard Avedon. During his visit, Avedon took a well-known portrait of Brodovitch. Leaning heavily on the crutches necessary for his injured hip, Brodovitch's arched eyebrows seem to signify an amused detachment at Avedon's request for a photograph. While we can see that physically Brodovitch was in a poor state, his eyes are still questioning, scrutinizing, alert to Avedon's every move. This is one of the last portraits of Alexey Brodovitch. He died two years later, on 15 April 1971.

A student in a Design Lab session once asked Brodovitch the question, What was it that made somebody want to be a photographer? Brodovitch replied "Someone who had the biological urge to press the shutter."[12] Brodovitch's own designs and photographs understood that when art is divided from life it has no great significance. In this respect his teachings, or more accurately his provocations, were not something to be learned by rote or emulated; they were directed at making the individual student develop his or her own unique vocabulary. Brodovitch said:

Every photograph is really giving a personal visual report on something.... [T]he problem of the photographer is to discover his own language, a visual ABC's to explain the event. The photograph is not only a pictorial report; it is also a psychological report. It represents the feelings and point of view of the intelligence behind the camera.[13]

Refracted through the prism of his own personality, Brodovitch willingly converted the experiences of modernity into the production of his work. Throughout his life, this openness and sensitivity to his environment was marked, in equal amounts, by moments of celebration and tragedy. From the joyous memories of Paris in *Ballet* to the torment of alcoholism on Ward's Island, instances of pain or happiness manifested themselves in the need to produce creative acts as "psychological reports." The photographer Bruce Davidson recollected a vivid example of Brodovitch's urgent need to articulate an instance of personal misfortune. "I remember one of his classes vividly," Davidson noted. "A storm had hit the Eastern seaboard. Brodovitch came late into the group of painters, sculptors, and designers who waited for him. He began by telling of the destruction of the storm on his farm. He told of riding horseback along the beach, where large birds lay embedded in the wet sand. He saw trees that he knew, down everywhere, and the roof partly gone from his barn. The destruction would take more than his lifetime for nature to renew. I think I saw Brodovitch the man in a moment when the personal pain of destruction created in him the need to communicate."[14] Brodovitch offered an insight into his compulsion to constantly give form to ideas, emotions, and fears when he asked the question:

What forces to create? Curiosity, escape from self, normality, abnormality, intuition, desire for knowledge of the unknown – Who or What? We cannot explain. Art and religion are mysteries which we can discover only by will, courage, trust, desire, need, patience and work. Work, work, and more work.[15]

Photographers, designers, and artists who responded to Brodovitch's elevated expectations discovered that they had to push themselves to the limit to satisfy his weary eye. Examining their work, he demanded nothing less than a permanent revolution of style and substance. It was a exacting approach that compelled involvement and disavowed moments of reflection, satisfaction, or contentment in what was produced. For some, this approach was deleterious to their creative spirit. For others, it was a pivotal encounter when they discovered something new about themselves; when Brodovitch's influence became part of their visual sensibility, sustaining their creative endeavors for many years to come. In 1999, Harvey Lloyd had this to say:

My God, is it thirty-five years later or more, he's still there.... That seed never leaves. That implant is part of your brain and part of your unconscious and part of what you do. And when you don't know it's operating, it's there, and it's an amazing thing.[16]

Alexey Brodovitch, Le Thor, France, 1969. Photograph by Richard Avedon.
After breaking his hip in 1967, Brodovitch moved to Le Thor, a small village not far from his family in Avignon. This well-known portrait is one of the last photographs taken of Brodovitch before he died in 1971.

In 1972, one year after he had passed away, Brodovitch was posthumously awarded a Doctor of Fine Arts degree from the institution that had introduced him to American life in 1930. The dean of faculty of what was now known as the Philadelphia College of Art, George R. Bunker, organized an exhibition to celebrate the occasion, "Alexey Brodovitch and His Influence." In the elegant catalogue that accompanied the exhibition, various students and colleagues pay their respects to his lasting influence. In a fitting epitaph to Brodovitch's enduring legacy, Frank Zachary recounted this touching story:

Alexey Brodovitch once owned two bull terriers – Fearless and his son, Mischa. He was greatly attached to these dogs and they in turn expressed a most uncommon devotion to him: their rapport with Brodovitch seemed almost human, it was as though they understood and were responding to the sensibility of this extraordinary artist teacher – a sensibility so exquisite and refined that anyone who was touched by him felt it with the impact of a physical force.

When Mischa grew up, he developed a deadly animosity towards his father and they fought often.... To maintain peace, Brodovitch – then living on an old Chester County farmstead – kept Fearless in one part of the house and Mischa in another, and exercised them at different times of the day. But this soon became an intolerable burden and Brodovitch was faced with giving up one of his beloved pets. At this time my two young daughters were clamouring for a new dog to replace one we had just lost, so we inherited Mischa....

Brodovitch did not see Mischa until five years later when he came to a dinner party at my home. The scene remains vivid in my mind. I had answered the doorbell and Brodovitch was standing there as I shall always picture him – lean Borzoi-like features, taut, slightly stooped figure, elegant and vital, a true Russian aristocrat straight out of the pages of Turgenev. Suddenly, a white thunderbolt shot past me and hurtled into Brodovitch's arms, almost knocking him down. It was Mischa.... It was a strangely affecting sight and I was moved, for the dog's behavior seemed to symbolize feelings of loyalty, devotion, and gratitude I myself felt for Brodovitch; deep, personal emotions I could not analyze but which I knew were shared by everyone who worked and studied with him.

The party broke up soon after midnight. We coaxed Mischa into an upstairs bedroom and locked him in, so that he would not run after Brodovitch's car. I could swear there were tears in Mischa's eyes when Brodovitch patted him and said goodbye. That is how I best remember my friend and master, Alexey Brodovitch.[17]

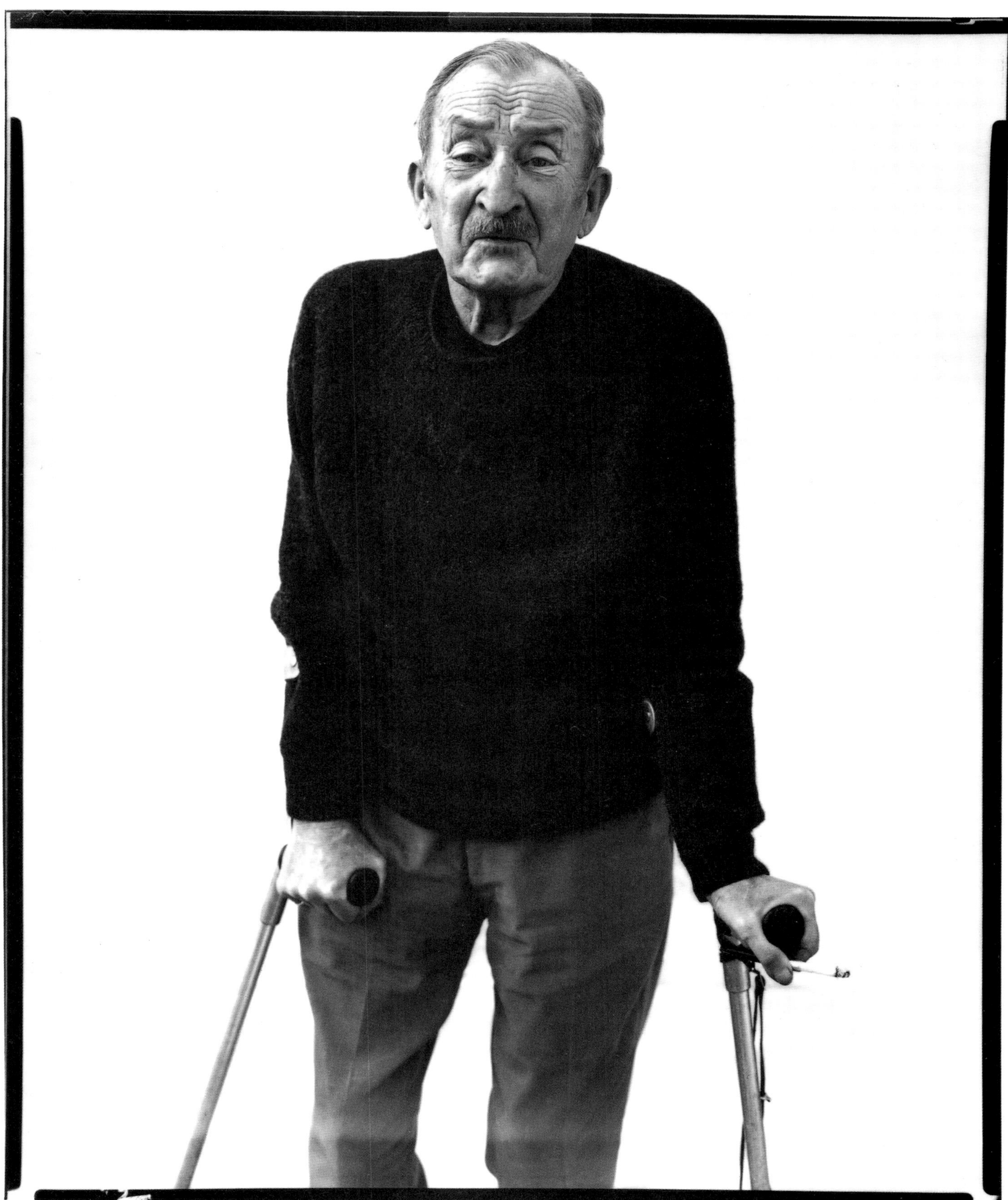

Notes

Introduction and Chapter 1

Epigraph. William Wiser, *The Crazy Years: Paris in the Twenties* (London: Thames and Hudson, 1983), 88.

1 Harvey Lloyd, interview by the author and Edward Dimsdale, 1999.

2 The life of an émigré is one of constant reinvention. Articles of the past are an expense few can afford to keep in the forced departure from their homes. Many hold on to their history through rituals, ceremonies, or simply memories. Following the map of Alexey Brodovitch is like any historical search into an émigré life: It is frequently fragmented and in many places seems uninhabited. As a result, researching his life is regularly a succession of disjointed journeys and historical blind alleys. This is especially the case with his early life in Russia and Paris. However, an increasing body of historical research into these areas enables us to paint a picture of the life the young Alexey Brodovitch would have faced.

3 George Bunker, *Alexey Brodovitch and His Influence* (Philadelphia: Philadelphia College of Art, 1972), 13–14.

4 Alexey Brodovitch, "Brodovitch on Brodovitch," *Camera* (February 1968): 6.

5 On the occasion of the birth of his sister, Brodovitch recounts another time he used his new camera: "A few years later, my sister was born in our apartment in St. Petersburg. I remember a lot of doctors, nurses running from the kitchen with hot water, my father all in white. My mother on a table ... glistening surgical instruments. I understood nothing, but I crawled under the table and tried to take pictures with my box camera. Obviously I was unsuccessful, and all I got was photos of the doctor's legs." Ibid.

6 "The traditions of this city are distinctively modern, growing out of the city's existence as a symbol of modernity in the midst of a backward society; but Petersburg traditions are modern in an unbalanced, bizarre way, springing from the imbalance and unreality of the Petrine scheme of modernization itself. In response to more than a century of brutal but abortive modernization from above, Petersburg [...] engender[ed] and nourish[ed], through the nineteenth century and into the twentieth, a marvellous array of experiments in modernization from below." Marshall Berman, *All That is Solid Melts Into Air: The Experience of Modernity* (New York: Verso, 1995), 285.

7 A. Bely, *Petersburg* (London: Penguin Press, 1995), 55.

8 Georg Simmel, "Metropolis and Mental Life," *Metropolis: Centre and Symbol of Our Times,* ed. Phillip Kasinitz (London: Macmillan Press, 1995), 31.

9 The commercial growth of Russia was both late compared to the rest of Europe and condensed into an insanely short period of time.

10 "If there was one state where revolution was believed to be not only desirable but inevitable, it was the empire of the tsars." Eric J. Hobsbawm, *The Age of Empire, 1875–1914* (London: Weidenfeld and Nicolson), 292.

11 Ibid.

12 Brodovitch, "Brodovitch on Brodovitch," 6–19.

13 Ibid., 19.

14 Ibid.

15 Ibid.

16 Ibid.

17 "Unlike the avant gardes of 1880–95, those of the new century, apart from the survivors of the older generation, were not attracted by radical politics. They were a-political [...] Only war, the October Revolution and the apocalyptic mood which both brought with them were to fuse revolution in the arts and society once again, thus casting a retrospective red glow over Cubism and constructivism, which had no such associations before 1914." Hobsbawm, *The Age of Empire,* 230–31.

18 Michel Brodovitch, interview by the author, April 2001.

19 Harold Rosenberg, "The Fall of Paris," In *Art in Theory, 1900–1990: An Anthology of Changing Ideas,* eds. Charles Harrison and Paul Wood (Oxford: Blackwood Publishers, 1993), 542. First published in Rosenberg, *The Tradition of the New* (London: 1962).

20 Brodovitch, "Brodovitch on Brodovitch," 25. It is worth noting here that in charting Brodovitch's early days in Russia and Paris it is difficult to ascertain what is true and what is invention. According to some of Brodovitch's relatives he was a notorious embellisher of the truth. Michel Brodovitch, interview.

21 Nathalie Cattaruzza, "Paris: The Formative Years, 1920–1930," in *The Enduring Legacy of Alexey Brodovitch* (New York: The Cooper Union for the Advancement of Science and Art, 1994), 23.

22 Charles S. Mayer, "The Impact of the Ballets Russes on Design in the West, 1909–1914," in *The Avant-Garde Frontier: Russia Meets the West,* eds. Gail Harrison Roman and Virginia Hagelstein Marquardt (Florida: University of Florida Press, 1992), 19.

23 "If you are lucky enough to have lived in Paris ... then wherever you go it stays with you like a movable feast." Ernest Hemingway, quoted in Carol Mann, *Paris: Artistic Life in the Twenties and Thirties* (London: Laurence King Publishing, 1996), 77.

24 Karim Sednaoui, *Alexey Brodovitch, His Work, His Influence* (Derby, UK: Trent Polytechnic and Derby College of Art, 1974), 7. Cattaruzza, "Paris: The Formative Years" 23.

25 Michel Brodovitch, interview.

26 Andy Grundberg, *Brodovitch* (New York: Harry N. Abrams, 1989), 37.

27 Brodovitch, "Brodovitch on Brodovitch," 25. The role this poster played in the future direction of Brodovitch's career cannot be overestimated. In many photos we can see it tacked up behind his desk; it was something that held immense value for him. As Nathalie Cattaruzza has commented: "Throughout his life Alexey Brodovitch was proud of this prize-winning poster, as he was of his brief stay at the Ballets Russes. Although several fires burned down his personal archives, he pinned this poster to his studio wall as late as 1964." Cattaruzza, "Paris: The Formative Years," 24.

28 As Robert Block, the director of the art department for the Parisian department store Aux Trois Quartiers and a future Brodovitch collaborator, realized: "The more intense life becomes the harder it is to distract the attention of individuals from their daily occupations by outside things; and thus arises the necessity of finding new forms of publicity every day." Robert Block, "The Publicity of a French Store," *Commercial Art* (November 1929): 196.

29 Steven Heller and Seymour Chwast, *Graphic Styles: From Victorian to Post-Modern* (London: Thames and Hudson, 1994), 128.

30 Cattaruzza, "Paris: The Formative Years," 24.

31 Brassai, *Brassai: Letters to My Parents* (Chicago: The University of Chicago Press, 1997), 64.

32 However, this exhibit did not meet with universal approval. As Douglas and Madeleine Johnson noted in *The Age of Illusion: Art and Politics in France, 1918–1940* (London: Thames and Hudson, 1987), the L'Espirit Nouveau pavilion was "intended to be reassembled as a dwelling house at the end of the exhibition. Designed as a machine for modern living, the house was the cause of much controversy and spent part of the exhibition surrounded by a fence to render it invisible," 75.

33 "After this exhibition I dropped everything for advertising." Brodovitch, "Brodovitch on Brodovitch," 25.

34 For many designers the 1925 exhibition simply highlighted how little resonance their work held for the future. This was the case for the couturier Paul Poiret: "All the theatrical elegance of the Belle Époque was personified in Paul Poiret as he stood on the deck of his flagship Orgues dressed in *smoking* and top hat, offering champagne to the remnants of his upper-crust clientele. But the socialites were outnumbered by a file of window-shoppers strolling from one beautifully appointed barge to the next: they had come to look, not buy. Nothing in Poiret's champagne manner and seigneurial hauteur he had learned from his idol and predecessor Jacques Doucet hinted at the impending bankruptcy or revealed a desperate captain of a sinking ship." Wiser, *The Crazy Years,* 146.

35 Cattaruzza, "Paris: The Formative Years," 26.

36 Ibid.

37 Robert Block "has working with him the publicity artist Brodovitch, whose name is a guarantee of success. All the Parisian publishers have tried in vain to entice him away." "The Publicity of a French Store," 200.

38 Karim Sednaoui's dissertation on Brodovitch suggests that during the 1926–27 period Brodovitch possibly worked for the large printing houses Deberny-Peignot, and Tolmer and Draeger.

39 Block, "The Publicity of a French Store," 196–98.

40 Paul Rand, *Thoughts on Design* (New York: Wittenburn Schultz, 1946), 2.

41 Being one of Brodovitch's most public designs, the temporary facade of the store was apparently so successful that it remained in place for many years.

42 In 1930, Brodovitch designed the interiors of Serge Koussevitzky's house, and Lucienne Long's boutique in Cannes. No images exist of these designs.

43 Grundberg, *Brodovitch,* 39. These designs are by no means original. The mix of forms seen here can be observed in other French poster artists of the period such as A. M. Cassandre and Pierre Masseau. However, Brodovitch's work for Aux Trois Quartiers did still play a significant role in the transformation of visual culture throughout Paris in the twenties.

44 In June 1928 Brodovitch actually exhibited a collection of his paintings with Alexeïeff at the Povolotzky gallery, 13, rue Bonaparte. According to Cattaruzza, "The Polish owner, Jacques Povolotzky, editor and owner of the library La Cible, became the defender of the Parisian non-objective artists: Kupka, Gleizes and Gallien [...] Thus, while specializing in Parisian geometric art, his open attitude toward other European artists encouraged him to exhibit Brodovitch." Cattaruzza, "Paris: The Formative Years," 23.

45 Its full title is actually *A Brief History of Moscovia and Other less-known Countries lying Eastward of Russia as far away as Cathay.*

46 Brodovitch, "Brodovitch on Brodovitch," 45.

47 Brodovitch to Charles Coiner, 5 October 1962. Syracuse University Library, Syracuse University, New York.

Chapter 2

Epigraph. Marvin Israel, quoted in Bunker, *Alexey Brodovitch and His Influence* (Philadelphia: Philadelphia College of Art, 1972), 32.

1 Barbara Haskell, *The American Century: Art and Culture, 1900–1950* (New York: Whitney Museum of Art, 1999), 236.
2 Virginia Smith, "Launching Brodovitch," *The Enduring Legacy of Alexey Brodovitch* (New York: The Cooper Union for the Advancement of Science and Art, 1994), 4. I am indebted to Smith's work on this aspect of Brodovitch's life.
3 Alexey Brodovitch, "What Pleases the Modern Man," *Commercial Art* (August 1930): 60–70.
4 Smith, "Launching Brodovitch," 5.
5 Brodovitch, "What Pleases the Modern Man," 60–70.
6 "Many individuals would be sensitive to the beauty of common objects, without artistic intention, if the preconceived notion of the objet d'art were not a bandage over their eyes. Bad visual education is the cause of this tendency." Fernand Léger, "The Aesthetic of the Machine" (1924), quoted in Herschel B. Chipp, *Theories of Modern Art: A Source Book by Artists and Critics* (Berkeley, Calif.: University of California Press, 1986), 277.
7 Smith, "Launching Brodovitch," 6.
8 Charles Coiner, "Revolution on Pine Street." Unpublished essay, p. 2. Syracuse University Library, Syracuse University, New York. Pine Street was the location of PMSIA.
9 Smith, "Launching Brodovitch," 6.
10 Ibid.
11 Harvey Lloyd, interview, 1999.
12 Lorraine Wild, "Exploring the Roots of Modern American Graphics," *Industrial Design* 30 (July/August 1983), 25.
13 Coiner, "Revolution on Pine Street," 3. Brodovitch's desire to have complete control over the creative process was, as Coiner notes, achieved without "compromising his talent or his principles." In a country where division of labor is the norm, this is a relatively unusual occurrence. As he goes on to say, "[a]rtists who are true to their ideals and maintain a standard of work to be proud of and who refuse to contribute to the banality of American advertising are few and far between. Brodovitch is one of them. But even more importantly these same standards are being projected with few exceptions by the growing list of his students." Ibid., 4–5.
14 "Graduates of these early classes found prominent jobs. Robert Greenwell became art director of RCA Records, Victor Trasoff, art director of CBS, Mary Fullerton, assistant to Brodovitch at *Harper's Bazaar* and art director of *Mademoiselle*, David Steck at *Life*, Alfred Lowrey, art director at *Good Housekeeping*, *American Weekly*, and *Newsweek*, Nelson Gruppo, art director of *Stage*, *Promenade*, and *This Week*, Joe Jones at *House Beautiful*, Roy Faulconer, Stewart Graves, Elizabeth Lovett, Ed Schartzer with N. W. Ayer and Son. Joseph Gering at *Brides*. The Philadelphia School became a 'prep school' for agencies and magazines around the country, disseminating Brodovitch's influence." Smith, "Launching Brodovitch," 12.
15 Ibid., 12. Abridged.
16 Cattaruzza, "Paris: The Formative Years," 26.
17 Grundberg, *Brodovitch*, 70.
18 Brodovitch, "Brodovitch on Brodovitch," 45.
19 Rand, *Thoughts on Design*, 107.
20 Grundberg, *Brodovitch*, 57.
21 Brodovitch, "What Pleases the Modern Man," 63.
22 Smith, "Launching Brodovitch," 13.
23 Heller and Chwast, *Graphic Styles*, 160.
24 Carmel Snow and Mary Louise Aswell, *The World of Carmel Snow* (New York: McGraw-Hill, 1962), 90.
25 Smith, "Launching Brodovitch," 15.
26 Ibid.
27 Coiner, "Revolution on Pine Street," 4.
28 Smith, "Launching Brodovitch," 15.
29 Grundberg, *Brodovitch*, 59.
30 Snow and Aswell, *The World of Carmel Snow*, 91.
31 Frances McFadden, quoted in Bunker, *Alexey Brodovitch and His Influences*, 33.
32 Owen Edwards, "Visual Dynamics: The Magic of Graphic Design," in *The American Magazine*, eds. Amy Janello and Brennon Jones (New York: Harry N. Abrams Inc., 1991), 160.
33 These dates indicate the issue of *Harper's Bazaar* referred to.
34 Polly Devlin, *Vogue Book of Fashion Photography* (New York: Simon & Schuster, 1979), 121.
35 Erté, *Things I Remember* (London: Peter Owen Press, 1974), 116. Erté goes on to say that William Randolph Hearst was not very pleased with the termination of his contract. In a letter to Snow, Hearst apparently commented: "I think the Cassandre covers are showy – let us say striking, as a more amiable word. I do not know exactly what they mean. I do not suppose it is necessary that I should know," p. 116. As with Brodovitch's appointment, Hearst seems to have submitted to Snow's superior judgement.
36 Devlin, *Vogue Book of Fashion Photography*, 120. The other key figure central to the transformation of the American magazine was T. E. Cleland at *Fortune* magazine. In the midst of a depression Cleland produced a decadently luxurious magazine that sold for the princely sum of $1.00.
37 Wild, "Exploring the Roots of Modern American Graphics," 58.
38 M. F. Agha, "Graphic Arts in Advertising," *American Union of Decorative Artists and Craftsmen*, by R. L. Leonard, et al. (New York: Ives Wasburn, 1931), 139.
39 Edward Steichen, *My Life in Photography* (London: W. H. Allen and Company, 1963).
40 Nancy Hall-Duncan, *History of Fashion Photography* (New York: A Chanticleer Press Edition, Alpine Book Co., 1977), 77.
41 Snow and Aswell, *The World of Carmel Snow*, 88–90.
42 Grundberg, *Brodovitch*, 63–7
43 George Herrick, "Alexey Brodovitch," *Art and Industry*, (July–December 1940): 169.
44 Quoted in Charles Reynolds, "Focus on Alexey Brodovitch," *Popular Photography* (December 1961): 80.
45 R. Roger Remington and Barbara. J. Hodik, *Nine Pioneers in American Graphic Design* (Cambridge: MIT Press, 1989), 38.
46 Tom Maloney, "Fashion and Color," *US Camera Annual 1957*: 72.
47 Remington and Hodik, *Nine Pioneers*, 38.
48 Frank Zachary, interview by the author and Edward Dimsdale, 1999.
49 Alfred Tolmer, *Mise en Page* (London: The Studio, 1930).
50 Roland Barthes, *The Grain of the Voice: Interviews 1962–1980* (Berkeley, Calif.: University of California Press, 1991), 59.
51 Ibid., 58.
52 William Owen, *Magazine Design* (London: Laurence King, 1991), 54.
53 Brodovitch, "Brodovitch on Brodovitch," 45.
54 Harvey Lloyd, "Alexey Brodovitch," *Photography* (February 1964): 18.
55 Quoted in Bunker, *Alexey Brodovitch and His Influence*, 33.
56 Quoted in Reynolds, "Focus on Alexey Brodovitch," 81.
57 Ibid., 107.
58 Quoted in Ann Thomas, *Lisette Model* (Ottawa: National Gallery of Canada, 1990), 99.
59 Quoted in Reynolds, "Focus on Alexey Brodovitch," 80.
60 Quoted in Jane Livingston, *The New York School: Photographs 1936–1963* (New York: Stewart, Tabori and Chang, 1992), 337.
61 Ibid.
62 Janet Malcolm, "Men Without Props." *Diana and Nikon* (New York: Aperture, 1997), 40.
63 Snow and Aswell, *The World of Carmel Snow*, 155. After 1948 a fall in advertising revenue resulted in the *Junior Bazaar* being incorporated into *Harper's Bazaar*.
64 Quoted in Hall-Duncan, *History of Fashion Photography*, 136.
65 Alexander Liberman, *Alex: The Life of Alexander Liberman* (New York: Alfred A. Knopf, 1995).
66 David Bordwell and Kristin Thompson, *Film Art: An Introduction* (London: McGraw-Hill, 1997), 480.
67 Sergei Eisenstein, "Montage of Attractions," *The Film Sense* (London: Faber and Faber, 1986), 182–3.
68 Ibid., 183.
69 Quoted in Susan Compton, *Russian Avant-Garde Books: 1917–34* (London: The British Library, 1992), 96.
70 Quoted in Bunker, *Alexey Brodovitch and His Influence*, 35.
71 Quoted in Martin Harrison, "Lillian Bassman," *Graphis* 298, no. 51 (July/August 1995): 33.
72 Ted Croner, interview by the author and Edward Dimsdale, 1999.
73 Snow and Aswell, *The World of Carmel Snow*, 203.
74 Ted Croner, interview, 1999.
75 Henry Wolf, "Hall of Fame," *Communication Arts* 14, no. 4 (1972): 28.

Chapter 3

Epigraph. J. Krishnamurti, *Education and the Significance of Life* (London: Gollancz Paperbacks, 1992), 11.

1 Quoted in Grundberg, *Brodovitch*, 129.
2 Quoted in Smith, "Launching Brodovitch," 15.
3 Quoted in Lloyd, "Alexey Brodovitch," 19.
4 L. Moholy-Nagy, "New Education–Organic Approach," *Art and Industry* (March 1946): 66–7.
5 Walter Gropius, "The Theory and Organization of the Bauhaus" (1923), in *Art in Theory, 1900–1990: An Anthology of Changing Ideas*, 338.
6 Quoted in Lloyd, "Alexey Brodovitch," 19.
7 Quoted in Reynolds, "Focus on Alexey Brodovitch," 87.
8 Quoted in Bunker, *Alexey Brodovitch and His Influence*, 13.
9 J. Krishnamurti, *Education and the Significance of Life*, 14.
10 Ted Croner, interview, 1999.
11 Quoted in Reynolds, "Focus on Alexey Brodovitch," 86.
12 Quoted in Peter Larson, "Life as a Brodovitch Student," *Photography* (February 1964): 21.
13 Quoted in Grundberg, *Brodovitch*, 132.
14 Harvey Lloyd, interview, 1999.
15 Larson, "Life as a Brodovitch Student," 20.
16 Quoted in Reynolds, "Focus on Brodovitch," 86.
17 Ibid.
18 Ted Croner, interview, 1999.
19 Quoted in Reynolds, "Focus on Alexey Brodovitch," 89.
20 Quoted in Lloyd, "Alexey Brodovitch," 18.
21 Ibid.
22 Alexey Brodovitch, "Brodovitch on Photography," *Popular Photography* (December 1961): 107.
23 Hans Namuth, *Contact: Theory* (New York: Lustrum Press, 1980), 134.
24 "Brodovitch on Photography," 92.
25 Quoted in Bunker, *Alexey Brodovitch and His Influence*, 10–13.

26 Alexey Brodovitch and Inge Bondi, "The Photographer's 'Two Masters,'" *Print* (March 1959): 27.
27 Harvey Lloyd, interview, 1999.
28 Ralph Steiner, *Ralph Steiner: A Point of View* (New York: Columbia University Press, 1979), 17.
29 Patricia Bosworth, *Diane Arbus: A Biography* (New York: W. W. Norton and Company, 1994), 122–3.
30 Martin Harrison, *Appearances: Fashion Photography Since 1945* (London: Jonathan Cape, 1991), 74.
31 Harvey Lloyd, interview, 1999.
32 Quoted in Smith, "Launching Brodovitch," 11.
33 Peter Basch, interview by the author and Edward Dimsdale, 1999.
34 Quoted in Reynolds, "Focus on Alexey Brodovitch," 87.

Chapter 4

Epigraph. Alexey Brodovitch, "Brodovitch on Photography," *Popular Photography* (December 1961), 92.
1 Ibid., 81.
2 Christopher Phillips, "Brodovitch on *Ballet*," *American Photographer* (December 1981): 80. The title of this article is misleading, as it includes virtually no comments by Brodovitch on the production of this groundbreaking book.
3 Ibid.
4 Edwin Denby, *Ballet* (New York: J. J. Augustin, 1945), 11–12.
5 Quoted in Livingston, *New York School: Photographs 1936–1963*, 290.
6 A. G. Bragaglia, "Futurist Photodynamism," in *Futurist Manifestos*, ed. Umbro Apollonio (London: Thames and Hudson, 1973), 44–45. Outside of photography one could also look to the dance performances choreographed by Oscar Schlemmer in 1927. In these productions the dancer wore a black costume and had long white poles attached his arms, legs and torso. Performed against a black backdrop the effect was that in action the body disappeared, replaced by the white lines tracing the dancers movements.
7 Ted Croner, interview, 1999.
8 W. J. Naef, "The Making of an American Photographer," *André Kertész: Of Paris and New York* (London: Thames and Hudson, 1985), 117.
9 Pierre Borhan, "Introduction: The Double of a Life," *André Kertész: His Life and Work*, ed. Pierre Borhan (Boston: Bulfinch Press, 1994), 29.
10 E. Paul, "A Mood from the Dim Past," *Saturday Review of Literature*, 19 May 1945. Quoted in Borhan, "Introduction: The Double of a Life," 29.
11 Fritz Henle, George Walsh, Colin Naylor, and Michael Held, eds., *Contemporary Photographers* (London: Macmillan Publishers, 1982), 337.
12 Ibid.
13 Ibid.
14 Quoted in William A. Ewing, *The Photographic Art of Hoyningen-Huene* (London: Thames and Hudson, 1998), 138.
15 Quoted in Reynolds, "Focus on Alexey Brodovitch," 86.
16 Quoted in Jane Livingston, "The Art of Richard Avedon," *Evidence* (London: Jonathan Cape, 1995), 33.
17 Malcolm, "Men without Props," 42.
18 John Szarkowski, *Looking at Photographs: 100 Pictures from the Collection of The Museum of Modern Art* (Italy: Idea Editions, 1980), 168.
19 Brodovitch, "Brodovitch on Photography," 84.
20 Grundberg, *Brodovitch*, 108.
21 Richard Avedon and Truman Capote, *Observations* (New York: Simon & Schuster, 1959), 150.
22 "David Attie: The Persistence of Vision," *Photography Annual 1962*, 21.

Chapter 5

Epigraph. Frank Zachary, interview by the author and Edward Dimsdale, 1999.
1 Ibid.
2 Ibid.
3 Steven Heller, *Paul Rand* (London: Phaidon Press, 1999), 90.
4 Frank Zachary, interview, 1999.
5 Ibid.
6 Ibid.
7 Ibid.
8 Michel Brodovitch, interview.
9 A Lissajous figure is produced through the intersection of two sinusoidal curves at right angles to each other. They were most famously used by Saul Bass in the opening credits of Alfred Hitchcock's 1958 film *Vertigo*.
10 Rand, *Thoughts on Design*, 2.
11 The company Photo-Lettering ceased operation in the late 1980s. A revival of Brodovitch's font was recreated by designer Nico Schweizer based on selected original letters of "Al-bro" and is now sold by Lineto.com under the name "Albroni."
12 Steven Heller, "Portfolio: Alexey Brodovitch," *Design Literacy: Understanding Graphic Design* (New York: Allworth Press, 1997), 42.
13 Peter Basch, interview, 1999.
14 Ibid.

Chapter 6

Epigraph. Alexey Brodovitch in "Focus on Alexey Brodovitch," *Popular Photography* (December 1961): 80.
1 Brodovitch to Charles Coiner, 13 October 1962. Syracuse University Library, Syracuse University, New York.
2 Ibid.
3 "Please let me know when you will be back in Philadelphia. I would like to see you to show you the dummy of the book." Brodovitch to Charles Coiner, undated. Syracuse University Library, Syracuse University, New York.
4 In a letter to Coiner from Brodovitch dated 22 June 1963, Brodovitch notes that "When I was in hospital, my mail was so badly disorganised and neglected, that I have not found several important letters including yours." Syracuse University Library, Syracuse University, New York.
5 Brodovitch to Charles Coiner, 6 October 1962. Syracuse University Library, Syracuse University, New York.
6 Harvey Lloyd, interview, 1999.
7 Ibid.
8 Quoted in Reynolds, "Focus on Alexey Brodovitch," 87.
9 Charles Reynolds, "Alexey Brodovitch: 1900–1971," *Popular Photography* (September 1971): 60.
10 Brodovitch, "Brodovitch on Brodovitch," 45.
11 Quoted in Reynolds, "Focus on Alexey Brodovitch," 87.
12 Peter Basch, interview, 1999.
13 Quoted in Reynolds, "Focus on Alexey Brodovitch," 82.
14 Quoted in Bunker, *Alexey Brodovitch and His Influence*, 16.
15 Brodovitch, introduction to "Brodovitch on Brodovitch," 45.
16 Harvey Lloyd, interview, 1999.
15 Quoted in Bunker, *Alexey Brodovitch and His Influence*, 7–9.

Bibliography

Books by Alexey Brodovitch

Ballet. New York: J. J. Augustin, 1945.

Books illustrated by Alexey Brodovitch

Dostoevsky, Fyodor. *Contes Fantastiques* (Paris: La Pléiade, 1928).

Hawes, Elizabeth. *Fashion is Spinach* (New York: Random House, 1938).

Lorrain, Jean. *Monsieur de Bougrelon* (Paris: La Pléiade, 1928).

Milton, John. *A Brief History of Moscovia* (London: Blackmore Press, 1929).

Pushkin, Aleksander S. *Nouvelles* (Paris: La Pléiade, 1928).

Books designed by Alexey Brodovitch

Attie, David, and Bill Manville. *Saloon Society* (New York: Duell, Sloan, and Pierce, 1960).

Avedon, Richard, and Truman Capote. *Observations* (New York: Simon & Schuster, 1959).

Breuer, Marcel. *Sun and Shadow* (New York: Longmans, Green and Co., 1956).

Bush, Christopher. *Dead Man's Music* (New York: Doubleday Doran, 1932).

Guerrero, Pedro, and H. H. Arnason. *Calder* (New York: Studio Vista, 1966).

Henle, Fritz, and Elliot Paul. *Paris* (Chicago: Ziff Davis, 1947).

Hoyningen-Huene, George. *Egypt* (New York: J. J. Augustin, 1943).

———. *Hellas: A Tribute to Classical Greece* (New York: J. J. Augustin, 1943).

Kertész, André. *Day of Paris* (New York: J. J. Augustin, 1945).

Maloney, Tom. *3 Poems* (New York: W. Morrow & Co., c. 1935).

Smith. Charles Edward. *The Jazz Record Book* (New York: Smith and Durrell, 1942).

Snow, Carmel, and Mary-Louise Aswell. *The World of Carmel Snow* (New York: McGraw-Hill, 1962).

Steeman, André. *The Night of the 12th–13th* (c. 1933).

Toussaint, Franz. *La Sultane de l'Amour* (Paris: André Delpeuch Press, 1927).

Wells, Carolyn. *Fuller's Earth* (New York: J. B. Lippincott, 1932).

Catalogues/annuals designed by Alexey Brodovitch

New Poster International Exposition catalogue (Philadelphia: Pennsylvania Museum of Art, 1937).

Sears Roebuck catalogue (1939).

Ninth Ballet Theatre Annual (New York, 1949).

Selected periodicals designed by Alexey Brodovitch

Harper's Bazaar, October 1934–August 1958.

Portfolio: No. 1, 1950; No. 2, 1950; No. 3. 1951.

Articles by Alexey Brodovitch

"What Pleases the Modern Man." *Commercial Art* (August 1930).

"Brodovitch on Photography." *Popular Photography* (December 1961).

"Unforgettable." *Popular Photography* (June 1964).

"Brodovitch on Brodovitch." *Camera* (February 1968).

Alexey Brodovitch and Inge Bondi. "The Photographer's 'Two Masters.'" *Print* (March 1959).

Articles and books on Alexey Brodovitch

Block, Robert. "The Publicity of a French Store." *Commercial Art* (November 1929).

———. "L' Expression graphique des Trois Quartiers." *Arts et Métiers Graphiques* (1930).

Bauret, Gabriel. *Alexey Brodovitch* (Paris: Assouline, 1998).

———. "From Russia with Love." *The Guardian Weekend* (April 10, 1999).

Bunker, George. *"Alexey Brodovitch and His Influence."* (Philadelphia: Philadelphia College of Art, 1972).

Carroll, Mark. "Brodovitch and Portfolio." *Typographic* (October 1986).

Cato, Bob. "Brodovitch." *Art Center Review* (November 1989).

———. "Alexey Brodovitch" *ID*, Vol. 37 (January/February 1990).

Coiner, Charles. "Revolution on Pine Street." Unpublished essay. Syracuse University Library, Syracuse University, New York.

Depuy, R. L. "Alexey Brodovitch: A Graphic Alchemist." *Gebrauchsgraphik* (January 1930).

Devlin, Polly. *The Vogue Book of Fashion Photography* (New York: Simon and Schuster, 1979).

di Constanzo, Diane. "Book Reviews: Rebels and Innovators." *ARTnews* (April 1990).

Downes, Bruce. "Brodovitch and *Ballet*." *Popular Photography* (September 1945).

Ebin, John David. "A Master Teaches the Experts." *Photography* (January 1955).

Edwards, Owen. "Zen and the Art of Alexey Brodovitch." *American Photographer* (June 1979).

Esten, John. "Alexey Brodovitch." In *Contemporary Photographers*. George Walsh, Michael Held, Colin Naylor, eds. (London: Macmillan Publishers, 1982).

Ettenberg, Eugene M. "The Remarkable Alexey Brodovitch." *American Artist* (December 1961).

Fernández, Horacio, et al. *Fotografia Pública: Photography in Print 1919–1939* (Madrid: Museo Nacional Centro de Arte Reina Sofia/Aldeasa, 2000).

Finke, J. A. "Profile: Alexey Brodovitch." *Upper and Lower Case* (March, 1977).

Fowle, Geoff. "Alexey Brodovitch." *Design*, No. 494 (February 1990).

Frayling, Christopher. "Imagineering." *Times Literary Supplement* (March 16, 1990).

Friedl, Christian. "Mode et photographie: Mise en page." *Beaux Arts Magazine*, No. 167 (April 1998).

Grundberg, Andy. *Brodovitch* (New York: Harry N. Abrams, 1989).

Gubbins, Bill. "Alexey Brodovitch." *Print* (Sept./October 1999).

Gutterman, Scott. "Alexey Brodovitch." *Print* (July/August 1990).

Guimond, James. *American Photography and the American Dream* (Chapel Hill and London: University of North Carolina, 1991).

Hall-Duncan, Nancy. *History of Fashion Photography* (New York: A Chanticleer Press Edition, Alpine Book Co., 1977).

Harrison, Martin. *Appearances: Fashion Photography Since 1945* (London: Jonathan Cape, 1991).

Hartney, Eleanor. "The Russian Revolutionary." *Harper's Bazaar* (September 1989).

Heller, Steven. *Design Literacy: Understanding Graphic Design* (New York: Allworth Press, 1997).

Heller, Steven, and Elinor Pettit. *Graphic Design Time Line* (New York: Allworth Press, 2000).

Herrick, George. "Alexey Brodovitch." *Art and Industry* (November 1940).

Hurlbert, Allen F. "Alexey Brodovitch: The Revolution in Magazine Design." *Print* (January 1969).

Janello, Amy, and Brennon Jones. *The American Magazine* (New York: Harry N. Abrams Inc., 1991).

King, Emily. "Alexey Brodovitch." *Journal of Design History* 13:2 (2000).

Krauss, Felix, Jr. "Modern Photography." *Tricolor* (June 1945).

Larson, Peter. "Life as a Brodovitch Student." *Photography* (February 1964).

Lemagny, Jean-Claude, and André Rouillé. *A History of Photography* (Cambridge, U.K.: Cambridge University Press, 1987).

Livingston, Jane. *The New York School: Photographs 1936–1963* (New York: Stewart, Tabori and Chang, 1992).

———. "The Art of Richard Avedon." *Evidence* (London: Jonathan Cape, 1995).

Lloyd, Harvey. "Alexey Brodovitch." *Photography* (February 1964).

Maingois, Michel, et al. "Hommage à Alexey Brodovitch." *Zoom* (November/December 1971).

Maloney, Tom. "Fashion—and Color." *US Camera Annual* (New York, 1957).

Owen, William. *Magazine Design* (London: Laurence King, 1991).

Phillips, Christopher. "Brodovitch on *Ballet*." *American Photographer* (December 1981).

Pittel, Christine. "In Short." *New York Times Book Review* (January 7, 1990).

Purcell, Kerry William. "Alexey Brodovitch." *Baseline Magazine*, No. 31 (2000).

Remington, R. Roger. "Coming to America." *ID* (May/June, 1989).

Remington, R. Roger, and Barbara J. Hodik. *Nine Pioneers in American Graphic Design* (Cambridge, Mass.: MIT Press, 1989).

Remington, R. Roger. *The Enduring Legacy of Alexey Brodovitch* (New York: The Cooper Union for the Advancement of Science and Art, 1994).

Reynolds, Charles. "Focus on Alexey Brodovitch." *Popular Photography* (December 1961).

———. "Alexey Brodovitch: *1900–1971*." *Popular Photography* (September 1971).

Rose, Ben. "Alexey Brodovitch." *Infinity* (June 1971).

Sednaoui, Karim. *Alexey Brodovitch, His Work, His Influence* (Derby, U.K.: Trent Polytechnic and Derby College of Art, 1974).

Snyder, Jerome. "Art Directors Club New York: 51st Annual Exhibition of Advertising, Editorial and Television, Art and Design, Inception of the Hall of Fame." *Graphis* 28:163 (1973).

Soupault, Philippe. "Alexey Brodovitch." *The Bulletin* (Paris) (August 1930).

Steinberg, Claire. "Alexey Brodovitch: *1900–1971*." *Photography Annual* (1972).

Stuttaford, Genevieve. "Nonfiction: Brodovitch." *Publishers Weekly* (October 13, 1989).

Tourdjman, Georges. *Alexey Brodovitch* (Paris: Grand-Palais, 1982).

Wild, Lorraine. "Exploring the Roots of Modern American Graphics," *Industrial Design* 30 (July/August 1983).

Witkin, Lee D., and Barbara London. *The Photograph Collector's Guide* (Boston: New York Graphic Society, 1979).

Index

Numbers in **bold** refer to captions and their corresponding illustrations.

Author's Acknowledgments

This book would never have been written without the help of various friends, colleagues, and members of my family.

Firstly, I am indebted to Edward Dimsdale. Visiting New York with Edward in 1999 to interview students of Brodovitch, our aim was to investigate Brodovitch's life in America with the intention of producing a documentary film (a project still to be realized). Many of the interviews from that enjoyable journey have found their way into this monograph—in this respect they are as much Edward's as mine. Special thanks are due to Peter Basch, Ted Croner, Harvey Lloyd, Charles Reynolds, Roger R. Remington, and Frank Zachary. All of whom kindly invited us into their homes and offices and permitted us to interrogate them for stories about Brodovitch's life.

Secondly, I would like to acknowledge those people and institutions that have enabled me to uncover aspects of Brodovitch's oeuvre hidden from view for many decades. These include: the National Art Library at the Victoria and Albert Museum; the British Library; Brighton University Library; the University of Sussex Library; Syracuse University Library; the University of Arts, and especially Sara J. Macdonald. I would particularly like to extend my gratitude to The Rochester Institute of Technology and Kari Horowicz.

For their generous help, my sincere gratitude goes out to Vince Aletti, Michel Brodovitch, and Elizabeth Crisp. I would also like to thank Hans Dieter Reichert for his role in bringing this publication to fruition.

For their belief in the importance of this project I would also like to thank Karen Stein and Megan McFarland at Phaidon Press.

Finally, I began writing this book when my dearest daughter Isabella was only three months old. Without the help of my wife Joanna Purcell, I would have never completed this project. I am forever thankful for her patience and love. This book is dedicated to her.

Illustration Credits

Courtesy Vince Aletti. Magazines photographed by Mark Luttrell: 4, 39, 58–62, 67–73, 76–97,
© www.artkane.com: 122
© David Attie: 112, 113, 114–15, 180–92
© Richard Avedon: 178, 263
Courtesy Richard Avedon: 52, 125, 172–77, 260
Avery Architectural and Fine Arts Library, Columbia University in the City of New York: 256
Courtesy N.W. Ayer & Partners, New York: 105
Courtesy Steven Bluttal: 171
Alexey Brodovitch, courtesy Rochester Institute of Technology, Archives & Special Collections, Rochester, New York: 131, 140–43, 249, 250, 255
Courtesy Michel Brodovitch, Paris: 11 left, 12, 13, 15, 16 top, 19, 37, 56, 98 bottom, 99, 100–1, 109, 126, 252–53, 258, 259
© Henri Cartier-Bresson/Magnum Photos: 202
© Ted Croner/Courtesy Howard Greenberg Gallery: 116–17, 120
Culver Pictures: 11 right
Courtesy Ed Dimsdale. Photographed by Ian Bavington Jones: 133–39, 144–49
Courtesy Jan van der Donk, New York: 150, 151 (bottom)
George Karger/Timepix: 6
© Estate of André Kértész: 152, 154–64
© Estate of André Kértész, courtesy Martin Parr: 153
© Harvey Lloyd: 119
The Minneapolis Institute of Arts: 21
Léon Bakst, Projet de décor pour le ballet Shéherezade/ Musée des Arts Décoratifs, Paris/Laurent-Sully Jaumes: 17
Reproduced from *The Modern Poster* by Stuart Wrede (New York: The Museum of Modern Art, 1988): 23
© Lida Moser: 257
© Hans Namuth Estate, Center for Creative Photography, University of Arizona, Tucson: 124
The New York Public Library: 49 bottom
Courtesy Irving Oaklander: 34, 35, 63
Courtesy R. Roger Remington: 48, 49 top
Walter Sanders/Timepix: 65
Roy Stevens, courtesy Richard Avedon: 107
© Georges Tourdjman: 123, 127, 128, 129, 195, 247
Courtesy Alexandra Truitt: 102–3
The University of the Arts. University Libraries. University Archives: 2, 9, 18, 20, 26–31, 36, 45, 46, 47, 50, 51, 53, 54–55, 110
Courtesy Kerry William Purcell: 16, 24, 25, 33, 42, 74, 98 top, 151 top
© Zebra Press, Editors: George S. Rosenthal & Frank Zachary: 197–99, 204–43. Original magazines courtesy Nico Schweizer, photographed by Beth Phillips.

Publisher's Acknowledgments

The Publisher would like to thank Vince Aletti, Richard Avedon, and Steven Heller for generously lending materials from their collections.

Phaidon Press Limited
Regent's Wharf
All Saints Street
London N1 9PA

Phaidon Press Inc.
180 Varick Street
New York, NY 10014

www.phaidon.com

First published 2002
Reprinted in paperback 2011

ISBN 978 0 7148 6317 7

A CIP catalogue record for this book is available from the British Library.

Designed by Hans Dieter Reichert
Printed in Hong Kong